ALSO BY JAMES WOOD

NONFICTION
The Broken Estate
The Irresponsible Self
How Fiction Works
The Fun Stuff
The Nearest Thing to Life

FICTION
The Book Against God
Upstate

SERIOUS NOTICING

SERIOUS NOTICING

SELECTED ESSAYS
1997–2019

James Wood

FARRAR, STRAUS AND GIROUX | NEW YORK

Farrar, Straus and Giroux
120 Broadway, New York 10271

These essays originally appeared, in slightly different form, in *The New Yorker*,
London Review of Books, and *The New Republic*.

Grateful acknowledgment is made for permission to reprint lines from
"Sea and Sand." Words and music by Peter Townshend. Copyright © 1973
Fabulous Music Ltd. Copyright renewed. All rights administered in the USA and
Canada by Spirit Four Music, Suolubaf Music, and ABKCO Music. International
copyright secured. All rights reserved. Reprinted by permission of Hal Leonard LLC.

Library of Congress Control Number: 2019951661
ISBN: 978-0-374-26116-0

Our books may be purchased in bulk for promotional, educational,
or business use. Please contact your local bookseller or the Macmillan
Corporate and Premium Sales Department at 1-800-221-7945, extension
5442, or by e-mail at MacmillanSpecialMarkets@macmillan.com.

www.fsgbooks.com
www.twitter.com/fsgbooks • www.facebook.com/fsgbooks

1   3   5   7   9   10   8   6   4   2

Contents

Introduction   1

The Fun Stuff: Homage to Keith Moon   15

What Chekhov Meant by Life   34

Serious Noticing   49

Saul Bellow's Comic Style   74

Anna Karenina and Characterisation   93

Joseph Roth's Empire of Signs   109

Paul Auster's Shallowness   129

Hysterical Realism   144

Bohumil Hrabal's Comic World   164

George Orwell's Very English Revolution   179

Jane Austen's Heroic Consciousness   207

Cormac McCarthy's *The Road*   222

'Reality Examined to the Point of Madness': László
    Krasznahorkai   240

Wounder and Wounded   254

On Not Going Home   270

The Other Side of Silence: Rereading W. G. Sebald   294

Becoming Them   315

Don Quixote's Old and New Testaments   325

Dostoevsky's God   338

Helen Garner's Savage Honesty   358

The All and the If: God and Metaphor in Melville   372

Elena Ferrante   393

Virginia Woolf's Mysticism   407

Job Existed: Primo Levi   426

Marilynne Robinson   447

Ismail Kadare   458

Jenny Erpenbeck   479

Packing My Father-in-Law's Library   493

ACKNOWLEDGEMENTS   509

SERIOUS NOTICING

Introduction

I WAS TAUGHT HOW to read novels and poems by a brilliant poststructuralist critic called Stephen Heath. I have an image in my mind of Dr Heath holding a sheet of paper – the hallowed 'text' – very close to his eyes, the physical proximity somehow the symbolic embodiment of his scrutinising avidity, while he threw out his favourite question about a paragraph or stanza: 'what's at *stake* in this passage?' He meant something more specific, professionalised and narrow than the colloquial usage would generally imply. He meant something like: what is the dilemma of meaning in this passage? What is at stake in maintaining the appearance of coherent meaning, in this performance we call literature? How is meaning wobbling, threatening to collapse into its repressions? Dr Heath was appraising literature as Freud might have studied one of his patients, where 'What is at stake for you in being here?' did not mean 'What is at stake for you in wanting to get healthy or happy?' but almost the opposite: 'What is at stake for you in maintaining your chronic unhappiness?' The enquiry is suspicious, though not necessarily hostile.

This way of reading could broadly be called deconstructive. Put simply, deconstruction proceeds on the assumption that literary texts, like people, have an unconscious that frequently betrays them: they say one thing but mean another thing. Their own figures of speech (metaphors, images, figurative turns of phrase) are the slightly bent keys to their unlocking. The critic can unravel – deconstruct – a text by reading it as one might read a Freudian slip. And just as an awareness of how people unconsciously defend and betray themselves enriches our ability to comprehend them, so a similar awareness enriches our comprehension of a piece of literature. Instead of agreeing with people's self-assessments, we learn how to read them in a stealthy and contrary manner, brushing them against their own grain. At university, I began to understand that a poem or novel might be self-divided, that its intentions might be beautifully lucid but its deepest motivations helplessly contradictory. Indeed, deconstruction tends to specialise in – perhaps over-emphasise – the ways in which texts contradict themselves: how, say, *The Tempest* is at once anti-colonialist in aspiration and colonialist in assumption; or how Jane Austen's novels are both proto-feminist and patriarchally structured; or how the great novels of adultery, like *Anna Karenina* and *Madame Bovary* and *Effi Briest*, dream of female transgression but simultaneously enforce punishment for that transgression. Critical intelligence is made more complex and sophisticated by an awareness that literature is an always-frail ideological achievement, only ever a sentence away from dissolution. My own reading of literature was permanently altered by this new understanding, and my critical instincts (especially when teaching) are still often deconstructive.

But alongside Dr Heath's question lies the looser, perhaps more generous usage preferred by writers and interested readers. When a book reviewer, or someone in a creative writing workshop, or a fellow author complains, 'I just couldn't see what was *at stake* in the book', or 'I see that this issue matters to the writer, but she didn't manage to make me feel that it was *at stake* in the novel', a different statement is also being made about meaning. The common implication here is that meaning has to be earned, that a novel or poem creates the aesthetic environment of its importance. A novel in which the stakes are felt to be too low is one that has failed to make a case for its seriousness. Writers are fond of the idea of earned stakes and unearned stakes; a book that hasn't earned its effects doesn't deserve any success.

I'm struck by the differences between these two usages. Both are central to their relative critical discourses; each is close to the other and yet also quite far apart. In Stakes[1] (let's call it), the text's success is suspiciously scanned, with the expectation, perhaps hope, that the piece of literature under scrutiny will turn out to be productively unsuccessful. In Stakes[2], the text's success is anxiously searched for, with the assumption that the piece of literature's lack of success cannot be productive for reading, but simply renders the book not worth picking up. The first way of reading is non-evaluative, at least at the level of craft or technique; the second is only evaluative, and wagers everything on technical success, on questions of craft and aesthetic achievement. Stakes[1] presumes incoherence; Stakes[2] roots for coherence. Both modes are interestingly narrow, and their narrowness mirrors each other. Not to think about literature evaluatively is not to think like a writer – it cuts literature off from the instincts and ambitions of the very people who created it. But to think only in terms of evaluation, in terms of craft and technique – to think only of literature as a settled achievement – favours those categories at the expense of many different kinds of reading (chiefly, the great interest of reading literature as an always *un*settled achievement). To read only suspiciously (Stakes[1]) is to risk becoming a cynical detective of the word; to read only evaluatively (Stakes[2]) is to risk becoming a naïf of meaning, a connoisseur of local effects, someone who brings the standards of a professional guild to bear on the wide, unprofessional drama of meaning.

Alas, each kind of reading tends to exclude the other. Formal academic study of modern literature began around the start of the twentieth century. But of course, for centuries before that, literary criticism existed outside the academy, practiced *as literature* by writers. In English alone, that tradition is a very rich one, and includes – to name just a few – Johnson, De Quincey, Hazlitt, Coleridge, Emerson, Arnold, Ruskin, Woolf, Lawrence, Eliot, Orwell, Jarrell, Hardwick, Pritchett, Sontag. One of the moving things about Coleridge's extraordinary book *Biographia Literaria* (the book that coins the term 'practical criticism', which in turn became the watchword of academic close reading) is that what he is most earnestly trying to do – amidst the crazy theorising and neologising and channelling of Fichte – is to convince his readers, through a series of passionately detailed close readings, that his friend and literary competitor William Wordsworth is England's greatest poet. That is what is at *stake* for Coleridge. It's one writer speaking about and to another.

This writerly critical tradition continues to flourish, both in and outside the academy. Of course, nowadays even non-academic literary criticism (I mean criticism written for a general audience) has been shaped and influenced by formal literary study. Many writers have studied literature at university, academics and writers teach together, attend conferences and festivals together, and sometimes almost speak the same language (think of Coetzee's fiction and academic post-colonialist discourse, Don DeLillo's fiction and academic postmodern critique, Toni Morrison's fiction and academic critiques of race). The rise and steady institutionalisation of academic literary criticism means that the long tradition of literary criticism is now really two traditions, the academic (Stakes[1]) and the literary-journalistic (Stakes[2]), which sometimes flow into each other but more often away from each other. Too often, Stakes[1] imagines itself in competition with, disdainful of, or simply inhabiting a different realm from Stakes[2], and vice versa.

This book gathers essays and reviews written over the last twenty years. Most of them are long book reviews, published for a general audience in general-interest magazines or literary journals (*The New Republic*, *The New Yorker* and the *London Review of Books*). These pieces belong to the journalistic or writerly critical tradition that comes before and comes after the academic critical tradition; they are marked by that academic tradition but are also trying to do something distinct from it. I like the idea of a criticism that tries to do three things at once: speaks about fiction as writers speak about their craft; writes criticism journalistically, with verve and appeal, for a common reader; and bends this criticism back towards the academy in the hope of influencing the kind of writing that is done there, mindful that the traffic between inside and outside the academy naturally goes both ways. Edmund Wilson stole the phrase 'triple thinker' from one of Flaubert's letters, and I want to steal it from Wilson. Such a threefold critic – writerly, journalistic, scholarly – would ideally be doing this kind of triple thinking; that, at least, has been my aspiration over the last twenty years, and probably since 1988, when I wrote my first review for the *Guardian*. Which is to say, in this book you'll encounter a criticism interested in both kinds of 'what's at stake?' questions; I think that Stakes[1] and Stakes[2] have no need to look down their noses at each other.

What, *ideally*, does this kind of triple thinking look like? In his essay 'Music Discomposed', the philosopher Stanley Cavell says that the critic's first gesture is: 'You have to *hear* it.' Why, he asks, do you have to hear it? Because, he says, with a deliberate risk of tautology, 'if I don't *hear* it, I don't *know* it', and works of art are 'objects of the sort that can only be *known in sensing*'. And again, at the further risk of excessive simplicity and tautology, Cavell writes: 'what I see is *that* (pointing to the object). But for *that* to communicate you have to see it too. Describing one's experience of art is itself a form of art; the burden of describing it is like the burden of producing it.'

I like this emphasis. When I write about a novel or a writer, I am essentially bearing witness. I'm describing an experience and trying to stimulate in the reader an experience of that experience. Henry James called the critic's task 'heroically vicarious'. Most of the time it feels pretty unheroic, to be honest; but it certainly feels vicarious. It's like playing, to a friend, a piece of music you really love. There is that moment when you stand next to this person, hopeful and intense as you anxiously scan your friend's face, to see if he or she is hearing the same thing you heard. How thrilling it is when the confirmation arrives; and how easily disappointed one can be (though we all learn to hide it) when the friend turns after a minute or two and says, 'You can turn it off, this isn't doing much for me.'

You are trying to get the listener to hear (or see) the same thing as you, to have the same kind of experience. Criticism is just such an adventure in sameness. The journalistic review-essay differs from the academic essay in the amount and quality of this sameness, the amount and quality of Cavellian 'pointing at the artwork' that has to be done. After all, the review-essay involves not just pointing at something, but pointing at it while re-describing it. The analogy is less 'You have to *hear* it' than 'Listen, I have to *play it for you on the piano.*' This re-voicing takes the form, overwhelmingly in book reviews, of paraphrase and quotation. It's disdained as 'plot summary' and often it's done carelessly, so poorly that it is no re-voicing at all. But quotation and re-description are at the heart of the book review and at the heart of that experience that Cavell calls 'creative'.

This passionate re-description is, in fact, pedagogical in nature. It happens in classrooms whenever the teacher stops to read out, to re-voice, the passage under scrutiny. Sometimes all we remember of a teacher is a voice, and that is as it should be. Academic criticism is wary of what used to be called 'the heresy of paraphrase'. The very thing that makes a review or essay into a vital narrative is discouraged in academic writing. We warn students – for perfectly good reasons – to avoid merely retelling or rephrasing the contents of a book. If you catch yourself doing that, we tell them, you're probably not doing criticism, you're not being analytical enough. But we should encourage students to do it better, for there is a quality of implicit intelligence in subtle paraphrase that is itself an act of analysis. And besides, doesn't much academic avoidance of paraphrase have to do, really, with anxiety or snobbery? Scholars don't want to be caught in the act of *primacy* when they are supposed to have read the book a thousand times; God forbid that anyone should think we are encountering a text for the first time! *Of course* we all remember the ins and outs, the ups and downs, the twists and turns of *Waverley* or *Vanity Fair* or *Under the Volcano*! Don't we? Yet the journalistic review *is* an act of primacy; to paraphrase is to dare a kind of innocence; subtle paraphrase is a kind of wise unlearning. And paraphrase is witness.

I have called this kind of critical re-telling a way of writing *through* books, not just about them.[1] This writing-through is often achieved by using the language of metaphor and simile that literature itself uses. It involves a recognition that literary criticism is unique because one has the privilege of performing it in the same medium one is describing. When Coleridge writes of Swift that 'he had the soul of Rabelais but dwelling in a dry place', or when Henry James says that Balzac was so devoted to his work that he became a kind of 'Benedictine of the actual' (a phrase he liked so much he plagiarised himself and also applied to Flaubert); when Pritchett laments that Ford Madox Ford never fell into that 'determined stupor' out of which great artistic work comes; when Woolf complains

---

1 See 'Virginia Woolf's Mysticism', pp. 407–425.

that E. M. Forster is too anxious a narrator, too keen to interrupt his characters, 'like a light sleeper who is always being woken by something in the room' – these writers are producing images that are qualitatively indistinguishable from the metaphors and similes in their so-called 'creative' work. They are speaking to literature in its own language, a large part of which is metaphorical.

So we perform. And we perform in proximity, exulting in the fact that, dolphin-like, we are swimming in the element that nourishes us. Our prose is our connection to the work of art we are re-voicing. Art critics, music critics, dance critics – to change the metaphor – have to board the boat unnaturally or a little awkwardly, from the front or the bow; we get to board the boat ideally, as one should, from the side, amidships. We write as if we expect to be read; we write like the roses Eliot describes in 'Burnt Norton' – roses 'that had the look of flowers that are looked at'.

The philosopher Ted Cohen, in his book *Thinking of Others: On the Talent for Metaphor*, quotes from a paper written in 1949, by another philosopher, Arnold Isenberg. That paper was called 'Critical Communication'. According to Cohen, Isenberg undermines the common notion that by describing an artwork, the critic is producing a *reason* in support of his or her value judgement. It's not about producing reasons, says Isenberg. All the critic can hope to do is, by drawing attention to certain elements of the artwork – by re-describing that artwork – induce in his or her audience a *similar view* of that work. This way, in Isenberg's phrase, the critic can achieve a 'sameness of vision' in his or her audience (i.e. a sameness of vision between audience and critic). Ted Cohen goes on to point out that this is actually a brilliant description of the use of metaphor: 'When your metaphor is "X is Y" you are hoping that I will see X as you do, namely as Y, and, most likely, although your proximate aim is to get me to see X in this way, your ultimate wish is that I will feel about X as you do.' So the critical act is a metaphorical act. For Cohen, identification with someone or something else is essentially metaphorical. The critic says, in effect, 'I will work to enable you to see the text as I do', and does so by enacting a sameness of vision, which is an act of figurative identification – because it is as if the critic were saying, 'I will get you to agree with me that the tiles on that roof over there look just like an armadillo's back; I will get you to see those roof tiles as I see them' (or whatever simile one has in mind). All I would add to Cohen's commentary is that if this 'sameness of vision' is effectively metaphorical, then the language of metaphor – the writer-critic's own use of metaphor – must be the embodied language of that process, the very enactment of it: a sameness of vision which is in some ways a sameness of writing.

In that spirit, I'll close with two examples of sameness of vision, sameness of writing. The first is from Virginia Woolf's biography of the art critic and curator Roger Fry; the other from my own experience. Woolf describes hearing Roger Fry give a public lecture in London – a stiff, formal affair, with the critic in evening dress and holding a long pointer.

All that he had done again and again in his books. But here there was a difference. As the next slide slid over the sheet there was a pause. He gazed afresh at the picture. And then in a flash he found the word he wanted; he added on the spur of the moment what he had just seen as if for the first time. That, perhaps, was the secret of his hold over his audience. They could see the sensation strike and form; he could lay bare the very moment of perception. So with pauses and spurts the world of spiritual reality emerged in slide after slide – in Poussin, in Chardin, in Rembrandt, in Cézanne – in its uplands and its lowlands, all connected, all somehow made whole and entire, upon the great screen in the Queen's Hall. And finally the lecturer, after looking long through his spectacles, came to a pause. He was pointing to a late work by Cézanne, and he was baffled. He shook his head; his stick rested on the floor. It went, he said, far beyond any analysis of which he was capable. And so instead of saying, 'Next slide,' he bowed, and the audience emptied itself into Langham Place.

For two hours they had been looking at pictures. But they had seen one of which the lecturer himself was unconscious – the outline of the man against the screen, an ascetic figure in evening dress who paused and pondered, and then raised his stick and pointed. That was a picture that would remain in memory together with the rest, a rough sketch that would serve many of the audience in years to come as the portrait of a great critic, a man of profound sensibility but of exacting honesty, who, when reason could penetrate no further, broke off; but was convinced, and convinced others, that what he saw was there.

It is all here, in this beautiful passage: criticism as passionate creation ('as if for the first time'); criticism as modesty, as the mind putting the 'understanding' into abeyance ('he was baffled'); criticism as simplicity and near-silence ('It went, he said, far beyond any analysis of which he was capable'); criticism as sameness of vision and re-description ('was convinced, and convinced others, that what he saw was there'). Fry 'found the word he wanted', but Woolf, using narrative much as she does in *To the Lighthouse*, withholds from us what that word exactly was; slowly, gradually, 'found the word he wanted' cedes to wordless humility and the fierce but unuttered conviction that 'what he saw was there': a movement whereby the audience began to experience what Fry saw.

A few years ago, I was in Edinburgh, and went with my father to hear the pianist Alfred Brendel give an illustrated talk about Beethoven's Piano Sonatas. We were late, and arrived at the hall breathless and sweaty. But all was serene inside. Brendel sat at a table, with a concert grand piano behind him. He talked – or mumbled, rather – from his lecture notes, peering down at his text through thick spectacles. He had a strong Austrian accent, unaffected by decades of living in England. Every so often he would turn to the piano to play a few bars, as illustration. But something remarkable occurred when he quoted: even to play a short phrase, he became not a quoter but a performer, not merely a critic but an artist-critic: physically, he had to enter the trance-like state in which he performs whole concerts (his customary shudderings, phantom mastication, closed eyes, swooning and tilting); he could not *blandly* quote the music, in the way that you might read a line from French without bothering to put on the 'proper' French accent. He had to become, as it were, French. In this sense, *he could not quote*. He could only recreate; which is to say, he could only create. It was intensely frustrating to hear, again and again, three bars of the most beautiful Beethoven, perfectly performed, only to have them break off and be replaced by the pianist's inaudible Viennese mumbling. Play on, play on, don't talk! I soundlessly urged. The mumbling quickly became of no interest or importance; I was living for the next pianistic performance, I wanted to swing from beauty to beauty, high above the dun currents of the prosaic. His 'quotes' overwhelmed his commentary; he was approaching Walter Benjamin's idea of a book entirely made of quotations.

Perhaps the analogy with literary criticism is not quite perfect, because the literary critic lacks this precise ability to inflect his chosen quotes as the musician performs his. But let Brendel's wordy mumbling stand for a kind of literary criticism condemned to exteriority, a writing-about rather than a writing-through the text, a flat commentary, banished from the heart of the creative. And let Brendel's performance on the piano, his inability to quote without also recreating, stand for the kind of criticism that is a writing *through* a text, the kind of criticism that is at once critique and re-description: sameness.

Listen, I have to play it for you on the piano.

2019

The Fun Stuff:
Homage to Keith Moon

I HAD A TRADITIONAL musical education, in a provincial English cathedral town. I was sent off to an ancient piano teacher with the requisite halitosis, who lashed with a ruler at my knuckles as if they were wasps; I added the trumpet a few years later and had lessons with a younger, cheerier man, who told me that the best way to make the instrument 'sound' was to imagine spitting paper pellets down the mouthpiece at the school bully. I sang daily in the cathedral choir, an excellent grounding in sight-reading and performance. I still play the piano and the trumpet.

But what I really wanted to do, as a little boy, was play the drums, and of those different ways of making music, only playing the drums still makes me feel like a little boy. A friend's older brother had a drum kit, and as a twelve-year-old I gawped at the spangled shells of wood and skin, and plotted how I might get to hit them, and make a lot of noise. It wouldn't be easy. My parents had no time for 'all that thumping about', and the prim world of ecclesiastical and classical music, which meant so much to me, detested rock. But I waited until the drums' owner was off at school and sneaked into the attic, where they gleamed, fabulously inert, and over the next few years I taught myself how to play them. Sitting behind the drums was also like a fantasy of driving (the other great prepubescent ambition), with my feet established on two pedals, bass drum and hi-hat, and the willing dials staring back at me like a blank dashboard . . .

Noise, speed, rebellion: everyone secretly wants to play the drums, because hitting things, like yelling, returns us to the innocent violence of childhood. Music makes us want to dance, to register rhythm on and with our bodies. So the drummer and the conductor are the luckiest of all musicians, because they are closest to dancing. And in drumming, how childishly close the connection is between the dancer and the dance! When you blow down an oboe, say, or pull a bow across a string, an infinitesimal, barely perceptible hesitation – the hesitation of vibration – separates the act and the sound; for trumpeters, the simple voicing of a quiet middle C is more fraught than very complex passages, because that brass tube can be sluggish in its obedience. But when a drummer needs to make a drum sound, he just . . . hits it. The stick or hand comes down, and the skin bellows. The narrator of Thomas Bernhard's novel *The Loser*, a pianist crazed with dreams of genius and obsessed with Glenn Gould, expresses the impossible longing to *become* the piano, to be at one with it. When you play the drums, you *are* the drums.

The drummer who *was* the drums, when I was a boy, was the Who's Keith Moon, though he was already dead by the time I first heard him. He *was* the drums not because he was the most technically accomplished of drummers, but because his many-armed, joyous, semaphoring lunacy suggested a man possessed by the antic spirit of drumming. He was pure, irresponsible, restless childishness. At the end of early Who concerts, as Pete Townshend smashed his guitar, Moon would kick his drums and stand on them and hurl them around the stage, and this seems a logical extension not only of the basic premise of drumming, which is to hit things, but an inevitable extension of Moon's drumming, which was to hit things exuberantly. In the band's very early days, the managers of clubs would complain to Townshend about his drummer. We like you guys, they would say, but get rid of that madman on the drums, he's too loud. To which Moon succinctly replied: 'I can't play quiet, I'm a rock drummer.'

The Who had extraordinary rhythmic vitality, and it died when Keith Moon died, on 7 September 1978. I had hardly ever heard any rock music when I first listened to albums like *Quadrophenia* and *Who's Next*. My notion of musical volume and power was inevitably circumscribed by my fairly sheltered, austerely Christian upbringing – I got off on classical or churchy things like the brassy last bars of William Walton's First Symphony, or the chromatic last movement of the *Hammerklavier* Sonata, or the way the choir bursts in at the start of Handel's anthem *Zadok the Priest*, or the thundering thirty-two-foot bass pipes of Durham Cathedral's organ, and the way the echo, at the end of a piece, took seven seconds to dissolve in that huge building. Those are not to be despised, but nothing had prepared me for the ferocious energy of the Who. The music enacted the mod rebellion of its lyrics: 'Hope I die before I get old'; 'Meet the new boss, same as the old boss'; 'Dressed right, for a beach fight';

'There's a millionaire above you, / And you're under his sus-picion'. Pete Townshend's hard, tense suspended chords seem to scour the air around them; Roger Daltrey's singing was a young man's fighting swagger, an incitement to some kind of crime; John Entwistle's incessantly mobile bass playing was like someone running away from the scene of the crime; and Keith Moon's drumming, in its inspired vandalism, was the crime itself.

Most rock drummers, even very good and inventive ones, are timekeepers. There is a space for a fill or a roll at the end of a musical phrase, but the beat has primacy over the curlicues. In a regular 4/4 bar, the bass drum sounds the first beat, the snare the second, the bass drum again hits the third (often with two eighth notes at this point), and then the snare hits the bar's final beat. This results in the familiar 'boom-DA, boom-boom-DA' sound of most rock drumming. A standard-issue drummer, playing along, say, to the Beatles' 'Carry That Weight', would keep his 4/4 beat steady through the line 'Boy, you're gonna carry that weight, carry that weight, a long time', until the natural break, which comes at the end of the phrase, where, just after the word 'time', a wordless, two-beat half-bar readies itself for the repeated chorus. In that half-bar, there might be space for a quick roll, or a roll and a triplet, or some-thing fancy with snare and hi-hat – really, any variety of filler. The filler is *the fun stuff*, and it could be said, without much exaggeration, that nearly all the fun stuff in drumming takes place in those two empty beats between the end of a phrase and the start of another. Ringo Starr, who interpreted his role fairly modestly, does nothing much in that two-beat space: mostly, he just provides eight even, straightforward sixteenth notes (da-da-da-da / da-da-da-da). In a good cover version of the song, Phil Collins, an extremely sophisticated drummer who was never a modest performer with Genesis, does a tight six-stroke roll that begins with featherlight delicacy on a tom-tom and ends more firmly on his snare, before going back to the beat. But whatever their stylistic differences, the modest and the sophisticated drummer share an understanding that there is a proper space for keeping the beat, and a much smaller space for departing from it, like a time-out area in a classroom. The difference is just that the sophisticated drummer is much more often in time-out, and is always busily showing off to the rest of the class while he is there.

Keith Moon ripped all this up. There is no time-out in his drumming, because there is no time-in. It is *all fun stuff*. The first principle of Moon's drumming was that drummers do not exist to keep the beat. He did keep the beat, of course, and very well, but he did it by every method except the traditional one. Drumming is repetition, as is rock music generally, and Moon clearly found repetition dull. So he played the drums like no one else – and not even like himself. I mean that no two bars of Moon's playing ever sound the same; he is in revolt against consistency, he is always vandalising repetition. Everyone else in the band gets to improvise, so why should the drummer be nothing more than a condemned metronome? He saw himself as a soloist playing with an ensemble of other soloists. It follows from this that the drummer will be playing a line of music, just as, say, the guitarist does, with undulations and crescendos and leaps. It further follows that the snare drum and the bass drum, traditionally the ball and chain of rhythmic imprisonment, are no more interesting than any of the other drums in the kit; and that you will need lots of those other drums. Lots and lots. By the mid-1970s, when Moon's kit was said to be 'the biggest in the world' – and what a deliciously absurd conceit, anyway! – he had two bass drums and at least twelve tom-toms, arrayed in stacks like squadrons of spotlights; he looked like a cheerful boy who had built elaborate fortifications for the sole purpose of destroying them. But he needed all those drums, as a flute needs all its stops or a harp its strings, so that his tremendous bubbling cascades, his liquid journeys, could be voiced: he needed not to run out of drums as he ran around them.

Average musical performance, like athletic prowess and viticulture – and perhaps novel-writing? – has probably improved in the last century. Nowadays, more and more pianists can brilliantly run off some Chopin or Rachmaninov in a concert hall, and the guy at the local drum shop is probably technically more adept than Keith Moon was. YouTube, which is a kind of permanent Special Olympics for show-offs, is full of young men wreaking double-jointed virtuosity on fabulously complex drum kits rigged up like artillery ranges. But so what? They can also backflip into their jeans from great heights and parkour across Paris. Moon disliked drum solos and did not perform them; the only one I have seen is pretty bad, a piece of anti-performance art – Moon sloppy and mindless, apparently drunk or stoned or both, and almost collapsing into the drums while he pounds them like pillows. He may have lacked the control necessary to sustain a long, complex solo; more likely, he needed the kinetic adventures of the Who to provoke him into his own. His cheerful way of conceding this was his celebrated remark that 'I'm the best Keith

Moon-style drummer in the world'. Which was also a way of saying, 'I'm the best Who-style drummer in the world.'

Keith Moon-style drumming is a lucky combination of the artful and artless. To begin at the beginning: his drums always sounded good. He hit them nice and hard, and tuned the bigger tom-toms low (not for him the little eunuch toms of Kenney Jones, who palely succeeded him in the Who, after Moon's death). He kept his snare pretty 'dry'. This isn't a small thing. The talentless three-piece jazz combo at your local hotel ballroom – dinner-jacketed old-timers hacking through the old favourites – almost certainly features a so-called drummer whose sticks are used so lightly that they barely embarrass the skins, and whose snare – wet, buzzy, loose – sounds like a repeated sneeze. A good dry snare, properly struck, is a bark, a crack, a report. How a drummer hits the snare, and how it sounds, can determine a band's entire dynamic. Groups like Supertramp and the Eagles seem soft, in large part, because the snare is so drippy and mildly used (and not just because elves are apparently squeezing the singers' testicles).

There are three great albums by the Who, and these are also the three greatest Moon records: *Live at Leeds* (1970), a recording of an explosive concert at Leeds University on 14 February 1970, generally considered one of the greatest live albums in rock; *Who's Next* (1971), the most famous Who album; and *Quadrophenia* (1973), a kind of successor to *Tommy*, a 'rock opera' that nostalgically celebrates the 1960s mod culture that had provoked and nourished the band in its earlier days. On these are such songs as 'Substitute', 'My Generation', 'See Me, Feel Me/Listening to You', 'Won't Get Fooled Again', 'Baba O'Riley', 'Bargain', 'The Song Is Over', 'The Real Me', '5.15',

'Sea and Sand' and 'Love, Reign o'er Me'. There is no great difference between the live concert recordings and the studio songs – all of them are full of improvisation and structured anarchy, fluffs and misses; all of them seem to have the rushed gratitude of something achieved only once. From which emerges the second great principle of Moon's drumming: namely, that one is always performing, not recording, and that making mistakes is simply part of the locomotion of vitality. (In the wonderful song 'The Dirty Jobs', on *Quadrophenia*, you can hear Moon accidentally knock his sticks together three separate times while travelling around the kit. Most drummers would be horrified to be caught out on tape like this.)

For Moon, this vitality meant trying to shape oneself to the changing dynamics of the music, listening as much to the percussive deviations of the bass line as to the steady, obvious line of the lead singer. As a result, it is impossible to separate him from the music the Who made. The story goes that, in 1968, Jimmy Page wanted John Entwistle on bass and Keith Moon on drums for his new band; and, as sensational as this group might have been, it would not have sounded like either Led Zeppelin or the Who. If Led Zeppelin's drummer, John Bonham, were substituted for Moon on 'Won't Get Fooled Again', the song would lose half its passionate propulsion, half its wild excess; if Moon sat in for Bonham on 'Good Times, Bad Times', the tight stability of that piece would instantly evaporate.

Bonham's drumming sounds as if he has thought about phrasing; he never overreaches himself, because he seems to have so perfectly measured the relationship between rhythmic order and rhythmic deviation: his superb but tightly limited breaks on the snare, and his famously rapid double strokes on the bass drum, are constantly played against the unvarying solidity of his hi-hat, which keeps a steady single beat throughout the bars. (In a standard 4/4 bar, the hi-hat sounds the four whole beats, or perhaps sounds eight beats in eighth notes.) That is the 'Bonham sound', heard in the celebrated long solo – one of devilish complexity – in 'Moby Dick', on the live album *The Song Remains the Same*. Everything is judged, and rightly placed: astonishing order. Moon's drumming, by contrast, is about putting things in the wrong place: the appearance of astonishing disorder. You can copy Bonham exactly; but to copy Moon would be to bottle his spilling energy, which is much harder.

The third great Moon principle, of packing as much as possible into a single bar of music, produces the extraordinary variety of his playing. He seems to be hungrily reaching for everything at once. Take, for instance, the bass drum and the cymbal. Generally speaking, drummers strike these with respectable monotony. You hit the crash cymbal at the end of a drum roll, as a flourish, but also as a kind of announcement that time-out has, boringly enough, ended, and that the beat must go back to work. Moon does something strange with both instruments. He tends to 'ride' his bass drum: he keeps his foot hovering over the bass drum pedal as a nervous driver might keep a foot on a brake, and strikes the drum often, sometimes continuously throughout a bar. When he breaks to do a roll around the toms, he will keep the bass drum going simultaneously, so that the effect is of two drummers playing together. Meanwhile, he delights in hitting his cymbals as often as humanly possible, and off the beat – just before or after the logical moment – rather as jazz and big-band drummers do. The effect of all these cymbals being struck is of someone shouting out at unexpected moments while waiting in line – a yammer of exclamation marks. (Whereas his habit of entering a song by first crashing a cymbal and then ripping around the kit is like someone bursting into a quiet room and shouting: 'I'm here!')

So alive and free is this drumming that one tends to emphasise its exuberance at the expense of its complexity. But the playing on songs like 'Won't Get Fooled Again' or 'Bargain' or 'Love, Reign o'er Me' or 'The Song Is Over' is extremely complex: in addition to the intricate cymbal work, Moon is constantly flicking off little triplets (sometimes on the toms, but sometimes with his feet, by playing the two bass drums together); using a technique known as the paradiddle to play one tom against another; and doing press rolls and double-stroke rolls (methods by which, essentially, you bounce the sticks on the drum to get them to strike faster notes), and irregular flams on the snare drum (a flam involves hitting the drum with the two sticks not simultaneously but slightly staggered, and results in a sound more like 'blat' than 'that'). New technology allows listeners to isolate a song's individual players, and the astonishing isolated drum tracks from 'Won't Get Fooled Again' and 'Behind Blue Eyes' can be found on YouTube. On 'Won't Get Fooled Again', the drumming is staggeringly vital, with Moon at once rhythmically tight and massively spontaneous. On both that song and 'Behind Blue Eyes', you can hear him do something that was instinctive, probably, but which is hardly ever attempted in ordinary rock drumming: breaking for a fill, Moon fails to stop at the obvious end of the musical phrase and continues with his rolling break, over the line and into the start of the next phrase. In poetry, this failure to stop at the end of the line, this challenge to metrical closure, this desire *to get more in*, is called enjambment. Moon is the drummer of enjambment.

For me, this playing is like an ideal sentence of prose, a sentence I have always wanted to write and never quite had the confidence to: a long, passionate onrush, formally controlled and joyously messy, propulsive but digressively self-interrupted, attired but dishevelled, careful and lawless, right and wrong. (You can encounter such sentences in Lawrence's prose, in Bellow's, sometimes in David Foster Wallace's.) Such a sentence would be a breaking out, an escape. And drumming has always represented for me that dream of escape, when the body forgets itself, surrenders its awful self-consciousness. I taught myself the drums, but for years I was so busy being a good boy that I lacked the courage to own any drums. One could timidly admit to playing them, only if that meant that one never actually played them. At school, I did play in a rock band, but I kept the fact very quiet. The kids I played rock music with did not overlap with the world of classical music. Drumming was a notional add-on, a supplement to the playing of 'proper' instruments, a merely licensed rebellion. At school, the classical music path was the scholastic path. Choir school was like being at conservatory – daily rehearsal and performance. And then, later, as a teenager, to work hard at the piano, to sing in the choir, to play the trumpet in a youth orchestra, to pass exams in music theory, to study sonata form in Beethoven, to sit for a music scholarship, to talk to one's parents about Bach (or even, daringly, the Beatles!), to see the

London Symphony Orchestra at the Albert Hall, even just to fall asleep during *Aida* – all this was *approved*, was part of being a good student. Nowadays, I see schoolkids bustling along the pavement, their large instrument cases strapped to them like diligent coffins, and I know their weight of obedience. Happy obedience, too: that cello or French horn brings lasting joy, and a repertoire more demanding and subtle than rock music's. But fuck the laudable ideologies, as Roth's Mickey Sabbath puts it: subtlety is not rebellion, and subtlety is not freedom, and sometimes it is rebellious freedom that one wants, and only rock music can deliver it. And sometimes one despises oneself, in near middle age, for still being such a merely good student.

Georges Bataille has some haunting words (in *Erotism*) about how the workplace is the scene of our domestication and repression: it is where we are forced to put away our Dionysianism. The crazy sex from the night before is as if forgotten; the drunken marital argument of the weekend is erased; the antic children have disappeared; all the writhing, passionate music of life is turned off; and the excremental body is fraudulently clothed – a false bourgeois order dresses you, and dismissal and quick retirement await you if you don't obey. But Bataille might also have mentioned school, for school is work, too, work before the adult workplace, and school tutors the adolescent in repression and the rectitude of the bourgeois order, at the very moment in life when, temperamentally and biologically, one is most Dionysiac and most enraged by the hypocritical ordinances of the parental league.

So adolescents quickly get split in two, with an inner and outer self, a lawless sprite inside and a lawful ambassador outside: rock music, or your first sexual relationship, or reading, or writing poetry, or probably all four at once – why not? – represent the possibilities for inward escape. And playing rock is different again from playing classical music, or from writing poetry or painting. In all these other arts, though there may be trance-like moments and even stages of wildness and excess, the pressure of creating lasting forms demands discipline and silence, a charged, concentrated precision; mindful of Pascal's severe aphorism about the importance of staying quietly in a room, one does just that – one *did* just that, even at the age of sixteen – and stares at the sheet of paper, even if the words are not coming. Writing and reading, beautiful as they are, still carry with them the faintest odour of the exam room. (It is exam-silent in the room where I write these words, and how terrible, in a way, is this disjunction between literary expression and the violence of its content!) Rock music, though, is noise, improvisation, collaboration, theatre, exuberance, showing off, truancy, pantomime, aggression, bliss, tranced collectivity. It is not concentration so much as fission.

Imagine, then, the allure of the Who, whose vandalising velocity was such an incitement to the adolescent's demon sprite: 'I'm wet and I'm cold, / But thank God I ain't old,' sang young Roger Daltrey on *Quadrophenia*, in a song about a 'mod' teenager (named Jimmy, no less) who gets thrown out of his home:

> Here by the sea and sand
> Nothing ever goes as planned
> I just couldn't face going home.
> It was such a drag on my own.

> They finally threw me out.
> My mum got drunk on stout.
> My dad couldn't stand on two feet
> As he lectured about morality.

It is no accident that punk got a fair amount of its inspiration from the Who (the Sex Pistols often performed 'Substitute'), or that, a generation later, a band like Pearl Jam would devotedly cover 'Love, Reign o'er Me'. (Or that Chad Smith, the volcanic drummer of the Red Hot Chili Peppers, has cited Moon as an influence.) Here was a band that, in one obvious way, embodied success, but that, in a less obvious way, dared failure – I mean the large amount of improvisation in their songs, the risky, sometimes loose, excess of their concert performances, the violent earnestness of so many of the lyrics. And the epicentre of this successful failure, this man who wanted to pack as much of *the fun stuff* into his playing as humanly possible, was Keith Moon.

The Who were a kind of performance-art band: there was plenty of calculation amid the carelessness. Pete Townshend was a graduate of the Ealing art school (whose other musical alumni from the 1960s were Freddie Mercury and Ronnie Wood) and has sometimes claimed that the idea of smashing his guitar on stage was partly inspired by Gustav Metzger's 'auto-destructive art' movement. That high tone is quite Townshendian. But in one way, it is hard not to think of Keith Moon's life as a perpetual 'happening'; a gaudy, precarious, self-destructing art installation, whose gallery placard simply reads: 'The Rock-and-Roll Life, Late Twentieth Century'. In a manner that is also true of his drumming, he seemed to live at once naively and self-consciously: utterly spontaneous in his scandalous misbehaviour, and yet also aware that this is how one *should* live if one is a famous and rich rock musician. His parody is very hard to separate from his originality; his parody *is* his originality. This is one of the most charming elements of his posture behind the drum kit: he is always clowning around – standing up sometimes, at other times puffing out his cheeks like Dizzy Gillespie, grimacing and grinning like a fool in some *opera buffa*, twirling his sticks, doing silly phantom rolls just above the skins of the drums. A child might think that Moon was a circus performer. His drumming, like his life, was a serious joke.

Nowadays, Moon would probably be classed as having both ADHD and bipolar disorder; fortunately for the rest of us, he grew up in post-war, non-therapeutic Britain and medicated himself with booze, illegal drugs and illegal drumming. Born into a modest, working-class household in north London in 1946, Moon had a paltry education. He was restless, hyperactive and often played to the gallery. An art teacher described him as 'retarded artistically, idiotic in other respects', and the authorities were doubtless relieved when he left school at the age of fifteen. 'You never felt, "One day he is going to be famous,"' a friend told Tony Fletcher, Moon's biographer. 'You felt more likely that he was going to end up in prison.'

He had little formal training on the drums. As Gogol's brilliant prose, or Richard Burton's swaggering acting, embodies the temperamental exhibitionism of its creator, so Moon's playing is an extension of his theatrical hyperactivity. His mother noticed that he got bored easily and quickly lost interest in his train set or Meccano. Throughout his short life, he was seemingly addicted to practical jokes: he set off cherry bombs in hotels, dressed up as Adolf Hitler or Noël Coward, rode a wheelchair down an airport staircase, smashed up hotel rooms, drove a car into a swimming pool, and got arrested for breaching the peace. On planes, Moon might do his 'chicken soup' routine, which involved carrying a can of Campbell's chicken soup on board, emptying it, unseen, into a sick bag, and then pretending to retch violently. At which point he 'would raise it, and pour the sicklike soup back into his mouth, offering up a hearty sigh of relief while innocently inquiring of fellow passengers what they found so disgusting'. There was a relentlessness, a curious, drunken patience, to this theatricalism, which often needed preparation and forethought, and certainly demanded a kind of addicted commitment. 'Keith wore the Nazi uniform like something of a second skin, donning it intermittently for the next six or seven years,' writes Tony Fletcher. *Six or seven years.* His alcoholism and coke snorting were certainly addictions, but perhaps they were merely the solvents needed to maintain the larger, primal addiction to joking and play-acting.

Performance is a way of sublimely losing oneself, and there is a sense in which Moon as drummer was another role alongside Moon as Hitler, Moon as Noël Coward, Moon as arsonist, Moon as sick-bag buffoon, and Moon as crazy 'rock star'. ('I don't give a damn about a Holiday Inn room,' he grandly said after some act of vandalism. 'There's ten million of them exactly the same.') But 'role' suggests choice, freedom, calculation, whereas these roles don't seem to have been chosen so much as depended on. Or to put it another way: despite all the gaiety and partying, the only performance that seems to have truly liberated Moon was the one he enacted behind the drum kit. I often think of Moon and Glenn Gould together, despite their great differences. Both started performing as very young men (Moon was seventeen when he began playing with the Who, Gould twenty-two when he made his first great recording of the *Goldberg Variations*); both were idiosyncratic, revolutionary performers for whom spontaneity and eccentricity were important elements (for instance, both enjoyed singing and shouting while playing); both men had exuberant, pantomimic fantasy lives – Gould wrote about Petula Clark's 'Downtown', and appeared on Canadian television and radio in the guise of invented comic personae such as Karlheinz Klopweisser and Sir Nigel Twitt-Thornwaite, 'the Dean of British conductors'; both were gregarious and essentially solitary; neither man practised very much (at least, Gould claimed not to practise, and it is impossible to imagine Moon having the patience or sobriety to practise); and with both men, all the other performing (Gould's hand-washing and coat-wearing and melodramatic, pill-popping hypochondria) has the slightly desperate quality of mania – except the performance behind the instrument, which has the joyous freedom of true escape and self-dissolution: Gould *becomes* the piano, Moon *becomes* the drums.

For both Moon and Gould, the performer's life was very short – Gould abandoned concert performance at the age of thirty-one; Moon was dead by the age of thirty-two and had not played well for years. He had perhaps eight really great drumming years, between 1968 and 1976. Throughout this period, he was ingesting ludicrous volumes of drink and drugs. There are stories of him swallowing twenty or thirty pills at once. In San Francisco, in 1973, he had taken so many depressants (perhaps to come down from a high, or to deal with pre-concert nerves) that, after slopping his way through several songs, he collapsed and had to be taken to the hospital. When his stomach was pumped, it was found to contain quantities of PCP, a drug described by Fletcher as 'used to put agitated monkeys and gorillas to sleep'. What magically happened on stage, while Moon was being carted away, was incised, years ago, on my teenage cerebellum. Pete Townshend asked the crowd whether anyone could come up and play the drums. Scott Halprin, a nineteen-year-old, and presumably soon to be the most envied teenager in America, got onto the stage and played with the Who. 'Everything was locked into place,' Halprin later said of the gargantuan drum kit; 'anyplace you could hit there would be something there. All the cymbals overlapped.'

Both Moon and Gould were rather delicate, even handsome young men who coarsened with age and developed a thickness of feature, an almost simian rind. At twenty, Moon was slight and sweet, with a bowl of black hair upended on his head, and dark, dopey eyes, and the arched eyebrows of a clown. By the end of his life, he looked ten years older than he was – puffy, heavy, his features no longer sweetly clownish but slightly villainous – Bill Sykes, played by Moon's old drinking friend Oliver Reed, the arched eyebrows now thicker and darker, seemingly painted on, as if he had become a caricature of himself. Friends were shocked by his appearance. He was slower and less inventive, less vital, on the drums; the album *Who Are You*, his last record, attests to the decline. Perhaps no one was very surprised when he died, from a massive overdose of the drug Heminevrin, a sedative prescribed for alcohol withdrawal symptoms. 'He's gone and done it,' Townshend told Roger Daltrey. Thirty-two pills were found in his stomach, and the equivalent of a pint of beer in his blood. His girlfriend, who found him, told a coroner's court that she had often seen him pushing pills down his throat, without liquid. Almost exactly two years later, John Bonham died from asphyxiation, after hours of drinking vodka. He was less than a year older than Moon.

There are two famous Glenn Gould recordings of the *Goldberg Variations*: the one he made at the age of twenty-two, and the one he made at the age of fifty-one, just before he died. The opening aria of that piece, the lucid, ornate melody that Gould made his own, sounds very different in each recording. In the young man's version, the aria is fast, sweet, running clear like water. In the middle-aged man's recording, the aria is half as fast, the notes so magnetically separated that they seem almost unrelated to one another. The first aria is cocky, exuberant, optimistic, vital, fun, sound-filled; the second aria is reflective, seasoned, wintry, grieving, silence-haunted. These two arias stand facing each other, separated by almost thirty years, as the gates of a life. I prefer the second version; but when I listen to the second, how I want to *be* the first!

2010

What Chekhov Meant by Life

WHAT DID CHEKHOV MEAN by 'life'? I wondered this while uncomfortably watching a Broadway production of *A Doll's House*. Mild, slippery Chekhov once told Stanislavsky, with soft surprise as if it were something too obvious to say: 'But listen, Ibsen is no playwright! . . . Ibsen just doesn't know life. In life it simply isn't like that.' No, in life it simply isn't like that, even while sitting in a theatre. It was summer. Outside, the Broadway traffic sounded like an army that is getting close but which never arrives. The fantastic heat was sensual, the air-conditioners dripping their sap. Everything was the usual noisy obscurity. Yet inside, here was Ibsen ordering life into three trim acts, and a cooled audience obediently laughing and tutting at the right moments, and thinking about drinks at the interval – the one moment of Chekhovian life being that, in the lobby, the barman could be heard putting out glasses, tuning up his little cocktail orchestra. The clinking was disturbing Ibsen's simpler tune.

A Doll's House tells the story of a woman's subjection to, and eventual escape from, her husband. Ibsen does not make Nora's husband, Torvald, monstrous so much as uncomprehending. And yet he cannot resist telling us how foolishly uncomprehending Torvald is. Nora deceives her husband in order to protect him; he discovers the deception and is furious. Towards the end of the play, Nora tells him that she is leaving him because she has never been more than his toy. Torvald 'forgives' her for her deception. Nora cries because Torvald cannot understand. 'Why are you crying?' asks Torvald. 'Is it because I have forgiven you for your deception?' At this moment, the audience snickered knowingly. Poor, foolish Torvald, who thinks he can make things all right by forgiving his wife! Surely Chekhov's objection to Ibsen was founded in the feeling that Ibsen is like a man who laughs at his own jokes. Ibsen's people are too comprehensible. We comprehend them as we comprehend fictional entities. He is always tying the moral shoelaces of his characters, making everything neat, presentable, knowable. The secrets of his characters are knowable secrets, not the true privacies of Chekhov's people. They are the bourgeois secrets: a former lover, a broken contract, a blackmailer, a debt, an unwanted relative.

But Chekhov's idea of 'life' is a bashful, milky complication, not a solving of things. We can get a good understanding of this from the notebook he kept. This notebook was, in effect, the mattress in which he stuffed his stolen money. It is full of enigmas in which nothing adds up, full of strange squints, comic observations, and promptings for new stories.

Instead of sheets – dirty tablecloths.

The dog walked in the street and was ashamed of its crooked legs.

They were mineral water bottles with preserved cherries in them.

In the bill preserved by the hotel-keeper was, among other things: 'Bugs – fifteen kopecks.'

He picked his teeth and put the toothpick back into the glass.

A private room in a restaurant. A rich man, tying his napkin round his neck, touching the sturgeon with his fork: 'At least I'll have a snack before I die' – and he has been saying this for a long time, daily.

If you wish women to love you, be original; I know a man who used to wear felt boots summer and winter, and women fell in love with him.

Chekhov thinks of detail, even visual detail, as a story, and thinks of story as an enigma. He was not interested in noticing that the roofs of a town look like armadillo shells, or that he was confused about God, or that the Russian people represented the world-spirit on a troika. He was drawn neither to the statically poetic nor to the statically philosophical. Detail is hardly ever a stable entity in Chekhov's work; it is a reticent event. He found the world to be as deeply evasive as he was himself – life as a tree of separate hanging stories, of dangling privacies. For him a story did not merely begin in enigma, but ended in enigma too. He has a character in 'Concerning Love' complain that 'decent Russians like ourselves have a passion for problems that have never been solved'. Chekhov had such a passion for problems, but only if complaint might stay unrequited. The writer Ivan Bunin said that Chekhov loved to read out random oddities from the newspapers: 'Babkin, a Samara merchant, left all his money for a memorial to Hegel!' The attraction of such tales, one suspects, was that a newspaper imagines that it has explained a story when all it has done is told one. Bunin supplied a true anecdote about a deacon who ate all the caviare at a funeral party; Chekhov used this at the beginning of 'In the Ravine'. His writing, which is strewn with unsolved details, is a kind of newspaper of the intimate fantastic. In this respect, his stories are like tales of crime in which nobody is a criminal.

There is no introspection in Chekhov's notebook. Everything has the same hard, found, random quality. We can infer as much of Chekhov's personality from one entry as from all of them together. A friend said that he 'lacked gaiety, and his fine, intelligent eyes always looked at everything from a distance'. From the various memoirs by relatives and friends, we can imagine a man who always seemed a little older than himself, as if he were living more than one life. He would not make himself transparent: he was approachable but unknowable. He had an arbitrary smile, and a comic's ability to make strange things seem inevitable. When an actor asked him to explain what kind of writer Trigorin is, in *The Seagull*, he replied: 'But he wears checkered trousers.' He had a horror of being the centre of attention. He delivered his judgements in a tone of weary generosity, as if they were so obvious that he had simply missed someone else saying them earlier. He was deeply charming; seasonally, a different woman fell in love with him. On this picture has been built the Anglo-American vision of Chekhov, in which the writer resembles the perfect literary Englishman – a writer of the religion of no religion, of instincts rather than convictions, a governor of ordinary provinces whose inhabitants may be unhappy or yearning for change, but who eventually learn to calm down and live by the local laws. D. S. Mirsky, the Russian critic who lived in England, argued that Chekhov was popular in England because of his 'unusually complete rejection of what we may call the heroic values'. But this idea of Chekhov as the nurse of the prosaic is far from the truth, and Chekhov's writing, which is odd, brutal, despairing and unhappily comic, gives no excuse for it.

The fullest biography to appear in English, by Donald Rayfield, clouds the soft Anglo-American idea of Chekhov, which is a good thing. In this account Chekhov is still charming, tactful, and decent. He is still the man who bought new books for the library of his home town, who dispensed free medicine and became a hospital inspector near his farm at Melikhovo. But we also see that Chekhov's life was a long flight into his work. He ran from human connections. There is something cruel, even repulsive, in a man who was so sensitive to pain, about the way Chekhov encouraged women to fall in love with him, and then, month by month, cancelled their ardour. He would reply scantily or not at all to their letters. His most productive writing years, between 1892 and 1900, were spent on his Melikhovo estate, about fifty miles south of Moscow, where he lived with his dutiful sister, Masha, and his parents. Here he tried to ration unnecessary involvement with people. Chekhov had the temperament of a philanderer. Sexually, he preferred brothels or swift liaisons.

His one loyalty was to his family, for whom he became the breadwinner while at medical school in Moscow. He was born in Taganrog, in southern Russia, in 1860. His father, Pavel, may be seen as the original of all Chekhov's great portraits of hypocrites. Pavel was a grocer, but he failed at everything he touched except religious devotion. In between flogging his children – he was exceptionally cruel – he became kapellmeister of the cathedral choir, where his love of the liturgy made services interminable. In church, 'Pavel never compromised over his favourite quality, splendour.' He was horribly pious. There is the story of Pavel finding a rat in a barrel of olive oil in his shop. 'He was too honest to say nothing, too mean to pour the oil away, too lazy to boil and re-filter it. He chose consecration: Father Pokrovsky conducted a service in the shop.'

Chekhov would become a writer who did not believe in God, hated physical cruelty, fought every sign of 'splendour' on the page, and filled his fiction with hypocrites. The ghost of Pavel can be found everywhere in Chekhov, in the complacent Dr Ragin in 'Ward No. 6', who lectures his abused patients at the local asylum about Marcus Aurelius and the importance of stoicism, and in the fatuous priest in 'In the Ravine' who, at dinner, comforts a woman who has just lost her baby while pointing at her with 'a fork with a pickled mushroom on the end of it . . .' Yet the son did not abandon the father. Once the Chekhovs had moved to Moscow, Anton calmly assumed the sustenance of his whole family. He checked his dissolute elder brothers with that strange, sourceless maturity of his, which sometimes gives him the air of being the sole possessor of a clandestine happiness. There are eight rules by which 'well-bred people' live, he told his brother Nikolai in a long letter. You restrain yourself sexually; you do not brag. 'The truly gifted are always in the shadows, in the crowd, far from exhibitions.' Until Donald Rayfield gained access to previously censored archives, the last line of this letter has always been soothed into English as: 'You have to relinquish your pride:

you are not a little boy any more.' But the actual version runs: 'You must drop your fucking conceit . . .' It is good to tear our idea of Chekhovian perfection with these little hernias. We should see the lapses, the mundanities, the coarseness, the sexual honesty which Russian censors and English worshippers removed. Chekhov is still philo-Semitic and a supporter of women's rights. But every so often his letters fall, show a little bulge of prejudice – 'Yids' appear from time to time, and women are verbally patted.

The Chekhov family lived off Anton's literary earnings. These were small at first. Chekhov wrote hackishly for six years – comic stubs, sketches, cartoons and colourings for newspapers. (His mature work, of course, has a briskness, and sometimes a slapping, educative motion reminiscent of the form of a cartoon or sketch.) His meeting with Alexei Suvorin, the owner of the newspaper *Novoye Vremya*, was the foundation of his greatest writing. Suvorin had had his eye on Chekhov's writing. From 1887 until 1900, he was Chekhov's patron and deepest correspondent. He was also the writer's opposite, so Chekhov had to function like Suvorin's kidney, extracting the businessman's poisons – his anti-Semitism (they quarrelled over the Dreyfus affair when Chekhov announced himself a Dreyfusard), his artistic conservatism, his wariness of the slightest political radicalism. Suvorin was reviled by most enlightened thinkers, and Chekhov's alliance with him was often scorned. But then Chekhov also became friendly with Gorki, and his fiction was sometimes simultaneously claimed by both right and left: the pantomime horse of politics fighting inside itself for front and back legs, and then collapsing on stage.

'The Steppe' (1888) was the first story to appear in a 'thick journal': Chekhov was a renowned writer for the rest of his life. He was only twenty-eight, and the story has its hesitations, such as a weakness for lurid theatrical gargoyles (Moses and Solomon, the Jewish traders) which seem Dickensian but which are lifted from Gogol. But much of the beauty of mature Chekhov is here; it is just an early footprint made by a lighter man. In particular, the bashful pace of the writing, which moves at the aimless, random speed of the imagination. We follow a little boy, Yegorushka, who is going to a new school, and who has hitched a ride with two men – a wool trader called Kuzmichov, and a priest called Father Christopher. As they leave the boy's home village, at the start of the journey, they pass the cemetery in which his father and his grandmother are buried. Chekhov's description drifts.

From behind the wall cheerful white crosses and tombstones peeped out, nestling in the foliage of cherry trees and seen as white patches from a distance. At blossom time, Yegorushka remembered, the white patches mingled with the cherry blooms in a sea of white, and when the cherries had ripened the white tombs and crosses were crimson-spotted, as if with blood. Under the cherries behind the wall the boy's father and his grandmother Zinaida slept day and night. When Grandmother had died she had been put in a long, narrow coffin, and five-copeck pieces had been placed on her eyes, which would not stay shut. Before dying she had been alive, and she had brought him soft poppy-seed bun rings from the market, but now she just slept and slept.

Woolf and Joyce admired Chekhov, and, faced with little Yegorushka's drifting thought, one sees why. (Just as, watching the didactic *A Doll's House*, one sees why George Bernard Shaw admired Ibsen.) For this is a form of stream-of-consciousness, more natural and less showy than Anna Karenina's mania at the end of Tolstoy's novel. 'Before dying, she had been alive . . . but now she just slept and slept.' This is not only how a small boy thinks, but how all of us think about the dead, privately: *Before dying, she had been alive*. It is one of those obviously pointless banalities of thought, an accidental banality which, being an accident, is never quite banal. But something deeper about Chekhov's art is revealed a page later, when Yegorushka cries because he misses his mother, and Father Christopher comforts him. 'Never mind son,' the priest says. 'Call on God. Lomonosov once travelled just like this with the fishermen, and he became famous throughout Europe. Learning conjoined with faith yields fruit pleasing to God. What does the prayer say? "For the glory of the Creator, for our parents' comfort, for the benefit of church and country." That's the way of it.' Of course, Father Christopher is offering no comfort at all; he is self-involved. His solace has no dramatic point, in the Ibsen sense. He is speaking his mind, literally. He speaks in the same apparently arbitrary manner as the boy thinks. This use of stream-of-consciousness would, in later years, become the basis of Chekhov's innovation in stagecraft; it is also his innovation in fiction. Chekhov sees the similarities between what we say to ourselves and what we say to others: both are failed privacies. Both are lost secrets, the former lost somewhere between our minds and our souls, the latter lost somewhere between each other. Naturally, this kind of mental speech, whether turned inward or outward, has the arbitrary quality of memory or dream. It *is* memory or dream. And this is why it seems comic, because watching a Chekhov character is like watching a lover wake up in bed, half awake and half dreaming, saying something odd and private which means nothing to us because it refers to the preceding dream. In life, at such moments, we sometimes laugh and say: 'You're not making any sense, you know.' Chekhov's characters live in these two states.

'The Bishop', a late story which Chekhov completed in 1902, two years before he died, is a good example of this new fluency in storytelling. A dying cleric starts to think about his childhood . . . and suddenly, he is adrift. He remembers 'Father Simeon, who was very short and thin, but who had a terribly tall son (a theological student) . . . Once his son lost his temper with the cook and called her "Ass of Jehudiel", which made Father Simeon go very quiet, for he was only too ashamed of not being able to remember where this particular ass was mentioned in the Bible.' Such richness, such healthy secularism of detail! Yet the great novelty of Chekhov is not in discovering or inventing such details and anecdotes – you can find details as good in Tolstoy and Leskov. It is in their placement, their sudden flowering, their lack of apparent point, as if Chekhov's characters were coming across something unwanted, certainly unexpected. The thought seems to be thinking the characters. It is the movement of free consciousness in literature for perhaps the first time: neither Austen nor Sterne, neither Gogol nor Tolstoy, allow their characters quite this relationship to memory.

The great pleasure of seeing Chekhov develop as a writer, from 'The Steppe' to 'The Lady with the Dog' eleven years later, is to see the way he discovers and enlarges this idea of apparently arbitrary detail. It becomes the very principle of Chekhov's prose style. Nabokov once complained about Chekhov's 'medley of dreadful prosaisms, ready-made epithets, repetitions'. But Chekhov's metaphors, nature-scenes and visual details are often finer than Nabokov's (and invariably finer than Tolstoy's) because they have an unexpectedness that seems to break away from literature. He sees the world not as a writer might see it but as one of his characters might. This is the case even when he is telling a story as 'Chekhov', apparently from outside a character's head. 'From somewhere far off came the mournful, indistinct cry of a bittern, sounding just like a cow locked up in a shed.' This is not an obviously poetic likeness; it is how a villager might think of a bittern's cry. 'A cuckoo seemed to be adding up someone's age, kept losing count and starting again.' A girl about to burst into tears, 'her face oddly strained as if her mouth were full of water'. (The key there is the word 'oddly'. Oddly to whom? To the other characters in the room, one of whom is Chekhov: he is no longer a writer.) The noise, in a poor village, of 'an expensive-sounding accordion'.

More completely than any writer before him Chekhov became his characters. A great story like 'Gusev' is impossible without this identification. It is set on a boat returning to Russia. In the sick-bay, a stupid peasant called Gusev is dying. The other patients make fun of his primitive imagination – he thinks that the winds are chained up somewhere like dogs to a wall, and that it is stormy because they have been let loose.

As Gusev lies in the ship, he recalls his home village, and we see that his imagination is not primitive. Soon, he dies, and is buried at sea, wrapped in a sail. 'Sewn up in the sailcloth,' writes Chekhov, 'he looked like a carrot or radish: broad at the head and narrow at the feet.' As he falls into the sea, clouds are massing. Chekhov writes that one cloud looks like a triumphal arch, another like a lion, a third like a pair of scissors. Suddenly we realise that Chekhov sees the world as Gusev does. If Gusev is foolish then so is Chekhov! Why is it more foolish to think of the wind as a chained dog as Gusev does, than to think of a cloud as a lion or a corpse as a radish, as Chekhov does? Chekhov's very narration disappears into Gusev's.

In 1890, Chekhov made a long journey to Sakhalin, a prison island off the coast of Siberia. He saw Russia's human leavings on Sakhalin, a kind of living death-camp. Near the end of the book-length report he published in 1895, he describes seeing a murderer being given ninety lashes. Then this Chekhovian detail – a whining military medical assistant who asks a favour. 'Your worship, please let me see how they punish a prisoner.' There were times, wrote Chekhov, when 'I felt that I saw before me the extreme limits of man's degradation . . .' Chekhov believed in the importance of good schools and medicine. But Sakhalin intensified his meliorism. At Melikhovo, the estate he bought in 1892, he helped to build a new school, gave freely of his medical expertise. His greatest stories became darker, more absolving. Prisons are everywhere in them: even the lovers in 'The Lady with the Dog', published in 1899 while Chekhov was first involved with his future wife, Olga Knipper, feel trapped in a cage, 'and it was impossible to escape from it, just as though you were in a lunatic asylum or a convict chain-gang!' The bleak 'Gusev' (1890) was seeded when Chekhov saw two men die on board the ship bringing him back from Sakhalin. 'Ward No. 6' (1892) is set in an asylum. A complacent doctor, who has ignored the sufferings of his patients, finds that his own mind is lapsing. He in turn is thrown into the asylum. From the window, he can see the town prison: 'There's reality for you!' thinks the doctor. He dies in the asylum, and as he leaves consciousness he goes on a mental safari, and Chekhov awards him one of those gorgeous lunges, one of those random aerations or white apertures that are so distinctive a feature of his work: 'A herd of deer, extraordinarily beautiful and graceful, which he had been reading about on the previous day, raced past him; then a peasant woman stretched out a hand to him with a registered letter . . .' These stories have a rather frantic humanism: Chekhov wrote to Suvorin in 1898 that the writer's task was to 'stand up for the guilty if they have already been condemned and punished'. This was a year after he made his first public stand, on behalf of Dreyfus.

What did Chekhov believe in? In his essay on the writer, the philosopher Lev Shestov suggested (approvingly) that Chekhov had 'no ideal, not even the ideal of ordinary life'. His work, he said, murmurs a quiet 'I don't know' to every problem. Certain Soviet critics decided that Chekhov's 'hopeless' characters were not prophetic enough about the imminent revolution – too pessimistic about Russia's future. But because Chekhov's stories confound philosophy they do not necessarily lack it. Susan Sontag is surely right when she suggests that

Chekhov's writing is a dream of freedom – 'an absolute freedom,' wrote Chekhov, 'the freedom from violence and lies'.
And freedom is not merely political or material in his work. It
is a neutral saturate, like air or light. How often he describes
a village, and then, at the village's edge – 'the open fields'! The
narrator of 'Man in a Case' remembers the freedom of being
a child when his parents went out, 'and we would run around
the garden for an hour or so, revelling in perfect freedom'. And
because Chekhov is truthful, because he is not a Tolstoy who
will shuffle his characters towards the light of the Godhead,
or a Gorki who will lead his characters to instinctive socialism, he must admit that freedom is not always attractive to us,
and that it frightens us. Perhaps freedom is only the freedom
not to exist? 'Oh how nice not to exist,' cries Chebutykin in
Three Sisters. Often we notice that his characters long to escape
into a freedom whose vastness depends on its non-existence.
Moscow is not just an impossibility for the three sisters. It
does not exist, because their desire for it has made it disappear.
Perhaps the gap between yearning for a new life – the most
familiar gesture of Chekhov's characters, and one the writer
saw first-hand amongst his own family – and yearning for no
life, is small. But whatever happens to Chekhov's characters,
however they yearn, they have one freedom that flows from
his literary genius: they act like free consciousnesses, and not
as owned literary characters. This is not a negligible freedom.
For the great achievement of Chekhov's beautifully accidental
style, his mimicking of the stream of the mind, is that it allows
forgetfulness into fiction. Buried deep in themselves, people
forget themselves while thinking, and go on mental journeys.
Of course, they do not exactly forget to be themselves. They

forget to act *as purposeful fictional characters*. They mislay their scripts. They stop being actors, Ibsen's envoys.

We see this most beautifully in one of Chekhov's earliest stories, 'The Kiss', written when he was twenty-seven. A virginal soldier kisses a woman for the first time in his life. He hoards the memory of it, and bursts to tell his fellow soldiers about his experience. But when he does tell them, he is disappointed because his story takes only a short minute to tell, yet 'he had imagined it would take until morning'. One notices that many of Chekhov's characters are disappointed by the stories they tell, and somewhat jealous of other people's stories. But to be disappointed by one's own story is an extraordinarily subtle freedom in literature, for it implies a character's freedom to be disappointed not only by his own story but, by extension, by the story Chekhov has given him. The soldier forgets that he is in Chekhov's story because he has become so involved in his own. His own story is bottomless, and yearns to last all night; Chekhov's story 'takes only a minute to tell'. In Chekhov's world, our inner lives run at their own speed. They are laxly calendared. They live in their own gentle almanac, and in his stories the free inner life bumps against the outer life like two different time-systems, like the Julian calendar against the Gregorian. This was what Chekhov meant by 'life'. This was his revolution.

1997

Serious Noticing

I

FOR THE LAST TWENTY YEARS or so, I have returned again and again to a remarkable story, written by Anton Chekhov when he was twenty-seven.[1] It's called 'The Kiss'. A regiment of soldiers has been billeted in a provincial town. The owner of the town's biggest house invites the officers to tea and a ball. One of them, a naive staff-captain named Ryabovich, does not find it as easy as his confident peers to dance with the women. He is 'a short, round-shouldered officer in spectacles and with whiskers like a lynx's'. He watches his fellow officers talk easily and flirtatiously with the women.

> In the whole of his life he had never once danced, nor had he ever put his arm round the waist of a respectable woman . . . There was a time when he envied the confidence and go of his comrades and suffered mental anguish; the awareness that he was timid, round-shouldered and drab, that he had lynx-like whiskers and no hips, hurt

1 See 'What Chekhov Meant by Life,' pp. 34–48.

him profoundly, but with the passing of the years he had become inured to this, so that now, as he looked at his comrades dancing or conversing loudly, he no longer experienced envy, only a feeling of wistful admiration.

To hide his embarrassment and boredom, he goes wandering in the large house and gets lost, ending up in a dark room. Here, writes Chekhov, 'as in the ball-room, the windows were wide open and there was a scent of poplar, lilac, and roses'. Suddenly, behind him, he hears rushed footsteps. A woman approaches and kisses him. They both gasp, and both instantly realise that she has kissed the wrong man; she quickly retreats. Ryabovich returns to the ballroom, his hands shaking. Something has happened to him.

> His neck, which had just been embraced by soft fragrant arms, seemed to have been bathed with oil; at the spot on his cheek by his left moustache where the unknown woman had kissed him, there was a slight, pleasant, cold tingling, such as you get from peppermints, and the more he rubbed the spot, the more pronounced this tingling became, whilst the whole of him, from top to toe, was filled with a new, peculiar feeling that grew and grew . . . He felt he wanted to dance, run into the garden, laugh out loud . . .

The incident grows in size and importance in the young soldier's mind. He has never kissed a woman before. In the ballroom he looks at each of the women in turn, and convinces himself that *she* was the one. That night, when he goes to bed, he has the sensation that 'someone had been kind to him and made him happy, that something unusual, absurd, but extremely good and full of joy, had taken place in his life'.

The next day the regiment breaks camp and moves on. Ryabovich cannot stop thinking about the kiss, and a few days later, at dinner, while his fellow officers are chatting and reading the newspapers, he summons the courage to tell his story. He does tell it, and a minute later falls silent. Because it only took a minute to tell. And Ryabovich is amazed, writes Chekhov, 'to find that the story had taken such a short time. He had thought he could go on talking about the kiss all night.' To add to the sense of failure, his fellow officers seem either bored by his short tale or sceptical of its veracity. Eventually the regiment returns to the town where the event took place. Ryabovich hopes for another invitation to the big house. But it doesn't happen, and he wanders down to a river near the house, feeling cynical and disillusioned. There are some sheets hanging over the rail of the bridge, 'and for no good reason' he touches one of the sheets. 'How absurd! . . . How stupid it all is!' he thinks, as he gazes at the water.

There are two absolutely lancing sentences in this story: 'In that minute he had told it all and was quite amazed to find that the story had taken such a short time. He had thought he could go on talking about the kiss all night.'

What a *serious noticer* a writer must be to write those lines. Chekhov appears to notice everything. He sees that the story we tell in our heads is the most important one, because we are internal expansionists, comic fantasists. For Ryabovich, his story has grown bigger and bigger, and has joined, in real time, the rhythm of life. Chekhov sees that Ryabovich, painfully, does and doesn't need an audience for his story. Perhaps Chekhov is also jokily suggesting that, unlike Chekhov, the captain wasn't much of a storyteller. For there is the inescapable irony that Chekhov's own story, while taking a bit longer than a minute to tell, does not take all evening to read: like many of his tales, it is brisk and brief. Had Chekhov told it, people would have listened. Yet Chekhov also suggests that even the story we have just read – Chekhov's brief story – is not the whole account of Ryabovich's experience; that just as Ryabovich failed to tell it all, so perhaps Chekhov has not told it all. There is still the enigma of *what* Ryabovich wanted to say.

'The Kiss' is a story about a story, and reminds us that one definition of a story might be that it always produces more of them. A story is story-producing. There is Chekhov's tale; there is the discrete incident that befalls Ryabovich; and there is the untold, bottomless story that Ryabovich makes, and fails to make, of that incident. No single story can ever explain itself: this enigma at the heart of story is itself a story. Stories produce offspring, genetic splinters of themselves, hapless embodiments of their original inability to tell the whole tale.

Stories are *dynamic combinations of surplus and lack*: disappointing because they must end, and disappointing because they cannot really end. A real story is endless, but it disappoints because it is begun and ended not by its own logic but by the coercive form of the storyteller: you can feel the pure surplus of life trying to get beyond the death which authorial form imposes. The story Ryabovich would ideally tell, the one that would take all evening and not a mere minute, might be the whole story of his life – something like the tale Chekhov has been telling us, though doubtless much longer and less shapely. It would not just recount the incident in the dark room, but might tell us about Ryabovich's shyness, his innocence of women, his sloping shoulders and lynx-like whiskers. It might recount things not mentioned by Chekhov, the kinds of episodes that a novel might find room for – his parents (how his father bullied him, and his mother indulged him); how his decision to become a soldier was undertaken partly to please his father, and was never something Ryabovich wanted to do; how he dislikes and rather envies his fellow officers; how he writes poetry in his spare time, but has never shared a single line with anyone; how he dislikes his lynx-like whiskers, but needs them because they obscure an area of pitted skin.

But just as Ryabovich's one-minute story is not really worth telling, is not really a story, so the shapeless story that would take all evening is too shapeless, is not enough of a story, either. Ryabovich, one suspects, needs a Chekhovian eye for detail, the ability to notice well and seriously, the genius for selection. Do you think that Ryabovich mentioned, when he told his tale to his fellow soldiers, that the darkened room smelt of lilac, poplar and roses? Do you think that Ryabovich mentioned that when the woman kissed him, his cheek glowed, as if brushed with peppermint? For details represent those moments in a story where form is outlived, cancelled, evaded. I think of details as nothing less than bits of life sticking out of the frieze of form, imploring us to touch them. Details are not, of course, just *bits of life*: they represent that magical fusion, wherein the maximum amount of literary artifice (the writer's genius for selection and imaginative creation) produces a simulacrum of the maximum amount of non-literary or actual life, a process whereby artifice is then indeed *converted into (fictional, which is to say, new) life*.

Details are not lifelike but irreducible: things-in-themselves, what I would call lifeness itself. The detail about the peppermint, like the tingle felt by Ryabovich on his cheek, lingers for us: all we have to do is rub the spot.

Henry Green's novel *Loving* (1945) is set in an Anglo-Irish country house, and deals largely with the lives of its cockney servants. There is a moment in that book not unlike Chekhov's 'The Kiss' (and Green was a keen student of Chekhov), when the young housemaid, Edith, enters the room of her mistress, Mrs Jack, to open the curtains and bring the morning tea. Edith gets a shock, because Mrs Jack is in bed with Captain Davenport, who is not her husband. As Captain Davenport quickly disappears under the sheets, Mrs Jack sits upright, naked, and Edith runs from the room. She had seen, writes Green in a memorable phrase, 'that great brilliant upper part of' Mrs Jack, 'on which, wayward, were two dark upraised dry wounds shaking on her'. Edith is shocked but secretly thrilled – partly because it happened to her and not anyone else; partly because, for an innocent young woman, the witnessing of this scene is an initiation, at one remove, into the glamour of adult sexual relations (though Green doesn't tell us this explicitly); partly because it's something to wield in her encounters with Charley Raunce, the butler, with whom she has been increasingly flirtatious.

As in Ryabovich's case, Edith's story is intensely valuable to her, a treasure to be both hoarded and haplessly given away. 'Well then isn't this a knock out,' she crows to Charley Raunce. 'An' it happened to me . . . after all these years.' Charley, always cautious when Edith seems to be one erotic step ahead of him, is not as happy as she is. 'Well, aren't you glad?' she asks, insistently. 'You're going to try and take that from me?'

> Why [she continues] there's all those stories you've had, openin' this door and seeing that when you were in a place in Dorset and lookin' through the bathroom window in Wales an' suchlike . . . and now it's come to me. Right a'bed they was next to one another. Stuff that in your old smelly pipe and smoke it.

When Raunce tries to dismiss the singularity of Edith's experience, by claiming that the former butler, Mr Eldon, also caught Mrs Jack and her lover in bed, Edith bursts out in splendid indignation: 'D'you stand there an' tell me Mr Eldon had come upon them some time? Just as I did? That she sat up in bed with her fronts bobblin' at him like a pair of geese the way she did to me?' It's a beautiful outburst: you don't easily forget that brilliant, almost Shakespearean neologism, 'fronts', or the idea of breasts bobbling like a pair of geese.

Detail is always *someone*'s detail. Henry Green's own diction is eloquent, lyrical and sharply particular. As the literary author, as the modernist author in the third person, he describes Mrs Jack's breasts as 'dry upraised wounds'. I think he means nothing sinister by this. Like a good painter, he is getting us to look harder than we usually do at a nipple – the way the darker skin around it can look like tender scar tissue (hence 'wounds'). But Edith makes the story her own by seeing *her* details, using her words and similes. Isn't there a moving quality of desperation about Edith's need to keep the story hers? She fears that Raunce will take it away from her, she wants her story to be the equal of Mr Raunce's stories from Dorset and Wales; and the very force of her language seems an attempt to ensure that whatever Mr Eldon saw, he did not see what *she* saw, because he did not see it as vividly and pungently as she did.

Like Ryabovich and Edith, we are the sum of our details. (Or rather, our details exceed the sum of our details; we fail to compute.) The details *are* the stories; stories in miniature. As we get older, some of those details fade, and others, paradoxically, become more vivid. We are, in a way, all internal fiction writers and poets, rewriting our memories.

I find that my memory is always yeasting up, turning one-minute moments into loafing, ten-minute reveries. Displacement also adds its own difficulties. I sometimes feel, for instance, that I grew up not in the 1970s and '80s but in the 1870s and '80s. I doubt I would feel this if I still lived in Britain, but the vanishing of certain habits and traditions, and my leaving that country for the United States in 1995, combine to make my childhood seem ridiculously remote. Often, in conversation in the States, I'm about to start a story about some aspect of my childhood, some memory, and I stop, aware that I can't quite heave into narrative the incommunicable mass of obscure and distant detail. I would have to explain too much – and then I would not have a story, would not have details, but explication; or my story would have to begin too early and end too late: it would take all evening to tell.

I was born in 1965, and grew up in a northern English town, Durham, home to a university, a majestic Romanesque cathedral and surrounded by coalfields, many of them now abandoned. Every house had a hearth and fire, and coal, rather than wood, was used as domestic fuel. Every few weeks, a lorry arrived, piled with lumpy burlap sacks; the coal was then poured down a chute into the house's cellar – I vividly remember the volcanic sound, as it tumbled into the cellar, and the drifting, blueish coal-dust, and the dark, small men who carried those sacks on their backs, with tough leather pads on their shoulders.

I went to school in Durham, an ecclesiastical institution strong in subjects like Latin, history and music. I sang in the cathedral choir, a kind of glorious indentured servitude – we performed evensong every day, and three services on Sundays. Every afternoon, we lined up in two equal columns, to walk from the school to the cathedral – dressed in thick black capes that were clasped at the neck, and black mortar boards with frondy purple tassels. The dormitories were so cold in the morning that we learned how to dress in bed. The school's headmaster, the Reverend Canon John Grove, was probably only in his early fifties, but seemed to us a fantastically antique figure. He was a bachelor and a clergyman, and wore the uniform of his calling: a black suit, a black buttonless shirt, a thick white clerical collar. (In a poem by the Scottish poet Robin Robertson, whose father was a minister, there is the wonderful detail that his father's clerical collar was a strip of white plastic cut from a bottle of washing-up liquid.) Except for the band of white starch round his neck, Canon Grove was entirely colourless – his ancient Oxford shoes were black, his thick spectacles were black, the pipe he smoked was black. He seemed to have been carbonised centuries ago, turned into ash, and when he lit his pipe, it seemed as if he was lighting himself. Like all children, we were fascinated by the match held over the pipe-bowl, by the flame steadily journeying along the flimsy match, entranced by the sucking noises of the smoker, and the way the flame halted its horizontal passage at these moments and then briefly disappeared vertically into the bowl. And always there was the question: how can he hold the match alight for so long, with such reptilian imperviousness?

This headmaster was quite a kind soul, in his way, but he stuck to the codes of punishment he understood. Boys guilty of major sins were given 'six of the best', six hard, stinging smacks on the arse, with the back of a large, flat, wooden hairbrush. By the time I left this school, at the age of thirteen, I was triumphant about how many 'whacks' of the hairbrush I had accumulated – 106, to be precise. It seems a measure of this *pastness* that when I announced this enormous sum to my parents, they had no impulse to complain about the school and merely enquired, mildly, 'Whatever have you been up to?' There were marvellous teachers – a Latin master who said that we should begin our essays 'with a bang, as Bacon began his essay on gardens: "God Almighty first planted a garden." Try to emulate Bacon.' A history teacher who strode into class one day, took off his black gown and tossed it onto his table, upended the contents of a wastepaper bin onto that table, then proceeded to take the contents of a boy's desk and hurl them onto that table, at which point he stood behind it and grandly declaimed: 'In 1482, England was in a mess!'

Sometimes, at home, I found a tramp sitting in a chair in the kitchen, drinking a cup of tea and eating a sandwich my mother had made for him. Tom came every so often for a bite to eat before hitting the road again. He was epileptic, and once had a fit while in our kitchen, rocking back and forth, his eyes tightly closed, his hands twisting the dirty cloth of his trousers. Many years later, poor man, he fell into a fire while having a fit, and died. He had never been on a train, a fact that riveted me when I was a little boy. He had almost no concept of London, or even of the south of England. When I eventually went away down south, to university, Tom, who liked stamps, asked me to bring back any I might find, as if the south of England were a foreign country.

The cathedral is still there – massive, grey, long, solemn – but much of the rest of that world has disappeared. The coalfields were already in serious decline when I was growing up, and most of the collieries had already closed. Coal is no longer as potent or as popular – or as native – as it once was in England. Of course, this also means that fewer men go underground to hack at coal-seams in dangerous conditions, as Orwell described so vividly in *The Road to Wigan Pier*. Fortunately, striking a child's bottom with a hard object is no longer considered an appropriate punishment; there probably isn't a school in Britain where systematic corporal punishment is still allowed, an astonishingly rapid development that began almost as soon as I entered my teens. And I doubt that tramps come round for sandwiches and tea – though they certainly still go somewhere for sandwiches and tea. When I describe this world to my twelve-year-old daughter and ten-year-old son, I seem to grow whiskers and a frock coat: they stare with amused eyes at a father now absurdly prehistoric. They live in a much gentler but oddly sanitised world, in which the only discipline at school seems to be a murmured 'time-out' from the teacher, and illnesses like epilepsy happen out of sight. No one smokes much, certainly not teachers, and pipes are known only from old movies and photographs.

Of course, I don't want my children to have exactly the same childhood as I did: that would almost be a definition of conservatism. But I would like them to be assaulted by the pungency, by the vivid strength and strangeness of *detail*, that I was as a child; and I want them to notice and remember. (I'm also aware that worrying about lack of pungency is a peculiarly middle-class, Western affliction; much of the world is full of people suffering from a surfeit of bloody pungency.) The carbonised clergyman; dressing in bed; Tom sitting by the kitchen drinking his sweet tea; the coal-men with their leather jackets – you have your equivalent details, the whatness or thisness of your own stories.

Here is a paragraph by the Bosnian-American writer Aleksandar Hemon. It is from his story 'Exchange of Pleasant Words', about a drunken and exuberant family reunion – what the family calls a Hemoniad – in rural Bosnia. The viewpoint is that of a teenager, close to the ground, and drunk:

> The noxious, sour manure stench coming from the pigsty; the howling of the only piglet left alive; the fluttering of fleeting chickens; pungent smoke coming from moribund pig-roast fires; relentless shuffling and rustling of the gravel on which many feet danced; my aunts and other auntly women trodding the *kolomiyka* on the gravel, their ankles universally swollen, and their skin-hued stockings descending slowly down their varicose calves; the scent of a pine plank and then prickly coarseness of its surface, as I laid my head on it and everything spun, as if I were a washing machine; my cousin Ivan's sandaled left foot tap-tapping on the stage, headed by its rotund big toe; the vast fields of cakes and pastries arrayed on the bed (on which my

grandmother had expired), meticulously sorted in chocolate and non-chocolate phalanxes.

Hemon, who left his native Sarajevo in 1992 and now lives in
Chicago, loves lists – and when he has such good inherited
material, why wouldn't he? Notice, in particular, 'the howling
of the only piglet left alive', and the phalanxes of cakes and
pastries arrayed on the *same bed* that the grandmother has
expired on.

In ordinary life, we don't spend very long looking at things
or at the natural world or at people, but writers do. It is what
literature has in common with painting, drawing, photography.
You could say, following John Berger, that civilians merely see,
while artists look. In an essay on drawing, Berger writes that
'To draw is to look, examining the structure of experiences. A
drawing of a tree shows, not a tree, but a tree being looked at.
Whereas the sight of a tree is registered almost instantaneously,
the examination of the sight of a tree (a tree being looked at)
not only takes minutes or hours instead of a fraction of a second, it also involves, derives from, and refers back to, much
previous experience of looking.' Berger is saying two things,
at least. First, that just as the artist takes pains – and many
hours – to examine that tree, so the person who looks hard at
the drawing, or reads a description of a tree on the page, learns
how to take pains, too; learns how to change seeing into looking. Second, Berger seems to argue that every great drawing of
a tree has a relation to every previous great drawing of a tree,
since artists learn by both looking at the world and by looking
at what other artists have done with the world. Our looking is
always mediated by other representations of looking.

Berger doesn't mention literary examples. But in the novel, think of the famous tree in *War and Peace*, which Prince Andrei rides past first in early spring, and then, a month later, in late spring. On his second journey, Andrei doesn't recognise the tree, because it is so changed. Before, it had been leafless and wintry. Now, it is in full bloom, surrounded by other trees similarly alive: 'Juicy green leaves without branches broke through the stiff, hundred-year-old bark, and it was impossible to believe that this old fellow had produced them.' Prince Andrei notices the tree in part because he too has changed: its healthy blossoming is related to his own.

Seventy or so years later, in his novel *Nausea*, Jean-Paul Sartre surely has in mind Tolstoy's two tree descriptions when he has his protagonist, Antoine Roquentin, experience the pivotal epiphany of the novel while looking at and thinking about a tree. When Roquentin looks at his tree, he brings to it his own speculative habits. He looks very hard at this chestnut, and especially at its roots: the bark, black and blistered, looks like boiled leather, he feels. He sees its 'compact sea-lion skin . . . that oily, horny, stubborn look', and he likens the curve of the root as it enters the ground to a 'big, rugged paw'. The epiphany that Roquentin has is an early version of Sartrean existentialism: he feels that the tree, like everything in the park, including himself, is absolutely superfluous, and has no necessity.

What is more interesting, perhaps, than his philosophy is his revelation: that what exists is simply there – what exists 'lets itself be *encountered*, but you can never *deduce* it' (Sartre's italics). As long as he has this revelation, 'I *was* the root of the chestnut tree. Or rather I was all consciousness of its existence.

Still detached from it – since I was conscious of it – and yet lost in it, nothing but it.' And when, later, he tries to formulate the philosophical conclusion from this visionary moment, he notices that he is struggling with words, whereas when he stood under the tree 'he touched the thing . . . That root . . . existed in so far that I could not explain it.' On the one hand, this experience of looking at things is intensely self-conscious – for if the drawing of a tree is not a tree but 'a tree being looked at', then the verbal description of a tree is not a tree but 'a tree being looked at being described'. This is the formal, or theoretical, side of surplus. But on the other hand, the tree is also pure detail for both Andrei and Roquentin – it is nothing but a tree; it exists, as Sartre puts it, in so far as it *cannot be explained*. We are detached from details, says Sartre (because they are not identical to us); but we are also – paradoxically – nothing but these details (a tree, its bark, its roots, and so on), as Andrei and the tree are one and the same. This irreducibility is the other aspect of the life-surplus I am trying to define: the enigmatic side of surplus. Just as detail is both intensely self-conscious and intensely self-annulling, so detail, as I suggested earlier, is both high artifice (the self-conscious exercise of creative power) and the magical opposite of artifice (lifeness; what Sartre calls 'the thing'). Karl Ove Knausgaard, a writer greatly engaged in the project of simultaneously describing and analysing detail, does his own version of Tolstoy's and Sartre's descriptions, in a magnificent page-long sketch of a tree in Volume Three of *My Struggle*:

It was strange how all large trees had their own person-
alities, expressed through their unique forms and the aura

created by the combined effects of the trunk and roots, the bark and branches, the light and shadow. It was as if they could speak. Not with voices, of course, but with what they were, they seemed to *stretch* out to whoever looked at them. And that was all they spoke about, what they were, and nothing else. Wherever I went on the estate or in the surrounding forest, I heard these voices, or felt the impact these extremely slow-growing organisms had.

II

What is *serious noticing*? In Saul Bellow's novella *Seize the Day*, Tommy Wilhelm, who is in his forties, helps an old man, Mr Rappaport, across the street. He takes him by the arm, and is struck by the man's 'big but light elbow'. It might not seem the most extraordinary piece of writing, but consider for a moment the precision of the paradox – the bone of the elbow is large because the old man is skinny and gnarled; but it is unexpectedly light, because Mr Rappaport is *just* skin and bone, and is gradually disappearing into his own longevity. I like to imagine the youngish writer sitting at his manuscript in 1955 or so, and trying to imagine (or perhaps remembering and imagining) the exact experience of holding an aged elbow in his hand: '*big . . . big but . . . big but light!*'

In the same novel, Tommy Wilhelm is running through the health club of a hotel, looking for his elderly father, who is getting a massage. As he rushes from room to room, he briefly catches sight of two men playing ping-pong; they have just come out of the steam-bath and are wearing towels round their waists: 'They were awkward and the ball bounded high.'

Again, imagine that youngish writer at his desk. He sees, in his mind's eye, his protagonist running from room to room; he sees his protagonist notice the two men in their towels. Often with great writers, it is instructive to stop at the point in a sentence, or in a metaphor, or in a perception, where the ordinary writer might come to a halt. The ordinary writer might have Tommy Wilhelm catch sight of the two men playing ping-pong and leave it at that ('Two men in towels were playing ping-pong'). Bellow will not leave it at that. He sees that the men are made awkward by their towels, and that, as a consequence, they are playing ineptly. Fearful that their towels will slip, they are just pretending to play – and so 'the ball bounded high'.

Just as great writing asks us to look more closely, it asks us to participate in the transformation of the subject through metaphor and imagery. Think of the way D. H. Lawrence describes, in one of his poems, the 'drooping Victorian shoulders' of a kangaroo; or how Aleksandar Hemon (again) describes horse-shit as looking like 'dark, deflated, tennis balls', or how Elizabeth Bishop describes a taxi meter staring at her 'like a moral owl', or how the novelist and poet Adam Foulds notices a blackbird 'flinching' its way up a tree. The critic Christopher Ricks once proposed that a fairly good test of literary quality is if a sentence or image or phrase of a writer comes to your mind unbidden when you are, say, just walking down the street. But you might also be standing in front of a tree. And if you should see a bird climbing the trunk of a tree, you will see indeed that it *flinches its way up*. Speaking of streets, right now the street I live on is being dug up. New sewers are being laid, a project that has already taken months.

Each day, there is much drilling, digging, opening up of the ground; and then towards mid-afternoon the workmen patch the holes with metal plates, or with gravel, so that cars can drive over them. The next day the whole process begins again, with full Promethean horror. At least four times a week I think of Nabokov's great defamiliarising joke in *Pnin*, about how the workmen come back day after day to the same spot in the road, to try to find the lost tool they accidentally entombed.

In fiction, of course, a good deal of apparently external noticing is simultaneously internal noticing – as is the case when Prince Andrei looks at the tree, or when Anna Karenina, famously, notices the size of her husband's ears, after her encounter on the train with Vronsky. Her noticing is itself noticeable, worthy of our notice, because it tells us something about her transformation. John Berger's phrase, 'examining the structure of experiences', nicely applies to this internal, or double, aspect of novelistic noticing. For fiction's chief difference from poetry and painting and sculpture – from the other arts of noticing – is this internal psychological element. In fiction, we get to examine the self in all its performance and pretence, its fear and secret ambition, its pride and sadness. It is by noticing people seriously that you begin to understand them; by looking harder, more sensitively, at people's motives, you can look around and behind them, so to speak. Fiction is extraordinarily good at dramatising how contradictory people are. How we can want two opposed things at once: think of how brilliantly Dostoevsky catches this contradiction, how we love and hate at the same time, or how quickly our moods, like clouds on a windy day, scud from one shape to another.

Often, in life, I have felt that an essentially novelistic understanding of motive has helped me to begin to fathom what someone else really wants from me, or from another person. Sometimes, it is almost frightening to realise how poorly most people know themselves; it seems to put one at an almost priestly advantage over people's souls. This is another way of suggesting that in fiction we have the great privilege of seeing how people make themselves up – how they construct themselves out of fictions and fantasies and then choose to repress or forget that element of themselves.

I've mentioned Dostoevsky's characters, who go back to the eighteenth-century Diderot, and to Lermontov's great hero, Pechorin (late 1830s), and forward to the narrator of Thomas Bernhard's novel *The Loser*, a wonderful book narrated by a man who is convinced that his friend, a pianist named Wertheimer, who has committed suicide, was 'a loser'. The narrator means by that word (*Der Untergeher* is the German title, which means one who is drowning or sinking – 'going under') that when he and Wertheimer were young, they were both desperate to be great pianists. They studied with Glenn Gould, and deeply envied Gould's pianistic genius. By comparison with Gould, who of course 'made it' as an internationally famous pianist, the narrator and his friend Wertheimer are 'losers'. They have not succeeded, and are obscure provincials. But over the course of the book, the narrator's desperate need to present his friend as a loser, to exempt himself from that dread category, and ultimately his distasteful tendency to see Wertheimer's suicide as the ultimate mark of his loserdom, become highly suspect. We slowly see that the narrator may not be entirely sane, that he has a kind of murderous envy of

Gould, a competitive rivalry with Wertheimer and a deep guilt over Wertheimer's suicide. And that he is in love with both Gould and Wertheimer. Of all this he seems largely unaware. The reader is privy to the narrator's fantasy, a fantasy more enraged and systematic than that of Chekhov's officer perhaps, but different in degree, not in kind.

III

What do writers do when they seriously notice the world? Perhaps they do nothing less than rescue the life of things from their death – from two deaths, one small and one large: from the 'death' which literary form always threatens to impose on life, and from actual death. Which is to say, they rescue us from our death. I mean the fading reality that besets details as they recede from us – the memories of our childhood, the almost-forgotten pungency of flavours, smells, textures: the slow death that we deal to the world by the sleep of our attention. Growing older, says Knausgaard, is like standing in front of a mirror while holding another behind one's head, and seeing the receding dance of images – 'becoming smaller and smaller as far as the eye could see'. Knausgaard's world is one in which the adventure of the ordinary – the inexhaustibility of the ordinary as a child once experienced it ('the taste of salt that could fill your summer days to saturation') – is steadily retreating; in which things and objects and sensations are pacing towards meaningless-ness. In such a world, the writer's task is to rescue the adventure from this slow retreat: to bring meaning, colour, and life back to the most ordinary things – to football boots and grass, to cranes and trees and airports, and even to Gibson guitars and Roland amplifiers and Old Spice and Ajax. 'You could still buy Slazenger tennis rackets, Tretorn balls, and Rossignol skis, Tyroka bindings and Koflack boots,' he writes.

> The houses where we lived were still standing, all of them. The sole difference, which is the difference between a child's reality and an adult's, was that they were no longer laden with meaning. A pair of Le Coque football boots was just a pair of football boots. If I felt anything when I held a pair in my hands now it was only a hangover from my childhood, nothing else, nothing in itself. The same with the sea, the same with the rocks, the same with the taste of salt that could fill your summer days to saturation, now it was just salt, end of story. The world was the same, yet it wasn't, for its meaning had been displaced, and was still being displaced, approaching closer and closer to meaninglessness.

Literature, like art, pushes against time's fancy – makes us insomniacs in the halls of habit, offers to rescue the life of things from the dead. A story is told about the artist Oskar Kokoschka, who was leading a live drawing class. The students were bored and doing dull work, so Kokoschka whispered to the model and told him to collapse to the ground. Kokoschka went over to the prone body, listened to his heart, pronounced him dead. The class was deeply shocked. Then the model stood up, and Kokoschka said: 'Now draw him as though you were aware he was alive and not dead!' What might that painting, in fiction, of a live body look like? It would paint a body that was truly alive, but in such a way that we might be able to see that a body is always really dying; it would understand that life is shadowed by mortality, and thus make a death-seeing metaphysics of Kokoschka's life-giving aesthetics. (Isn't this what makes serious noticing truly *serious*?) It might read like this passage from a late story by Saul Bellow, 'Something to Remember Me By'. It is a paragraph about a drunken Irishman, McKern, who has passed out on a couch: 'I looked in at McKern, who had thrown down the coat and taken off his drawers. The parboiled face, the short nose pointed sharply, the life signs in the throat, the broken look of his neck, the black hair of his belly, the short cylinder between his legs ending in a spiral of loose skin, the white shine of the shins, the tragic expression of his feet.' This is perhaps what Kokoschka had in mind: Bellow is painting, in words, a model, who might or might not be alive: a painting that threatens at any moment to become a still life. So his character looks very hard at McKern, the way an anxious young parent does at a sleeping baby, to check that it is still alive. And he is still alive – just: *the life signs in the throat*.

Although Nabokov was too competitive to say anything decent about his peer Saul Bellow, it is hard to read this description of a man asleep without thinking of Nabokov's words, in one of his lectures, on how the great writer 'models a man asleep':

To minor authors is left the ornamentation of the commonplace: these do not bother about any re-inventing of the world; they merely try to squeeze the best they can out of a given order of things, out of traditional patterns of fiction . . . But the real writer, the fellow who sends planets spinning and models a man asleep and eagerly tampers with the sleeper's rib, that kind of author has no given values at his disposal: he must create them himself. The art of writing is a very futile business if it does not imply first of all the art of seeing the world as the potentiality of fiction.

Nabokov's is a highly self-serving and romantic view of the author, who seems to have no indebtedness to any other author; indeed, in Nabokov's mythology, this writer, who fashions humans from ribs, is God Himself, which might well mean Vladimir Vladimirovich Nabokov.

But Kokoschka and Nabokov have hold of a central truth. Surely it is no surprise that we so often remember details that concern the deaths of real people ('famous last words', and so on) and fictional characters. Isn't this because at such moments writers are snatching the details of life, and the life of details, from the extinction that surrounds and threatens them? Montaigne, in his essay 'Of Cruelty', writes about the last minutes of Socrates's life, and how he is said to have scratched his leg. 'By that quiver of pleasure that he feels in scratching his leg after the irons were off, does he not betray a sweetness and joy in his soul at being unfettered by past discomforts and prepared to enter into the knowledge of things to come?' But whereas Montaigne is essentially pre-novelistic, because he has a tendency to moralise about such details, and sees this moment as an example not of accident but of forthright moral vigour, a later writer like Tolstoy sees such a gesture as accidental or automatic – as life just instinctively desiring to extend itself beyond death. I am thinking of the moment witnessed by Pierre in *War and Peace*, when he sees a young Russian, blindfolded and about to be executed by firing squad, fiddle with his blindfold, perhaps in order to make it a little more comfortable.

This is the life-surplus, pushing itself beyond death, out-living death. Think of Tolstoy's Ivan Ilyich. As he nears his death, at the moment of greatest loneliness, he remembers the plums of his childhood, and the way that when you got down to the pit of the fruit, *the saliva would flow*. When Bellow's character Moses Herzog sees lobsters behind the glass of a Manhattan fishmonger, he sees their 'feelers bent', pressed up against the glass – the complaint of life against its deathly imprisonment. When the contemporary American novelist Rachel Kushner sees a squashed cockroach on a New York pavement, she sees its long wispy antennae 'swiping around for signs of its own life'. In Lydia Davis's story 'Grammar Questions', the narrator comes to the conclusion that her dying father is pure negation, has become nothing more than the adverb 'not' (hence the story's title) – and yet what she remembers, what *extends out* of her story, is the way her father is frowning as he lies in his sickbed, as if irritated. She has seen this frown many times in her life: it is what Bellow would call a 'life sign'.

To notice is to rescue, to redeem; to save life from itself. One of the characters in Marilynne Robinson's novel *Housekeeping* is described as a girl who 'felt the life of perished things'. In the same book, Robinson writes of how Jesus raised Lazarus from the dead, and even restored the severed ear of the soldier who came to rescue him, 'a fact that allows us to hope the res-urrection will reflect a considerable attention to detail'. I like the idea that heaven might reward us for what we have lost by paying attention to detail, that heaven must perforce be a place of serious noticing. But perhaps we can bring back life, or extend life, here on earth, by doing the same: by applying what Walter Benjamin once called 'the natural prayer of the soul: attentiveness'. We can bring the dead back by applying the same attentiveness to their shades as we apply to the world around us – by looking harder: by transfiguring the object. Benjamin's phrase comes in a letter to Adorno about Kafka; and perhaps Adorno was recalling this idea of attentiveness when he wrote, in *Negative Dialectics*, that 'if the thought really yielded to the object, if its attention were on the object, not on its category, the very objects would start talking under the lingering eye'.

See, there they are, talking to us: the poplar, the lilac and the roses. That peppermint tingle. The kiss.

2014

Saul Bellow's Comic Style

I

EVERYONE IS CALLED a 'beautiful writer' at some point or other, just as all flowers are eventually called pretty. 'Stylists' are crowned every day, of steadily littler kingdoms. But of course, there are very few really fine writers of prose. This is not surprising, since a prose is a vision, a totality. Great stylists should be as rare as great writers. Saul Bellow is probably the greatest writer of American prose of the twentieth century – where greatest means most abundant, various, precise, rich, lyrical. (Far more consistently fine than Faulkner, say.) This seems a relatively uncontroversial claim. The august raciness, the Melvillean enormities and cascades ('the limp silk fresh lilac drowning water'), the Joycean wit and metaphoricity, the lancing similes with their sharp American nibs ('he was meteor-bearded like John Brown'), the happy rolling freedom of the daring, uninsured sentences, the prose absolutely ripe with inheritance, bursting with the memories of Shakespeare and Lawrence, yet prepared for modern emergencies, the Argus eye for detail, and controlling all this, the firm metaphysical intelligence – all this is now thought of as Bellow's, as 'Bellovian'.

Reading Bellow is a special way of being alive; his prose is germinal. There is an image in *Ravelstein* in which the narrator describes how his neurologist, Dr Bax, coaxed his very ill patient back from death to life: 'Dr Bax, like a shrewd Indian scout of the last century, pressed his ear to the rail and heard the locomotive coming. Life would soon be back, and I would occupy my seat in the life-train. Death would shrink to its former place at the margin of the landscape.' This lovely metaphor, celebrating life, also enacts it; the prose is in fact the life-train. Again and again, Bellow's writing reaches for life, for the human gust. Joyce is his only obvious twentieth-century rival. Indeed, sometimes they are eerily close. In *A Portrait of the Artist as a Young Man*, Joyce alights for a moment on Mr Casey, whose fingers could not be straightened out: 'And Mr Casey told him that he had got those three cramped fingers making a birthday present for Queen Victoria.' In *Humboldt's Gift* we come across the Russian Bath in Chicago: 'On the second floor there had always lived aged workingstiffs, lone Ukrainian grandfathers, retired car-line employees, a pastry cook famous for his icings who had to quit because his hands became arthritic.' It is a curious historical reversal – like Bruckner sounding Mahlerian – that Joyce can sometimes sound like Bellow, or that nothing sounds more like Bellow than Lawrence's description of the Rhine, from his short story 'The Border Line': 'old Father Rhine, flowing in greenish volume'.

This life-sown prose moves fast, logging impressions with broken speed. Rereading *Herzog* one encounters too many marvels to record: there is Herzog's mistress, Renata, sparkily described as 'certainly not one of those little noli me tangerines'. And there is a brief memory of Strawforth, a fat schoolboy, with his 'fat curling thumbs', and a rabbi, 'short-bearded, his nose violently pitted with black'. And Nachman, who played the harmonica in the lavatory stalls: 'You heard the saliva in the cells of the tin instrument as he sucked and blew.' And the light bulb that Herzog remembers at home, 'which had a spike at the end like a German helmet. The large loose twist of tungsten filament blazed.' Herzog recalls his asthmatic brother, Willie, in the grip of a breathing fit: 'Trying to breathe he gripped the table and rose on his toes like a cock about to crow.'

Of course, there is Valentine Gersbach and his wooden leg, 'bending and straightening gracefully like a gondolier'. There is the hospital Herzog remembers being in as a child, where the icicles hung from the hospital roof 'like the teeth of fish, clear drops burning at their tips', and the Christian lady who comes to the young Herzog to read from the Bible, her hatpin sticking out from the back of her head 'like a trolley rod'. Passing a fish shop, Herzog pauses to look at the catch: 'The fish were packed together, backs arched as if they were swimming in the crushed, smoking ice, bloody bronze, slimy black-green, gray-gold – the lobsters were crowded to the glass, feelers bent.' In New York, Herzog passes a demolition crew, and this passage flows out, one of the great examples of urban realism, at once lyrical and robustly particular:

At the corner he paused to watch the work of the wrecking crew. The great metal ball swung at the walls, passed easily through brick, and entered the rooms, the lazy weight browsing on kitchens and parlors. Everything it touched wavered and burst, spilled down. There rose a white tranquil cloud of plaster dust. The afternoon was ending, and in the widening area of demolition was a fire, fed by the wreckage. Moses heard the air, softly pulled toward the flames, felt the heat. The workmen, heaping the bonfire with wood, threw strips of molding like javelins. Paint and varnish smoked like incense. The old flooring burned gratefully – the funeral of exhausted objects. Scaffolds walled with pink, white, green doors quivered as the six-wheeled trucks carried off fallen brick. The sun, now leaving for New Jersey and the west, was surrounded by a dazzling broth of atmospheric gases.

Given so much, it might be easy for a reader to become blasé. Good writers tend to raise one up like canal-locks, so that one swims at their level, and forgets the medium that supports one. After a while, the reader might take for granted Bellow's exuberance of detail, might not notice that the squares of the harmonica are called 'cells', that the tungsten filament in the bulb is seen not only as large, but wonderfully as 'loose', that the icicles have clear drops 'burning at their tips' (the paradox of heat at the end of something cold, yet superbly right as a description of ice melting into water; and compare, incidentally, Lawrence, seeing oranges in a grove in Italy, 'hanging like hot coals in the twilight'), or that the demolition ball, hard at work, is yet seen as 'lazy' and 'browsing' – and browsing *on* kitchens and parlours (Bellow adds prepositions to his verbs, as Lawrence does when he has a woman walking behind her lover 'gloating on him from behind', or: 'Banford turtled up like a fighting cock').

One realises, with a shock, that Bellow has taught one how to see and hear, has opened the senses. Until this moment one had not really thought of the looseness of a light-bulb filament, one had not heard the saliva bubbling in the harmonica, one had not seen well enough the nose pitted with black pores, and the demolition ball's slow, heavy selection of its victims. A dozen very good writers – the Updikes, the DeLillos – can render you the window of a fish shop, and do it very well, but it is Bellow's genius to see the lobsters 'crowded to the glass' and their 'feelers bent' by that glass – to see the riot of life in the dead peace of things. Flaubert told Maupassant that 'talent is a slow patience', and that 'there is a part of everything which is unexplored, because we are accustomed to using our eyes only in association with the memory of what people before us have thought of the thing we are looking at. Even the smallest thing has something in it which is unknown. We must find it.' Bellow is Flaubertian in this sense: either, by force of metaphorical wit, he makes us seize new connections and linkages – 'the toes of his bare feet were pressed together like Smyrna figs'; cats with 'grenadier tails'; a man's 'dry-cereal mustache' – or he notices what is unexplored: 'Her throat was ever so slightly ringed or rippled by some enriching feminine deposit.'

II

There are three main areas of comedy in Bellow: the comedy of ideas, the comedy of spiritual or religious yearning, and the comedy of the body. Bellow has been so often discussed – mistakenly, I think – in the context of his many 'ideas', that it is easy to forget that many of his heroes are failures or clowns in thought; the comedy of the novels has much to do with the prospect of the inefficacy of ideas, the piles of intellectual slack which truss these schlemiels like babies. 'Oh so much human thread being wound on the most trivial spools,' the narrator laments in *More Die of Heartbreak*. And Herzog wonders if thought can wake him from the dream of his mad existence, in which he runs chaotically from wife to mistress. 'Not if it [thought] becomes a second realm of confusion, another more complicated dream, the dream of intellect, the delusion of total *explanations*.' Out of this disjunction, between the rage to explain and the rage to experience, Bellow creates a distinctive modern irony – witty, heated, cerebral. He universalises and simultaneously mocks the universalising impulse: 'Cops have their own way of ringing a doorbell. They ring like brutes. Of course, we are entering an entirely new stage in the history of consciousness,' thinks Charlie Citrine, in his characteristic jumble, in *Humboldt's Gift*.

Moses Herzog is an adult child, flooded with memories of his close, stifling family life. He recalls his immigrant father, with his stern, furious face. Herzog hangs his head before great ideas, as a child might before his father. His intellectual patrimony is both parent and tyrant, and Herzog's wild and frequently funny letters to the great dead – 'Dear Doktor Professor Heidegger, I should like to know what you mean by the expression "the fall into the quotidian." When did it happen?' – are like a son's wartime letters to his family, written at the battlefront. Nietzsche and Kierkegaard are, in effect, our parents, and we moderns are like spoiled children, bloated with a wealth we do not know how to spend wisely. Tommy Wilhelm, in *Seize the Day*, complains that 'the fathers were no fathers and the sons no sons'.

This comedy is not only an intellectual or academic comedy; we are not merely laughing at the delusions of intellectuals, but experiencing the pathos of their aspirations. And sometimes, these comic creatures are not formal intellectuals at all, as Tommy Wilhelm is not, in *Seize the Day*, yet they wrestle comically with ideas. Perhaps nothing is more movingly comic in the whole of Bellow than the scene in *The Adventures of Augie March* in which Einhorn, a Chicago autodidact, writes an obituary of his father for the local newspaper. Stiff, clumsy, noble, the obituary is foolishly, ambitiously 'intellectual', and the reader is able to see, in a paragraph, the quavering pretensions of a generation of intelligent American Jews:

> Einhorn kept me with him that evening; he didn't want to be alone. While I sat by he wrote his father's obituary in the form of an editorial for the neighborhood paper. 'The return of the hearse from the newly covered grave leaves a man to pass through the last changes of nature who found Chicago a swamp and left it a great city. He came after the Great Fire, said to be caused by Mrs O'Leary's cow, in flight from the conscription of the Hapsburg tyrant, and in his life as a builder proved that great places do not have to be founded on the bones of slaves, like the pyramids of Pharaohs or the capital of Peter the Great on the banks of the Neva, where thousands were trampled in the Russian marches. The lesson of an American life like my father's,

in contrast to that of the murderer of the Strelitzes and of his own son, is that achievements are compatible with decency. My father was not familiar with the observation of Plato that philosophy is the study of death, but he died nevertheless like a philosopher, saying to the ancient man who watched by his bedside in the last moments . . .' This was the vein of it, and he composed it energetically in half an hour, printing on sheets of paper at his desk, the tip of his tongue forward, scrunched up in his bathrobe and wearing his stocking cap.

I doubt that this could be bettered by Dickens or Joyce. We begin the obituary in laughter and end it in tears, in a sublime dapple of emotions. Everything is here, beautifully ventriloquised: the clumsy, ungrammatical pompousness of the unpractised writer ('leaves a man to pass through the last changes of nature who found Chicago a swamp . . . saying to the ancient man who watched by his bedside'), the rambling, feebly channelled anarchy ('He came after the Great Fire, said to be caused by Mrs O'Leary's cow'), the intellectual exhibitionism which is in fact the purest non sequitur ('My father was not familiar with the observation of Plato that philosophy is the study of death, but he died nevertheless like a philosopher'), the autodidact's historical allusions hanging off the sentences ('in flight from the conscription of the Hapsburg tyrant'), and finally Einhorn's affecting, foolhardy American optimism, whereby this new land apparently proves that 'great places do not have to be founded on the bones of slaves'. No bones of slaves in America, indeed! – a marvellous idiocy of optimism.

III

Bellow's bodies are funny; he is a great portraitist of the human form, Dickens's equal at the swift creation of instant gargoyles. There is not only Valentine Gersbach in *Herzog*, but Victor Wulpy, the great art critic and theorist, in 'What Kind of Day Did You Have?', who is dishevelled and 'wore his pants negligently'; and Cousin Riva in 'Cousins': 'I remembered Riva as a full-figured, dark-haired, plump, straight-legged woman. Now all the geometry of her figure had changed. She had come down in the knees like the jack of a car, to a diamond posture'; and Pierre Thaxter in *Humboldt's Gift*, whose penis lengthens and contracts like a trombone; and Professor Kippenberg, in 'Him with His Foot in His Mouth', a great scholar with bushy eyebrows 'like caterpillars from the Tree of Knowledge'.

What function do these exuberant physical sketches have? First, there is a simple joy to be had from reading the sentences. The description of Professor Kippenberg's bushy eyebrows as resembling caterpillars from the Tree of Knowledge is not just a fine joke; when we laugh, it is with appreciation for a species of wit that is properly called metaphysical. We delight in the curling process of invention whereby seemingly incompatible elements – eyebrows and caterpillars and Eden; or women's hips and car-jacks – are combined. Thus, although we feel after reading Bellow that most novelists do not really bother to attend closely enough to people's physical shapes and dents, his portraiture does not exist merely as realism. We are not just encouraged to see the lifelikeness of Bellow's characters, but to partake in a creative joy, the creator's joy in *making* them look like this. This is not just how people look; they are also sculptures, pressed into by the artist's quizzical and ludic force. In 'Mosby's Memoirs', for instance, a few lines describe a Czech pianist performing Schoenberg. 'This man, with muscular baldness, worked very hard upon the keys.' Certainly, we quickly have a vision of this 'muscular baldness'; we know what this looks like. (Richter, in a word.) But then Bellow adds: 'the muscles of his forehead rising in protest against *tabula rasa* – the bare skull', and suddenly we have entered the surreal, the realm of play: how strange and comic, the idea that the muscles of the man's head are somehow rebelling against the bareness, the blankness, the *tabula rasa*, of his bald head.

Bellow's way of seeing his characters also tells us something about his metaphysics. In his fictional world, people do not stream with motives; as novelists go, he is no depth psychologist. Instead, his characters are embodied souls. Their bodies are their confessions, their moral camouflage faulty and peeling: they have the bodies they deserve. Victor Wulpy, a tyrant in thought, has a large, tyrannical head; Valentine Gersbach, the adulterer with the roving eye, is hobbled by his lameness; Max Zetland, a reproving, withholding father, has an unshavable cleft or pucker in his chin, and when he smokes, 'he held in the smoke of his cigarettes'. It is perhaps for this reason that Bellow is rarely found describing young people; even his middle-aged characters seem old. For in a sense he turns all his characters into old people, since the old helplessly wear their essences on their bodies, like hides; they are seniors in moral struggle.

Like Dickens, and to some extent like Tolstoy and Proust, Bellow sees humans as the embodiments of a single dominating essence or law of being, and makes repeated reference to his characters' essences, in a method of leitmotif. As, in *Anna Karenina*, Stiva Oblonsky always has a smile, and Anna a light step, and Levin a heavy tread, each attribute the accompaniment of a particular temperament, so Max Zetland has his reproving pucker, and Sorella, in *The Bellarosa Connection*, her forceful obesity, and so on. In *Seize the Day*, probably the finest of Bellow's earlier works, Tommy Wilhelm sees the great crowds walking in New York, and seems to see 'in every face the refinement of one particular motive or essence – *I labor, I spend, I strive, I design, I love, I cling, I uphold, I give way, I envy, I long, I scorn, I die, I hide, I want.*'

IV

As for the comedy of religious or spiritual yearning: Bellow's characters are repeatedly tempted by visions of escape – sometimes mystical, sometimes religious, and often Platonic (Platonic in the sense that the real world is felt to be not the real world but only a place where the soul is in exile, a place of mere appearances). Charlie Citrine, in *Humboldt's Gift*, with his anthroposophical leanings, is the most celebrated example. Tommy Wilhelm, in *Seize the Day*, imagines a different world, one suffused with love, and Woody Selbst, in 'A Silver Dish', is full of the 'secret certainty that the goal set for this earth was that it should be filled with good, saturated with it', and sits and listens, religiously, to all the Chicago bells ringing on Sunday. Yet the story he recalls is a tale of shameful theft and trickery, an utterly secular story. The narrator of 'Cousins' admits that he has 'never given up the habit of referring all truly important observations to that original self or soul' (referring here to the Platonic idea that man has an original soul from which he has been exiled, and back to which he must again find a path). But again, the spur of his revelations is completely secular – a shameful court case involving a crooked cousin.

Bellow's characters all yearn to make something of their lives in the religious sense; and yet this yearning is not written up religiously, or solemnly. It is written up comically: our metaphysical cloudiness, and our fierce, clumsy attempts to make these clouds yield rain, are full of hilarious pathos in his work. In this regard, Bellow is perhaps most tenderly suggestive in his lovely late story 'Something to Remember Me By' (surely a gentle homage to Isaac Babel's story 'My First Fee'). The narrator, now old, recalls a single day from his adolescence, in Depression-blighted Chicago. He was, he recalls, a child dreamy with religious and mystical ideas, of a distinctly Platonic nature: 'Where, then, is the world from which the human form comes?' he asks rhetorically. On his jobs delivering flowers in the city, he always used to take one of his philosophical or mystical texts with him. On the day under remembrance, he becomes the victim of a cruel prank. A woman lures him into her bedroom, encourages him to remove his clothes, throws them out of the window, and then flees. The clothes disappear, and it is his task then to get home, an hour away across freezing Chicago, to the house where his mother is dying and his stern father waits for him, with 'blind Old Testament rage'.

The boy is clothed by the local barman and earns his fare home by agreeing to take one of the bar's regulars, a drunk called McKern, to McKern's apartment. Once there, the boy lays out the drunk and then cooks supper for McKern's two motherless young daughters – he cooks pork cutlets, the fat splattering his hands and filling the little apartment with pork smoke. 'All that my upbringing held in horror geysered up, my throat filling with it, my guts griping,' he tells us. But he does it. Eventually, the boy finds his own way home, where his father, as expected, beats him. Along with his clothes, he has lost his treasured book, which was also thrown out of the window. But, he reflects, he will buy the book again, with money stolen from his mother. 'I knew where my mother secretly hid her savings. Because I looked into all books, I had found the money in her *mahzor*, the prayer book for the High Holidays, the days of awe.'

There are coiled ironies here. Forced by the horridly secular confusions of his day to steal, the boy will take this money to buy more mystical and unsecular books, books which will no doubt religiously or philosophically instruct him that *this* life, the life he is leading, is not the real life. And why does the boy even know about his mother's hiding place? Because he looks 'in all books'. His bookishness, his unworldliness, are the reasons that he knows how to perform the worldly business of stealing. And where does he steal this money from? From a sacred text. So then, the reader thinks, who is to say that *this* life, the life our narrator has been so vividly telling us about, with all its embarrassments and Chicago vulgarities, is not real? Not only real, but also religious in its way – for the day he has just painfully lived has also been a kind of day of awe, in which he has learned much, a secular High Holiday, complete with the sacrificial burning of goyish pork.

This lovely tale, both wistful and comic, throws out at us, in burning centrifuge, the secular-religious questions: What are our days of awe? And how shall we know them?

V

Saul Bellow was nearly born in Russia. His father, Abraham Belo, came to Lachine, Quebec, in 1913, and Bellow was born in June 1915. He lived in Quebec for eight years before his father moved the family to Chicago, in 1924. Abraham Bellow went to work at Dworkin's Imperial Baking Company. Repeatedly, in novels and stories, Bellow has his protagonist dream back to the days of Bellow's childhood on Saint Dominique Street in Lachine, or to the later years just east of Humboldt Park, in Chicago. Though *Dangling Man*, his first novel, is more contained than any of his later work, the true Bellovian note bursts through at one moment, when Joseph is polishing his shoes, and recalls doing the same as a child in Montreal:

> I have never found another street that resembled St Dominique . . .
>
> Little since then has worked upon me with such force as, say, the sight of a driver trying to raise his fallen horse, of a funeral passing through the snow, or of a cripple who taunted his brother. And the pungency and staleness of its stores and cellars, the dogs, the boys, the French and immigrant women, the beggars with sores and deformities

whose like I was not to meet again until I was old enough to read of Villon's Paris . . . a cage with a rat in it thrown on a bonfire, and two quarreling drunkards, one of whom walked away bleeding, drops falling from his head like the first slow drops of a heavy rain in summer, a crooked line of drops left on the pavement as he walked.

The reference to Villon, the blood dripping heavily 'like the first slow drops of a heavy rain in summer' – it is all here, in little form, in Bellow's first novel, written in his late twenties. In *Herzog*, Saint Dominique Street becomes Napoleon Street, and Herzog recalls 'my ancient times. Remoter than Egypt':

Up and down the street, the brick-recessed windows were dark, filled with darkness, and schoolgirls by twos in their black skirts marched toward the convent. And wagons, sledges, drays, the horses shuddering, the air drowned in leaden green, the dung-stained ice, trails of ashes. Moses and his brothers put on the caps and prayed together,
   '*Ma tovu ohaleha Yaakov . . .*'
   'How goodly are thy tents, O Israel.'
   Napoleon Street, rotten, toylike, crazy and filthy, riddled, flogged with harsh weather – the bootlegger's boys reciting ancient prayers. To this Moses's heart was attached with great power. Here was a wider range of human feeling than he had ever again been able to find. The children of the race, by a never-failing miracle, opened their eyes on one strange world after another, age

after age, and uttered the same prayer in each, eagerly loving what they found. What was wrong with Napoleon Street? thought Herzog. All he ever wanted was there. His mother did the wash, and mourned . . . His sister Helen had long white gloves which she washed in thick suds. She wore them to her lessons at the conservatory, carrying a leather music roll . . . On a summer night she sat playing and the clear notes went through the window into the street. The square-shouldered piano had a velveteen runner, mossy green as though the lid of the piano were a slab of stone. From the runner hung a ball fringe, like hickory nuts. Moses stood behind Helen, staring at the swirling pages of Haydn and Mozart, wanting to whine like a dog. Oh, the music! thought Herzog.

One of the significances of Bellow's career is that in the age of Beckett he has retained the soul-pungency of the nineteenth-century novelists, and the metaphysical leanings of the great Russians. He is like an earlier generation of writers in his determination to deliver his characters from the inessential. He once wrote that when we read 'the best nineteenth and twentieth century novelists, we soon realise that they are trying in a variety of ways to establish a definition of human nature'. In most contemporary literature, however, 'this power to understand the greatest human qualities appears to be dispersed, transformed, or altogether buried'. In his Nobel lecture, he wrote that 'There is another reality, the genuine one, which we lose sight of. This other reality is always sending us hints, which, without art, we can't receive. Proust calls these hints our "true impressions."'

At the risk of sounding apocalyptic, we might say that Bellow has extended the life of the novel. He has reprieved realism, held its neck back from the blade of the postmodern; and he has done this by revivifying realism with modernist techniques. His prose is densely 'realistic', and yet it is hard to find in it any of the usual conventions of realism. People do not walk out of houses and onto streets, his characters do not have 'dramatic' conversations, it is almost impossible to find sentences in Bellow along the lines of 'He put down his drink and left the room.' That is because most Bellovian detail appears as memory in his novels, as scenes which are filtered through a remembering mind. So detail is modern in Bellow because it is always the impression of a detail; yet his details have an unmodern solidity – they are indeed 'true impressions'.

> My ancient times. Remoter than Egypt. No dawn, the foggy winters. In darkness, the bulb was lit. The stove was cold. Papa shook the grates, and raised an ashen dust. The grates grumbled and squealed. The puny shovel clinked underneath. The Corporals gave papa a bad cough. The chimney in their helmets sucked in the wind. Then the milkman came in his sleigh. The snow was spoiled and rotten with manure and litter, dead rats, frogs. The milkman in his sheepskin gave the bell a twist . . . And then Ravitch, hung over, came from his room, in his heavy sweater . . .

Herzog is recalling this scene, hence that aspect, so strong in Bellow, of a kind of emotional cubism, whereby the mind returns repeatedly, but with variations, to the same details, and ponders and reponders. It is a relaxed stream-of-consciousness, disguised by its relaxation so that it almost seems as if it were conventional realism. Of course, Bellow learned from Joyce that the stream-of-consciousness gives realism new life, because it absolves realism of having to persuade in the conventional way. A standard realist account might try to convince us that the scene in Herzog's kitchen was happening as we witness it, or as another character witnessed it. In such a convention, for us to 'believe' in the milkman would necessitate the conjuring into life of that milkman – a plausible description of his existence. But the memory can select and assert, can pounce on one small detail – the bulb with its large loose twist of tungsten – precisely because these events have happened long ago, and there is no pressure to convince us; there is not the pressure of simultaneity in which realism often awkwardly finds itself ('She entered the door and gave a sharp cough'). Bellow is using detail not to persuade us of the existence of something but almost the opposite – to confirm its absence. Realism is elegiac, a branch of consciousness in Joyce and Bellow.

Bellow's prose moves between different temporalities, between the immediate and the traditional, present time and memory time, the short-lived and the long-lived. The narrator of 'Something to Remember Me By' writes that at home, inside the house, they lived by 'an archaic rule; outside, the facts of life'. Bellow's prose marvellously moves in similar ways, between the 'archaic' or traditional, and the immediate, dynamic 'facts of life'. It may not be an ideal style, but then no such thing exists: of course there are registers which Bellow cannot fathom, or has not chosen to fathom. But it grandly exuberates with more diverse elements – lyricism, comedy, realism, vernacular – than any other contemporary English prose, and in America it deserves more praise than Bellow's now elderly canonicity perhaps encourages.

2001

Anna Karenina and Characterisation

EVERYONE WHO READS TOLSTOY feels that it is an experience different in kind, not just degree, from reading the other great novelists. But how, and why? Rather as one is supposed to approach an elephant not from the front but the side, the critic finds himself becoming, alongside Tolstoy's massive straightforwardness, a mere poser of angles. The transparency of Tolstoy's art – realism as a kind of neutral substrate, like air – makes it very difficult to account for, and more often than not one blusters in tautologies. Why are his characters so real? Because they are so individual. Why does his world feel so true? Because it is so real. And so on. Even Tolstoy himself was forced into paradox when once defending his writing. In a letter to his friend Nikolai Strakhov, written in 1876, he argued that *Anna Karenina* was not a collection of ideas that could be abstracted from the book, but a network: 'This network itself is not made up of ideas (or so I think), but of something else, and it is absolutely impossible to express the substance of this network directly in words: it can be done only indirectly, by using words to describe characters, acts, situations.'

The novel's opening provides an example of Tolstoy's easy fullness. Stiva Oblonsky, vigorous and well-born, simple, handsome, 'cheerful and content', the possessor of an habitually kind smile, has been having an affair with the former governess of his children. Unfortunately his wife, Dolly, has found out, and Stiva miserably recalls the recent evening when, returning from the theatre and 'holding a huge pear for his wife' (we are two pages into the novel and already Tolstoy's succulence of detail is bearing fruit), he found her not in the drawing room but in their bedroom, holding an incriminating letter.

But Stiva is incapable of depression, really. Like many of Tolstoy's men, he has a self-sufficiency which is almost solipsistic. As in Shakespeare, Tolstoy's characters feel real to us in part because they feel so real to themselves, take their own universes for granted. What can Stiva do about his wife's unhappiness? Life tells him to go on living, in obliviousness, and that is all. In effect, he forgets about it. Instead, he takes what is clearly a customary pleasure in the rituals of waking and dressing. He puts on his 'grey dressing gown with the light-blue silk lining', and we see him 'drawing a goodly amount of air into the broad box of his chest', going to the window 'with the customary brisk step of his splayed feet, which so easily carried his full body . . .' A barber arrives, and with his 'glossy, plump little hand' sets about 'clearing a pink path between his long, curling side-whiskers'. Then Stiva sits down to breakfast and opens 'the still damp newspaper'.

Tolstoy generally starts his characterisation with the description of a body, and the body will tend to fix a character's essence. This essence is then repeatedly referred to in the novel. This is the method of 'leitmotif' from which Thomas Mann and Proust both learned a good amount. Stiva's smile appears at the beginning of the novel, and never, as it were, goes away. In the first thirty pages of the book he three times stops someone's hand by raising his (the barber, his secretary, and Levin) – isn't he really stopping the reader, as it were, raising his hand to us and, in effect, saying, 'Watch me, I am full of commanding life'? Stiva's sister, Anna Karenina, also has 'a quick step, which carried her rather full body with such strange lightness'. And these essences are both physical and moral. It might be said that, morally speaking, both Stiva and Anna have too light a tread, are not grounded enough – unlike, say, Levin, Tolstoy's great hero and spokesman in the novel, who is described as 'a strongly built, broad-shouldered man', and is first seen 'pacing around' outside Stiva's office. Anna's husband, Alexei Karenin, is cold, dutiful, an unimaginative Petersburg bureaucrat, and far too grounded in the wrong way: he is first seen at the Petersburg station, by Vronsky, who is irritated by the way Karenin walks, 'swinging his whole pelvis and his blunt feet'. As Tolstoy repeats the appearance of these essences, so they take on a life of their own, begin to seem as if they are repeating of their own accord. And the characters respond to each other's essences. For instance, Veslovsky, an unwanted houseguest, has an annoying habit of tucking his fat legs under him when he sits, and is defined by this one habit. Levin picks up on this motif, and complains that what he dislikes about Veslovsky is his habit of 'tucking his legs under'.

Stiva Oblonsky, like many of Tolstoy's characters, cannot help being himself, cannot help being his essence, and his essence is his body: simple, broad, sybaritic, and rather too light-footed. But such merry forcefulness is of course infectious, and Stiva is the kind of man who gives out a life-heat which others delight in being warmed by. His valet, Matvei, enjoys helping to dress his 'pampered body', and a few pages later, when Stiva and Levin have lunch at the Anglia restaurant, the old Tartar waiter cannot help smiling with pleasure at Oblonsky's relish of the food. The reader is infected in the same way, and a curious transaction begins to occur – remember that the novel is only a few pages old – whereby we too yearn to be in the presence of a man so self-sufficient that he would probably barely notice us. With delight, we watch Oblonsky eat, 'peeling the sloshy oysters from their pearly shells', we see the Tartar waiter, 'his tails flying over his broad hips', and we see Levin sulking – Levin, the prig from the country, the self-competing moralist, who would rather be eating 'white bread and cheese' and is offended by these 'surroundings of bronze, mirrors, gas-lights, Tartars . . .'

It is the same throughout the novel. Tolstoy's details are superbly dynamic. Think of Alexei Karenin, in a fury with Anna, putting his portfolio under his arm, and gripping it so tightly with his elbow 'that his shoulder rose up'; or the merchant Ryabinin, wearing 'high boots wrinkled at the ankles and straight on the calves'. Or Levin, in the wonderful scene after his successful wooing of Kitty, waiting with ecstatic impatience in his hotel room for the hour when he can go and announce his intentions to Kitty's parents. Meanwhile, in the next bedroom of the hotel, 'they were saying something about machines and cheating, and coughing morning coughs'. Later in the book, when Kitty and Levin are married, he watches her combing her hair, and sees 'the narrow parting at the back of her round little head, which kept closing the moment she drew her comb forward'. And there is Levin's housekeeper, Agafya Mikhailovna, who, 'while carrying a jar of freshly pickled mushrooms to the cellar, slipped, fell, and dislocated her wrist'. Or Dolly, sitting down to talk to the miserable Karenin, and finding only the children's schoolroom private enough. So they sit down 'at a table covered with oilcoth cut all over by penknives'.

These details are surely a large aspect of the 'network' which Tolstoy mentions in his letter. First, how vividly and exactly true his descriptions are: the 'still damp newspaper', or the people next door coughing in the morning. But further, one notices that his details are almost always propelled by function, by life-movement – by work, in fact. Agafya is not carrying any pickled mushrooms, but ones 'freshly pickled', ones she has recently pickled; the merchant's boots are wrinkled that way by movement, just as Kitty's narrow hair-parting opens and closes only when she touches it, and Karenin's arm goes up when he squeezes too tightly.

Something flows from this which makes Tolstoy feel very different from other modern realists. He is not interested in telling us what things look like to him, and he is not interested in telling us what they resemble. This is why he eschews simile and metaphor at these moments. Tolstoy's similes are often of the blandly universal kind: 'He felt like a man does when he enters a shop and sees things that are too expensive for him', and so on. (Nabokov rightly noticed that at this kind of metaphor, Tolstoy is not very good.) When Flaubert writes of the long tail of steam flowing from a train's funnel as the train makes its passage through the countryside, and likens it to 'a gigantic ostrich feather whose tip kept blowing away' (in *Sentimental Education*), it is very beautiful, but nevertheless a stylist is being a stylist. It is how Flaubert sees the world. Yet in Tolstoy, as in Chekhov, reality appears in his novels as it might appear not to a writer but to the characters.

When Flaubert describes the train, he is freezing it into pictorial arrest, and claiming it as his own. But reality in *Anna Karenina* is what the characters share, and reality is in the present, as the work of movement occurs in the present. Flaubert's train, as soon as it becomes style, becomes somewhat superfluous, and not least because metaphor, even the greatest metaphor, tends to insist on the accidental: we are meant to notice that X *happens* to resemble Y. Yet one of the powerful oddities we feel when reading Tolstoy is that though everything is extraordinarily free – Tolstoy does as he pleases as a novelist, even inhabiting the thought and mental speech of Levin's dog, Laska, on several occasions – everything also feels curiously inevitable. This is partly because reality is not the novelist's toy in Tolstoy but his characters' necessary food. Proust, in an enigmatic paragraph on *Anna Karenina* and *War and Peace*, writes that each feature of these novels, though supposedly 'observed' (i.e. stylised, 'accidental', 'literary'), is actually 'the garment, the proof, the example of a law the novelist has identified, a rational or irrational law'. Each gesture, each word, each action, says Proust, being only the signifying of a law, makes us feel that we are 'moving inside a multitude of laws'. Proust may well be gesturing, in part, to this sense of inevitability in Tolstoy, of physical detail as the product of the laws of dynamism: in the morning the newspaper will still be damp and people will cough morning coughs, and when people use their boots they will wrinkle, and oilcloth is always already scratched, and when you comb your hair a small hole opens and closes. The writer who uses metaphor is always describing the world hypothetically, as it might be; Tolstoy is simply describing the world as it necessarily is.

Tolstoy began writing *Anna Karenina* in 1873, though he told his wife in 1870 that he was planning a novel about a married woman disgraced by adultery. As in the case of *Madame Bovary*, an actual event occurred which perhaps propelled the novel. In January 1872, Anna Stepanovna Pirogov, the mistress of a neighbouring landowner, threw herself under a train after being abandoned by her lover. Tolstoy went to look at the body at the station, and was deeply affected. There are familial similarities between the novels about fallen women that were written in the second half of the nineteenth century. Anna, like Emma Bovary, reads novels. Hardy's Tess, like Anna, is full-bosomed. Indeed, all three women are sensuous to the point of irresponsibility. Men cannot help being seduced by them, which of course is not thought to be the fault of men; Levin, after meeting Anna late in the novel, accuses himself of having yielded to her 'cunning influence'. Yet *Tess*, *Madame Bovary* and *Anna Karenina*, while carrying the germs of male blame, produce their own antibodies, as it were, so that their doomed heroines are finally sympathised with rather than judged, written into rather than written off. There is a reason that the great age of novelistic character, the nineteenth century, was really the great age of female fictional character. These are heroines who are trying to escape society's imprisonment of them: it is because they seek to escape a world that merely characterises them as types that these women become true characters.

Originally, Tolstoy planned a novel that would condemn Anna for her sin. In the early drafts she is a fat and somewhat vulgar creature, and her cuckolded husband a saintly figure. Most of the novel's spaciousness, as we now know it, did not exist: Levin scything with the peasants, his marriage to Kitty (their fertile domesticity the wholesome 'answer' to the sterile carnality of Anna and Vronsky), Kitty's family the Shcherbatskys (the old prince, Kitty's father, one of Tolstoy's finest small roles: it's hard not to smile with pleasure when recalling his term for one of the rooms at his club: 'the clever room'). There was none of this, and instead, a relentless concentration on the adulterous triangle. But as Richard Pevear has written, as Tolstoy worked on his book, 'he gradually enlarged the figure of Anna morally and diminished the figure of the husband; the sinner grew in beauty and spontaneity, while the saint turned more and more hypothetical'.

Two objections to *Anna Karenina* are commonly made. One is that the great scything scenes – or later, the chapters when Levin and others go hunting – are tedious or unnecessary. Turgenev and, later, James felt that the novel had no architecture; they are nowadays thirded by A. N. Wilson, in his biography of Tolstoy, in which he writes that 'the extended Levin passages are not obviously justifiable in aesthetic terms ... There is nothing artistic, nothing planned about these interludes.' Now, it is all very well to view Tolstoy as a beast of instinct who can outrun the nervous zoologists of form, and it is true that Tolstoy is, in a sense, the great anti-formalist. But he himself insisted that his novel had an invisible architecture. It seems worthwhile trying to find it.

Some of the novel's power – yet another of the qualities that make reading Tolstoy different in kind from reading other novelists – has to do with the way in which Tolstoy slows down the tempo of realism so that it no longer has the artificial pace of most realist novels, but rather has the more ample lento of life as we live it from day to day. Of course, the pages in which Levin scythes grass with the peasants are in themselves beautiful: 'The tall grass softly twined around the wheels and the horse's legs, leaving its seeds on the wet spokes and hubs.' Very touching is the little picture of one of the peasants, an old man working alongside Levin, who, upon finding mushrooms in the long grass, bends down each time and puts them in his pocket, muttering to himself, 'Another treat for my old woman.'

And these pages calm the conventional speed of novelistic realism. As Levin, amazed by how strenuous the work is, loses all sense of the day, so the novel loses its sense of the day. Vronsky falls from his horse, in the famous racing scene, on about page 200. We relive the race again, this time from Anna's perspective. Then, over the next eighty pages, Kitty goes to a German spa and meets the saintly Varenka; Sergei visits his brother, Levin, in the country; Levin scythes with the peasants; Dolly comes with her children to the country; and we see Alexei Karenin in pain and anger as he begins to live with the news that Anna finally gave him at the races: that she loves Vronsky, that 'I listen to you and think about him. I love him, I am his mistress, I cannot stand you, I'm afraid of you, I hate you . . .' But over these hundred pages we do not once visit Vronsky, until around page 300. And what does Tolstoy now write? 'Waking up late the day after the races, Vronsky put on his uniform jacket without shaving or bathing . . .' A hundred pages have elapsed for us, and yet, for Vronsky, barely an evening. And it has probably taken the average reader about an evening to read those hundred pages. The reader may be reading at the same speed at which Vronsky is living. It is difficult to think of a better example of 'real time'.

A more serious charge concerns Tolstoy's didacticism. Isn't Levin first bullied by Tolstoy into an identification with the peasants, and then, nearer the end of the book, towards a very Tolstoyan Christianity (three parts ethics to one part theology)? The book ends as Levin commits his life to 'faith in God, in the good, as the sole purpose of man', to 'that life of the soul which alone makes life worth living and alone is what we value'. There is certainly something propagandistic about elements of the scything scenes. It is always hard not to laugh at Tolstoy when he writes of the peasants that 'the long, laborious day had left no other trace in them than merriment'.

But in fact, Levin's relations with the peasants are pictured with a sense of comic absurdity, for Levin, like most of the characters in the novel, is solipsistic. It is clear enough to the reader that Levin uses the peasants for his own moral hygiene. Later in the book, Tolstoy will make one of the finest episodes in the novel from the comedy of Levin's solipsism: his certainty, once he has won Kitty, that everyone else in the world shares his rapture. Returning to his hotel after his evening with his future wife, Levin falls into conversation with Yegor, the lackey on duty. Levin asks Yegor if, when he got married, he loved his wife. 'Of course I loved her,' says Yegor. 'And Levin saw that Yegor was also in a rapturous state and intended to voice all his innermost feelings.' A sly sentence, this, for does Levin think that Yegor is intending to voice all Yegor's innermost feelings, or does Levin assume that Yegor intends to voice all Levin's innermost feelings? We never really know, because a bell rings, and Yegor leaves to answer it. The next morning, Levin decides that even the cabbies outside the hotel 'evidently knew everything'. Levin's self-involvement is delightful in these pages, but it complicates our earlier reading of his scything with the peasants, as Tolstoy surely means it to do.

Besides, the argument that Levin's sermonising ratiocination forces our free sense of him, that it bruises his autonomy, assumes that he has such an autonomy, that Tolstoy 'the artist' is spoiled by Tolstoy 'the preacher'. But Tolstoy is never really a pure enough artist for his characters to have the kind of purity which can be violated. His approach to character is always paradoxical: his characters are fixed as essences, and ever-changing as people. It is Levin's fixed essence that he will always have 'a desire to be better, which never left him', though this does not mean we will always know how he will act. It is Karenin's essence that he is cold, despite the fact that, at one moving and unexpected moment in the novel, he sobs like a child and warmly forgives both Vronsky and Anna. In time, he returns to his essential coldness and refuses to grant Anna her divorce.

If Tolstoy's characters have a different kind of reality than do those of other novelists, it is because they are both inevitable and unpredictable, universal and private, and that while they are certainly their own individuals, we are always aware of who their maker is. Tolstoy has a pre-modern primitivism which puts me in mind of the famous Alfred Jewel, a ninth-century English object on which is written, in reference to King Alfred, 'Alfred caused me to be made.' There is a way in which, despite their autonomy, Tolstoy's characters all bear the stamp: 'Tolstoy caused me to be made.' Think of that very early scene when Levin and Stiva meet. Though we hardly know them, Levin and Stiva are already vivaciously established as characters and as essences. Tolstoy tells us that they have been friends for years and have loved each other. And then, in familiar mode, he breaks in and informs us that 'in spite of that, as often happens between people who have chosen different ways, each of them, while rationally justifying the other's activity, despised it in his heart'. In most other writers, this authorial meddling would be very dangerous: the characters have just been invented, and here is the author sticking his fat fingers into the web, telling us not only what to think about them, but that there is a law which regulates how certain people feel about each other.

Yet the incursion – this is one of many throughout the novel – does not destroy the individuality of Stiva and Levin, because their individuality lies precisely in the different and unpredictable ways they embody universal laws. Coleridge said that 'as in Homer all the deities are in armour, even Venus', so 'in Shakespeare all the characters are strong'. By strong, he means what he elsewhere says about Lady Macbeth, that she is, 'like all in Shakespeare, a class individualized'. John Bayley, in his great book on Tolstoy, tells us that in the early plans of *War and Peace*, Count Rostov appeared merely as Count Prostoy:

prostoy means, in Russian, 'honest, simple'. Is this the artist or the preacher at work? Both, surely: it is not that Tolstoy begins with an idea (in the sense of an abstraction), but that he begins with a truth, a large truth about Rostov.

In *Anna Karenina*, too, the characters are heirs to universal emotions, as Hamlet is. When Levin feels that the whole world must be aware of his love of Kitty, he feels something individually true, and also generally true about the solipsism of infatuation. One could imagine Stiva feeling the same thing, or even Vronsky. When Anna and Vronsky argue, and he says 'experimenced' by mistake, and she wants to laugh, many readers will acknowledge a characteristic subtlety of Tolstoyan detail. But it would be hard to say that this tells us anything strongly individual about either Anna or Vronsky; it is more that our pleasure, in recognising such a detail, is in recognising its broad human applicability. Yes, we say to ourselves, that is what happens in arguments. We might say then that Tolstoy's characters have feelings that are peculiar to themselves but not *that* peculiar. Paradoxically, they differ from each other while sharing this universality, something suggested by the fact that nearly all the men in *Anna Karenina* are described by Tolstoy as 'handsome': Vronsky, Levin, Stiva, but also Levin's old beekeeper, and Dolly's driver, and even Veslovsky, the unwelcome visitor. All these men share a kind of law of manliness, and so, in this, resemble each other. Similarly, two different babies – Levin's and Anna's – are pictured in exactly the same way, as having fat little wrists that look as if cord has been tied around them. This is surely not a slip on Tolstoy's part; he is merely repeating the universal essence of babyhood.

In most novels, we see characters search for themselves, or lose themselves, or build themselves. In Tolstoy, the difficulty is in being anything other than oneself. It is what Tolstoy meant when, in late life, he said: 'As I was at five, so I am now.' This may be why he has such an interest in those moments when his characters find themselves forced to play roles, or when the natural sounds artificial, sounds unlike itself: to Nikolai Rostov on the field of Austerlitz, the crying of the wounded sounds feigned. It is always moving in *Anna Karenina* when we see a character struggling with the essence that is surging though him. Once Anna has truly left him, Karenin is so miserable that, very uncharacteristically, he thinks of speaking about his sadness to his office manager. But even caught in this uncharacteristic gully, Karenin has been more characteristic than he can know. For, Tolstoy tells us, he has prepared in advance, like the good bureaucrat he is, an opening line: 'He had already prepared the phrase: "You have heard of my grief?"' It is so comically stiff that we almost weep with laughter for poor Karenin. Of course, he says nothing.

Reading *Anna Karenina* again, one is struck by the self-absorption of the novel's characters. Vronsky, we are told, 'was not in the habit of noticing details'. Once he has declared his love to Anna, at the little station where the Petersburg train stops during the night, he gets back into his carriage, and 'he now seemed still more proud and self-sufficient. He looked at people as if they were things.' Alexei Karenin finds it impossible to imagine what it is like to be Anna. He tries for a second, and abandons the attempt: 'To put himself in thought and feeling into another being was a mental act alien to Alexei Alexandrovich.' Even Dolly and Kitty, the sympathetic mothers, fail to see that Anna is not merely 'pathetic' in her isolation – Kitty's slightly condescending word to Dolly, when, very late in the book, Anna visits them – but opium-sodden and close to suicide.

There is a powerful tension between the 'sloshy' shared world of the novel – Tolstoy's fat notation of textures, substances, atmospheres – and the selfish interiority of many of the characters, who live in their own worlds. Accordingly, the most affecting incidents occur when the world breaks in upon these fantasists – when, for example, Vronsky first sees Alexei Karenin, meeting Anna at the Petersburg station, and thinks, 'Ah, yes, the husband!' Tolstoy adds: 'Only now did Vronsky understand clearly for the first time that the husband was a person connected with her.'

The paradox of the world of *Anna Karenina* is that it is a highly shared world (families who know each other, and so on), shared by solipsists. Anna, whose face is repeatedly described as 'sympathetic', is the only character who is not solipsistic; and yet her sensitivity is a stale liberty, for she has no actual world on which to practise her understanding. Deprived of society, she begins to wither – indeed, she is made solipsistic by a solipsistic society that refuses to see her properly. Vronsky's habit of not noticing details proves to be fatal for her. Nothing is finer in the book than its last hundred pages, in which Tolstoy shows the creeping disintegration of Vronsky and Anna's relationship. Again and again, Anna struggles with her essence, which is freedom, irrepressibility. Every day, Vronsky goes out into society to claim his freedom. But she cannot do that. Society forbids it. Jealous and resentful, she reflects, 'He has all the rights and I have none.' Every day she promises to herself that she will not voice her resentment when Vronsky returns, and every day she plays truant with that promise, unable not to be herself. As she falls under the wheels of the train, she has, in a way, finally merged with her essence. For we are told that this woman with a light step 'fell on her hands under the carriage, and with a light movement, as if preparing to get up again at once, sank to her knees'. Light in step when we met her, she is now light unto death.

2001

Joseph Roth's Empire of Signs

I

WITH JOSEPH ROTH, you begin – and end – with the prose. The great delight of this Austrian novelist, who wrote in the 1920s and 1930s, lies in his strange, nimble, curling sentences, which are always skewing into the most unexpected metaphors. It is rare to find luminous powers of realism and narrative clarity so finely combined with a high poetic temperature. Joseph Brodsky said that there is a poem on every page of Roth, and certainly Roth's almost nervous fondness for metaphor recalls the image-blessed, image-sick prose of another poet, Osip Mandelstam, sooner than that of any novelist.

Like Mandelstam's, Roth's details and images are often not primarily visual, in the usual Flaubertian sense. He isn't especially interested in describing the exact colour-shade of a man's moustache, and then likening it, say, to rolled filaments of copper (though he is perfectly capable of writing this way). Instead, he comes at his images from behind, or sideways, and then climbs towards something at once magical and a little abstract. In *The Emperor's Tomb* (1938), he pictures a businessman talking about his prospects in the Austro-Hungarian

Empire during the First World War: 'As he spoke he stroked both sides of his mutton-chop whiskers as if he wished to caress simultaneously both halves of the monarchy [i.e. Austria and Hungary].'

This level of magical abstraction can be found in all of Roth's novels, from the earliest, *The Spider's Web* (1923), to his last published work, *The Tale of the 1002nd Night* (1939). *The Spider's Web* is a generally rather crude and flat book, but Roth's next novel, *Hotel Savoy* (1924), suggests the power of the more mature writer. It tells the story of Gabriel Dan, who has spent three years in a Siberian POW camp and who has ended up in an unnamed Eastern European town, as a resident of the enormous Hotel Savoy, which is full of the refugees of war – Poles, Germans, Russians, Serbians and Croats. This early book already shows a deep command of simile and metaphor. 'My room – one of the cheapest – is on the sixth floor, number 703. I like the number – I am superstitious about them – for the zero in the middle is like a lady flanked by two gentlemen, one older and one younger.' Dickens, and more acutely Gogol, may have influenced Roth, but probably the strongest impression was made by Viennese journalism, in particular the practice and perfection of the *feuilleton*, or short literary article. *Feuilletons* were brief sketches, sometimes arguments but often exquisite descriptive snatches. Karl Kraus was an earlier master of the form; in the 1920s, when Roth started writing them, Alfred Polgar was the most celebrated exponent. Walter Benjamin called Polgar 'the German master of the small form'. In 1935, writing in honour of Polgar's sixtieth birthday, Roth said that he considered himself Polgar's pupil: 'He polishes the ordinary until it becomes extraordinary . . . I have learned this *verbal carefulness* from him.'

The brevity of the *feuilleton* put every sentence under pressure, packing it with twice the usual energy. Polgar, in one of his pieces, describes a man's cane in very Rothian style: 'A small walking-stick made out of rhinoceros hide danced between his fingers. It was a woolly light-yellow in colour and looked like a pole of thickened honey.' These articles – Benjamin's essays are stylistic cousins – often proceed in a pretty shuffle, as if each sentence were a new beginning. The writing is essentially aphoristic, even when not obviously so, because each sentence attains the status of aphorism. Kraus described the aphorism as both half the truth and one and a half times the truth, and this might also stand as a description of metaphor, certainly of metaphor as it appears in Roth's work, where the similes are both magically untrue and magically more than true.

Roth, in effect, novelised the techniques of the *feuilleton*, producing fictions that behave as if they are always about to end, and which therefore always include one more superb phrase before the deferred closure. His books are highly patterned, but each sentence is a discrete explosion. There is, for example, the disagreeable Lord von Winternigg in Roth's greatest novel, *The Radetzky March* (1932), who rides through the garrison town in his barouche: 'small, ancient and pitiful, a little yellow oldster with a tiny wizened face in a huge yellow blanket . . . he drove through the brimming summer like a wretched bit of winter.' Or, from the same novel, this passing scene-setter: 'It was getting dark. The evening fell vehemently into the street.' Or again, from the same novel, the description of the peasant Onufrij, and his effort to write his name: 'The beads of sweat grew on his low brow like transparent crystal boils . . . These boils ran, ran down like tears wept by Onufrij's brain.' And from *The Emperor's Tomb*: 'All little stations in all little provincial towns looked alike throughout the old Austro-Hungarian Empire. Small and painted yellow, they were like cats lying in the snow in winter and in the sun in summer.' Or: 'The lonely lantern which stood before it reminded one of an orphan vainly trying to smile through its tears.' From *Flight without End* (1927): 'It was an icy night, so cold that at first I thought even a shout must freeze the instant it was uttered, and so never reach the person called.' Or: 'The lady's smoothly shaved legs lay side by side like two similarly clad sisters, both in silk sheaths.' Or: the waiters 'moved about like gardeners; when they poured coffee and milk into the cups, it was as if they were watering white flower-beds. Trees and kiosks stood on the kerbs, almost as if the trees were selling newspapers.' From *Right and Left* (1929): 'In the gloaming, only the silver birches in the little wood opposite would shimmer, standing amongst the other trees like slips of days among ancient nights.'

Joseph Roth was born in 1894 on the rim of the Habsburg Empire in Brody, Austrian Galicia, which is now part of Ukraine. Until David Bronsen established the facts in his German-language biography, the record of Roth's life was an evocative smudge, a rumour worthy of the shadowy border town in which he was born – a town about which, in different versions, he writes repeatedly in his fiction.

Brody had a sizeable Jewish population, but it appears that in later life Roth would conceal his Jewishness, claiming that his father, a businessman from Galicia called Nachum, had been an Austrian government official, and even, on one occasion, a Polish count. Such fantasies may have had their origin in Viennese anti-Semitism, or more likely in Roth's conservative romanticism, and his almost naive love of the Austro-Hungarian military. It was no doubt easier to invent a fictitious father once the real one had disappeared: while Joseph was still a boy, Nachum went mad and was locked away in a German asylum. As readers are bound to notice, Roth's fiction is painfully concerned with the relationship of son and father, with absent or useless fathers and damaged, aimless sons. The rawest treatment of this theme is in *Zipper and His Father* (1928), the portrait of a young man, Arnold Zipper, who is spiritually ruined by his service on the front during the First World War, and by his father's thoughtless support for that war.

The Radetzky March is Roth's deepest consideration of fathers and sons. The novel's formal beauty flows from its dynastic current, which irrigates the very structure of the book. We begin with Captain Joseph Trotta, who inadvertently saved the young Emperor Franz Joseph's life at the Battle of Solferino in 1859. Thanks to this, the Captain is ennobled and the doomed, quixotic Trotta line established, each generation less heroic, but more absurdly quixotic, than its predecessor. Baron Trotta's son, Franz, is only a dutiful district captain in a garrison town in Austrian Silesia; but Franz's son, Lieutenant Carl Joseph Trotta, who is the novel's real protagonist, is more spectacularly unhappy – first in the Cavalry, from which he discharges himself, and then in the Infantry, where he dies a foolish death during the First World War.

Hanging like a golden cloud over Lieutenant Trotta's head is the reputation of his grandfather, the 'Hero of Solferino'. Young Trotta can never match this heroism, not least because it was accidental; part of his affliction is precisely that he strives to emulate a quality that was, originally, not the product of striving. Roth beautifully expands this into a larger celebration and critique of the Austro-Hungarian Empire: Lieutenant Trotta comes to represent an entire generation of enfeebled young men, living off the recessive heroism of an earlier imperial age, and unable to achieve by force of will what was once achieved by instinct. What remains changeless, however, is the Emperor Franz Joseph himself, who ascended to the throne in 1848, and reigned until his death in 1916. The Emperor is the omnipresent yet absent father of all the Empire's inhabitants; in a sense, he is both father and grandfather to Lieutenant Trotta, because his long reign has spanned the generations. The Emperor, of course, is the true hero of Solferino, under whose heroic reputation Trotta lives and fails. Whenever Trotta sees, in a café, the standard portrait of the Emperor 'in the sparkling white uniform', it merges in his memory with an old family portrait of his grandfather. The Trotta and Habsburg dynasties are one, a conflation which, characteristically, Roth both idealises and mocks.

History marked Joseph Roth's life at least twice, viciously. First came the assassination of the Emperor's nephew Franz Ferdinand in Sarajevo in June 1914. This, followed by Franz Joseph's death in 1916, started the unravelling of the Austro-Hungarian Empire. In at least half of Roth's thirteen novels comes the inevitable, sabre-like sentence, or a version of it, cutting the narrative in two: 'One Sunday, a hot summer's day, the Crown Prince was shot in Sarajevo.' Then there was the Anschluss. The news of the German occupation in 1938 precipitated a collapse of morale in Roth, who was exiled in Paris at the time, and drinking heavily. He died fourteen months later, in May 1939. Nevertheless, he was able to make the Anschluss the dramatic epilogue of *The Emperor's Tomb*, which is a kind of sequel to *The Radetzky March*, extending the story of the Trotta family (via a cousin of Lieutenant Carl Joseph) from 1914 to 1938.

So Roth lived through light and then twilight and then darkness, seeing his beloved Empire mutate into a neglected and unmonarchical Austria and finally disappear into Hitler's pouch. The Empire was already on the verge of dissolution when Roth became a student at the University of Vienna in the summer of 1914. He joined up in 1916 and a year later was sent to the Galician front. He returned from the war with tales of capture by the Russians and a forced march across Siberia, a history he awards Franz Tunda in *Flight without End*, and Gabriel Dan in *Hotel Savoy*. But he probably never saw combat, serving instead in the army's press office. During the next ten years, living on and off in Berlin, he wrote the novels which would make him unpopular with the Nazis: in particular *Flight without End*, which tells the story of a man who returns from the war and grows steadily more disenchanted with the confident rise of German 'culture'; and *Right and Left*, which logs the growth of fascism in Germany during the 1920s.

Roth fled to Paris in 1933, a year after *The Radetzky March* had made him celebrated. There, he marinated himself in drink and in the impossibility of his romantic nostalgia. His solution to the advance of the Nazis seems to have been a proposal to restore the Habsburg monarchy. He 'renounced' his Jewishness in 1935, calling himself a Catholic. He died in 1939, apparently attended, at his deathbed, by a priest, a rabbi, and a representative of the league for the restoration of the Habsburgs.

II

For the citizens of the Austro-Hungarian Empire, especially those who, like Stefan Zweig and Joseph Roth, were of a nostalgic and idealising cast, Sarajevo was momentous not because it precipitated the First World War, but because the First World War precipitated the collapse of the adored Habsburg Empire, the impossible archipelago of different countries and races that, like a child's cartographic fantasy, stretched northwards from Vienna to take in Prague, eastwards to include Moravia, Silesia and some of what is now Poland, and southwards from Vienna to include Croatia and Bosnia–Herzegovina, which it annexed in 1908. The Austro-Hungarian Empire was, of course, the nineteenth-century incarnation of the earlier Holy Roman Empire; it was the pampered child of more than five hundred years of historical privilege, looked after since 1848 by its spiritual father and commander-in-chief, the Emperor Franz Joseph, who ruled until his death in 1916. Two years later, the Empire had disappeared, and the Habsburg dynasty faded out of history into historiography, and out of succession into the little monthly coups of the society gossip pages.

Roth is the great elegist of that empire; Robert Musil its great analyst; Kafka its dark allegorist. Roth's most characteristic novels are portraits of men who, either infatuated with the Empire, or merely unthinkingly dependent on it, are disappointed by it in some way or another, and who subsequently lose their way, or fall into aimlessness and finally despair. Generally, this hero will have left the embrace of the Austrian army, which stands in for the Empire, either because the First World War has just ended, or because he has been discharged in cloudy circumstances (like Baron Taittinger in *The Tale of the 1002nd Night*). In the course of the novel, this hero may travel either to the rim of empire (the border districts), or to the centre (to Vienna). In the border towns, amongst Cossacks and Jews, the hero may fight in the Great War, may die (as Lieutenant Trotta does in 1916, in *The Radetzky March*), or may be captured by the Russians and sent to Siberia (as Trotta's cousin is in *The Emperor's Tomb*, and Franz Tunda is in *Flight without End*). If he survives, he must return to hollow, postwar Vienna, like poor, aimless Arnold Zipper in *Zipper and His Father*, or like Andreas Pum, the protagonist of *Rebellion*, Roth's third novel.

Roth's novels delight in, insist on, the uniformity of the Empire and its livery in all its varied lands; they enact a kind of fictive imperialism of their own, imposing the same conditions on different characters in different books. In Roth's novels, Sunday lunch in the Empire is always noodle soup, brisket of beef, and cherry dumplings. In spring, the laburnums flower and the new sunlight makes the silverware in the Vienna coffee-houses sparkle. The governmental officers are moustachioed and upright, like waxworks.

In the border districts, there is always a Hotel Bristol, where the hero puts up for a while, and a tavern where Russians pay their entire savings to cross into the Empire. The larks trill, the frogs croak, and everywhere can be seen the portrait of the beloved Emperor, and everywhere can be heard bands playing evocative martial tunes, first and foremost 'The Radetzky March'.

But even at their most nostalgic, his novels also exaggerate and mock the presence of the Empire in its citizens' lives. If Roth loved the Empire because it imposed an imperial uniformity on so many different peoples, it is also seen in his books as a kind of tyranny, almost a totalitarianism, so that Roth and Kafka have more in common than might at first seem to be the case. His novels so insist on the Empire that they end up gesturing towards the impossibility of realising it. Roth's elegy suggests to the reader not simply that the Empire is dead and gone, but that it could never, in reality, have equalled the absurd dreams Roth cherished of it. Roth, one feels, was elegiac for the Empire even when the Empire existed, because it was not alive enough for his idea of it. Thus his novels, which were all, of course, written after the collapse of the Empire, are elegies twice over: in a sense, they are elegies for an *original* feeling of elegy.

So it is that Roth's greatest novels squeeze, simultaneously, comedy and romanticism from their depiction of the Austro-Hungarian Empire. The romanticism *is* comedy, because the unwieldy human diversity of the Empire is both magnificent and absurd. In *The Emperor's Tomb*, published in 1938, Roth has his hero, Franz Ferdinand Trotta, describe the extraordinary human resources of the Empire:

The brilliant variety of the Imperial Capital and Residence [i.e. Vienna] was quite visibly fed . . . by the tragic love which the Crown Lands bore to Austria: tragic, because forever unrequited. The gypsies of the Puszta, the Huzulen of Subcarpathia, the Jewish coachmen of Galicia, my own kin the Slovene chestnut roasters of Sipolje, the Swabian tobacco growers from the Bacska, the horse breeders of the Steppes, the Osman Sibersna, the people of Bosnia and Herzegovina, the horse traders from the Hanakei in Moravia, the weavers from the Erzgebirge, the millers and coal dealers of Podolia: all these were the open-handed providers of Austria; and the poorer they were, the more generous. So much trouble and so much pain so freely offered up as though it were a matter of course and in the natural order of things, so as to ensure that the centre of the Monarchy should be universally acclaimed as the home of grace, happiness and genius.

This is Roth, in high nostalgia, in 1938, after the Nazis had occupied Austria. But there is something terribly unstable about the passage ('and the poorer they were, the more generous') and this seems intentional, as if it should be difficult for the reader to tell if Roth is entirely in earnest: what empire could possibly be such a utopia? Roth relishes the strange, crooked proper names (the Osman Sibersna, the coal dealers of Podolia), which he rolls on the tongue like a lyric poet listing the proper names of flowers (saxifrage, amaranths, myrtles). The nouns become almost abstract, lift out of reference and hover in the unaccountable, where they cannot be verified or really known: where is Podolia?

When Roth is at his most extravagant, his very extravagance is a form of sad irony. This is supremely true of *The Radetzky March*, which is full of magnificently romantic, despairing prose. At one marvellous moment, for instance, Lieutenant Trotta takes his mistress to Vienna to see the annual Corpus Christi procession, in which the different regiments of the vast Empire parade before the Viennese:

> The light-blue breeches of the infantry were radiant. Like the serious embodiment of ballistic science, the coffee-brown artillerists marched past. The blood-red fezzes on the heads of the azure Bosnians burned in the sun like tiny bonfires lit by Islam in honour of His Apostolic Majesty [i.e. the Emperor]. In black lacquered carriages sat the gold-decked Knights of the Golden Fleece and the black-clad red-cheeked municipal councillors . . . And the lieutenant's heart stood still yet pounded fiercely – a challenge to medical science. Over the slow strains of the anthem, the cheers fluttered like small white flags amid huge banners painted with coats of arms.

'The blood-red fezzes on the heads of the azure Bosnians burned in the sun like tiny bonfires lit by Islam in honour of His Apostolic Majesty.' One reads this glorious passage as Roth intends us to, in the spirit one feels Roth wrote it in, which is childish wonderment. This is a dream, in which even metaphor is co-opted by the Empire, and red hats become oblatory fires for Franz Joseph. This combination of the childishly romantic and the surreally ironic or comic, of realism and excess, innocence and sophistication, gives Roth's writing a paradoxical air. It is at once modern and old-fashioned. His gifted translator, Michael Hofmann, has noted how many different textures can be found in a Roth novel: 'the caricatures of Grosz, the semi-abstract gorgeousness of Klimt, and the freewheeling, home-made, modern inventions of Paul Klee'. To which I would add only the streaming, ruddy fullness of Ilya Repin, the Repin of those famous large canvases of soldiers eating and laughing. Which means, in novelistic terms (more or less): Tolstoy (and perhaps also Babel). Here, for example, in a rich, streaming passage, Roth celebrates the horsemanship of the Cossacks, who are found on the edges of the Empire:

> In the vast plain between the two border forests, the Austrian and the Russian, the sotnias of the borderland Cossacks, uniformed winds in military formations, raced around on the mercuric ponies of their homeland steppes, swinging their lances over their tall fur caps like lightning streaks on long wooden poles – coquettish lightning with dainty pennons. On the soft, springy, swampy ground, the clatter of hooves could barely be heard . . . It was as if the Cossacks were soaring over the meadows . . . With their strong yellow horse teeth, the saddled Cossacks, in mid-gallop, lifted their red-and-blue handkerchiefs from the ground, their bodies, suddenly felled, ducked under the horses' bellies, while the legs in the reflective boots still squeezed the animals' flanks. Other riders flung their lances high into the air, and the weapons whirled and obediently dropped back into the horsemen's raised fists – they returned like living falcons into their masters' hands.

Still other riders, with torsos crouching horizontal along the horses' backs, human mouths fraternally pressing against animal mouths, leaped through wondrously small rounds of iron hoops that could have girded a small keg.

In such passages, there is no greater modern writer than Joseph Roth (Babel, whom he resembles, lacks his scope), none more appealing in his capacity to combine the novelistic and the poetic, to blend lusty, undamaged realism with sparkling powers of metaphor and simile.

III

If there is something a little sickly in Roth's love of the Empire, Roth's characteristic hero is a little sickly too – sick with love for empire but also made sick *by* empire. And Thomas Mann, a considerable influence on Roth, had shown that a fictional hero who has been made sick by the epoch he lives in – like Hans Castorp in *The Magic Mountain* – can be used by the novelist to offer a critique of the sickness of that epoch.

This is the case with *Rebellion*, written in 1924, when the thirty-year-old Roth still considered himself something of a leftist. The story is fabular. Andreas Pum has come back from the war without a leg. He is a simple, loyal subject of the Empire, who unquestioningly believes that the government will provide him with a pension and a small job for life. Things go well for him at first. The authorities do indeed issue Andreas with a permit to play a barrel-organ, and Andreas spends his days churning out sentimental songs and patriotic marches for appreciative crowds. He finds a kindly war-widow to marry.

But a chance incident inverts his life: he becomes involved in a scuffle with a wealthy industrialist, and assaults a policeman who intervenes. His organ permit is taken away, and he is imprisoned.

Andreas's time inside is only six weeks, but they are fateful weeks. During this period, he ages terribly, and turns into a silent rebel, mentally siding with those malcontents, Communists, angry war veterans and other agitators he had always previously despised and disdainfully called 'heathens'. On his release, Andreas feels that life has become a prison. The old Empire he had always believed in has steamrolled over him. One of the novel's recurring symbols is the lavish official summons that Andreas receives, with its imperial eagle stamped on it; Andreas has become nothing but the prey of the Empire. *Rebellion* ends mordantly: Andreas can only find work as a lavatory attendant at one of the Vienna cafés, now run by his successful friend Willi, and Roth tells us that Andreas has 'decided that he would like to be a revolutionary', like the firebrands he reads about 'in the newspapers that the café supplied him with'. But at the café lavatory all his newspapers are 'generally a couple of days old by that stage, and the news he got was no longer news when he chopped the newspaper into rectangles and hung them on nails in tidy packages. Willi was constantly telling him to economize on expensive toilet tissue.' In other words, the gentlemen of the Empire wipe their arses on such revolutionaries, and by extension, on such mental revolutionaries as Andreas.

Andreas is more rebellious than Lieutenant Trotta in *The Radetzky March*, or Arnold Zipper in *Zipper and His Father*, or Baron Taittinger in *The Tale of the 1002nd Night*, who are all curiously indifferent to their aimlessness, but no less defeated than them. Roth's heroes are victims of the Habsburg Empire, contaminated by what they so love, which is the paternal security and presence of the Empire. Baron Taittinger, who is discharged from the army for dishonourable conduct, drifts without purpose and then kills himself. 'I think he lost his way in life,' a colleague memorialises. 'A man can lose his way!' A friend describes Arnold Zipper as having fallen into 'indifference, melancholy, indecision, weakness, and lack of critical faculty', and blames this collapse on Arnold's father, and his father's entire generation: 'All our fathers are responsible for our bad luck. Our fathers belong to the generation that made the war.'

But really, it is the Empire that is being blamed, and the great father-of-all, Franz Joseph. In *Hotel Savoy*, Gabriel Dan notices that all the other hotel residents, who, like him, are refugees of the Empire, blame the hotel for their misfortune and stasis: 'Every piece of bad luck came to them through this hotel and they believed that Savoy was the name of their misfortune.' Like the Austrian army, the Hotel Savoy is one of Roth's microcosms of the Empire. It is the Empire that is really 'the name of their misfortune'.

But why does the Empire so disappoint its citizens? Partly because, like Roth's, their love of it is desperate and uncontainable. And partly because, as Roth's novels so delicately suggest, the Empire is not quite a reality, is not itself quite containable. Not only love for it, but comprehension of it, will always exceed the reality. Robert Musil writes about this in *The Man without Qualities*, when he praises the Empire as a place that allowed its citizens 'inner space', partly because it did not really exist. The Empire, writes Musil, is 'only just, as it were, acquiescing in its own existence. In it one was negatively free, constantly aware of the inadequate grounds for one's own existence.'

Roth seems to have cherished the 'inadequate grounds' of the existence of the Empire. His novels delight in the fact that the Empire was functionally inefficient – the Austrian army, for instance, was famously feeble – but efficient at glamour; in other words, he loved the rhetoric of empire, and loved that the Empire was first and foremost a rhetoric. There is a constant sense in his fiction that such a fantastic assemblage of different peoples could only really be magical, fictional – as if it could only really exist *for* the novel (those blood-red fezzes). Roth enjoys the Empire as a fictional form, as something analogous to the novel itself. For Roth, and for his heroes, the Empire is too magical for life, but not too magical for the novel.

And his novels, correspondingly, are not just about the Empire; they enact it symbolically, using an empire of signs to create the closed world of his novels, and to insist on its dreamlike inescapability. Roth's imagery pulls its comedy and its magic from this insistence. There is the man already encountered, in *The Emperor's Tomb*, who is seen rubbing both sides of his whiskers, 'as if he wished to caress simultaneously both halves of the monarchy'. In *The Radetzky March*, Roth makes sympathetic fun of Trotta's father, the dutiful district captain, when he describes how thin and gaunt he has become. The district captain resembles 'one of the exotic birds at the Schönbrunn Zoo – creatures that constitute Nature's attempt to replicate the Habsburg physiognomy within the animal kingdom'. And in *Zipper and His Father*, the regulars sit in a Vienna café, as if it were 'a besieged garrison in a castle'.

Roth uses this unreal world, in which everything interlocks for the glory of the Empire, both to elegise a lost time of uniformity and security, and, more interestingly, to so exaggerate the uniformity of the Empire that a kind of disappointment and mockery of it must result. For how can such imperial intrusion – in which the very birds in the zoo have taken on the Habsburg physiognomy, and even a café is like a garrison – not verge on the totalitarian or tyrannous, as Andreas Pum discovers? For instance, one of Roth's best achievements in *The Radetzky March* is the evocation of the slow, eternal repetitions of routine in the Empire. There is a marvellous description of Sunday lunch as Trotta recalls it, with the local town band playing 'The Radetzky March' outside the dining-room windows, and the Trotta family consuming brisket of beef and cherry dumplings, a meal which never varies, on any Sunday of the year. But the book is also a devastating portrait of the inertia of the habitual, and of the oppression of uniformity, and all the best comedy in the novel flows from this apprehension. After all, that café in Vienna may well resemble a 'garrison' to its deluded patrons but it is into just such a coffee-house that a man will stride, as at the end of *The Emperor's Tomb*, to announce that the city has been occupied by the Germans. Roth's characters are made the more vulnerable to history by their refusal of it. Above all, they are people who are acted on; the Empire is their fate and the source of their infantilisation, inasmuch as they have handed over their volition to the great present-absent father, Franz Joseph. The army is the imperial institution which manages this childhood. Lieutenant Trotta, gazing up in cafés at the portrait of the Supreme Commander-in-Chief, is the most pathetic example. When Baron Taittinger, in *The Tale of the 1002nd Night*, is discharged from the Cavalry, he is at a loss, and Roth has a lovely phrase about how Taittinger must act as if he were a newly recruited civilian. In Roth's fiction, to be discharged from the army is like being rusticated from the Empire.

These ironies and comedies enliven and complicate Roth's conservatism. Roth sees that Lieutenant Trotta in *The Radetzky March* thinks he is conserving his patrimony by honouring his grandfather's name and joining the army. But Roth makes us see that Trotta is letting that patrimony congeal by not extending it. Roth describes Gabriel Dan as having 'fallen prey' to the Hotel Savoy, and elsewhere in that book a character remarks: 'A man lays his head on a block – it is a Jewish destiny.' Seen in this light, and despite Roth's difficult relations with his own Jewishness, all of his self-defeating heroes, even the gentiles, are ultimately Jewish.

Because the Empire is everything to Roth's characters, they tend to convert everything, even metaphysics, into the terms of the Empire; they make a religion of the Habsburgs. This is constantly hinted at in *Rebellion*: 'Then he remembered he didn't have his permit anymore. All at once he felt he was alive, but without any authority to live. He was nothing anymore!' So reflects Andreas, when his organ-grinder's permit is taken away. It is the Empire that gives him authority to exist, that tells him what to do, and promises to look after him. In Roth's novels, marching orders are more than merely figurative. They are everything. But at some critical moment in a life, they will not be enough.

The Empire is a religion in Roth's novels, the God that failed, and it fails its citizens rather as God may fail its more desperate believers, by being indescribable, by being *too much*. This religion produces both devotion and a secular rebellion against that religion. Roth's wish-fulfilment sows the seeds of its own disappointment, and this frustration is shared with his embattled fictional heroes, who are epic heroes in a mere age of the novel, junior Don Quixotes, all, as it were, going at life with inappropriate weaponry. It might be said that Roth's novels are war novels without any real war in them. Again one thinks of Kafka, and not just because in *Rebellion* Andreas is promised in prison that a shadowy 'Director' will help him to gain an early release. Kafka once famously said that 'there is infinite hope, but not for us'. In Roth's sad comic world, there is an infinite Empire, but not for us.

1999

Paul Auster's Shallowness

ROGER PHAEDO HAD NOT SPOKEN to anyone for ten years. He confined himself to his Brooklyn apartment, obsessively translating and re-translating the same short passage from Rousseau's *Confessions*. Ten years ago, a mobster named Charlie Dark had attacked Phaedo and his wife. Phaedo was beaten to within an inch of his life; Mary was set on fire and survived just five days in the ICU. By day, Phaedo translated; at night he worked on a novel about Charlie Dark, who was never convicted. Then he drank himself senseless with Scotch. He drank to drown his sorrows, to dull his senses, to forget himself. The phone rang, but he never answered it. Sometimes, Holly Steiner, an attractive woman across the hall, would silently enter his bedroom, and his bed, and expertly rouse him from his stupor. At other times, he made use of the services of Aleesha, a local hooker. Aleesha's eyes were too hard, too cynical, and they bore the look of someone who had already seen too much. But the curious thing was that, despite this hardness, Aleesha looked identical to Holly; it was impossible to tell them apart, as if she were Holly's double. And it was Aleesha who brought Roger Phaedo back from the dead, from the darkness. One afternoon, she was wandering naked through Phaedo's apartment. In his small office, she saw two enormous manuscripts: two piles, neatly stacked. One, the Rousseau translation, each page covered with almost identical words; the other, the novel about Charlie Dark. She started leafing through the novel. 'Charlie Dark!' she exclaimed. 'I knew Charlie Dark! He was one tough cookie. That bastard was in the Paul Auster gang. I'd love to read this book, baby, but I was always too lazy to read long books. Why don't you read it to me?' And that is how the ten-year silence was broken. For no good reason, but no bad one either, Phaedo decided to please Aleesha. He sat down and started reading the opening paragraph of his novel, the paragraph you have just read . . .

Yes, that is a parody of Paul Auster's fiction, an attempt to shrink *l'eau d'Auster* into a sardonic sac. It is unfair, but diligently so: it reduces most of the familiar features of his work. A protagonist, almost always male, often a writer or intellectual, certainly a reader, lives monkishly, coddling a loss – a deceased or divorced wife, dead children, a missing brother. Violent accidents perforate the narratives, both as a means of insisting on the contingency of existence and as a means of keeping the reader reading – a woman drawn and quartered in a German concentration camp, a man beheaded in Iraq, a woman severely beaten by a man with whom she is about to have sex, a boy kept in a darkened room for nine years and periodically beaten, a woman accidentally shot in the eye, and so on. The narratives conduct themselves like realistic stories, except for a slight lack of conviction, and a general atmosphere of the B movie. People say things like: 'You're one tough cookie, pal', or 'Yeah well, my pussy's not for sale', or 'It's an old story, pal. You let your dick do your thinking for you, and that's what happens.' A visiting text – Chateaubriand, Rousseau, Hawthorne, Poe, Beckett – is elegantly slid into the host book. There are doubles, alter egos, doppelgängers, and appearances by a character named Paul Auster. At the end of the story, the hints that have been punctually scattered like mouse droppings lead us to the postmodern hole in the book where the rodent got in – the revelation that some or all of what we have been reading has probably been imagined by the protagonist. Hey, Roger Phaedo invented Charlie Dark! It was all in his head.

Paul Auster's novel *Invisible*, though it has charm and vitality in places, conforms to the Auster model. It is 1967. Adam Walker, a young poet studying literature at Columbia, mourns the loss of his brother, Andy, who drowned in a lake ten years before the novel opens. At a campus party, Adam meets the flamboyant and sinister Rudolf Born, Swiss by birth, of German-speaking and French-speaking parentage. Born is a visiting professor, teaching the history of the French colonial wars, about which he appears to have decided views. 'War is the purest, most vivid expression of the human soul,' he tells a startled Adam. He tries to get Adam to sleep with his girlfriend. Later in the book, we learn that he has worked clandestinely for the French government, or possibly as a double agent.

Perhaps because Rudolf Born is so obviously a figure from spy movies – Auster should have called his novel *The Born Supremacy* – he never sounds remotely like a fastidious and well-educated French-speaking European of the 1960s. He says things like 'Your ass will be so cooked, you won't be able to sit down again for the rest of your life', or 'We're still working on the stew' (about a lamb navarin!), or 'Rudolf the First . . . the bright boy with the big dick. All I have to do is pull it out of my pants, piss on the fire, and the problem is solved.' He takes an immediate interest in Adam and gives him money to set up a literary magazine: 'I see something in you, Walker, something I like,' he says, sounding oddly like Burt Lancaster in *Local Hero*, 'and for some inexplicable reason I find myself willing to take a gamble on you.' For 'some inexplicable reason', indeed: Auster anxiously confesses his own creative lack.

This being an Auster novel, accidents attack the narrative like automobiles falling from the sky. Walking one evening along Riverside Drive, Born and Walker are held up by a young black man, Cedric Williams. 'The gun was pointed at us, and just like that, with a single tick of the clock, the entire universe had changed,' is Walker's banal gloss. Born refuses to hand over his wallet, draws a switchblade and ruthlessly stabs the young man (whose gun, it turns out, was unloaded). Walker runs away, returns a little later, but the body is gone. He knows he should call the police, but Born sends a threatening letter the next day: 'Not a word, Walker. Remember: I still have the knife, and I'm not afraid to use it.' Full of shame, Walker eventually goes to the police, but Born has already left for Paris.

One might tolerate the corny Born, and his cinema-speak, if Adam Walker, who narrates much of the novel in one way or another, were not himself such a bland and slack writer. He is supposed to be a dreamy young poet, but is half in love with easeful cliché. Born 'was just thirty-six, but already he was a burnt-out soul, a shattered wreck of a person'. Adam has an affair with Born's girlfriend, but 'deep down I knew it was finished'. Born was 'deep in his cups by the time he poured the cognac'. 'Why? I said, still reeling from the impact of Born's astounding recitation about my family.' And so on. At times, the prose seems to be involved in some weird, breathless competition to fit the greatest number of shopworn objects into its basket:

> After torturing myself for close to a week, I finally found the courage to call my sister again, and when I heard myself spewing out the whole sordid business to Gwyn over the course of our two-hour conversation, I realized that I didn't have a choice. I had to step forward. If I didn't talk to the police, I would lose all respect for myself, and the shame of it would go on haunting me for the rest of my life.

There are things to admire in Auster's fiction, but the prose is never one of them, though he is routinely praised for the elegance of his sentences. (A review of *Invisible* in *The New York Times*, likening Auster to Freud, Husserl and Goethe, called it 'contemporary American writing at its best: crisp, elegant, brisk'.) The most second-hand sentences in my opening parody, the ones most thickly lacquered with laziness (about being beaten to within an inch of his life, drinking to drown his sorrows, and the prostitute's eyes being too hard and having seen too much), are taken verbatim from Auster's previous work. *Leviathan* (1992), for instance, is supposedly narrated by an American novelist, a stand-in for Paul Auster called Peter Aaron, who tells us about the doomed life of another writer, a friend named Benjamin Sachs. But Peter Aaron can't be much of a writer. He talks thus about his former wife, Delia: 'Guilt is a powerful persuader, and Delia instinctively pushed all the right buttons whenever I was around.' He describes Benjamin Sachs's first novel like this: 'It's a whirlwind performance, a marathon sprint from the first line to the last, and whatever you might think of the book as a whole, it's impossible not to respect the author's energy, the sheer gutsiness of his ambitions.' Lest you are tempted to chalk all this up to an unreliable narrator – 'that's the point, he's *supposed* to write in clichés' – consider August Brill, the seventy-two-year-old literary critic who narrates Auster's novel *Man in the Dark* (2008). Like Nathan Zuckerman in *The Ghost Writer*, he lies awake in a New England house, inventing fantastic fictions. (He imagines a parallel universe in which America is not at war in Iraq, but engaged in a bitter civil war over the fate of the 2000 election.) But when he thinks about actual America, his language is sodden with cliché. Recalling the Newark riots of 1968, he describes a member of the New Jersey State Police, 'a certain Colonel Brand or Brandt, a man of around forty with a razor-sharp crew cut, a square, clenched jaw, and the hard eyes of a marine about to embark on a commando mission'. (It is this same Brill who later says to his granddaughter, 'You're one tough cookie, kid.')

Clichés, borrowed language, bourgeois *bêtises*, are intricately bound up with modern and postmodern literature. For Flaubert, the cliché and the received idea are dozy dogs obstructing the difficult path of precision and beauty, beasts to be toyed with, then slain. *Madame Bovary* italicises examples of foolish or sentimental phrasing, the better to notice them in

all their lividness on the page. Charles Bovary's conversation is
likened to a pavement, over which many people have walked;
twentieth-century literature, violently conscious of mass culture, extends this idea of the self as a kind of borrowed tissue,
full of other people's germs. Among modern and postmodern
writers, Beckett, Nabokov, Richard Yates, Thomas Bernhard,
Muriel Spark, Don DeLillo, Martin Amis and David Foster
Wallace have all employed and impaled cliché in their work.
Wallace's late writing about modern boredom belongs obviously enough to that long Flaubertian tradition. Paul Auster
is probably America's best-known postmodern novelist; his
New York Trilogy must have been read by thousands who do
not usually read avant-garde fiction. But while Auster clearly
shares some of this interest in mediation and borrowedness –
hence, his cinematic plots and rather bogus dialogue – he
does nothing with cliché except use it. Cliché is under no
significant pressure in his work; it just holds its soft hands with
firmer words in the usual way.

This seems bewildering, on its face, but then Auster is a
peculiar kind of postmodernist. Or is he actually a postmodernist? Eighty per cent of a typical Auster novel proceeds in
a manner indistinguishable from American realism; the other
20 per cent does a kind of wan postmodern surgery on the 80
per cent, often fiddling with the veracity of the plot, so as to
cast doubt on its status. Nashe, in *The Music of Chance* (1990),
sounds as if he has sprung from a Raymond Carver story (except
that Carver would have written more interesting prose):

> He drove for seven straight hours, paused momentarily to
> fill up the tank with gas, and then continued for another

six hours until exhaustion finally got the better of him. He was in north-central Wyoming by then, and dawn was just beginning to lift over the horizon. He checked into a motel, slept solidly for eight or nine hours, and then walked over to the diner next door and put away a meal of steak and eggs from the twenty-four-hour breakfast menu. By late afternoon, he was back in the car, and once again he drove clear through the night, not stopping until he had gone halfway through New Mexico.

One reads Auster's novels very fast, because they are lucidly written, because the grammar of the prose is the grammar of the most familiar realism (i.e. the kind of recognisable 'realism' that is in fact comfortingly artificial), and because the plots, full of sneaky turns and surprises and violent irruptions, have what *The New York Times* once called 'all the suspense and pace of a bestselling thriller'. There are no semantic obstacles, lexical difficulties or syntactical challenges. The books fairly hum along. But Auster is not a realist writer, of course. Or rather, his local narrative procedures are indeed uninterestingly realist, while his larger narrative games are anti-realist or surrealist; which is a fancy way of saying that his sentences and paragraphs are quite conventional, and obey the laws of physics and chemistry, and his larger plots are almost always ridiculous. Nashe, in *The Music of Chance*, inherits money from his father and goes on the road. Eventually, he meets a professional poker player named Jack Pozzi (the name suggestive of jackpot, and also of Pozzo from *Waiting for Godot*). 'It was one of those random, accidental encounters that seem to materialize out of thin air.' For no very obvious or credible reason, Nashe decides to tag along with Pozzi: 'It was as if he finally had no part in what was about to happen to him.' The pair end up in the Pennsylvania mansion of two eccentric millionaires, Flower and Stone. Pozzi loses all Nashe's money on a poker game, and the unfortunate duo suddenly owe ten thousand dollars to Flower and Stone, who exact repayment by putting them to work on their estate: their job will be to build, by hand, a huge wall in a field. A trailer is prepared for their quarters. The estate has become a Sisyphean prison yard for Nashe and Pozzi, with Flower and Stone as unreachable gods (Flower's name perhaps gesturing at God's soft side, Stone's at punishment). Nashe gnashes his teeth in this pastoral hell.

Or take what is probably Auster's best novel, *The Book of Illusions* (2002). David Zimmer, a professor of literature, holes up in Vermont, where he mourns the death of his wife and two sons in a plane crash. 'For several months, I lived in an alcoholic blur of grief and self-pity.' By chance, he sees a silent film starring Hector Mann, a brilliant actor who disappeared in 1929, and who, it was thought, never made a film again. Zimmer decides to write a book about Mann, and the best part of the novel is Auster's painstaking and vivid fictional re-creation of the career of a silent-movie actor of the 1920s. But the story soon hurtles into absurdity. After his book on Hector Mann is published, Zimmer receives a letter from Mann's wife, Frieda: Mann is alive, though dying, in New Mexico; Zimmer must come at once. He does nothing about the letter, and one evening a strange woman named Alma arrives at Zimmer's house. She orders him, at gunpoint, to the New Mexico ranch. Second-rate dialogue is copiously exchanged: 'I'm not your friend . . . You're a phantom who wandered in from the night, and now I want you to go back out there and leave me alone,' Zimmer tells Alma, in one of those predictable moments of ritual temporary resistance we know so well from bad movies ('Well, buddy, you can count me out of this particular bank heist').

Alma explains to Zimmer that Hector Mann did not die in 1929 but disappeared, to hide the traces of a murder: Mann's fiancée accidentally shot his jealous girlfriend. The rest of the book speeds along like something written by a hipper John Irving – Zimmer goes to the ranch with the mysterious Alma; meets Hector Mann, who then dies almost immediately; Alma kills Hector's wife, and then commits suicide. And at the end, making good on many helpful suggestions throughout the book, we are encouraged to believe that David Zimmer invented everything we have just read: it was the fiction he needed to raise himself from the near death of his mourning.

What is problematic about these books is not their postmodern scepticism about the stability of the narrative, which is standard-issue fare, and amounts, anyway, to little more than weightless fiddling. What is problematic is the gravity and emotional logic that Auster seems to want to extract from the 'realist' side of his stories. Auster is always at his most solemn at those moments in his books that are least plausible and most ragingly unaffecting. One never believes in Nashe's bleak solitude, or David Zimmer's alcoholic grief. In *City of Glass*, Quinn, the protagonist, decides to impersonate a private investigator (who happens to be named Paul Auster).

Though he is a solitary writer, and has never done any detective work before, he takes on a case that involves protecting a young man from a potentially violent and insane father, whom he must shadow. He pursues this lunatic father with desperate fervour throughout the book. The motive? Quinn's loss of his wife and son, who died several years before the book begins. Quinn, writes Auster, 'wanted to be there to stop him. He knew he could not bring his own son back to life, but at least he could prevent another from dying. It had suddenly become possible to do this, and standing there on the street now, the idea of what lay before him loomed up like a terrible dream. He thought of the little coffin that held his son's body and how he had seen it on the day of the funeral being lowered into the ground.'

This is the kind of balsa-wood backstory that is knocked into 'realist' Hollywood plots every day. Now, a certain kind of comic postmodernist could play such stuff for laughs, might concede that the 'realistic' material is just as jokey or artificial as the non-realistic material – much as, say, the early postmodern Irish writer Flann O'Brien brilliantly undermines all conventional motive and consequence in his novel *The Third Policeman*. But Auster seems to believe in the actuality of his characters' motives, even if the reader never does. Thus, while Flann O'Brien is truly funny, Auster is only ever unwittingly funny. In *The Book of Illusions*, an excruciating example of this unintended comedy occurs when Alma tells David Zimmer that Hector Mann and Frieda had a son, Thaddeus, or Tad for short, who died at the age of three. Imagine the effect it had on them, she says. Zimmer, who lost Marco and Todd, his two sons, in the plane crash that also killed his wife, replies that of course he can imagine such pain. Alma, realising her mistake, embarrassedly apologises. 'Don't be sorry,' says Zimmer. 'It's just that I know what you're talking about. No mental gymnastics required to understand the situation. Tad and Todd. It can't get any closer than that, can it?' The reader has the urge to blow a Flann O'Brien-size raspberry at Auster's laughable seriousness. Zimmer sounds less like a grieving father than a canny deconstructionist leading a graduate seminar. But Auster is death-suited and thin-lipped here, wanting from the sober scene both the emotional credibility of conventional realism and a frisson of postmodern wordplay (a single letter separates the two names, and *Tod* is German for 'death').

What Auster often gets instead is the worst of both worlds: fake realism and shallow scepticism. The two weaknesses are related. Auster is a compelling storyteller, but his stories are assertions rather than persuasions. They assert themselves: they hound the next revelation. Because nothing is persuasively assembled, the inevitable postmodern disassembly leaves one largely untouched. (The disassembly is also grindingly explicit, spelled out in billboard-size type.) Presence fails to turn into significant absence, because presence was not present enough. This is Auster's great difference from postmodern novelists like José Saramago or the Philip Roth of *The Ghost Writer* and *The Counterlife*. Saramago's realism is deeply ironic, and his scepticism feels real. Roth's narrative games emerge naturally out of his consideration of ordinary human ironies; they do not start life as allegories about the relativity of mimesis (though they may become them, and then feed back into the consideration of ordinary human ironies). Saramago and Roth both assemble and disassemble their stories in ways that seem fundamentally grave. They are ironists, and the irony has deep roots.

Despite all the games, Auster is really the most unironic of contemporary writers. Return to Adam Walker's profession of mortification in *Invisible*:

> After torturing myself for close to a week, I finally found the courage to call my sister again, and when I heard myself spewing out the whole sordid business to Gwyn over the course of our two-hour conversation, I realized that I didn't have a choice. I had to step forward. If I didn't talk to the police, I would lose all respect for myself, and the shame of it would go on haunting me for the rest of my life.

A narrator who trades in such banalities is difficult to credit, and the writer who lends him those words seems uninterested in persuading us that they mean anything. But once again, here is an Auster character keen to persuade us, in words of air, of the gravity of his motives, the depths of his anguish: 'This failure to act is far and away the most reprehensible thing I have ever done, the low point in my career as a human being.' It forced me to 'confront my own moral weakness, to recognize that I had never been the person I thought I was'. This shame supposedly determines the course of Walker's life. A year later, in Paris, he runs into Born again, and hatches a plan for revenge that will involve informing Born's fiancée of his murderous past. Walker has never been a vengeful person, 'has never actively sought to hurt anyone, but Born is in a different category, Born is a killer, Born deserves to be punished, and for the first time in his life Walker is out for blood'.

You will notice that the novel's narration has switched from first person to third person – and that the novel's prose has not adjusted its awfulness. The switch in narration is less complex than it seems. An Austerian framing device is in operation. Walker's account of how he met Born in 1967 (the first section of the novel) is revealed, in the novel's second section, to be a manuscript, which he has been working on as an adult, and which he has sent to his old Columbia friend James Freeman, now a well-known writer. Freeman is the only person in possession of this text, which recounts Walker's youthful adventures in New York and Paris, and which moves between first-, second- and third-person narration. The second section of Walker's narrative contains a scandalous (and quite touching) account of the incestuous affair Walker carried on with his sister, Gwyn, in the summer of 1967, just before he left for Paris. Auster's writing stirs in this passage about taboo-breaking, almost as if the radicalism of the content challenges something in his prose: the story has a vividness and pathos largely absent from the rest of the book.

Later in the novel, after the death of Adam Walker, James Freeman sends Walker's manuscript to Gwyn, who denies the incest. The reader is free to infer, if he or she so wishes, that Walker invented the relationship with his sister, in part as a way of compensating for the grief of his lost brother. Perhaps he also invented Born's murder of Cedric Williams, and for similar reasons? Unwisely, the novel ends by returning to its least plausible character, Rudolf Born, who is glimpsed, in the present day, now fat and old, and living on a Caribbean island, looked after by servants in expensive isolation like some kind of Dr No gone to seed. The vitality of the passage about Adam Walker's possible incest is squeezed at either end of the novel by the flamboyantly unreal Born.

The classic formulations of postmodernism, by theorists and philosophers like Maurice Blanchot and Ihab Hassan, emphasise the way that contemporary language abuts silence. For Blanchot, as indeed for Beckett, language is always announcing its invalidity. Texts stutter and fragment, shred themselves around a void. Perhaps the strangest element of Auster's reputation as an American postmodernist is that his language never registers this kind of absence at the level of the sentence. The void is all too speakable in Auster's work. The pleasing, slightly facile books come out almost every year, as tidy and punctual as postage stamps, and the applauding reviewers line up like eager collectors to get the latest issue. Peter Aaron, the narrator of *Leviathan*, whose own prose is so pressureless, claims that 'I have always been a plodder, a person who anguishes and struggles over each sentence, and even on my best days I do no more than inch along, crawling on my belly like a man lost in the desert. The smallest word is surrounded by acres of silence for me.'

Not enough silence, alas.

2009

Hysterical Realism

I

A GENRE IS HARDENING. It is becoming possible to describe the contemporary 'big, ambitious novel'. Familial resemblances are asserting themselves, and a parent can be named: Dickens. Such recent novels as Rushdie's *The Ground Beneath Her Feet*, Pynchon's *Mason & Dixon*, DeLillo's *Underworld*, David Foster Wallace's *Infinite Jest*, and Zadie Smith's *White Teeth* overlap rather as the pages of an atlas expire into each other at their edges.

The big contemporary novel is a perpetual motion machine that appears to have been embarrassed into velocity. It seems to want to abolish stillness, as if ashamed of silence. Stories and sub-stories sprout on every page, and these novels continually flourish their glamorous congestion. Inseparable from this culture of permanent storytelling is the pursuit of vitality at all costs. Indeed, vitality is storytelling, as far as these books are concerned. A parody would go like this. If a character is introduced in London (call him Toby Awknotuby, i.e. 'To be or not to be' – ha!) then we will be swiftly told that Toby has a twin in Delhi (called Boyt: an anagram of Toby, of course), who, like Toby, has the same very curious genital deformation, and that their mother belongs to a religious cult based, oddly enough, in the Orkney Islands, and that their father (who was born at the exact second that the bomb was dropped on Hiroshima) has been a Hell's Angel for the last thirteen years (but a very curious Hell's Angel group, devoted only to the fanatical study of very late Wordsworth), and that their mad left-wing aunt, Delilah, was curiously struck dumb when Mrs Thatcher was elected prime minister in 1979, and has not spoken a single word since.

Is this a caricature, really? Recent novels by Rushdie, Pynchon, DeLillo, Wallace, and others, have featured a great rock musician who, when born, began immediately to play air guitar in his crib (Rushdie); a talking dog, a mechanical duck, a giant octagonal cheese and two clocks having a conversation (Pynchon); a nun called Sister Edgar who is obsessed with germs and who may be a reincarnation of J. Edgar Hoover, and a conceptual artist who is painting retired B-52 bombers in the New Mexican desert (DeLillo); a terrorist group devoted to the liberation of Quebec called the Wheelchair Assassins, and a film so compelling that anyone who sees it dies (Wallace). And Zadie Smith's novel features, among other things: a terrorist Islamic group based in north London with a silly acronym (KEVIN), an animal-rights group called FATE, a Jewish scientist who is genetically engineering a mouse, a woman born during an earthquake in Kingston, Jamaica in 1907, a group of Jehovah's Witnesses who think that the world is ending on 31 December 1992, and twins, one in Bangladesh and one in London, who both break their noses at about the same time.

This is not magical realism but what might be called hysterical realism. Storytelling has become a kind of grammar in these novels; it is how they structure and drive themselves on. The conventions of realism are not being abolished but, on the contrary, exhausted, overworked. Appropriately, then, one's objections should be made not at the level of verisimilitude but at the level of morality: this style of writing is not to be faulted because it lacks reality – the usual charge – but because it seems evasive of reality while borrowing from realism itself. It is not a cock-up but a cover-up.

One is reminded of Kierkegaard's remark that travel is the way to avoid despair. For these books share a bonhomous, punning, travelling serenity of spirit. (This is less true of *Infinite Jest* than of the other books; and Wallace's subsequent work represents a deepening of what can seem like puerility in his authorial voice.) Their mode of narration seems to be almost incompatible with tragedy or anguish. *Underworld*, the darkest of these books, nevertheless, in its calm profusion of characters and plots, its flawless carpet of fine prose on page after page, carries within it a soothing sense that it might never have to end, that another thousand or two thousand pages might easily be added. There are many enemies, seen and unseen, in *Underworld*, but silence is not one of them.

And that optimism is shared by readers, apparently. Again and again, books like these are praised for being brilliant cabinets of wonders. Such diversity! So many stories! So many weird and funky characters! Bright lights are taken as evidence of habitation. The mere existence of a giant cheese or a cloned mouse or three different earthquakes in a novel is seen as meaningful or wonderful, evidence of great imaginative powers. And this is because too often these features are mistaken for *scenes*, as if they constituted the movement or workings or pressure of the novel, rather than taken for what they are – props of the imagination, meaning's toys. The existence of vitality is mistaken for the drama of vitality.

What are these busy stories and sub-stories evading? One of the awkwardnesses evaded is precisely an awkwardness about the possibility of novelistic storytelling. This in turn has to do with an awkwardness about character and the representation of character in fiction, since human beings generate stories. It might be said that these recent novels are full of *inhuman stories*, whereby that phrase is precisely an oxymoron, an impossibility, a wanting-it-both-ways. By and large, these are not stories that could never happen (as, say, a thriller or a magic realist novel often contains things that could never happen); rather, they clothe people who could never actually endure the stories that happen to them. They are not stories in which people defy the laws of physics (obviously, one could be born in an earthquake); they are stories which defy the laws of persuasion. This is what Aristotle means when he says that in storytelling 'a convincing impossibility' (a man levitating, say) is always preferable to 'an unconvincing possibility' (say, the possibility that a fundamentalist group in London would continue to call itself KEVIN). And what above all makes these stories unconvincing is their very profusion, their relatedness. One cult is convincing; three are not. Cervantes has a famous story about two talking dogs, but it is only a few pages long, and feels more like a fable than an exercise in verisimilitude (he called it, precisely, 'an exemplary story').

Novels, after all, turn out to be delicate structures, in which one story judges the viability, the actuality, of another. Yet it is the relatedness of these stories which their writers seem to cherish, and propose as an absolute value. Each of these novels is excessively centripetal. The different stories all intertwine, and double and triple on themselves. Characters are forever seeing connections and links and hidden plots, and paranoid parallels. (There is something essentially paranoid about the idea that everything connects with everything else.) These novelists proceed like street-planners of old in south London: they can never name one street Ruskin Street without linking a whole block, and filling it with Carlyle Street, and Turner Street, and Morris Street, and so on. There is an obsession in these novels with connecting characters with each other, as information is connected on the Internet.

For instance, near the end of *White Teeth*, one of the characters, Irie Jones, has sex with one twin, called Millat; but then rushes round to see the other twin, called Magid, to have sex with him. She becomes pregnant; she will never know which twin impregnated her. But it is really Smith's hot plot which has had its way with her. In *Underworld*, everything and everyone is connected in some way to paranoia and to the nuclear threat. *The Ground Beneath Her Feet* suggests that a deep structure of myth, both Greek and Indian, binds all the characters together. *White Teeth* ends with a clashing finale, in which all the novel's characters – most of whom are now dispersed between various cults and fanatical religious groups – head towards the press conference which the scientist, Marcus Chalfen, is delivering in London, to announce the successful engineering of his mouse.

Alas, since the characters in these novels are not really alive, not fully human, their connectedness can only be insisted on; indeed, the reader begins to think that it is being insisted on precisely because they do not really exist. After all, hell is other people, actually; real humans disaggregate more often than congregate. So these novels find themselves in the paradoxical position of enforcing connections which are finally merely conceptual rather than human. The forms of these novels *tell* us that we are all connected – by the Bomb (DeLillo), or by myth (Rushdie), or by our natural multiracial multiplicity (Smith); but it is a formal lesson rather than an actual enactment.

An excess of storytelling has become the contemporary way of shrouding, in majesty, a lack; it is the Sun King principle. That lack is the human. Of course, there has been since modernism a crisis in how to create human character on the page. Since modernism, many of the greatest writers have been offering critique and parody of the idea of character, in the absence of convincing ways to return to an innocent representation of character. Certainly, the people who inhabit the big, ambitious contemporary novels have a showy liveliness, a theatricality, that almost succeeds in hiding the fact they are without life. This is much less true of Zadie Smith than of Rushdie; Smith's principal characters move in and out of human depth. Sometimes they seem to provoke her sympathy, at other times they are only externally comic.

But watch what she does with one of the many bit-parts in her large, inventive book. Smith is describing the founder of KEVIN, the fundamentalist Islamic group based in north London. She tells us that he was born Monty

Clyde Benjamin in Barbados in 1960, 'the son of two poverty-stricken barefoot Presbyterian dypsomaniacs', and converted to Islam at the age of fourteen. At eighteen, he fled Barbados for Riyadh, where he studied the Koran at Al-Imam Muhammad ibn Saud Islamic University. He was five years there, but he became disillusioned with the teaching, and returned to England in 1984. In Birmingham, he

> locked himself in his aunt's garage and spent five more years in there, with only the Qur'an and the fascicles of Endless Bliss for company. He took his food in through the cat-flap, deposited his shit and piss in a Coronation biscuit tin and passed it back out the same way, and did a thorough routine of press-ups and sit-ups to prevent muscular atrophy. The *Selly Oak Reporter* wrote regular bylines on him during this period, nicknaming him 'The Guru in the Garage' (in view of the large Birmingham Muslim population, this was thought preferable to the press-desk favoured suggestion, 'The Loony in the Lock-Up') and had their fun interviewing his bemused aunt, one Carlene Benjamin, a devoted member of the Church of Jesus Christ of Latter-Day Saints.

Clearly, Smith does not lack for powers of invention. The problem is there is too much of it. The passage might stand, microcosmically, for her novel's larger dilemma of storytelling: on its own, almost any of these details (except perhaps the detail about passing the shit and piss through the cat-flap) might be persuasive. Together, they vandalise each other: the Presbyterian dipsomaniacs and the Mormon aunt make impossible the reality of the fanatical Muslim. As realism, it is incredible; as satire, it is cartoonish; as cartoon, it is too realistic; and anyway, we are not led towards the consciousness of a truly devoted religionist. It is all shiny externality, a caricature.

II

It might be argued that literature has only rarely represented character. Even the greatest novelists, like Dostoevsky and Tolstoy, resort to stock caricature, didactic speaking over characters, repetitive leitmotifs, and so on. The truly unhostaged, the Chekhovs, are rare. *Buddenbrooks*, a first novel written by a writer only a year older than Zadie Smith when she wrote hers, makes plentiful use of the leitmotif, as a way of affixing signatures to different characters. (Yet how those tagged characters live!) Less great but very distinguished writers indulge in the kind of unreal, symbolic vitality now found in the contemporary novel – for instance the autodidact in Sartre's *Nausea*, who is somewhat unbelievably working his way alphabetically through an entire library, or Grand, the writer in *The Plague*, who writes the first line of his novel over and over again.

Dickens, of course, is the great master of the leitmotif (and Dostoevsky read and admired Dickens). Many of Dickens's characters are, as Forster rightly put it, flat but vibrating very fast. They are souls seen only through thick, gnarled casings. Their vitality is a histrionic one. Dickens has been the overwhelming influence on post-war fiction, especially post-war British fiction. There is hardly a writer who has not been touched by him: Angus Wilson and Muriel Spark, Martin Amis's robust comic gargoyles, Rushdie's outsize characters, the intensely theatrical Angela Carter, the Naipaul of *Mr*

Biswas, V. S. Pritchett, and now Zadie Smith. In America, Bellow's genius for grotesquerie and for vivid external description owes something to Dickens; and what was *Underworld* but an old-fashioned Dickensian novel like *Bleak House*, with an ambition to describe all of society on its different levels?

One obvious reason for the popularity of Dickens among contemporary novelists is that his way of creating and propelling theatrically alive characters offers an easy model for writers unable to, or unwilling to, create characters who are fully human. Dickens's world seems to be populated by vital simplicities. Dickens shows a novelist how to get a character launched, if not how to keep him afloat, and this glittering liveliness is simply easier to copy, easier to figure out, than the recessed and deferred complexities of, say, Henry James's character-making. (And I say this not merely as the apparently untouchable critic, but also guiltily, as an apprentice novelist whose own characters owe more than a little to the hard edges of Dickensian caricature.) Dickens makes caricature respectable for an age in which, for various reasons, it has become difficult to create character. Dickens licenses the cartoonish, coats it in the surreal, or even the Kafkaesque (the Circumlocution Office). Indeed, to be fair to contemporary novelists, Dickens shows that a large part of characterisation *is* the management of caricature.

Yet in Dickens there is always an immediate access to strong feeling, which tears the puppetry of his people, breaks their casings, and lets us enter them. Mr Micawber may be a caricature, a simple, univocal essence, but he feels, and he makes us feel. One recalls that very passionate and simple sentence, in which David Copperfield tells us: 'Mr Micawber was waiting for me within the gate, and we went up to his room, and cried very much.'

It is difficult to find a single moment like that in all the many thousands of pages of the big, ambitious, contemporary books. It has become customary to read seven-hundred-page novels, to spend hours within a fictional world, without experiencing anything really affecting or beautiful. Which is why one never wants to reread a book like *The Ground Beneath Her Feet*, while *Madame Bovary* is faded and creased with our rereadings. But that is partly because some of the more impressive novelistic minds of our age do not think that language and the representation of consciousness are the novelist's quarries any more. Information has become the new character. It is this, and the use made of Dickens, that connects DeLillo and the reportorial Tom Wolfe, despite the literary distinction of the former and the cinematic vulgarity of the latter.

So it suffices to make do with lively caricatures, whose deeper justification arises – if it ever arises – from their immersion in a web of connections. Zadie Smith has said, in an interview, that her concern is with 'ideas and themes that I can tie together – problem-solving from other places and worlds'. It is not the writer's job, she says, 'to tell us how somebody felt about something, it's to tell us how the world works'. Citing David Foster Wallace and Dave Eggers, she comments: 'these are guys who know a great deal about the world. They understand macro-microeconomics, the way the Internet works, math, philosophy, but . . . they're still people who know something about the street, about family, love, sex, whatever. That is an incredibly fruitful combination. If you can get the balance right. And I don't think any of us have quite yet, but hopefully one of us will.'

III

This is gently, modestly put. Smith may not actually believe what she says; she seems to me a writer who is quite interested in telling us 'how somebody felt about something' – it is one of her many strengths. And to give Smith her considerable due, she may be more likely to 'get the balance right' than any of her contemporaries, in part just because she sees that a balance is needed, and in part because she is very talented and still very young. At her best, she approaches her characters and makes them human; she is much more interested in this, and more naturally gifted at it, than Rushdie is, for example. To begin with, her minor Dickensian caricatures and grotesques, the petty filaments of *White Teeth*, often glow. Here, for instance, is a school headmaster, a small character who flares and dies within a few pages. But Smith captures his physical essence surely: 'The headmaster of Glenard Oak was in a continual state of implosion. His hairline had gone out and stayed out like a determined tide, his eye sockets were deep, his lips had been sucked backwards into his mouth, he had no body to speak of, or rather he folded what he had into a small, twisted package, sealing it with a pair of crossed arms and crossed legs.' This conjures a recognisable type, and indeed a recognisable English type, always in the process of withdrawing or disappearing – as Smith's highly Dickensian image suggests, always mailing himself out of the room. The headmaster is like Miss Dartle in *David Copperfield*: 'she brings everything to a grindstone and sharpens it, as she has sharpened her own face and figure . . . she is all edge.'

Smith, as Rushdie has said, is 'astonishingly assured'. About her, one is tempted to apply Orwell's remark that Dickens had rotten architecture but great gargoyles. The architecture is the essential silliness of her lunge for multiplicities – her cults and cloned mice and Jamaican earthquakes. Formally, her book lacks moral seriousness. But her details are often instantly convincing, both funny and moving. They justify themselves. She tells the story, really, of two families, the Joneses and the Iqbals. Archie Jones is married to a Jamaican woman, Clara Bowden, and is the father of Irie. He fought in the war, as a teenager, alongside Samad Iqbal, a Bengali Muslim from Bangladesh. The two men have been friends for thirty years, and now live near each other in north London. This is a bustling, desolate area, full of gaudy Indian restaurants and yeasty pubs and unclean laundromats. Smith amusingly captures its atmosphere. Any street in this region will include, 'without exception':

> one defunct sandwich bar still advertising breakfast
> one locksmith uninterested in marketing frills (KEYS CUT HERE)
> and one permanently shut unisex hair salon, the proud bearer of some unspeakable pun (*Upper Cuts* or *Fringe Benefits* or *Hair Today, Gone Tomorrow*).

Samad's wife, Alsana, is an engaging creation. She earns a living sewing black plastic garments, at home, that are bound 'for a shop called Domination in Soho'. (One of the many good jokes in this comic book.) Samad is a waiter at a restaurant in central London, an intelligent man, frustrated by his foolish occupation; and a moral man, frustrated by the lax country he lives in. He spends much of the novel in a fury – he is, precisely, a caricature more than a character – about England and English secularism. He is determined that his twin sons, Millat and Magid, will grow up in the ways of the Koran. But Millat, at least initially, has joined a tough street-gang, who speak 'a strange mix of Jamaican patois, Bengali, Gujarati and English', and hangs out on streets populated by 'Becks, B-boys, Indie kids, wide-boys, ravers, rude-boys, Acidheads, Sharons, Tracies, Kevs, Nation Brothers, Raggas and Pakis'. (This is what Smith means by bringing us the information. But this crocodile of youths has a time-bomb inside it; Colin MacInnes brought us the information about the London of the 1950s in *Absolute Beginners*, and where is that novel? At an absolute end.) Millat's brother, Magid, is a scientific rationalist, and apparently no more interested in Islam than his brother. But his father decides to send Magid, the better student, back to Bangladesh, for a safely religious education. The plan backfires, of course.

When Smith is writing well, she seems capable of almost anything. She more than justifies the excitement she has provoked. For example, at several moments, she proves herself very skilled at interior monologue, and brilliant, in several passages, at free indirect style:

'Oh Archie, you are funny,' said Maureen sadly, for she had always fancied Archie a bit but never more than a *bit* because of this strange way he had about him, always talking to Pakistanis and Caribbeans like he didn't even notice and now he'd gone and married one and hadn't even thought it worth mentioning what colour she was until the office dinner when she turned up black as anything and Maureen almost choked on her prawn cocktail.

That is a fabulous bit of writing, the narrative running on as if in the jumbled and prejudiced head of Maureen; how deftly that vicious little 'even' is placed in the sentence. Can't one immediately hear Maureen's voice, with its silly stress as it greedily alights on the stressed 'even'?

One of the novel's best chapters is a gently satirical portrait of the Chalfen family, middle-class north London intellectuals of impeccable smugness, with whom Millat, Magid and Irie become involved. (One of the Chalfen sons, Joshua, attends Glenard Oak school with the Jones and Iqbal children.) There is Marcus Chalfen, busy with his genetic experiments, and his wife, Joyce, who writes about gardening. She lives the politically unexamined life of the liberal who is sure that she is right about everything. Even her gardening books encode her bien pensant *pensées* about the importance of hybridity. Smith invents a long passage from one of them: 'In the garden, as in the social and political arena, change should be the only constant . . . It is said cross-pollinating plants also tend to produce more and better-quality seeds.'

But this same Joyce cannot help exclaiming, when Millat and Irie first appear in her house, about the delightful novelty of having 'brown strangers' in the house. By mocking the Chalfens, even gently, Smith works against the form of her own novel, and seems to guard against a Rushdie-like piety about the desirability of hybridity, an important novelistic negative capability which she then, alas, deforms by inserting a little Rushdie-like lecture of her own into the very same chapter: 'This has been the century of strangers, brown, yellow and white. This has been the century of the great immigrant experiment.' Far more powerful than such announcements on the authorial PA is a lovely moment when Marcus Chalfen puts his arms around his adored wife (the two are devoted, if a little complacently, to each other), 'like a gambler collecting his chips in circled arms', whereupon the fifteen-year-old Irie, whose parents are much less communicative, thinks 'of her own parents, whose touches were now virtual, existing only in the absences where both sets of fingers had previously been: the remote control, the biscuit tin, the light switches'.

But Smith is a frustrating writer, for she has a natural comic gift, and yet is willing to let passages of her book descend into cartoonishness and a kind of itchy, restless extremism. Here, for instance, is her description of O'Connell's, a bar and café where Archie and Samad have been regulars for many years. Comically, it is run by a family of Iraqis, 'the many members of which share a bad skin condition', but it has kept its Irish name, and various Irish accoutrements. It is where, we are told, Archie and Samad have talked about everything, including women:

> Hypothetical women. If a woman walked past the yolk-stained window of O'Connell's (a woman had never been known to venture inside) they would smile and speculate – depending on Samad's religious sensibilities that evening – on matters as far-reaching as whether one would kick her

out of bed in a hurry, to the relative merits of stockings or tights, and then on, inevitably, to the great debate: small breasts (that stand up) vs big breasts (that flop to the sides). But there was never any question of real women, real flesh and blood and wet and sticky women. Not until now. And so the unprecedented events of the past few months called for an earlier O'Connell's summit than usual. Samad had finally phoned Archie and confessed the whole terrible mess: he had cheated, he was cheating . . . Archie had been silent for a bit, and then said, 'Bloody hell. Four o'clock it is, then. Bloody hell.' He was like that, Archie. Calm in a crisis.

But come 4.15 and still no sign of him, a desperate Samad had chewed every fingernail he possessed to the cuticle and collapsed on the counter, nose squished up against the hot glass where the battered burgers were kept, eye to eye with a postcard showing the eight different local charms of County Antrim.

Mickey, chef, waiter and proprietor, who prided himself on knowing each customer's name and knowing when each customer was out of sorts, prised Samad's face off the hot glass with an egg slice.

This kind of writing is closer to the low 'comic' style of a farceur like Tom Sharpe than it ought to be. It squanders itself in a mixture of banality and crudity. And unlike many passages in the book, it cannot shelter behind the excuse that it is being written from within the mind of a particular character. This is Smith as narrator, as writer. Yet nothing we know about Samad (and nothing we later learn, incidentally) convinces us that Smith is telling the truth when she asks us to imagine this hot-headed Muslim talking about women's breasts; the topic seems, instead, to have been chosen by Smith from the catalogue of clichés marked 'Things Men Talk About in Bars'. And then there is the extremism of the language – Samad is not just anxious, but has bitten his fingers down to the cuticles, and has to be 'prised' off the counter 'with an egg slice'. It seems only a step from here to exploding condoms and the like. The language is oddly thick-fingered – from a writer capable of such delicacy – and stubs itself into the vernacular: that juvenile verb, 'squished', for instance. It comports bewilderingly with sentences and passages elsewhere that are precise and sculpted.

In general, the first half of *White Teeth* is strikingly better written than the second, which seems hasty, the prose and wild plots bucking along in loosened harnesses. Just as the quality of the writing varies, sometimes from page to page, so Smith seems unable to decide exactly the depth of her commitment to the revelation of character. Samad offers a good example. Overall, he's a caricature, complete with Indian malapropisms and Indian (or Bengali) 'temperament', for he has, really, only the one dimension, his angry defence of Islam. Yet every so often, Smith's prose opens out, into little holidays from caricature, apertures through which we see Samad tenderly, and see his frustrations, such as the restaurant he works in: 'From six in the evening until three in the morning; and then every day was spent asleep, until daylight was as rare as a decent tip. For what's the point, Samad would think, pushing aside two mints and a receipt to find fifteen pence, what is the point of tipping a man the same amount you would throw in a fountain to chase a wish.'

This is breathtaking, and peers into a depth of yearning: it is very fine to link the tip to money thrown into a well, and link both to Samad's large desires; and those 'two mints', roughly pushed aside! I wonder if Smith knows how good it is. For it's bewildering when, thirty pages later, she seems to leave Samad's interior and watch him from the outside, satirically. She is describing Samad's and Archie's war experiences, and the moment they first met. The tone wavers drastically around the mock-heroic. Archie has been staring at Samad, and Samad, all of nineteen, malapropistically demands: 'My friend, what is it you find so darned mysterious about me that it has you in such constant revelries? . . . Is it that you are doing some research into wireless operators or are you just in a passion over my arse?' We seem to be in the world of Tom Sharpe again.

Forty pages later, Smith has a funny passage about Samad trying and failing to resist the temptation of masturbation. Samad becomes, for a while, an enthusiastic masturbator, on the arrangement (with Allah) that if he masturbates, he must fast, as recompense: 'this in turn . . . led to the kind of masturbation that even a fifteen-year-old boy living in the Shetlands might find excessive. His only comfort was that he, like Roosevelt, had made a New Deal: he was going to beat but he wasn't going to *eat*.' As in the passage about O'Connell's, the question is one of voice. Again, Smith is not writing from inside Samad's head here; the sophomoric comparison to a boy in the Shetlands is hers. The reference to the New Deal is misplaced, and merely demonstrates the temptation that this style of writing cannot resist, of bringing in any kind of allusion. Equally, take that phrase, 'he was going to beat but he wasn't going to *eat*'. 'Beat' is not Samad's word; he would never use it. It is Smith's, and in using it she not only speaks over her character, she reduces him, obliterates him.

And so it goes on, in a curious exchange of sympathy and distance, affiliation and divorce, brilliance and cartoonishness, astonishing maturity and ordinary puerility. *White Teeth* is a big book, and does not deal in fractions: when it excites, and when it frustrates, it 'o'erflows the measure'. Indeed, its size tests itself, for one reason it disappoints has partly to do with the fact that it becomes clear that over the length of the book Smith's stories will develop, and develop wildly, but her characters will not. Yes, Smith's characters change – they change opinions, and change countries. Millat, once an urban rapper, becomes a fundamentalist terrorist; Joshua Chalfen, once a rationalist and loyal son of his scientist father, becomes an animal-rights freak. Yet whenever these people change their minds, there is always a kind of awkwardness in the text, a hiatus, and the change itself is always rapidly asserted, usually within a paragraph or two. It's as if the novel were deciding at these moments whether to cast depths on its shallows, and deciding against.

Which way will the ambitious contemporary novel go? Will it dare a picture of life, or just shout a spectacle? *White Teeth* contains both kinds of writing. Near the end, an instructive squabble occurs between these two literary modes. The scene is the conference room where Marcus Chalfen is delivering the news about the mouse. All of the book's major characters are present. Irie Jones is pregnant, and looks from Millat to Magid, and cannot decide which twin is the father of her child. But she stops worrying, because Smith breaks in, excitedly, to tell us that 'Irie's child can never be mapped exactly nor spoken of with any certainty. Some secrets are permanent. In a vision, Irie has seen a time, a time not far from now, when roots won't matter anymore because they can't because they mustn't because they're too long and they're too tortuous and they're just buried too damn deep. She looks forward to it.'

But it is Smith who made Irie, most improbably, have sex with both brothers, and it is Smith who decided that Irie, most improbably, has stopped caring who is the father. It is quite clear that a general message about the need to escape roots is more important than Irie's reality, what she might actually think. A character has been sacrificed for what Smith called, in that interview, 'ideas and themes that I can tie together – problem-solving from other places and worlds'. This is problem-solving all right. But at what cost? As Irie disappears under the themes and ideas, the reader perhaps thinks wistfully of Mr Micawber and David Copperfield, so beautifully uncovered by theme and idea, weeping together in an upstairs room.

2000

Bohumil Hrabal's Comic World

WHAT IS FUNNY and forlorn in the following sentence? 'A fortune-teller once read my cards and said that if it wasn't for a tiny black cloud hanging over me I could do great things and not only for my country but for all mankind.'

Instantly, a person opens before us like a quick wound: probably a man (that slight vibration of a swagger), grandiose in aspiration but glued to a petty destiny, eccentric and possibly mad, a talker, rowdy with anecdote. There is a comedy, and a sadness, in the prospect of an ambition so large ('for all mankind') that it must always be frustrated, and comedy, too, in the rather easy and even proud way that this character accepts his frustration: isn't he a bit pleased with the 'tiny black cloud' that impedes his destiny? – at least it is the mark of something. So this character may be grandiose in his ambition, but also in his fatalism. And isn't that phrase 'tiny black cloud' done with great finesse? It hints at a man whose sense of himself has so swelled that he now sees himself geographically, like a darkened area experiencing a bout of low pressure on a weather-map of Europe. 'Tiny', above all: a marvellous word, because it suggests that this man, while possibly proud of his handicap, might also disdain it, or believe that he could just brush it away whenever he wanted and get on with the business of doing great things.

Such are the goods packed in a typical comic sentence by the great Czech novelist Bohumil Hrabal, who died in 1997. The character relieving himself of this little confession is a garrulous cobbler, who admits to being 'an admirer of the European Renaissance', and is the narrator of *Dancing Lessons for the Advanced in Age*. But many of Hrabal's comic heroes are equally talkative. There is Hanta, the narrator of *Too Loud a Solitude*, who has been compacting waste for thirty-five years, and educating himself on the sly using the great books he rescues from the trash. He wanted to grow up to be a millionaire, he tells us, so that he could buy 'phosphorescent hands for all the city clocks' in Prague. Now he reads his rescued Kant and Novalis, and dreams of going on holiday to Greece, where he would like to visit Stagira, 'the birthplace of Aristotle, I'd run around the track at Olympia, run in my underwear'. Hanta doesn't take baths because he suspects them of spreading disease, 'but sometimes, when a yearning for the Greek ideal of beauty comes over me, I'll wash one of my feet or maybe even my neck'.

And there is Ditie, the picaresque hero of *I Served the King of England*, a waiter in a Prague hotel, who once served the Emperor of Ethiopia, and worked with a head waiter who once served the King of England. Ditie is usually wrong about everything – he marries a German athlete just as the Nazis are invading Czechoslovakia – but sometimes he says something wise or prescient, and whenever he is complimented for this, he replies, 'modestly': 'I served the Emperor of Ethiopia.' And there is Milos Hrma, the young, timid railway signalman in

Hrabal's most famous novel, *Closely Observed Trains*. When he discovers that the stationmaster may become an Inspector of State Railways, he is excited, and reverently asks: 'An inspector, like that . . . that's the same rank on the railways as a major in the Army, isn't it?' Yes, it is, says the stationmaster. 'Ah, and then,' Hrma cries, 'instead of the three small stars you'll have just one, but bordered with the inspector's field!'

Hrabal's obvious model for these buffeted heroes is the Czech soldier Svejk, Jaroslav Hašek's comic simpleton, who finds himself entangled in the First World War. Svejk is a kind of Sancho Panza, living on into an age that is no longer epic, not even comic. Hrabal deeply admired *The Good Soldier Svejk*, and in *Total Fears*, a selection of letters written to an American scholar of Czech literature, he praises the way Hašek's novel is 'written as though he tossed it off with his left hand, after a hangover, it's pure joy in writing'. Svejk resembles many of Hrabal's heroes, a 'little man' who seems to wander cheerfully into large historical events. As Svejk effectively talks himself into being arrested by a secret police-man, and is later sent to the front, so Hrabal's absurd waiter, Ditie, who has become rich, is outraged to hear that the Communists have arrested all the millionaires in the coun-try, but have somehow overlooked him. Since he has always wanted nothing more than to be a millionaire, he goes to the police, bank statements in hand, to argue that he should be immediately taken in. (He is, though not without some effort on his part.) Svejk's apparent idiocy hides an intelligence bent on thwarting the authorities with whom he only seems to comply; similarly, Hanta, the man who rescues books from the compacting machine in *Too Loud a Solitude*, is not only a uselessly learned autodidact, but a little rebel against a large book-censoring regime.

Like Hašek, Hrabal kept his ear close to the pub table. He sat for hours in his favourite Prague establishment, the Golden Tiger, listening to beer-fed stories. Those who knew him recall a man who liked to pass himself off as a beer-drinker rather than a writer, content to sit silently and gather – the community's generous beggar. Ondrej Danajek wrote a eulogy for Hrabal in 1997, and remembers 'a very spiritual artist and free-thinker with the ways and looks of a labourer. You were as likely to find him (maybe smiling shyly) in the already slightly drunk crowd at a Third Division football game as overhear him commenting on the game quoting Immanuel Kant or another of his philosophical gods.'

Hrabal, who was born in 1914 in Moravia, started writing poems under the influence of French Surrealism. The poems quickly squared their shoulders and became paragraphs: prose poems, epiphanic jottings, broken anecdotes. The *Prague Revue* (No. 5) has printed a number of these early poems, written in the 1940s, and many of them are touched with a characteristic Hrabalian oddity: 'In the little pub overhanging the river, in a corner by the window, I was reading. You were weeping, I too was weeping and the tubby landlady was weeping.'

In the early 1950s, he was a member of an underground literary group run by the poet Jiri Kolar. His poems had now become stories, but he did not submit them for publication. Instead, he read them aloud to the group's members (who included the novelist Josef Skvorecky). The tale is told – it is rather like those 'symbolic' stories about rulers that were collected by Tacitus and Plutarch – that one day

Hrabal overheard Kolar, who was selling dolls at the time, being asked: 'Kolar, do you have another death?' The question referred, apparently, to a marionette of the Grim Reaper, popular in Prague, but to Hrabal's ears, it suggested a new way of writing, whereby heterogeneous elements could be forced against each other, in a natural, comic manner, arising out of ordinary human business rather than the obviously surreal.

Hrabal began to experiment with an unlimited, flowing style, almost a form of stream-of-consciousness (he admired Joyce, Céline and Beckett) in which characters associate and soliloquise madly. He called it *pabeni*, to which the closest approximation, according to Skvorecky, is 'palavering'. This palavering is really anecdote without end. The lovely truancy with which Hrabal's work vibrates has to do with its hospitality to an abundance of stories. Often, one senses that Hrabal has taken a brief comic tale heard in the pub, and exaggerated its comic essence. The narrator of *Dancing Lessons* tells us, just in passing, of a man who hangs himself on the cross marking his mother's grave, at which the local priest becomes very angry because he has to reconsecrate the whole churchyard. Hanta, in *Too Loud a Solitude*, is accosted by a man who puts a knife to his throat, starts reciting a poem celebrating the beauties of the countryside at Ricany, then apologises, 'saying he hadn't found any other way of getting people to listen to his verse'. In *I Served the King of England*, a general arrives at the hotel where Ditie works. He is very greedy, but has a curious habit. After each sip of champagne and each capture of an oyster, he shudders with disgust and denounces what he has just consumed: 'Ah, I can't drink this swill!' This reminds me of Chekhov (Hrabal loved both Chekhov and Babel), who stole stories from the newspapers, and who kept a notebook full of enigmas, such as this one: 'A private room in a restaurant. A rich man, tying his napkin round his neck, touching the sturgeon with his fork: "At least I'll have a snack before I die" – and he has been saying this for a long time, daily.'

Chekhov is more gloomily scrupulous than Hrabal, who likes to heat his caught enigmas, his snatches of story and strange facts, so that they begin to emit a magical vapour. He is quite capable of a Chekhovian realism (Hanta recalls a village market, at which a woman was standing selling only 'two bay leaves'), but, always watchful for the splendid or sublime in a story – what he called 'the pearl on the bottom' of a tale – he more usually allows his garrulous narrators to run on, prolonging and stretching their stories. A peerless example occurs in *I Served the King of England*, which was written in the early 1970s, though not published until 1983. Ditie has been telling us about the different travelling salesmen who stayed at the Golden Prague Hotel. One of them represents a famous tailoring firm from Pardubice, and he has brought with him a revolutionary fitting technique. It involves putting pieces of parchment on the body of the client, and writing the measurements on them. Back at the workshop, the strips are taken and sewn together on a kind of tailor's dummy with a rubber bladder inside that is gradually pumped up until the parchment strips are filled out; they are then covered with glue, so that they harden in the shape of the client's torso. When the bladder is removed, the torso floats up to the ceiling, permanently inflated, and a cord with a name and address is tied to it. The client's mannequin 'is up there among several hundred colourful torsos, until he dies'.

Ditie, predictably, is enthralled by this absurd and wonderfully pointless innovation, and longs to order a new dinner jacket from this prestigious firm, 'so that I and my mannequin could float near the ceiling of a company that was certainly the only one of its kind in the world, since no one but a Czech could have come up with an idea like that'. He spends his savings and is fitted with a suit. He travels to Pardubice to pick it up, and this 'little man' (Ditie is, in fact, very short, and wears double-soled shoes) is overwhelmed by the social grandeur of the firm's torsos:

> It was a magnificent sight. Up near the ceiling hung the torsos of generals and regimental commanders and famous actors. Hans Albers himself had his suits made here, so he was up there too . . . A thin thread bearing a name tag dangled down from every torso, and the tags danced gaily in the breeze, like fish on a line. The boss pointed at a tag with my name and address on it, so I pulled it down. It looked so small, my torso. I almost wept to see a major-general's torso beside mine, and Mr Beranek the hotelkeeper's, but when I thought of the company I was in I laughed and felt better.

Hrabal may have heard from someone about a real company's mad scheme, but he takes the story and passes it through the madness of his escapist hero, and, in doing so, glazes it with a further strangeness. Hrabal is sometimes called a cinematic writer, probably because a successful film was made of *Closely Observed Trains*. Yet a curious element of scenes like this one is that, although they are pictorial, they retain a kind of hypothetical status, which is the status of dream. Isn't this scene, in some sense, Ditie's dream, despite the fact that it is undeniably happening? Hrabal's descriptions often have a paradoxical visibility and invisibility about them. They are vaporous. The invitation, we feel, is not simply for the reader to see these hanging torsos, but to imagine someone imagining them, which is a little different.

In some respects, Hrabal is an early magical realist, and superficially he resembles some of those contemporary writers who are fond of abundant stories, exotic coloration, jokes and puns, and farcical escapism: Rushdie, Grass, Pynchon, David Foster Wallace, and others. In novels by those writers, we have lately encountered terrorist groups with silly names, a genetically engineered mouse, two clocks having a conversation with each other, a giant cheese, a baby who plays air guitar in his crib, and so on. But this is more like hysterical realism than magical realism: it borrows from the real while evading it. These novels are profligate with what might be called inhuman stories: 'inhuman' not because they could never happen, but because they are not really about human beings. By contrast, Hrabal's magical stories are comic and human – they are really desires embodied. And as such they are, paradoxically, not as parasitical on the real as some magical realism. They inhabit a utopian province, the realm of laughter and tears. How funny and sad it is to imagine Ditie impressed by the celebrity of the dangling torsos, and how fine that Ditie is seen to be as impressed by the presence of the torso of Mr Beranek, the hotel-keeper, as he is by those of the major-generals and actors.

Hrabal was never a strongly ideological or allegorical writer. Nevertheless his first book of stories, *Lark on a String*, was withdrawn a week before it was due to be published, in 1959. It appeared four years later, as *Pearl on the Bottom*. According to Skvorecky, this book 'launched its author on a meteoric career that elevated him to peaks of popularity no other Czech writer had enjoyed before him'. *Dancing Lessons* appeared in 1964, *Closely Observed Trains* a year later. The film's success made Hrabal untouchable. Yet he could still be unprintable: once the Soviet tanks rolled in, Hrabal, who was always a prolific author (his collected works run to many volumes, and only a handful have been translated into English), was silenced again. Skvorecky left Czechoslovakia for Toronto, where he would publish Hrabal and others in émigré editions.

Hrabal began work on *I Served the King of England* during this period of prohibition, in the early 1970s. It was circulating in samizdat form by 1975, and Hrabal is said to have been especially keen for it to be formally published. Karl Srp, writing in the *Prague Revue*, has given a gripping (and often comically Hrabalian) account of how he and his colleagues in the Jazz Section of the Czech Musicians' Union semi-legally published the novel in 1983, in the form of a 'private' edition for its members. 'Boys,' said Hrabal, 'publish just one copy and I can go ahead and die.' They printed five thousand copies and distributed a leaflet telling people that they could come and collect the novel at the Jazz Section's offices. Hrabal's drinking friends were turning up, Srp writes, with beer coasters on which was written: 'Give him one copy of *I Served the King of England* – B. Hrabal.' Karl Srp and other members of the Jazz Section were imprisoned in 1986. Party members, having found boxes of the novel, sold them to each other as Christmas presents. Srp and his friends were released in 1988. 'Shortly afterwards,' as Skvorecky nicely cracks, 'Communism went bust.'

I Served the King of England is a joyful picaresque story, which begins with Baron Munchausen-like adventures, and ends in tears and solitude, a modulation typical of Hrabal's greatest work. Ditie, the book's narrator, is a cloud always chasing the sun of experience – a scudding, flighty, mobile simpleton, who naively pursues one world-historical event after another. Awarded a medal with a fine blue sash by the Emperor of Ethiopia for his exemplary service, he takes out the sash every so often and puts it on, just to remind himself and others what a personage he is. In fact, he is a fool, though he learns a fool's wisdom. When he marries the Nazi athlete, he is ostracised by his friends, and later imprisoned for collaboration. Released, he becomes a millionaire, and runs a successful hotel. 'But the guests who came now were sad, or if they were gay it was not the kind of gaiety I was used to, but a forced gaiety.' (The kind of humour later baptised by Kundera as 'laughable laughter', the forced laughter of those pure and in power, 'the angels'.) It is 1948. Hrabal shows subtlety in allowing this little shard of political critique to be wielded by such an unreliable and fantastical man.

Having forced the new Communist authorities to arrest him as a bona fide millionaire and confiscate his property, Ditie is eventually released and ends his days mending roads in a remote village, sharing his cottage with a horse, a dog and a goat. The novel has suddenly thinned out, as if Hrabal had been walking through a train and finally come to the last carriage, with almost no one in it. The ending is beautifully bereft. Sitting in the pub, Ditie asks each of the villagers where they would like to be buried. They are wordless. Ditie himself nominates a graveyard at the top of the local hill, and a grave straddling its crest, his body balanced like a boat, so that his remains would trickle down each side of the hill, one part into the streams of Bohemia, and the other part over the border into the Danube. In a rising aria, mixing both absurd aspiration and genuine solemnity, Ditie explains: 'I wanted to be a world citizen after death, with one half of me going down the Vltava into the Labe and on into the North Sea, and the other half via the Danube into the Black Sea and eventually into the Atlantic Ocean.'

As with the narrator of *Dancing Lessons* and his 'tiny black cloud', Ditie has expanded into the realms of geography. He has fulfilled, ridiculously, the Czechoslovak dream of being both a nation itself and something more than a nation: he is a posthumous citizen of the world at large. The depth of this desire, and its comic thwarting, are Hrabal's abiding themes. At one point, Ditie refers to the uncle of a colleague, an old bandmaster who wrote a number of polkas and waltzes for his military band in the time of the Habsburg Empire. Since this music is still played, says Ditie, the uncle always puts on his old Habsburg uniform when he goes out to chop wood. This is not so far, in impulse, from Hanta, the narrator of *Too Loud a Solitude*, who longs to run around the track at Olympia in his longjohns, fulfilling his dream of the Greek ideal of athleticism.

What is moving about all these characters is the enormity of the gulf between their aspiration and the limited means by which they often satisfy it: Ditie is, in a way, content to wear his Ethiopian medal and to dream of being a 'world citizen' in death. When Hanta feels like being 'Greek', he washes a leg or an arm, and reads a bit of Aristotle. And then, in a twist of the dialectic, the limited means of satisfaction come to seem equivalent in size to the original aspiration, come to seem a big enough fulfilment, and then become the source of a new kind of swagger for these characters: the old man chopping wood in his Austro-Hungarian uniform is not really defeated. Grandiose in ambition, grandiose in fatalism.

Hrabal's comedy, then, is complexly paradoxical. Holding in balance limitless desire and limited satisfaction, it is both rebellious and fatalistic, restless and wise. Politically, it is not a dependably radical humour: Hrabal described himself as one taught by Hašek to be 'a man of the Party of Moderate Progress, that is my modus vivendi in this Central Europe of mine'. His heroes want to be everything; but they are hardly aware of the size of those wants, and settle for less, without knowing that they are doing so.

It is a comedy of blockage, of displacement, entrapment, cancellation. Hardly surprising, then, that Hrabal sometimes said that he rooted his comedy in one of his favourite findings, a dry-cleaner's receipt, which read: 'Some stains can be removed only by the destruction of the material itself.' In *Total Fears*, Hrabal glancingly commends Freud's writing about comedy and jokes, and calls it 'typically Central European, and especially typical of Prague'. Freud, it may be remembered, distinguishes humour from comedy and the joke. He is concerned with 'broken humour' – 'the humour that smiles through tears'. This kind of humorous pleasure, he says, arises from the prevention of an emotion. A sympathy that the reader has prepared is blocked by a comic occurrence, and transferred onto a matter of secondary importance. In Ditie's case, the solemnity we feel as he contemplates death is comically blocked by his instructions for burial. This is blocked humour about blocked people. Hrabal, in Freud's terms, is a great humorist.

And a great writer. His finest book, *Too Loud a Solitude*, enacts an even more acute modulation, from early buoyancy to late despair. Hrabal, who himself worked for a while as a trash-compactor, creates, in Hanta, his subtlest 'idiot'. Hanta may also represent the closest Hrabal came to a self-portrait. (Hrabal, like Hanta, rescued books from the compacting machine, and built a library of them in the garage of his country cottage outside Prague.) Hanta's wide reading allows Hrabal to use all the mental resources of his hero, however insanely, and the result is a free-flowing prose of extraordinary flexibility, a prose with many interiors within interiors, like some of the Dutch Masters – or perhaps many false bottoms. That would be the proper, unsolemn, Hrabalian image.

Hanta is put out of work, effectively, by the arrival, on the outskirts of Prague, of a much larger, industrial-scale trash-compactor. He visits it, and does not like what he sees. It is clear that this machine does not simply compact trash, with the occasional discarded book, as his small press does, but is swallowing thousands of books. The books are lined up on lorries. It is a giant metal censor, and the harbinger of a sinister new era. But although Skvorecky describes this novel as Hrabal's 'poetic condemnation of the banning of books', this is too heavy a reading. For how nimbly Hrabal enacts a comic crescent around obvious political allegory. What is Hanta's response to this huge machine? He returns to his one-man press, and tries to increase his output by 50 per cent, so as to keep his job. As usual in Hrabal, political critique is slyly neutralised by the unreliability, indeed in this case the madness, of the narrator.

Hanta's increased production little avails him. He is sacked, and wanders through Prague, stopping every so often to drink a beer. He sits in the park, and watches naked children playing, noticing the stripes across their midriffs from the elastic in their pants. This sets in train a succession of observations and allusions, in a passage of stunning vivacity which runs on a thousand feet, a passage which alone and without any context at all, should secure Hrabal's prestige in world literature:

> Hasidic Jews in Galicia used to wear belts of loud, vivid stripes to cut the body in two, to separate the more acceptable part, which included the heart, lungs, liver and head, from the part with the intestines and sexual organs, which was barely tolerated. Catholic priests raised the line of demarcation, making the clerical collar a visible sign of the primacy of the head, where God in Person dips His fingers. As I watched the children playing naked and saw the stripes across their midriffs, I thought of nuns, who sliced head from face with one cruel stripe, stuffing it into the armour of the starched coif like Formula One drivers. Those naked children splashing away in the water didn't know a thing

about sex, yet their sexual organs, as Lao-tze taught me, were serenely perfect. And when I considered the stripes of the priests and nuns and Hasidic Jews, I thought of the human body as an hourglass – what is down is up and what is up is down – a pair of locked triangles, Solomon's seal, the symmetry between the book of his youth, the Song of Songs, and the *vanitas vanitatum* of his maturity in the Book of Ecclesiastes.

This torrent of speculation is true and wise and lofty and simultaneously madly comic (those nuns dressed in starched coifs like Formula One drivers). It is also the thought of a man in despair, the fruit of Hanta's thirty-five years of compacting trash and rescuing great books – a thief of ideas, his very mind a compacted bale of allusion. All this is aquiver in this short, flying passage.

On 3 February 1997, Bohumil Hrabal, sick and in despair, haunted by what he called his own 'loud solitude', and obsessed by the idea of 'jumping from the fifth floor, from my apartment where every room hurts', fell from the fifth floor of a hospital while he was trying to feed the pigeons. Some stains can only be removed by the destruction of the material itself. But if what is up is down, then what is down is up.

2001

George Orwell's
Very English Revolution

I

I VIVIDLY REMEMBER WHEN I first read George Orwell. It was at Eton, Orwell's old school. Not coming from a family with any Eton connections (a portion of my fees was paid by the school), I had refined a test: if a boy's father had gone there, then that boy's grandparents had been rich enough, in the early 1950s, to come up with the money. And if his grandparents had been rich enough, the chances were that his great-grandparents had had enough cash to send Grandpa there in the 1920s – and back and back, in an infinite regression of privilege. There were probably hundreds of boys whose family wealth stretched so far back, into the nineteenth and eighteenth centuries, that to all intents and purposes the origin of their prosperity was invisible, wallpapered over in layers and layers of luck.

It seemed extraordinary to a member of the upwardly mobile bourgeoisie that these boys were incapable of answering two basic questions: How did your family make its money? And how on earth did it hold on to it for so long? They were barely aware of their massive and unearned privilege; and this at a time of recession and Mrs Thatcher, while English fields became battlegrounds, and policemen on horseback fought armies of striking coal miners. I spent my time at that school alternately grateful for its every expensive blessing and yearning to blow it up. Into those receptive hands fell Orwell's pamphlet, written in 1941, 'The Lion and the Unicorn: Socialism and the English Genius', with its own war cry: 'Probably the battle of Waterloo *was* won on the playing-fields of Eton, but the opening of all subsequent wars have been lost there.' And also: 'England is the most class-ridden country under the sun. It is a land of snobbery and privilege, ruled largely by the old and silly . . . A family with the wrong members in control.'

'The Lion and the Unicorn' is a powerfully radical pamphlet, published at a time when Orwell thought that the only way for the British to beat the Nazis was to make the war a revolutionary one. British capitalism had been culpably inefficient. Its lords and captains – the old and silly – had slept through the 1930s, either colluding with or appeasing Hitler. There had been long periods of recession and unemployment. Britain had failed to produce enough armaments; he notes that as late as August 1939, British manufacturers were still trying to sell rubber, shellac and tin to the Germans. The Fascists, by contrast, stealing what they wanted from socialism and discarding all the noble bits, had shown how efficient a planned economy could be: 'However horrible this system may seem to us, it works.' Only by shifting to a planned, nationalised economy, and a 'classless, ownerless' society, could the British prevail. Revolution was not just desirable but necessary. And what was needed was more than just a change of heart but a structural dismantling, 'a fundamental shift of power. Whether it happens with or without bloodshed is largely an accident of time and place.'

During the 1940s, a social revolution did take place in Britain. Though it would not be Orwell's idea of a fundamental shift of power, Orwell's writing certainly contributed to the quieter change that occurred when the Labour Party won the 1945 election, ousted Winston Churchill, and inaugurated the welfare state. After the war, Orwell became most famous as a left-baiting anti-totalitarian, but he did not change his opinion that massive systemic change was necessary in order to make Britain a decent and fair country to live in – he always made the case for nationalisation of major industries, tight government regulation of income disparity (he proposed a system whereby the highest income did not exceed the lowest by more than ten to one), the winding up of the empire, the abolition of the House of Lords, the disestablishment of the Church of England, and reform of the great English boarding schools and ancient universities. This revolution, he thought, will be a curious, ragged, English thing: 'It will not be doctrinaire, nor even logical. It will abolish the House of Lords, but quite probably will not abolish the Monarchy. It will leave anachronisms and loose ends everywhere . . . It will not set up any explicit class dictatorship.' Nowadays, Orwell's imprecision about exactly how this revolution might come about seems telling, because despite the fighting talk ('At some point or other it may be necessary to use violence'), his vagueness seems a kind of wish fulfilment, as if, mimicking his own haziness, a nice muddled revolution might gently and spontaneously emerge from the

London fog. 'A real shove from below will accomplish it,' he writes. A shove – ah, that will do it.

But there is a difference between being revolutionary and being a revolutionary, and journalists aren't required to be tacticians. What is striking, to me, is that Orwell premises the economic viability of his socialistic planned economy on the economic success of the Nazis' planned economy, and, in turn, premises the viability of the planned economy only on its efficiency in wartime. Nazism worked, to use Orwell's verb, because it was good at producing tanks and guns in wartime, but how good would it be at hospitals and universities in peacetime? He doesn't say. So the example of efficient fascism is what inspires the hope of efficient socialism! Orwell seems never to have realised the political contradiction of this, at least explicitly. Unconsciously, he did perhaps realise it, because later works like *Animal Farm* and *Nineteen Eighty-Four* worry away at the fascistic temptation inherent in the socialistic, planned, collective economy – or the 'classless, ownerless society'.

This is not to suggest, as contemporary neoconservatives like Jonah Goldberg absurdly claim, that socialism is just fascism with a bleeding heart. Orwell never thought that. Despite the anti-totalitarian books, despite his reputation's later theft at the hands of the right wing and the neoconservatives, he remained revolutionary in spirit. But he never really reconciled his hatred of what he once called 'the power instinct' with a candid assessment of the power instinct that would have to be exercised to effect revolution. This was because, as he saw it, the ideal English revolution existed precisely to dismantle power and privilege, so how could it possibly end up replacing one kind of privilege with another?

The English just wouldn't do that. An actual revolution, in Russia, with its abuses of power and privilege, necessarily disappointed him, because it contaminated the ideal. Orwell became not so much anti-revolutionary as anti-revolution. He used an ideal revolution to scourge an actual one – which is a negative form of messianism, really.

When I first read 'The Lion and the Unicorn', I was so blinded by flag-waving lines like 'And if the rich squeal audibly, so much the better', and 'The lady in the Rolls-Royce car is more damaging to morale than a fleet of Goering's bombing planes', that I missed this incoherence. To someone surrounded by alien acres of privilege, Orwell's relentless attack on privilege seemed a necessary, obliterating forest fire: 'What is wanted is a conscious open revolt by ordinary people against inefficiency, class privilege and the rule of the old . . . We have got to fight against privilege.' Nowadays, I'm struck by the fact that throughout his work, Orwell is much more vocal about the abolition of power and privilege than about equitable redistribution, let alone the means and machinery of that redistribution. There is a fine spirit of optimistic destruction in his work, a sense that if we all just work hard at that crucial, negating 'shove from below', then the upper-class toffs will simply fade away, and things will more or less work out in the interests of justice. In 'The Lion and the Unicorn', there is a suggestive moment when Orwell writes that collective deprivation may be more necessary than political programmes: 'In the short run, equality of sacrifice, "war-Communism", is even more important than radical economic changes. It is very necessary that industry should be nationalised, but it is more urgently necessary that such monstrosities as butlers and "private incomes" should disappear forthwith.' In other words, let's agree to be a bit vague about the economic stuff, like industrial policy; and let's keep the serious rhetoric for the lady in the Rolls, about whom we can be militantly precise. This is the same Orwell who wrote in his wartime diary, 'The first sign that things are really happening in England will be the disappearance of that horrible plummy voice from the radio', and the same Orwell who, dying in an English nursing home, wrote in his notebook about the sound of upper-class English voices: 'And what voices! A sort of over-fedness, a fatuous self-confidence, a constant bah-bahing of laughter about nothing, above all a sort of heaviness and richness combined with a fundamental ill-will . . . No wonder everyone hates us so.' Getting rid of those accents was more than half the battle for Orwell.

So it is probably fair to say that Orwell was even more consumed by the spectacle of overweening privilege than by the spectacle of overwhelming poverty, despite the two great, committed books he wrote about the poor, *Down and Out in Paris and London* (1933) and *The Road to Wigan Pier* (1937). Again and again, Orwell returns to the abuse of power. In his long essay on Dickens, one of the finest he wrote, he marks Dickens down for not being revolutionary enough (Dickens is 'always pointing to a change of spirit rather than a change of structure'), yet applauds his 'real hatred of tyranny', and then turns back on himself to repeat the case that a purely moral critique of society is not quite sufficient, since the 'central problem – how to prevent power from being abused – remains unsolved'.

His nicely pugilistic essay on Tolstoy's hatred of *King Lear* is sceptical about Tolstoy's late, monkish religiosity, and sets up a binarism that is repeated two years later, in his essay on Gandhi. For Orwell, the humanist is committed to this world and its struggles, and knows that 'life is suffering'. But the religious believer wagers everything on the next life, and though the two sides, religious and secular, may occasionally overlap, there can be no ultimate reconciliation between them. Orwell suspects that when the bullying humanist novelist became a bullying religious writer, he merely exchanged one form of egoism for another. 'The distinction that really matters is not between violence and non-violence, but between having and not having the appetite for power.' The example he appends to this dictum is an interesting one: when a father threatens his son with 'You'll get a thick ear if you do that again', coercion is palpable and transparent. But, writes Orwell, what of the mother who lovingly murmurs, 'Now, darling, is it kind to Mummy to do that?' The mother wants to contaminate her son's brain. Tolstoy did not propose that *King Lear* be banned or censored, says Orwell; instead, when he wrote his polemic against Shakespeare, he tried to contaminate our pleasure. For Orwell, 'creeds like pacifism and anarchism, which seem on the surface to imply a complete renunciation of power, rather encourage this habit of mind'.

Orwell became increasingly obsessed with this kind of manipulative, insidious power; his repeated denunciations of those he thought wielded it – pacifists, anarchists, Communist fellow-travellers, naive leftists – reached a slightly hysterical pitch. But his terror of the tyrannical mother who lovingly murmurs at you while rearranging your brain makes the two novels written under that shadow, *Animal Farm* and *Nineteen Eighty-Four*, very powerful – indeed, the only two really fine fictions he ever produced. Reliably, the most appalling moments in *Nineteen Eighty-Four* come when the state has already read Winston Smith's mind and abolished his interiority. A man sits in a room and thinks: we expect the traditional realist novel to indulge his free consciousness and represent its movements on the page. When we are told, in effect, that this cannot happen in the usual way, because this man is being watched by the state, that this man fears even to betray himself by speaking aloud in his sleep, the shock, even sixty years after the book's publication, is still great. The all-seeing novelist becomes not the benign author but the dreaded telescreen, or the torturer O'Brien, who seems to know in advance what questions Winston will ask.

Eric Blair (Orwell's real name) was born in 1903, in Bengal, to a father who worked as a minor official in the Indian Civil Service; his mother was the daughter of a French teak merchant who did business in Burma. In a kind of morbid squirm, Orwell wrote that he belonged to the 'lower-upper-middle class', a station with prestige but no money. Such families went to the colonies because they could afford to play there at being gentlemen. But this self-description appears in *The Road to Wigan Pier*, where it must have seemed very important to scuff his social polish a bit. In fact, 'lower-upper class' would be a more accurate and compact portmanteau: he was the great-great-great-grandson of an earl, the grandson of a clergyman, and in later life kept up with Old Etonian chums such as Cyril Connolly, Anthony Powell and A. J. Ayer. At St Cyprian's, a preparatory school he was sent to at the age of eight, little Eric was inducted into a regime of violence and intimidation. According to his memoir 'Such, Such Were the Joys' (not published in Orwell's lifetime, for fear of libel), he was singled out for bullying because he was a poor boy, on reduced fees. There was soft and hard power here – Mummy and Daddy were both at work. The headmaster and his wife used Blair's depressed financial status as manipulative weapons. 'You are living on my bounty,' the headmaster would say, as he vigorously caned the little boy. His wife comes across as an understudy for O'Brien; she could make young Blair snivel with shame and gratitude, by saying things like 'And do you think it's quite fair to us, the way you're behaving? After all we've done for you? You do know what we've done for you, don't you?'

Having crammed for the Eton scholarship, which he won, Orwell then seems to have taken the next five years off, though he read an enormous amount in his own time. Eton was enlightenment itself after St Cyprian's, and he confessed to having been 'relatively happy' there. But he must have been painfully aware, as he had been at St Cyprian's, of not being able to keep up with wealthier boys. There was probably a more sophisticated version of the inquisition that he remembered from St Cyprian's, in which 'new boys of doubtful social origin' were bombarded with questions like: 'What part of London do you live in? Is that Knightsbridge or Kensington? How many bathrooms has your house got? How many servants do your people keep?' (I remember an updated edition of this.) Unable to win a scholarship to Oxford or Cambridge, Orwell joined the Indian Imperial Police, in Burma, in 1922. It was a peculiar decision, but as with the atheist who loves churches, it perhaps represented an unconscious form of rebellious espionage.

School provided Orwell with one of his lifelong obsessions, class; his experience as a colonial policeman provided a tutorial in the other, the abuse of power. The famous essays that come out of the time in Burma, including 'A Hanging' and 'Shooting an Elephant', are written with cool fire – a banked anger at administered cruelty. In the latter piece, Orwell is ashamed that he must kill a magnificent elephant simply to avoid losing face, as a policeman and white man, before a large Burmese crowd. In 'A Hanging', the horror of the execution – 'It is curious, but till that moment I had never realised what it means to destroy a healthy, conscious man' – is made more vivid by the triviality that surrounds the event, like rubbish around the base of a monument: Orwell describes a dog that bounds up and tries to lick the face of the condemned man, and he notices, in a celebrated moment, the prisoner swerve to avoid a puddle as he walks towards the gallows.

Orwell claimed that in a peaceful age he might have been a harmless, ornamental writer, oblivious to political obligation. 'As it is,' he wrote in 1946, 'I have been forced into becoming a sort of pamphleteer. First I spent five years in an unsuitable profession (the Indian Imperial Police, in Burma), and then I underwent poverty and failure.' That verb, 'underwent', suggests not coercion but voluntary self-mortification. The truth is that Orwell went to Paris in 1928 like hundreds of other poor aspiring artists, to see what he could produce. He did indeed run out of money, and ended up working as a dishwasher, or *plongeur*, in a Paris hotel. He had pneumonia and spent several weeks in a free hospital in Paris, in hideous circumstances, an experience he wrote up in 'How the Poor Die'. He returned to England, and tramped around London and Kent with the down-and-out, living like the homeless, on bread and butter and cups of tea, and putting up for the night at doss-houses, or 'spikes'. But he chose to do all this rather than, say, go and live with his parents, because he was scouting for material.

And what material! *Down and Out in Paris and London*, his first book, which he published in 1933, is in some ways his best (though *Homage to Catalonia* comes very close). There is a young man's porousness to impressions and details, a marvellous ear for speech, and a willingness to let anecdotes play themselves out. Five years later, he would write again about the poor, this time miners, steelworkers and the unemployed in Wigan and Sheffield, but they are hardly ever allowed to speak in *The Road to Wigan Pier*. As there are no voices, so there are no stories in the later book, no movement, just the tar of deprivation, which glues his subjects into their poverty. Orwell has become a pamphleteer, and is now doing rhetorical battle with fellow socialists. The earlier book, curiously, is a joyful, dynamic one. There is Boris, the unemployed Russian waiter and former soldier, who likes to quote Marshal Foch: '*Attaquez! Attaquez! Attaquez!*' There is the frighteningly precise account of hunger, and the worldly tips that Orwell enjoys passing on, such as eating bread with garlic rubbed on it – 'the taste lingers and gives one the illusion of having fed recently'. There are the vivid descriptions of the labyrinthine inferno in the bowels of the hotel where he works: 'As we went along, something struck me violently in the back. It was a hundred-pound block of ice, carried by a blue-aproned porter. After him came a boy with a great slab of veal on his shoulder, his cheek pressed into the damp, spongy flesh.' And there are characters like Bozo, a London pavement artist, who rattles on:

'The whole thing with cartoons is being up to date. Once a child got its head stuck in the railings of Chelsea Bridge. Well, I heard about it, and my cartoon was on the pavement before they'd got the child's head out of the railings. Prompt, I am.'

And on:

'Have you ever seen a corpse burned? I have, in India. They put the old chap on the fire, and the next moment I almost jumped out of my skin, because he'd started kicking. It was only his muscles contracting in the heat – still, it give me a turn. Well, he wriggled about for a bit like a kipper on hot coals, and then his belly blew up and went off with a bang you could have heard fifty yards away. It fair put me against cremation.'

Bozo, whose collar is always fraying, and who patches it with 'bits cut from his shirt tail so that the shirt hardly had any tail left', is both real and heightened. He is pure Dickens, and Orwell almost certainly worked up his speech like a good novelist. Who's to say that Orwell did not come up on his own with that simile, 'like a kipper on hot coals'? It perfectly fulfils one of the requests he would make thirteen years later in a well-known essay, 'Politics and the English Language', for 'a fresh, vivid, home-made turn of speech'. His own writing abounds with images of kipperlike pungency: 'In the West even the millionaire suffers from a vague sense of guilt, like a dog eating a leg of mutton.' In his novel *Coming Up for Air* (1939), the old bucolic town of Lower Binfield has unattractively expanded after the First World War and has 'spread like gravy over a tablecloth'.

But even if Orwell worked at his journalism like a good novelist, the strange thing is that he could not work at his novels like a good novelist. The very details that sharply pucker the journalism are rolled flat in the fiction. Orwell needed the prompt of the real to get going as a writer. One of the most vivid details in the novel *Keep the Aspidistra Flying* (1936) involves the impoverished hero, about to go to a genteel tea party, inking the skin of his ankles where it peeps through the threadbare sock. You don't forget this: it gives such new meaning to the phrase 'down-at-heel'. But Orwell saw it in Paris, first recorded it in *Down and Out*, and then recycled it years later in fiction. No one forgets the waiters and tramps and cooks in his first book, inking their heels, stuffing the soles of their shoes with newspaper, or squeezing a dirty dishcloth into the patron's soup as a revenge on the bourgeoisie; nobody forgets Mr Booker in *The Road to Wigan Pier*, who runs a tripe shop and has filthy fingers, and 'like all people with permanently dirty hands . . . had a peculiarly intimate, lingering manner of handling things'. But there is absolutely nothing memorable in the watery, vaudevillian description of the urban poor – 'the proles' – in *Nineteen Eighty-Four*; it is just neutered Gissing.

Orwell is famous for his easy, intimate, frank style, and for his determination that good prose should be as transparent as a windowpane. But his style, though superbly colloquial, is much more like a lens than a window. His narrative journalism directs our attention pedagogically; he believed, as he put it, that 'all art is propaganda'. There is a cunning control of suspense. The dog who bounds up to the prisoner in 'A Hanging' is introduced like this: 'Suddenly, when we had gone ten yards, the procession stopped short without any order or warning. A dreadful thing had happened – a dog, come goodness knows whence, had appeared in the yard.' Whatever dreadful thing one has been made to expect at that moment, it is unlikely to be a dog. The characteristic Orwellian formulation 'It is interesting that' or 'Curiously enough' works similarly; it generally introduces not some penny curiosity but a gold-plated revelation: 'Curiously enough, he was the first dead European I had seen,' he writes in 'How the Poor Die'. The man swerving to avoid the puddle in 'A Hanging' is passed off rather similarly, as a kind of found object, a triviality noticed by chance. But the essay is carefully structured around two examples of irrelevance, each of them suggestive of an instinctive solipsism. The dog who bounds up to the condemned man is living its own joyous, animal life, and this has nothing to do with the imminent horror; this incursion is then 'balanced' – in a formal sense – by the victim's 'irrelevant' swerve, which, among other things, is suggestive of a body or mind still moving at its own instinctual rhythm. The piece is highly choreographed.

He almost certainly got this eye for didactic detail from Tolstoy, who is masterful at the apprehension that forces a sudden reappraisal of reality, often a new awareness that another person is as real to him as you are to yourself. The man swerving round the puddle has an ancestor in the young Russian, in *War and Peace*, who is about to be executed by French soldiers, and irrelevantly fiddles with his blindfold, because it is too tight. Nikolai Rostov, in the same book, finds that he cannot kill a French soldier, because instead of seeing an enemy he sees 'a most simple, homelike face'. In 'Looking Back on the

Spanish War', Orwell is about to shoot a Fascist soldier, and then cannot, because 'he was half-dressed and was holding up his trousers with both hands as he ran'.

Orwell is wrongly thought of as the great neutral reporter, immune to the fever of judgement – the cool camera, the unbiased eyeball. He was attacked by Edward Said for propagating 'the eye-witness, seemingly opinion-less politics' of Western journalism: 'When they are on the rampage, you show Asiatic and African mobs rampaging: an obviously disturbing scene presented by an obviously unconcerned reporter who is beyond Left piety or right-wing cant,' wrote Said. I think that almost the opposite is true. Orwell may seem cool, because he does not flinch from violence and poverty and distress, but looks harder at it. Yet he seems to think about horror coolly only to watch it hotly. Henry Mayhew, whose reportage in *London Labour and the London Poor* (1861) is often compared to Orwell's writing about the poor, generally writes a notably detached prose. He goes around the London streets cataloguing and recording deprivation, an enlightened anthropologist. But there is nothing detached about Orwell's diction. In *Down and Out* and *The Road to Wigan Pier*, the world of poverty is frequently described as 'loathsome', 'disgusting', 'fetid', 'squalid'. In the Paris hotel where he works, there is 'the warm reek of food' and 'the red glare of a fire'. He works alongside 'a huge excitable Italian' and 'a hairy, uncouth animal whom we called the Magyar'. Back in England, tramping around the countryside with the homeless, he must share quarters in hostels with people who revolt him: 'I shall never forget the reek of dirty feet . . . a stale, fetid stink . . . the passage was full of squalid, grey-shirted figures.' In one doss-house, where the sheets 'stank so horribly of sweat that I could not bear them near my nose', a man is lying in bed with his trousers wrapped around his head, 'a thing which for some reason disgusted me very much'. Orwell is woken next morning

> by a dim impression of some large brown thing coming towards me. I opened my eyes and saw that it was one of the sailor's feet, sticking out of bed close to my face. It was dark brown, quite dark brown like an Indian's, with dirt. The walls were leprous, and the sheets, three weeks from the wash, were almost raw umber colour.

Notice, as ever, the crafty use of suspense ('some large brown thing'), and then the diction – 'like an Indian's' – that borrows from a nineteenth-century sensationalist like Wilkie Collins (a contemporary novelist like Ian McEwan has in turn learned quite a lot about narrative stealth and the control of disgust from Orwell).

Perhaps Orwell struck Said as dangerous because though politically didactic, he is rarely obviously sympathetic. On the contrary, he thrashes his subjects with attention. He punishes people with his own transferred masochism. In 'How the Poor Die', what stays with the reader is the description of the administration of the mustard poultice:

> I learned later that watching a patient have a mustard poultice was a favourite pastime in the ward. These things are normally applied for a quarter of an hour and certainly they are funny enough if you don't happen to be the person inside. For the first five minutes the pain is severe, but you

believe you can bear it. During the second five minutes this belief evaporates, but the poultice is buckled at the back and you can't get it off. This is the period the onlookers most enjoy.

First, there is the apparent coolness ('and certainly they are funny enough if you don't happen to be the person inside'). And then the heat – the leap to that last sentence, with its combination of Grand Guignol and unverifiable self-projection: how can he really know this? Isn't it actually the moment that *Orwell* might most enjoy as a spectator, even while hating it? Orwell says of Mr Booker that like all men with dirty hands he handled food in a lingering way, but it is *Orwell* whose eye cannot stop lingering on those dirty hands. In *Down and Out*, he cannot suppress the relish with which he tells us how many times he has seen the nasty fat pink fingers of the chef touching steak. Then he joyfully drives it home: 'Whenever one pays more than, say, ten francs for a dish of meat in Paris, one may be certain that it has been fingered in this manner . . . Roughly speaking, the more one pays for food, the more sweat and spittle one is obliged to eat with it.' The effect is both sadistic and masochistic, because Orwell does not exempt himself from the punishment: it is understood that, at some point, he, the Old Etonian, will be the diner, not the waiter; and indeed he seems, self-abnegatingly, to want to taste the sweat on the meat, as a salty political reminder. In a similar way, his rhetoric of disgust in *The Road to Wigan Pier* works so well because it involves us in his own difficult struggle to admire the working classes. If I can overcome my repulsion, he seems to say, then you can, too.

There is a long historical connection between revolution and Puritanism (with both a capital and lower-case *p*), and Orwell sings in that stainless choir. In Paris, he exults that all that separates the diners from the filth of the kitchen is a single door: 'There sat the customers in all their splendour – and here, just a few feet away, we in our disgusting filth.' He is like Jonathan Edwards, reminding his congregation that we are suspended over hell by 'a slender thread' and that an angry God can cut it when it pleases him. Throughout the 1930s and early 1940s, as Orwell's radicalism grows, this politics of the slender thread becomes more pronounced. It provides one of the best passages in *Wigan*, when he reminds us that our comfortable existence aboveground is founded on what men do beneath, in hellish conditions:

> Whatever may be happening on the surface, the hacking and shovelling have got to continue without a pause. In order that Hitler may march the goosestep, that the Pope may denounce Bolshevism, that the cricket crowds may assemble at Lord's, that the Nancy poets may scratch one another's backs, coal has got to be forthcoming.

And it is the same with empire – a stream of dividends 'flows from the bodies of Indian coolies to the banking accounts of old ladies in Cheltenham'.

II

It has become a slightly easy commonplace to note that Orwell's radicalism was conservative. He was a socialist artist but utterly anti-bohemian, a cosmopolitan who had worked in Paris and fought alongside Trotskyists in Spain but who was glad to get back home to lamb and mint sauce and 'beer made with veritable hops'. He wanted England to change and stay the same, and he became a great popular journalist in part because he was so good at defending the ordinary virtues of English life, as he saw them, against the menace of change; even when he is attacking something politically disagreeable – like the popular boys' comic *The Magnet*, featuring Billy Bunter, whose tales were set at a posh, Eton-like boarding school – he sounds as if he wants it to last forever. During the war, he wrote a weekly column for the left-wing *Tribune*, as well as squibs for the *Evening Standard*, in which he praised the solid food he liked – Yorkshire pudding, kippers, Stilton ('I fancy that Stilton is the best cheese of its type in the world'); attacked women's make-up ('It is very unusual to meet a man who does not think painting your fingernails scarlet is a disgusting habit'); asked why people use foreign phrases when 'perfectly good English ones exist'; and lamented the disappearance of the warming pan and the rise of the rubber hot-water bottle ('clammy, unsatisfying').

What makes his essays about Donald McGill's seaside postcards, and Dickens, and the decline of the English murder, and Billy Bunter so acute is that he was greatly talented at describing closed worlds, and adumbrating their conventions. If he pioneered what became cultural studies, it is because he could see that these worlds were both real (because they were produced by a living culture) and unreal (because they subsisted on their own peculiar codes). He transferred to the description of these extant fictional worlds precisely the talent he lacked as a novelist for non-existent worlds; he needed a drystone wall already up, so that he could bring his mortar to it and lovingly fill in the gaps. And he did the same with the greatest closed world, English life, reading the country as if it were a place both real and fictional, with its own narrative conventions. This semi-fictional England, beautifully described in 'The Lion and the Unicorn' and given body in his popular columns, was a rather shabby, stoical, anti-American, ideally classless place, devoted to small English pleasures like marmalade and suet pudding and fishing in country ponds, puritanical about large luxuries like the Ritz Hotel and Rolls-Royces, and suspicious of modern conveniences like aspirins, plate glass, shiny American apples, cars and radios. There is an undoubted comedy in Orwell's never having realised that what was obviously utopia to him might strike at least half the population as a chaste nightmare.

The biggest convention in this semi-fictional world is the working class. In *The Road to Wigan Pier*, Orwell says that he knows too much about working-class life to idealise it, and then proceeds to idealise it, like some Victorian genre painter. In the best kind of proletarian home, he says, 'you breathe a warm, decent, deeply human atmosphere', and a working-man has a better chance of being happy than an 'educated' one. He paints a nice picture: 'Especially on winter evenings after tea, when the fire glows in the open range and dances mirrored in the steel fender, when Father, in shirt-sleeves, sits in the rocking chair at one side reading the racing finals, and Mother sits on the other with her sewing, and the children are happy with a pen'orth of mint humbugs, and the dog lolls roasting himself on the rag mat.' What will that scene be like in two hundred years, he asks, in that utopia where there is no manual labour, and everyone is 'educated'? There will be no coal fire, he answers, and no horse racing, and the furniture will be made of rubber, glass and steel.

Like many radicals, Orwell has strong Rousseauian tendencies: the simpler, apparently more organic life of the countryside seemed a tempting birdsong compared to London's mechanised squawks. He could see that, with or without a revolution, post-war British society would be very different from the bucolic pre-1914 world in which he grew up, and uneasily he returns repeatedly to what lies ahead. For millions of people, he laments, the sound of the radio is more normal than the sound of birds. Modern life should be simpler and harder, he argues, not softer and more complex, and in a healthy world 'there would be no demand for tinned foods, aspirins, gramophones, gaspipe chairs, machine guns, daily newspapers, telephones, motor-cars, etc. etc.' Note that 'etc.' – there speaks the puritan, reserving the right to stretch his prohibitions, at cranky whim. In his novel *Coming Up for Air* (1939), the hero returns to the country town he remembers from childhood (based on Orwell's own childhood memories of the Thames Valley) to find that it has become an overdeveloped horror, full of flimsy new houses and orbital roads; it looks just like 'those new towns that have suddenly swelled up like balloons in the last few years, Hayes, Slough, Dagenham . . . That kind of chilliness, the bright red brick everywhere, the temporary-looking shop windows full of cut-price chocolates and radio parts.' The same new towns recur in 'The Lion and the Unicorn', when Orwell admits that life has improved for the working classes since 1918, and that people of an 'indeterminate social class' have emerged, in new towns and suburbs around London, places like 'Slough, Dagenham, Barnet, Letchworth, Hayes'. He acknowledges that this is the future; indeed, he says that this puzzling non-class will provide the 'directing brains' for the post-war socialist revolution. But he cannot really admire these people:

> It is a rather restless, cultureless life, centring round tinned food, *Picture Post*, the radio and the internal combustion engine . . . To that civilisation belong the people who are most at home in and most definitely *of* the modern world, the technicians and the higher-paid skilled workers, the airmen and their mechanics, the radio experts, film producers, popular journalists and industrial chemists.

Lest one is in any doubt as to what Orwell feels about this 'indeterminate class', it is just such people who, in *Nineteen Eighty-Four*, have emerged after the war, and who now run the totalitarian apparatus: 'The new aristocracy was made up for the most part of bureaucrats, scientists, technicians, trade-union organisers . . . These people, whose origins lay in the salaried middle class and the upper grades of the working class, had been shaped and brought together by the barren world of monopoly industry and centralised government.'

'Monopoly industry and centralised government' sounds pretty much like capitalism and socialism combined. And perhaps Orwell had, by the late 1940s, soured on the latter as well as the former. On the one hand, as Orwell saw it, capitalism produced unemployment and monopoly and injustice (i.e. England in the 1920s and 1930s); on the other hand, socialist collectivism produced totalitarianism and barren machine-progress (i.e. Soviet Russia). And both political economies seemed to point, willy-nilly, to the loathsome post-war world of plate glass and industrial chemists and rubber hot-water bottles. After the war, when Orwell was writing his two most famous books, he remained faithful to an *ideal* English revolution, while losing faith in actual socialism because, for all his acute powers of political prophecy, and his general approval of what the Labour Party stood for, he could not envisage a *realistic* English post-war future. (In *Nineteen Eighty-Four*, when Winston and Julia meet for their first, illicit lovemaking, they travel outside soulless London into the unspoiled rural world that Orwell grew up in.)

III

I sat up when I encountered Orwell's two references to the east London suburb of Dagenham, because that was where my father was born, in 1928, into exactly the 'indeterminate class' that Orwell cannot bring himself to admire. His father, my grandfather, ended up as a quality-control checker at the Ford factory that came to Dagenham in 1931, and my father's passage out of and up from that rather 'cultureless' world was the traditional one for bright working-class boys: he went to the Royal Liberty Grammar School, in Essex, founded in 1921 by the state, to aid boys like him, and then Queen Mary College, at London University, a product of late-Victorian charity, established in the East End to educate working men. He was good at science and went on to become a professor of zoology. (An equivalent social movement occurred in America, with the passage of the GI Bill of 1944.) Theoretically, Orwell had to approve of men like my father; practically, he could not, and in *The Road to Wigan Pier*, in perhaps the most scandalous paragraph he ever wrote, he announces that the working-class attitude to education is much sounder than the middle class's – they see through the nonsense of education, 'and reject it by a healthy instinct', and sensibly want to leave school as soon as possible. The working-class boy 'wants to be doing real work, not wasting his time on ridiculous rubbish like history and geography'. He should be bringing home a pound a week for his parents, not stuffing himself into silly uniforms and being caned for neglecting his homework.

'It's a good British feeling to try and raise your family a little,' says Mr Vincy in *Middlemarch*. George Eliot, the estate manager's daughter who ended up living in a grand house on Cheyne Walk, in Chelsea, understood that 'good British feeling'. But Orwell was suspicious of this indeterminate, petit bourgeois class, because it wanted to change itself first, and society second, if at all. Margaret Thatcher, born in 1925 to a Grantham shopkeeper, is the model of this kind of conservative class mobility. Orwell suspected Dickens of the same impulse, noting with displeasure that the novelist sent his eldest son to Eton. Dickens belonged, mentally, to the small urban bourgeoisie, a class that was just out for itself. That is why the great Dickens novels want to change things, but in fact leave everything in place. 'However much Dickens may admire the working classes, he does not wish to resemble them.' Orwell means this as a judgement against Dickens. But it is unwittingly comic. Why should Dickens have wanted to resemble the working classes? Why would anyone want to resemble the working classes, least of all the working classes themselves? (Ah, there speaks a true petit bourgeois!) But Orwell did – at least, somewhat. The upper-class masochist lived frugally, dressed down, and for most of his life, until *Animal Farm* and *Nineteen Eighty-Four*, earned very little. His sister said after his death that the kind of person he most admired was a working-class mother of ten children. But if the problem with wanting to get out of the working class is that someone is always left behind, then the problem with 'admiring' the working class is that admiration doesn't, on its own, help anyone to get out of it at all. (Tellingly, Orwell reported vividly on extreme poverty, but never reported as vividly on the kind of working-class life he was content to idealise.)

So the question that hangs over Orwell is the one that always hangs over so many well-heeled revolutionaries: did he want to level up society or level it down? The evidence points to the latter. The real struggle for this puritan masochist, the one that was personal – the one that was, ironically enough, *inherited* – was the struggle to obliterate privilege, and thus, in some sense, to obliterate himself. This was, at bottom, a religious impulse, and was not always politically coherent. In *Down and Out in Paris and London*, he pauses to consider the plight of the *plongeur*, working for hours and hours in hotels, so that wealthier people can stay in them. How is this bad situation to be mitigated? Well, says Orwell, hotels are just needless luxuries, so if people stopped going to them, there would be less hard work to do. 'Nearly everyone hates hotels. Some restaurants are better than others, but it is impossible to get as good a meal in a restaurant as one can get, for the same expense, in a private house.' As Larkin puts it in a poem, useful to get *that* learned. There is a similarly telling moment in Orwell's review of Hayek's *The Road to Serfdom*. There was much in the book to agree with, he said. (It was also admired by the young Margaret Thatcher.) But Hayek's faith in capitalist competition was overzealous: 'The trouble with competitions is that somebody wins them.' Not, you notice, that somebody loses them – which would mean raising those people up. Somebody wins them, and that cannot be allowed.

It is hardly fair to claim that Orwell did not earnestly long for the emancipation of the working classes; of course he did. But for all his longing to abolish class distinctions, he could barely credit actual class mobility. For although it may be true that the upwardly mobile working classes do not want fundamentally to change society, their very ascension does change it. (If Orwell had taken any interest in Scotland, he would have seen a relatively socially dynamic culture propelled by a serious stake in education.) Actual class mobility was probably unappealing to Orwell – unconsciously, of course – because he longed for a mystical revolution, a revolution in which England changed and stayed the same; and what seems to have guaranteed England's preservation for him was the idea of a static, semi-fictional working-class world of decency and good-tempered bus conductors and bad teeth. Change that, and you change England. Yet how can you have revolution and not change that? Thus Orwell stresses, throughout his work, 'equality of sacrifice' rather than equality of benefit. The former could be controlled, indeed is control itself; the latter might lead to the Ritz and the Rolls-Royce.

Orwell feared what he most desired: the future. But it is easy to gloat over Orwell's contradictions – to point out that he wrote so well about the drabness and horror of totalitarianism because he himself had a tendency to drab omnipotence; or that the great proponent of urban collectivity liked rural isolation (he wrote *Nineteen Eighty-Four* on the Hebridean island of Jura); or more simply, that the hater of private schools put his adopted son down for Westminster, one of the grandest London academies. So Orwell was contradictory: contradictions are what make writers interesting; consistency is for cooking. Instead, one is gratefully struck by how prescient Orwell was, by how much he got right. He was right about how capitalism had failed British society: subsequent post-war governments did indeed nationalise many of the major industries and utilities (though thankfully, Orwell did not live long enough to see many of them fail). He was right about education: although the private schools kept their autonomy, Oxford and Cambridge opened themselves up to state-aided students, exactly as Orwell had demanded in 1941, and the Butler Act of 1944 universalised free secondary-school education. He was right about colonialism (that he disliked Gandhi seems only to strengthen Orwell's position, by making it disinterested); right about totalitarianism. If his novelistic imagining of totalitarian horror now looks a bit dated, it is partly because his fiction provided the dusty epitaph on a dustier tombstone that he himself helped to carve; and anyway, his coinages, like 'Doublethink' and 'Newspeak' and 'Big Brother', now live an unexpectedly acute second life in the supposedly free West: to see Fox News go after President Obama or Bill Ayers for days on end is to think, simply, 'Hate Week.'

And Orwell's revolutionary mysticism turned out to be curiously precise: he was right not in spite of, but because of his contradictions. Although an Orwellian revolution never quite came about, an Orwellian victory did. In part, Hitler was defeated by the exercise of a peculiarly British – peculiarly Orwellian – combination of collectivity and individualism. (He marvelled, in the summer of 1945, that Britain had won the war without becoming either socialist or fascist, and with civil liberties almost intact.) This combination of conservatism and radicalism, of political sleepiness and insomnia, this centuries-long brotherhood of gamekeeper and poacher, which Orwell called 'the English genius', was also Orwell's genius, finding in English life its own ideological brotherhood. For good and ill, those English contradictions have lasted. If Orwell hammered so noisily at privilege that at times he couldn't hear the working classes eagerly knocking at the door to be admitted, it is because he knew the immense size of the obstacle they would face. To level an Orwellian emphasis, what is remarkable about British society today is not how much bigger the middle class is, but how little the upper classes have given up. The working classes got richer, but the rich got much richer. Britain has now elected its nineteenth Old Etonian prime minister – a Conservative, of course. The Orwell who wrote about the playing fields of Eton would be shocked to discover that, for all the transformations Britain has undergone, the lofty old school is still there, much as it always was, educating the upper classes to govern the country, wreck the City and have lovely house parties.

2010

Jane Austen's Heroic Consciousness

JANE AUSTEN FOUNDED CHARACTER and caricature at the same time – which is the essentially satirical, essentially English approach to fictional character. From her, Dickens learned that characters can survive on one large attribute and still be fat with life. From her, Forster learned that characters do not have to change to be real; they must merely reveal more of their stable essence as the novel progresses. Yet at the same time, the first stirrings of what would become Woolf's stream-of-consciousness are found in Austen – she invented a new, rapid semaphore for signalling a person's thought as it is happening. It is this innovation, the discovery of how to represent the brokenness of the mind's communication with itself, that constitutes her radicalism.

Jane Austen was a ferocious innovator, and her innovations were largely complete by the time she was twenty-four. This tells us something about the elusive mixture of application and instinct in her writing life. On the one hand, she shocked fiction forward from Samuel Richardson's epistolary mode; on the other, she left behind barely a word about her idea of fiction, of aesthetics, or of religion. We have only 160 letters by her, and most of them are rather tedious: the futile daily plough of seedless social events. But you can tell that she was a natural revolutionary in fiction. Almost as soon as she started writing squibs and family sketches as a teenager, she began to find new ways of representing fictional characters. These young experiments would soon bear fruit, as Austen began to create the room of heroines for which she is admired and loved.

Austen's heroines do not change in the modern sense, because they do not really discover things about themselves. They discover cognitive novelties; they probe for rectitude. As the novel moves forwards, certain veils are pierced and obstacles removed, so that the heroine can see the world more clearly. In the course of that process, more and more of the heroine's stable essence is revealed to us. Thus plot is inherently rational and problem-solving in Austen ('rational' was one of Austen's favourite words, and is used often by her heroines). The habitual stance of the Austen heroine is that of the reader, one who reads and reflects upon the material of the novel before her, and, when all that material is complete at the end of the novel, makes her decision. It is probably for this reason that readers so adore Austen's heroines – not because they are especially real or 'rounded', but because, like us, they are readers of the novel in question, and *thus on our side*. Elinor Dashwood in *Sense and Sensibility*, like Fanny Price in *Mansfield Park*, craves 'the relief of quiet reflection'. Elinor describes this process of reflection several times in *Sense and Sensibility*. When she reappraises Willoughby, she is 'resolved not only upon gaining every new light as to his character which her own observation or the intelligence of others could give her, but likewise upon watching his behaviour to her sister with such zealous attention, as to ascertain what he was and what he meant . . .' Elizabeth Bennet, at the end of *Pride and Prejudice*, finally sees Darcy as he really is, not as she mistook him – that is her triumph; she does not learn anything really decisive about herself. She is, perhaps, less proud and judgemental, but she has hardly transformed herself. Likewise Fanny Price. Fanny is, in some ways, a caricature of goodness, unchangeably good. The novel, showing its origins in stage-conventions (despite the fact that it is a book that appears to censure the stage), lays a stable characterological foundation within its first fifteen pages, and never deviates from it: Mrs Norris appears, and is wicked and garrulous; Lady Bertram enters, and takes up the posture she will maintain for the rest of the book, 'doing some long piece of needlework, of little use and no beauty, thinking more of her pug than her children, but very indulgent to the latter, when it did not put herself to inconvenience'; and Fanny Price will not deviate, either, from Edmund's early assessment: he is 'convinced of her having an affectionate heart, and a strong desire of doing right'.

Emma Woodhouse is the nearest Austen came to creating a character who discovers something about herself. Like Elizabeth Bennet, she must rationally solve a problem – which is the problem of who is right for whom, and ultimately, who is right for her – and the novel allows her to conduct several disastrous experiments. To that extent, she learns, at the end of the novel, what we have always known about her, that she is blind, headstrong, and foolish. But she too is essentially stable, for she is incorrigible. Indeed, isn't the incorrigibility of Austen's heroines what makes them so appealing? Don't we imagine that Emma will continue to act foolishly in the future, even with Mr Knightley by her side? One of the reasons that we know from the beginning of the novel that Emma is essentially good but wilful (as opposed to bad and hapless) is that we sense that Mr Knightley loves her, and we feel that Mr Knightley is a repository of the novel's highest values. A fairy-tale cradle protects Emma from real harm. A comparison can be made with a modern heroine, Isabel Archer in *The Portrait of a Lady*. Ralph Touchett is Isabel's higher understanding, her Mr Knightley. Yet in James's tragic, psychological vision, Ralph cannot save Isabel from herself. She must make mistakes for herself. Emma, by contrast, makes mistakes on behalf of others; for herself, she makes the right choice, and chooses Mr Knightley. In an early conversation, Mrs Weston says to Mr Knightley that Emma 'will never lead any one really wrong'. This observation the novel is about to prove untrue. But in the same conversation Mrs Weston says that 'she will make no lasting blunder', which is quite correct. Within this capsule, Emma's subjectivity rides.

Austen's heroines do not discover, then, what is best in themselves; they discover what is best *for* themselves and for others. Austen's work is not therapeutic but hermeneutic. As it happens, hermeneutic study was given its fullest development at this time by Friedrich Schleiermacher, the German theologian. But we know from contemporary texts that the words 'hermeneutical' and 'hermeneutics' were in wide currency in English long before Schleiermacher, and that they were applied to people as often as to the study of texts. Someone who understood other people, who attended to their secret meanings, who read people properly, might be called hermeneutical. Schleiermacher himself stressed repeatedly that hermeneutics could be applied to ordinary conversation as well as to the Scriptures. In 1829, in his Academy Address 'On the Concept of Hermeneutics', he referred to the art of reading 'significant conversations', and added: 'Who could move in the company of exceptionally gifted persons without endeavouring to hear "between" their words, just as we read between the lines of original and tightly written books? Who does not try in a meaningful conversation, which may in certain respects be an important act, to lift out its main points, to try to grasp its internal coherence, to pursue all its subtle intimations further?' This is what the Austen heroine does. Even the wild and undisciplined Emma is such a reader. When Mr Knightley finally proposes to Emma, Austen writes: 'While he spoke, Emma's mind was most busy, and, with all the wonderful velocity of thought, had been able – and yet without losing a word – to catch and comprehend the exact truth of the whole.'

This is the hermeneutic task of the Austen heroine, to which is added a distinctly Protestant, or even Evangelical, bent. For Austen's heroines also read themselves, and carry their spirit inside them. Henry Crawford asks Fanny, in *Mansfield Park*, for advice, and she replies: 'We have all a better guide in ourselves, if we would attend to it, than any other person can be.' Our inwardness is our God and our guide; we apply to it for aid. The inwardness of Austen's heroines is precisely what makes them heroic in the novels. This is measurable, because Austen maintains a hierarchy of consciousness: the people who matter think inwardly, and everyone else speaks. Or rather: the heroines speak to themselves, and everyone else speaks to each other. The heroines are the only characters whose inner thought is represented. And this speaking to oneself is often a secret conversation, which Austen almost invented a new technique, a precursor of modernist stream-of-consciousness, to represent. We can watch the development of this technique. Her first novel, *Sense and Sensibility* (1811), has almost none of this kind of stream-of-consciousness. *Sense and Sensibility* abounds in passages like this one, in which Austen's notation of excited thought seems to strain to outgrow itself, yet which stays inside conventional narrated thought: 'What felt Elinor at that moment? Astonishment, that would have been as painful as it was strong, had not an immediate disbelief of the assertion attended it. She turned towards Lucy in silent amazement, unable to divine the reason or object of such a declaration, and though her complexion varied, she stood firm in incredulity and felt no danger of an hysterical fit, or a swoon.' Lucy has just told Elinor that she is engaged to Robert Ferrars's brother, and Elinor is revolving this shock in her mind. But Austen stays outside Elinor, noting her change of colour, and calming the reader, as it were, with the promise that Elinor will not become hysterical. The reference to an external change – a change of colour – is significant, for it suggests that Austen is using the idea of the stage, that a character will physically register a shock, on the outside. Austen's point, of course, is that Elinor is not like one of these stage-actors; Elinor is too calm to register agitation as anything more than an almost invisible change of colour. She thinks 'in silent amazement', and is therefore inaccessible to us. ('What felt

Elinor at that moment?') Elinor, in this sense, anticipates the later Austen heroines: from an almost invisible blush, it is only a small increment for the novelist into the very mind of a character. Nevertheless, at this moment in Austen's development, we cannot enter Elinor's mind; her 'silent amazement' is actually silent.

Pride and Prejudice (1813) allowed Austen to burst into the interior of her heroine, Elizabeth Bennet. But she rations a gradual increase in the reader's access. At first, Elizabeth resembles Elinor; she does not speak to herself, except in Austen's indirect report. Slowly, her intensity deepens, and Austen's registration of Elizabeth's self-conversation begins to gather its mass. When she first hears that Darcy has separated Bingley and Jane, she goes to her room, where 'she could think without interruption of all that she had heard'. Here, Austen begins to expand the range of Elizabeth's mental revolutions, and we witness Elizabeth 'exclaiming' to herself bitterly about how poorly Jane has been used: 'All liveliness and goodness as she is! Her understanding excellent, her mind improved, and her manners captivating.' But this self-exclamation soon ends, the agitation having brought on a headache (a headache, tears, or sleep, will often end the representation of female inwardness in early Austen). Only twenty pages later, Elizabeth is unbound. Darcy has written to her, and she has taken the letter with her on a walk. She is alone. As she reads it, she is burnt with shame, and her speech to herself is rapidly broken up into different stumbling inroads:

'How despicably have I acted!' she cried. – 'I, who have prided myself on my discernment! – I, who have valued

myself on my abilities! who have often disdained the generous candour of my sister, and gratified my vanity, in useless
or blameable distrust. – How humiliating is this discovery! – Yet, how just a humiliation! – Had I been in love,
I could not have been more wretchedly blind. But vanity,
not love, has been my folly. – . . . Till this moment, I never
knew myself.'

This, in essence, is the stage soliloquy. In the course of
Mansfield Park (1814), and *Emma* (1816), Austen uses it with
ever greater sophistication, dispensing with quotation marks,
and blending the heroine's soliloquy with her own third-
person narration, so that she is able to move in and out of a
character as she pleases. At the same time, her heroine's mental
speech loses the last tinctures of the staginess that still clings to
Elizabeth's ('How despicably have I acted!'), becoming looser
and more conversational. Fanny Price is seen thinking to herself much earlier in *Mansfield Park* than Elizabeth is seen doing
the same in *Pride and Prejudice*; and of course, Emma fills the
entire book with her lively self-disputations: *Emma* is one large
mental chamber. Where before, Elizabeth had to roam outside
to express her thoughts, Emma's thought arises in the most
ordinary and domestic settings, among her puffs, powders and
billets-doux. Austen novelises the soliloquy, in effect:

The hair was curled, and the maid sent away, and Emma
sat down to think and be miserable. – It was a wretched
business, indeed! – Such an overthrow of everything she
had been wishing for! – Such a development of everything
most unwelcome! – Such a blow for Harriet! – That was

the worst of all. Every part of it brought pain and humiliation, of some sort or other; but, compared with the evil to
Harriet, all was light; and she would gladly have submitted
to feel yet more mistaken – more in error – more disgraced
by mis-judgment, than she actually was, could the effects
of her blunders have been confined to herself.

This is immensely supple, Austen marvellously extending what is called free indirect style, in which the author
describes the heroine's thoughts with such sympathetic agitation that the heroine seems to be writing the novel. In free
indirect style, though narration is still in the third person,
the heroine seems to flood the narration, forcing it onto her
side. ('It was a wretched business indeed! – Such an overthrow
of everything she had been wishing for!') In her later novels,
Austen tends to alternate free indirect style with a first-person
stream-of-consciousness. *Mansfield Park* abounds in examples
of the latter. Near the end of the book, Fanny, in Portsmouth,
receives a letter from Edmund. She is sure that Edmund will
marry Mary Crawford:

> As for the main subject of the letter – there was nothing in that
> to soothe irritation. She was almost vexed into displeasure,
> and anger, against Edmund. 'There is no good in this delay,'
> said she. 'Why is not it settled? – He is blinded, and nothing
> will open his eyes, nothing can, after having had truths before
> him so long in vain. – He will marry her, and be poor and
> miserable. God grant that her influence do not make him
> cease to be respectable!' – She looked over the letter again.
> '"So very fond of me!" 'tis nonsense all. She loves nobody

but herself and her brother. "Her friends leading her astray for years!" She is quite as likely to have led *them* astray. . . . "The only woman in the world, whom he could ever think of as a wife." I firmly believe it . . . Edmund, you do not know *me*. The families would never be connected, if you did not connect them. Oh! write, write. Finish it at once. Let there be an end of this suspense. Fix, commit, condemn yourself.'

In this superb passage, quite characteristic of the later novels, Austen combines third-person narration ('She looked over the letter again'), first-person soliloquy ('Edmund, you do not know *me*'), and scraps from Edmund's letter which are not quoted in first person, but which Austen turns into free indirect style in order to hurry the effect of the passage, and to stamp on the reader the sense of *Fanny's* thought, of *Fanny* having taken and converted Edmund's words into her own. As the paragraph develops, so third-person narration falls away, and we entirely enter Fanny's mind. This writing, moving between different modes, hurriedly capturing the very stammer of ratiocination, makes Austen a more radical novelist than, say, Flaubert. Flaubert never allows Emma Bovary quite such a broken self-conversation. Unlike the smoothly controlling Flaubert, Austen wants to capture the difficulty of solitary thought, and in this her modernity lies. This thought is a kind of concealment in all of Austen's novels except in the free and open *Emma*. Austen's heroines withdraw, or wait until visitors have departed, or go on walks, in order to think. (The two enormous modern changes that are found in Woolf and Joyce are that a character need go nowhere particular to think; and that thought need not have the gravity of emergency or agitation in order to earn its place. Thought is as natural as narration, and has in fact become narration.) Austen's heroines are separate, different from everyone else in the novels by virtue of their ability to speak to themselves. In *Mansfield Park* Mary Crawford asks Edmund if the young Fanny is 'out, or is she not?' Mary means presentable, socially adult, and Edmund replies that his cousin is an adult, 'but the outs and not outs are beyond me'. Mary comments, reprovingly, that 'it is much worse to have girls *not out*, give themselves the same airs and take the same liberties, as if they were …' Mary decides that Fanny is '*not out*', and seems obscurely irritated by the challenge that Fanny's being 'not out' represents. Austen no doubt implies another kind of 'out' or 'in', the 'out' of outwardness and the 'in' of inwardness. We might think of Austen's heroines, despite their vivacity, as always 'in', insofar as they are the only characters who hoard their thought, and who are seen to do so.

It is through inwardness that we get to know a character. Emma complains (to herself) that Jane Fairfax is 'so cold, so cautious! There was no getting at her real opinion. Wrapt up in a cloak of politeness, she seemed suspiciously reserved.' If Jane Fairfax seems reserved to us, as well as to Emma, it is because Austen never shows her speaking to herself. We feel we cannot 'get at her real opinion', because we do not witness her thinking it. But we are always close to Emma's real opinion, even if it is the wrong one. In this sense, Emma's reality is what is most right about her. We delight in the rightness of her reality even when she is wrong. When one says, then, that Austen's heroines are 'in', it is not that they are like Jane Fairfax, who seems lost to herself; rather that they are real to themselves, and thus to us. And they are heroines *because* of this quality of being 'in'. Austen refers to Emma as being in 'mental soliloquy', and while Austen's heroines are internal soliloquists, the obviously bad people in the novels are monologists, people who speak *at* others. Mr Collins, Mrs Norris, Miss Bates, Mrs Elton all speak as if on stage, to an audience. Austen's heroines, by contrast, speak to themselves, like people in a novel. Her heroines belong to the novel; her villains belong to the stage.

Her heroines belong to the novel; and indeed, they act not only like readers, but like novelists, too. Like novelists, her heroines enable people to speak through them, they are arrangers and conduits of others' feelings. Anne Elliot in *Persuasion* (1818) dislikes, for instance, that the Musgroves speak to each other through her, dislikes 'being treated with too much confidence by all parties, and being too much in the secret complaints of each house'. Like novelists, the heroines have to retreat to their study, to reflect, as it were, on their material, as if they were both writing and reading the material that the novel has presented them with. This is Anne Elliot's first instinct at the end of *Persuasion*, when she has won Wentworth: 'Anne went home to think over all that she had heard.' All of Austen's heroines retreat to a room of their own, often prompted by the intimacy of a letter (which functions a little like the written contract that allows female subjectivity). Like novelists, her heroines have the capacity of memory, while the rest of the characters have only 'pasts'. It is the heroines who must learn about these pasts, who must enquire into the past. When they are gregarious, these heroines have the novelist's genius for negative capability, the capacity to find justice in the other side, to act a role. Emma catches herself doing this in an argument with Mr Knightley: 'to her great amusement, [she] perceived that she was taking the other side of the question from her real opinion, and making use of Mrs Weston's arguments against herself.'

Mansfield Park makes perhaps the strongest case for the novel, and for the heroine's novelist-like powers. When the household at Mansfield Park decides to stage a play in the house (it is Kotzebue's *Das Kind der Liebe*, translated by Mrs Inchbald as *Lovers' Vows*), Fanny Price objects to the impropriety, in particular to the prospect of the ladies of the house acting in compromising roles with the gentlemen of the house. Fanny's objection, which appears to be supported by Austen and by the thrust of the entire novel, seems priggish, and has occasioned much comment, because Austen and her family used happily to stage, as children, amateur dramatics. But Austen's objection might be that the play does not act like a novel. Recall that Fanny's first response to the idea is to withdraw with the text of the play and read it like a novel. Though Austen does not say so, there is a sense in which the play is improper because, by forcing people to act in highly charged emotional situations, it might precipitate actual emotional situations, off stage, that should remain latent. In other words, the stage artificially speeds up dilemmas and relationships. Things ought to go at a novel's pace (and *Mansfield Park* is a lengthy, spacious novel) and not at the pace of two melodramatic hours on stage. Though we don't know it yet, Fanny is right. The play, which intimately throws together Henry Crawford and Maria Bertram (who is already engaged to her foolish neighbour, Rushworth), accelerates their flirtation: later in the book, Henry elopes with Maria, now married to the unfortunate Rushworth.

Austen's fiction is either celebrated or attacked for being conservative; but it is, of course, a strenuous argument on behalf of the deserving poor – deserving not because of gentility but because of goodness. Austen's ideal world, glimpsed in the puff of harmony that is exhaled at the end of her novels when the heroine gets her husband, would be an ethical meritocracy, in which the best dowry the heroine can bring to her match is her goodness. These best virtues are earned, not bestowed, and are internal. Austen's heroines are heroic because of their inwardness. Think of Anne Elliot at the end of *Persuasion*. She thinks that Captain Wentworth 'must love her', and she goes around the room, looking at her father and sister and Lady Russell, and feels inclined 'to pity every one, as being less happy than herself . . . Her happiness was from within.' Now Anne is in love, and is pitying those who are not, just as Levin does in *Anna Karenina* when he secures Kitty. But Austen's argument is stronger than that. Tolstoy describes Levin's happiness as a temporary advantage: he is in love, it is a gorgeous spasm of early love, it will pass. It is a sublime hallucination, really. But the whole of *Persuasion* – indeed, the whole of Austen's oeuvre – suggests that Anne will always be happier than those around her. Anne's horrible father and sister might, conceivably, fall in love, but Anne will still be happier than they will be. And why? Because her happiness is 'from within' and the others do not exist 'within'. They are 'out'. She is a heroine.

It is consciousness that makes one happy; consciousness is intelligence, and consciousness is inwardness. Even when the agitation of consciousness is not happy, it is always welcome, it is always good – and *a* good. Elizabeth Bennet likes to 'indulge in all the delight of unpleasant recollections'. I suspect that Jane Austen, so private, so enigmatic and contradictory, went through life as if she were the possessor of a clandestine happiness. Like her heroines, she saw things more clearly than other people and so pitied their cloudiness.

1998

Cormac McCarthy's
The Road

I

IN ADDITION TO the 9/11 novel, and the 9/11 novel that is pretending not to be a 9/11 novel, an old genre has been reawakened by new fears: the post-apocalyptic novel (which may well be, in fact, the 9/11 novel pretending not to be one). The possibility that familiar, habitual existence might be so disrupted within the next hundred years that crops will fail, warm places will turn into deserts and species will become extinct – that areas of the earth may become uninhabitable – holds and horrifies the contemporary imagination. This fear may not be as present, acute or knife-edged as the fear of nuclear annihilation that produced novels such as *A Canticle for Leibowitz* and *On the Beach* and movies such as *Fail-Safe* and *The Day After*, but it is more fatalistic and in its way more horrible, precisely because the catastrophe that climate fear imagines may be inevitable and incorrigible. And the temporal reprieve, the deferral of the worst to later generations, may not be any consolation at all. It may, strangely enough, increase the fear: are you more agonisingly afraid of something that will happen to yourself or of something that will happen to your children?

This – the increasingly well-documented horror that precedes all the 'greening' that is around us – may in part explain the recent cluster of new movies and novels that are set in a future world catastrophically changed or almost post-human: *The Children of Men*, the global-warming horror movie *The Day After Tomorrow*, Kazuo Ishiguro's novel about cloning, *Never Let Me Go*, Jim Crace's novel *The Pesthouse* and Cormac McCarthy's *The Road*. In his book *The Revenge of Gaia*, the scientist James Lovelock presents this hideous picture of the warmed world, sometime in the middle of this century:

> Meanwhile in the hot arid world survivors gather for the journey to the new Arctic centres of civilization; I see them in the desert as the dawn breaks and the sun throws its piercing gaze across the horizon at the camp. The cool fresh night air lingers for a while and then, like smoke, dissipates as the heat takes charge. Their camel wakes, blinks and slowly rises on her haunches. The few remaining members of the tribe mount. She belches, and sets off on the long unbearably hot journey to the next oasis.

Note the word 'survivors': post-apocalyptic minimalism is assumed.

Minimalism can be very good for the life of fiction: description, thrown back onto its essentials, flourishes as it justifies its own existence. Words are returned to their original function as names. The J. M. Coetzee who admires the way that Daniel Defoe has the shipwrecked Robinson Crusoe notice 'two shoes, not fellows' on the island shore, as proofs of other deaths, is the novelist who, in *Life & Times of Michael K*, thrillingly described, from the ground up as it were, Michael K's desperate, starving, solitary roaming through the dry wastes of rural South Africa. How will Michael K find his next meal? Where will he sleep? Prison fiction works in the same way. One day of Ivan Denisovich's will suffice for the telling, not just because Ivan's every day is the same, but because the fiction has slowed down to notice the smallest details, just as time has slowed down for Ivan. Inside prison, the scale of everything has changed: a decent piece of bread would be an unimaginable luxury for Ivan, and worth the lengthiest savouring.

In some ways, and despite Cormac McCarthy's reputation as an ornate stylist, *The Road* represents both the logical terminus and a kind of ultimate triumph of an American minimalism that became well known in the 1980s under the banner of 'dirty realism'. This was a prose of short declarative sentences, in which verbs docked quickly at their objects, adjectives and adverbs were turned away, parentheses and subclauses were shunned. An anti-sentimentality, learned mainly from Hemingway, was so pronounced as to constitute a kind of male sentimentality of reticence. Basic, often domestic activities were honoured in sentences of almost painfully repetitive simplicity. A generic parody might sound like this:

> He took the glass from the cupboard and set it on the table. He poured the bourbon into it, but did not drink it.

Instead, he went to the door and listened. Nothing except far away a squeal of tires, over on Route 9 probably. He walked back heavily to the table. Through the wall he could hear them arguing again.

This style, which quickly reaches the limits of its expressivity, produced one indisputably significant writer, Raymond Carver, and a thousand thin cousins. In 2005, it was born again in Cormac McCarthy's cynical, very bloody, very stripped-down thriller *No Country for Old Men*, which abounded in lucid, hard little paragraphs devoted to male activity – say, a man painstakingly dressing a wound or slowly cleaning his gun or chasing another man down a street. That book was slick and cinematic, but in *The Road* the same kind of minimalism comes alive. Dirty realism was sometimes unwittingly excruciating because one felt that the chosen fictional worlds – even impoverished ones, all those motels and trailers – deserved richer prose. But in *The Road* something strange happens to this ordinary descriptive language – the book describes a world without reference, without things, but does so in a language we associate with reference and domestic normality: the father pitches a tent, makes a home, the boy eats some beans, or washes himself, in a descriptive language little different from Hemingway's in the Nick Adams stories: 'He fixed dinner while the boy played in the sand' (a sentence not from Hemingway but from this novel). There is a powerful tension between reference (things, context) and its absence. McCarthy writes at one point that the father could not tell the son about life before the apocalypse: 'He could not construct for the child's pleasure the world he'd lost without constructing the loss as well and he thought perhaps the child had known this better than he.' It is the same for the book's prose style: just as the father cannot construct a story for the boy without also constructing the loss, so the novelist cannot construct the loss without the ghost of the departed fullness, the world as it once was.

Roughly ten years before the opening of the action of the novel, some kind of climacteric occurred: 'The clocks stopped at 1:17. A long shear of light and then a series of low concussions.' A kind of nuclear winter now grips an America – and presumably a world – that is largely unpeopled. Animals have disappeared, there are no birds, no cities – just burned-out buildings – no cars, no power, nothing. Corpses are everywhere. Black ash covers everything, and the weather is always grey: 'By day the banished sun circles the earth like a grieving mother with a lamp.' A father and a son, who remain unnamed, are making their way southward, in America, towards the sea, in the hope that they might find human community or just some activity on the coast. We learn that the son was born ten years ago, and that the boy's mother committed suicide rather than wander the world as a survivor. So the boy has never known anything else. The father has his memories of ordinary life before the catastrophe, but these are horridly incommunicable, and McCarthy beautifully catches the alienation between the two generations.

Short phrasal sentences, often just fragments, savagely paint the elements of this voided world. Food and survival are the only concerns. With no animals alive, the best chance is to come upon some old cache of tinned food in an abandoned house or farm: 'Mostly he worried about their shoes. That and food. Always food. In an old batboard smokehouse they found a ham gambreled up in a high corner. It looked like something fetched from a tomb, so dried and drawn. He cut into it with his knife.' McCarthy is not without a sense of the comic, and he knows how to keep his punchlines dry until the last moment. The couple rake through an old supermarket, for instance, and eventually come upon an unopened can of Coke. The boy does not know what this is; his father promises him it will be a treat:

> On the outskirts of the city they came to a supermarket. A few old cars in the trashstrewn parking lot. They left the cart in the lot and walked the littered aisles. In the produce section in the bottom of the bins they found a few ancient runner beans and what looked to have once been apricots, long dried to wrinkled effigies of themselves. The boy followed behind. They pushed out through the rear door. In the alleyway behind the store a few shopping carts, all badly rusted. They went back through the store again looking for another cart but there were none. By the door were two soft-drink machines that had been tilted over into the floor and opened with a prybar. Coins everywhere in the ash. He sat and ran his hand around in the works of the gutted machines and in the second one it closed over a cold metal cylinder. He withdrew his hand slowly and sat looking at a Coca Cola.
>
> What is it, Papa?
> It's a treat. For you.
> What is it?

Surely McCarthy is knowingly playing here – not only with the American iconicity of the Coke can, but with iconic artworks about American icons, like Edward Hopper's *Gas* (his painting, from 1940, of the archetypal American gas station), and Andy Warhol's Campbell's soup tins.

The Road will not let the reader go, and will horribly invade his dreams, too. The apocalyptic fiction genre is not a very distinguished one. It relies on formulaic scenery (those piles of burning tyres always seen in films, those gangs of feral children), and generally rather lazy or incoherent political futurism: for instance, if Britain, in *The Children of Men*, twenty years hence, is ruled by a totalitarian dictator who can round up immigrants and put them in cages, why can't this same all-powerful ruler clean up the rubbish? It is an interesting question as to why McCarthy succeeds so well. The secret, I think, is that McCarthy takes nothing for granted.

It is the common weakness of novels such as Walter Miller's *A Canticle for Leibowitz*, Doris Lessing's *The Memoirs of a Survivor*, P. D. James's *The Children of Men*, or even *A Clockwork Orange* and *Nineteen Eighty-Four*, that they are all to some extent science-fiction allegories in which the author extrapolates from the present, using hypothetical developments in the future to comment on crises that he or she sees as already imminent in contemporary society. Thus, in the post-nuclear age of *A Canticle for Leibowitz*, secularism will triumph and religions die; in Burgess's and Lessing's worlds, juvenile violence and waywardness have spun out of control (these two novels were written in 1962 and 1974, early in the two decades of 'the Sixties'); in James's Britain of twenty years hence, males have become infertile and immigrants are rounded up by a totalitarian government and put in cages. There is nothing wrong with any of this, except that some essential illusionistic pressure is taken off the novelist, who can then merely describe the life that we know but with a twist, the old world that most of us recognise but that is suddenly more horrid to live in.

McCarthy's vision is not much like this. *The Road* is not a science fiction, not an allegory, and not a critique of the way we live now, or of the-way-we-might-live-if-we-keep-on-living-the-way-we-do. It poses a simpler question, more taxing for the imagination and far closer to the primary business of fiction-making: what would this world without people look like, feel like? From this, everything else flows. What would be the depth of one's loneliness? What kind of tattered theology would remain? What would hour-to-hour, day-to-day experience be like? How would one eat, or find shoes? These questions McCarthy answers magnificently, with the exception of the theological issue (about which more in a moment).

McCarthy's devotion to detail, his Conradian fondness for calmly described horrors, his tolling, fatal sentences, make the reader shiver with fear and recognition. The Coke can is a good example: McCarthy is not afraid to stint the banal, and we are always aware of the contemporary American civilisation that has been overthrown by events; it pokes up out of the landscape like fingerposts. There is a barn in a field 'with an advertisement in faded ten-foot letters across the roofslope. See Rock City.' (So we are in Tennessee, the scene of many of McCarthy's novels.) There are old supermarkets, and abandoned cars, and guns, and a truck the father and son sleep a night in, and even a dead locomotive in a forest. The narrative is about last-ditch practicality, and is itself intensely practical. In one of the houses they enter, the father goes upstairs, looking for anything useful. A mummified corpse is lying in a bed, a blanket pulled up to its chin. Without sensitivity, the man rips the blanket from the bed and thieves it. Blankets matter. There is even a light meter, and the way McCarthy deals with this gives an idea of his patience with things. The man is reflecting on how monotonous the diurnal thin grey light has become:

> He'd once found a lightmeter in a camera store that he thought he might use to average out readings for a few months and he carried it around with him for a long time thinking he might find some batteries for it but he never did.

Again there is the slightly droll humour – the non-existent batteries kept for the punchline. This sort of ordinariness anchors the book. Jim Crace's *The Pesthouse*, by contrast, is finely written but afraid of banality. Mysteriously, in Crace's vision of life after catastrophe – his book is also set in America and also involves a couple trying to get to the coast – we have returned to the Middle Ages, as if all plastic and technological proof of our former existence had been utterly extinguished. McCarthy's single can of Coke, hallowed like a fossil, seems of course much more plausible than Crace's 'biblical' voiding of memory and evidence. Reviewers endlessly speak of McCarthy's biblical style, but in fact this novel is sagely humdrum.

McCarthy's prose combines three registers, two of which are powerful enough to carry his horrors. He has his painstaking minimalism, which works well here. Again and again, he alerts us, in this simpler mode, to elements of hypothetical existence we had not thought about: how angry we might be, for instance, at the world before our catastrophe. The man comes across some old newspapers and reads them: 'The curious news. The quaint concerns.' He remembers standing in the charred ruins of a library, where books lay in pools of water: 'Some rage at the lies arranged in their thousands row on row.' In this mode the novel succeeds very well at conjuring into life the essential paradox of post-apocalyptic struggle, which is that survival is the only thing that matters, but why bother surviving?

The second register is the one familiar to readers of *Blood Meridian* or *Suttree*, and again seems somewhat Conradian. Hard detail and a fine eye are combined with exquisite, gnarled, slightly antique (and even slightly clumsy or heavy) lyricism. It ought not to work, and sometimes it does not. But many of its effects are beautiful – and not only beautiful, but powerfully efficient as poetry. The shape of a city seen from far away, standing 'in the greyness like a charcoal drawing sketched across the waste'. The father and son stand inside a once grand house, 'the peeling paint hanging in long dry sleavings down the columns and from the bucked soffits'. The little boy has 'candlecolored skin', which perfectly evokes his grey, undernourished whiteness, in a grey light that is itself undernourished and entirely reliant on candlepower. The black ash that blows everywhere is seen as resembling a 'soft black talc', which 'blew through the streets like squid ink uncoiling along a sea floor'.

When McCarthy is writing at his best, he does indeed belong in the company of the American masters. In his best pages one can hear Melville and Lawrence, Conrad and Hardy. His novels are full of marvellous depictions of birds in flight, and *The Road* has a gorgeous paragraph, like something out of Hopkins:

> In that long ago somewhere very near this place he'd watched a falcon fall down the long blue wall of the mountain and break with the keel of its breastbone the midmost from a flight of cranes and take it to the river below all gangly and wrecked and trailing its loose and blowsy plumage in the still autumn air.

One of the most moving passages in the book concerns the eventual arrival of father and son at the sea. It is a great disappointment: their discovery reverses the ancient classical cry, in Xenophon, of 'Thalassa! Thalassa!' There is no one and nothing there, except a huge grey watery waste, and of course the loneliness of the couple is vilely exaggerated by the endless grey water – what McCarthy calls 'the endless seacrawl'. The sea is covered in ash.

> Beyond that the ocean vast and cold and shifting heavily like a slowly heaving vat of slag and then the grey squall line of ash. He looked at the boy. He could see the disappointment in his face. I'm sorry it's not blue, he said. That's okay, said the boy.

Yet McCarthy's third register is more problematic. He is an American ham. When critics laud him for being biblical, they are hearing sounds that are more often than not merely antiquarian, a kind of vatic histrionic groping, in which the prose plumes itself up and flourishes an ostentatiously obsolete lexicon. Blood Fustian, this style might be called. The father and son are here described as 'slumped and cowled and shivering in their rags like mendicant friars', that word 'mendicant' being one of McCarthy's regular favourites. He is almost always prompted to write like this by metaphor or simile, which he often renders as hypothesis or analogy, using the formulation 'like some': so the man, his face streaked with black from the rain, looks 'like some old world thespian' (an especially flagrant example here, since the son is looking at his father at this moment, and the fancy language stubbornly violates a child's point of view). In the following sentence, the word 'autistic', while comprehensible, seems simply incorrect, and somehow a little adolescent, and shakes one's confidence in the writer: 'He rose and stood tottering in that cold autistic dark with his arms outheld for balance while the vestibular calculations in his skull cranked out their reckonings.' It begins to snow at one point, and 'he caught it in his hand and watched it expire there like the last host of christendom'.

Still, as in Hardy and Conrad, who were both at times terrible writers, there is a sincerity, an earnestness, in McCarthy's vaudevillian mode that softens the clumsiness, and turns the prose into a kind of awkward secret message from the writer. Conrad, after all, was capable of this description of money, in *The Secret Agent*: it 'symbolised the insignificant results which reward the ambitious courage and toil of a mankind whose day is short on this earth of evil'. In the same novel, a cheap Italian restaurant in London is said to have 'the atmosphere of fraudulent cookery mocking an abject mankind in the most pressing of its miserable necessities'. Moreover, McCarthy's writing tightens up as the novel progresses; it is notable that the theatrical antiquarianism belongs largely to the first fifty or so pages, as the writer pushes his barque out into new waters.

II

All of McCarthy's remarkable effects notwithstanding, there remains the matter of his meanings. There is another vaude-villian strain in *The Road*, a troubling one, in the way the novelist manipulates his theological material. McCarthy's work has always been interested in theodicy, and somewhat shallowly. He likes to stage bloody fights between good and evil, and his commentary tends towards the easily fatalistic. There is nothing easy about the machinery of this book – the *mise en scène*, the often breathtaking writing, the terrifying concentration of the evocation – but there is something perhaps a little showy about the way that questions of belief are raised and dropped.

The questions could not have been avoided. A post-apocalyptic vision cannot but provoke dilemmas of theodicy, of the justice of fate; and a lament for the *Deus absconditus* is both implicit in McCarthy's imagery – the fine simile of the sun that seems to circle the earth 'like a grieving mother with a lamp' – and explicit in his dialogue. Early in the book, the father looks at his son and thinks: 'If he is not the word of God God never spoke.' There are thieves and murderers and even cannibals on the loose, and the father and son encounter these fearsome envoys of evil every so often. The son needs to think of himself as 'one of the good guys', and his father assures him that this is the side they are indeed on.

About halfway through *The Road*, the couple run into a pitiful old man in rags named Ely. The father asks Ely, in another of McCarthy's examples of drollery, how one would know if one were the last man on earth. 'I don't guess you would know it. You'd just be it,' replies Ely. 'I guess God would know it,' says the father, which suggests that some measure of faith has survived the end. Ely flatly asserts, 'There is no God,' and continues: 'There is no God and we are his prophets.' A little later in the conversation, the father again suggests that he sees his son as divine: 'What if I said that he's a god?' Ely replies: 'I hope that's not true what you said because to be on the road with the last god would be a terrible thing so I hope it's not true.' Ely suggests that it will be better when everybody has died. 'Better for who?' asks the father. For everybody, says Ely, closing the scene with a rather lovely peroration, of the kind that gives this book its clear, deep sound: 'When we're all gone at last then there'll be nobody here but death and his days will be numbered too. He'll be out in the road there with nothing to do and nobody to do it to. He'll say: Where did everybody go? And that's how it will be. What's wrong with that?'

But the idea that the boy may be the last god – an eschatological plot that is a kind of more philosophical version of *The Terminator* – lingers in the book, and is caught up again at the end. It is this ending that has surely prompted *USA Today* to draw attention to 'something vital and enduring about the boy's spirit', and the *San Francisco Chronicle* to talk of McCarthy's 'tale of survival and the miracle of goodness'. I wonder what 'redemptive' gloss Oprah Winfrey, who selected the novel for her remorselessly edifying book club, read into the novel's final pages? The father, who has been ailing, dies, and the son realises this in the morning. McCarthy's prose is movingly chaste; the reticent power of his minimalism is exactly what is needed:

> He slept close to his father that night and held him but when he woke in the morning his father was cold and stiff. He sat there a long time weeping and then he got up and walked out through the woods to the road. When he came back he knelt beside his father and held his cold hand and said his name over and over again.

Especially fine is the withheld passion of 'held his cold hand and said his name over and over again', because, in the rest of the novel, we rarely, if ever, witness the son calling his father 'Father' (or any intimate equivalent); those words of tenderness burst through only now, at the end of the novel, and only in reported description.

So the boy is alone, but not for long. He meets a man on the road. 'Are you one of the good guys?' he warily asks him. Yes, says the man. 'You dont eat people,' says the boy. 'No. We dont eat people.' So he joins the man's group, and in the novel's penultimate paragraph, a woman is seen embracing the boy, and saying, 'Oh . . . I am so glad to see you.' It is the only moment in the book in which anyone other than the boy's father has embraced him.

> She would talk to him sometimes about God. He tried to talk to God but the best thing was to talk to his father

and he did talk to him and he didnt forget. The woman
said that was all right. She said that the breath of God was
his breath yet though it pass from man to man through all
of time.

The woman seems to affirm that God, or some kind of God,
still exists, and is not annihilated by the end of his creation.
The boy is indeed a kind of last God, who is 'carrying the fire'
of belief (the father and son used to speak of themselves, in a
kind of familial shorthand, as people who were carrying the
fire: it seems to be a version of being 'the good guys'). Since
the breath of God passes from man to man, and God cannot
die, this boy represents what will survive of humanity, and also
points to how life will be rebuilt.

There is no obligation for *The Road* to answer an unanswer-
able dilemma like theodicy. But the placement of what looks
like a paragraph of religious consolation at the end of such a
novel is striking, and it throws the book off balance a little, precisely because theology has not seemed exactly central to the
book's enquiry. One has a persistent, uneasy sense that theodicy and the absent God have been merely exploited by
the book, engaged with only lightly, without much pressure
of interrogation. When Ely says, 'There is no God and we are
his prophets', the phrase seems a little trite in its neat paradox
of negation; when exactly the same phrase was used by the
nineteenth-century Danish novelist Jens Peter Jacobsen, in
his novel *Niels Lyhne*, it vibrated powerfully, because it arose
out of an extended, vehement and utterly engaged treatment,
crucial to nineteenth-century life, of the question of God's
existence.

In this respect, to compare McCarthy to Beckett, as some reviewers have done, is to flatter McCarthy. His reticence and his minimalism work superbly at evocation, but they exhaust themselves when philosophy presses down. The style that is so good at the glancing, the lyrical, the half-expressed, struggles to deal adequately with the very metaphysical questions that apocalypse raises. Beyond tiny hints, we have no idea what the father and son believe about God's survival, so there is no dramatised rendition, no aesthetically responsible account, of such a question.

The theological question stirred by apocalypse is, How will all this end? What will result? 'Please don't tell me how the story ends,' the father silently implores, early in the book. It is not the truth about the end of the world that he refers to, but the knowledge that it may end with him killing his son. He is haunted by this apprehension, and he cannot do it: that is why he dies and tells his son to go on without him. That the question of endings is transferred onto this personal dilemma is precisely what makes the novel, and especially its conclusion, so painfully affecting. But the end of the world is more than a personal matter; and what *The Road* gains in human interest it loses by being personal at the moment when it should be theological. The question of endings in apocalypse must be philosophical as well as merely personal, even in a novel. Will it be heaven or hell? Will it last forever, or be over in a flash?

Apocalyptic narrative is necessarily paradoxical. The end threatens, but in order for narrative to exist, in order for narrative to continue narrating, apocalypse must always be postponed. Behind much of *The Road* one can feel the pressure of Edgar's lines from *King Lear*: 'the worst is not / So long as we can say "This is the worst"'; as long as language can be used to recount the worst, then the worst has not arrived. Has 'the worst' already occurred (the destruction of *almost* everything we recognise as human), or is worse still ahead? And would *that* then be 'the worst'? When does narrative, language end? *The Road*'s solacing theological optimism blurs and finally evades these deepest of questions.

2007

'Reality Examined to the Point of Madness': László Krasznahorkai

'REALITY EXAMINED TO THE point of madness.' What would this look like, in contemporary writing? It might look like the fiction of László Krasznahorkai, the difficult, peculiar, obsessive, visionary Hungarian novelist, the author of six novels, only two of which are presently available in English, *The Melancholy of Resistance* (which appeared in Hungarian in 1989, and in English in 1998) and *War and War* (which appeared in 1999, and was translated in 2006), both published by New Directions. Post-war avant-garde fiction, like post-war conventional fiction, has tended to move between augmentation (abundance, immersion, getting more in) and subtraction (reduction, minimalism, lack, what Samuel Beckett called 'lessness'): Beckett started out as an augmenter, and ended his life as a subtractor. But this division is not really a sharp one, because augmentation in the avant-garde novel often looks like a kind of subtraction: augmentation takes the form of an intensification of the *sentence* rather than an intensification of the things that many people habitually associate with the novel – plots, characters, furniture, objects. A lot has already disappeared from this fictional world, and the writer concentrates on filling the sentence, using it to notate, produce and reproduce the tiniest qualifications, hesitations, intermittences, affirmations and negations of existence. This is one reason why very long, breathing, unstopped sentences, at once literary and vocal, are almost inseparable from the progress of experimental fiction since the 1950s. Claude Simon, Thomas Bernhard, José Saramago, W. G. Sebald, Roberto Bolaño, David Foster Wallace, James Kelman and László Krasznahorkai have used the long sentence to do many different things, but all of them have been, in one way or another, at odds with a merely grammatical realism, whereby the real is made to fall into approved units and packets.

This grammatical anti-realism is not necessarily hostile to the real; in fact, all of these writers could be called realists, of a kind. But the reality many of them are interested in is 'reality examined to the point of madness'. The phrase is László Krasznahorkai's, and of all these novelists, Krasznahorkai is perhaps the strangest. His tireless, tiring sentences – a single one can fill an entire chapter – feel potentially endless, and are presented without paragraph breaks. The poet George Szirtes, Krasznahorkai's translator, refers to his prose as 'a slow lava-flow of narrative, a vast black river of type'. It is often hard to know what Krasznahorkai's characters are thinking, because this author's fictional world hangs on the edge of a revelation that never quite comes. In the extraordinary *War and War*, Gyorgy Korin, an archivist and local historian from a provincial Hungarian town, is going mad. For the rest of the novel, he stands 'on the threshold of some decisive perception', but we never discover what that perception is. Here is a necessarily long quote from early in the book, as Krasznahorkai introduces Korin's relentless mental distortions:

because he didn't feel like going home to an empty apartment on his birthday, and it really was extremely sudden, the way it struck him that, good heavens, he understood nothing, nothing at all about anything, for Christ's sake, nothing at all about the world, which was a most terrifying realization, he said, especially in the way it came to him in all its banality, vulgarity, at a sickeningly ridiculous level, but this was the point, he said, the way that he, at the age of forty-four, had become aware of how utterly stupid he seemed to himself, how empty, how utterly blockheaded he had been in his understanding of the world these last forty-four years, for, as he realized by the river, he had not only misunderstood it, but had not understood anything about anything, the worst part being that for forty-four years he thought he had understood it, while in reality he had failed to do so; and this in fact was the worst thing of all that night of his birthday when he sat alone by the river, the worst because the fact that he now realized that he had not understood it did not mean that he *did* understand it now, because being aware of his lack of knowledge was not in itself some new form of knowledge for which an older one could be traded in, but one that presented itself as a terrifying puzzle the moment he thought about the world, as he most furiously did that evening, all but torturing himself in the effort to understand it and failing, because the puzzle seemed ever more complex and he had begun to feel that this world-puzzle that he was so desperate to understand, that he was torturing himself trying to understand was really the puzzle of himself and the world at once, that they were in effect one and the same thing, which was the conclusion he had so far reached, and he had not yet given up on it, when after a couple of days, he noticed that there was something the matter with his head.

The passage has many of Krasznahorkai's qualities: the relentless ongoingness of the syntax; the way Korin's mind stretches and then turns back on itself, like a lunatic scorpion trying to sting itself; the perfect comic placement of the final phrase ('something the matter with his head'). The prose has about it a kind of self-correcting shuffle, as if something were genuinely being worked out, and yet, painfully and humorously, the self-corrections never result in the correct answer. As in Thomas Bernhard, whose influence is felt on Krasznahorkai's work, a single word or compound ('puzzle', 'world-puzzle') is seized and worried at, murdered into unmeaning, so that its repetition begins to seem funny and alarming at once. Whereas the characters in Bernhard's work engage in elegant, even oddly formal, rants – which can be removed from the fictions and performed as bitterly comic set pieces – Krasznahorkai pushes the long sentence to its furthest extreme, miring it in a thick, recalcitrant atmosphere, a kind of dynamic paralysis in which the mind turns over and over to no obvious effect.

In *War and War* – whose epigraph is 'Heaven is sad' – Korin has found a manuscript in the archive where he works.

He came across the text, which seems to date from the early 1940s, in a box labelled 'Family Papers of No Particular Significance'. This text is a fictional narrative about four men, named Kasser, Falke, Bengazza and Toot, who have various adventures, from Crete, to Cologne, to the north of England, and in different periods of history. Korin is overwhelmed by the beauty of this unknown manuscript; at the moment he took it out of its box, 'his life changed forever'. Already unstable, he decides that the manuscript holds a religious or visionary answer to the 'puzzle' of his life. He feels sure that it is really 'speaking about the Garden of Eden', and decides that he must go to what he thinks of as '*the very centre of the world*, the place where matters were actually decided, where things happened, a place such as Rome had been, ancient Rome, where decisions had been made and events set in motion, to find that place and *then* quit everything'. He decides this place is New York. There, he will publish the manuscript by typing it up and putting it on the Internet. Then, he thinks, his life will come to an end.

László Krasznahorkai was born in Gyula, in southeast Hungary, in 1954. He has lived in both Germany and America, but his name is more familiar in Europe (in Germany, he is almost canonical, partly because of the amount of time he has spent there, and partly because of his fluent German). He is probably best known through the oeuvre of the director Béla Tarr, who has worked with Krasznahorkai on several films, including *Damnation*, *Werckmeister Harmonies* (Tarr's version of *The Melancholy of Resistance*), and the massive, overwhelming *Sátántangó*, which lasts for over seven hours. These bleak, cavernous works, which in their spectral black-and-whiteness, sparse dialogue and reticent scores seem constantly to be wanting to revert to silent pictures, offer a film-maker's analogue of Krasznahorkai's serpentine sentences in their extraordinarily long tracking shots, which can last as long as ten minutes: in *Werckmeister Harmonies*, the camera accompanies for many minutes two characters, Mr Eszter and Valuska, as they walk through the streets of a grey provincial town; the wordless, stretched ambulation seems almost to occur in real time. Throughout the film, the camera lingers on the blank, illuminated face of Valuska (a naive and troubled visionary) with the devotion of a believer kissing an icon. *Sátántangó* uses a complex tango-like structure (six steps forward, six back) to present the tableau of a collective farm on the brink of collapse. It is famous both for its monumental length and its long, uncut scenes, such as one of villagers drunkenly dancing (an intoxication that, according to Tarr, was not fictional).

Krasznahorkai's work tends to get passed around like rare currency. I first heard of *The Melancholy of Resistance* because a freakishly well-read Romanian graduate student handed me a copy, convinced I would like it. I opened it, was slightly excited and slightly alienated by the 'slow lava-flow of narrative', and then put the book on a shelf, in that resignedly optimistic way one deals with difficult work – one day, one day . . . The sense of somewhat cultic excitement persists, apparently. While I was taking notes on these books, a Hungarian woman stopped at my table in a café and intensely asked me why I was studying *this particular author*. She knew his work, indeed she knew the author (and had, she said, gone to see *Pulp Fiction* with him in Boston, when it came out), and she would like to talk to me now about *this writer* . . .

The excitement has something to do with Krasznahorkai's literary mysteriousness. Thomas Bernhard's world, by comparison, is at once reasonable and insane: a pianist and writer, say, recalls a friend who committed suicide and their interaction wth Glenn Gould. This book – Bernhard's *The Loser* – is an extreme form of unreliable first-person narration but at least conforms to a basic generic conventionality. Even if the sentences are difficult, such a world is comprehensible, even desperately logical. But the abysses in Krasznahorkai are bottomless and not logical. Krasznahorkai often deliberately obscures the referent, so that we have no idea what is motivating the fictions: reading him is a little like seeing a group of people standing in a circle in a town square, apparently warming their hands at a fire, only to discover, as one gets closer, that there is no fire, and that they are gathered around nothing at all.

In *War and War*, Korin is convinced of the transcendent importance of his discovered manuscript. He travels to New York, finds lodgings with a Hungarian interpreter, Mr Sárváry, gets a computer and begins to type up the text. But the desperation of his attachment to this text is equalled only by his inability to describe its actual import:

> It took no more than the first three sentences to convince him that he was in the presence of an extraordinary document, something so out of the ordinary, Korin informed Mr Sárváry, that he would go so far as to say that it, that

is to say the work that had come into his possession, was a work of astonishing, foundation-shaking, cosmic genius, and, thinking so, he continued to read and reread the sentences till dawn and beyond, and no sooner had the sun risen but it was dark again, about six in the evening, and he knew, absolutely knew, that he had to *do something* about the vast thoughts forming in his head, thoughts that involved making major decisions about life and death, about not returning the manuscript to the archive but ensuring its immortality in some appropriate place . . . for he had to make this knowledge the basis of the rest of his life, and Mr Sárváry should understand that this should be understood in its strictest sense, because by dawn he had really decided that, given the fact that he wanted to die in any case, and that he had stumbled on the truth, there was nothing to do but, in the strictest sense, to stake his life on immortality.

It is not just that this 'truth' upon which Korin has stumbled is not defined; it is also that Krasznahorkai recesses Korin himself: this passage is third-person description, but notice the strange, unstable way in which it veers between the report of a present activity ('he continued to read and reread the sentences till dawn'), the description of a mental state ('he had to *do something* about the vast thoughts forming in his head'), and an account of an unstoppable monologue that Korin is apparently delivering to Mr Sárváry ('something so out of the ordinary, Korin informed Mr Sárváry'). The result is that the entire passage, even those elements that seem anchored in objective fact, has the quality of hallucination.

One senses that Korin spends his entire time either manically talking to other people or manically talking to himself, and that there may not be an important difference between the two. Both Bernhard and Sebald similarly recess their characters, so that a character's stories and impressions are often told to someone else before being told to the reader, and everything gets, as it were, an extra layer of fictionality. As in Sebald, almost every page of *War and War* contains the phrase 'said Korin', or some variation thereon ('It was Hermes, said Korin, Hermes lay at the heart of everything'). At one moment we get this sublime confusion: 'believe me when I say, as I said before, he said, that the whole thing is unreadable, insane!!!'

In New York, Korin starts to tell first Mr Sárváry, and then Sárváry's partner, about the manuscript. Day after day, he sits in the kitchen, retelling the stories about Kasser, Falke, Bengazza and Toot. Krasznahorkai reproduces these strange and beautiful fictions – there are remarkable passages about Cologne Cathedral and Hadrian's Wall. Korin tells Sárváry's partner that as he reads the manuscript and types it up, he can 'see' these characters, because the text is so miraculously powerful: 'he could see their faces and expressions from the moment he started reading as clearly as anything . . . faces you see once and never forget, said Korin'. And slowly the reader confirms what he has suspected since the start, that Korin found no manuscript but is writing his own in New York; that 'the manuscript' is a mental fiction, a madman's transcendent vision. The 'said Korin' tag inevitably slips into the implied 'wrote Korin'. Reading, saying, writing, thinking and inventing are all mixed up in this novel, and inevitably get mixed up in the reader's mind, too.

Which is a way of suggesting that this is one of the most profoundly unsettling experiences I have had as a reader. By the end of the novel I felt that I had got as close as literature could possibly take me to the inhabiting of another person, and in particular the inhabiting of a mind in the grip of 'war and war' – a mind not without visions of beauty, but also utterly lost in its own boiling, incommunicable fictions, its own grotesquely fertile pain ('Heaven is sad'). This pain is gravely inscribed into the pages of *War and War* much as Korin feels that pain is inscribed into the pages of his own manuscript:

> the manuscript was interested in one thing only, and that was *reality examined to the point of madness*, and the experience of all those intense mad details, the *engraving* by sheer manic repetition of the matter into the imagination, was, and he meant this literally, Korin explained, as if the writer had written the text not with pen and words but with his nails, scratching the paper into the paper and into the mind.

Krasznahorkai is clearly fascinated by apocalypse, by broken revelation, indecipherable messages. To be always 'on the threshold of some decisive perception' is as natural to a Krasznahorkai character as thinking about God is to a Dostoevsky character; the Krasznahorkai world is a Dostoevskian one from which God has been removed. His novel *The Melancholy of Resistance* is a kind of comedy of apocalypse, a book about a God that not only failed but didn't even turn up for the exam. Less manic, less entrapped than *War and War*, it has elements of a traditional social novel; it is set in a provincial Hungarian town and features a range of vivid characters – the wicked, quasi-fascist Mrs Eszter, who is plotting to take over the town and appoint herself head of a committee for moral and social renewal; her sickly, philosophical husband, a musician who long ago resigned from his directorship of the town orchestra and spends his days on a chaise longue, thinking bitter and refined thoughts; János Valuska, a postman and visionary dreamer, who walks all day through the town 'considering the purity of the cosmos', and is mocked by people who think him simple or odd; and the kind of supporting cast you want in Central European comic novels (the drunken police chief, the hapless mayor).

But this kind of summary does no justice to the unfathomable strangeness of this novel. The town is in a state of decline and uncertainty: the street lights are out, rubbish is piling up uncollected. A travelling circus arrives, whose only attraction is an enormous whale, mounted in a curious, doorless truck, and some pickled embryos. The circus has been moving through the region, accompanied by a group of apparently aimless but oddly menacing onlookers, men who hang around the town's main square near the whale, waiting for something to happen. Everything is full of vague and doomy imminence, and Mrs Eszter sees her opportunity: if she can foment (or even manage) some kind of anarchy, blame the unrest on unnamed 'sinister forces', and then successfully quash that unrest, she may attain her desire, to head the 'tidy yard and orderly house movement'. The men do eventually go on the rampage, smashing up things and people, burning buildings. But why? We are never told. One of them states that 'we could not find a fit object for our disgust and despair, and so we attacked everything in our way with an equal and infinite passion'. The army is called in, and Mrs Eszter triumphs. Within fourteen days of taking charge, she has 'swept away the old and established the new'.

It is unclear whether the whale really had anything to do with the irruption of violence; Krasznahorkai mischievously dangles the possibility that the circus is a difficult artwork, that it was simply misread by everyone as an agent of apocalypse, in the way that all revolutionary and obscure artworks are misread (by implication, this novel included). Obviously, the whale is some kind of funny, gloomy allusion to Melville, and perhaps Hobbes: like the leviathan, like Moby-Dick, it is vast, inscrutable, terrifying, capable of generating multiple readings. But it is static, dead, immobile, and the Puritan God who makes Melville's theology comprehensible (however incomprehensible Melville's white whale is) has long vanished from this nightmarish town in the shadow of the Carpathians. Meaning scrambles for traction, and the sinister doorless truck that sits silently in the middle of the town square is also a joke about the Trojan Horse: naturally, in Krasznahorkai's world, the Trojan Horse is empty. No one gets out of it.

The Melancholy of Resistance is a difficult book, and a pessimistic one, too, since it seems to take repeated ironic shots at the possibility of revolution. The only resistance offered to Mrs Eszter comes in the form of Valuska (who is arrested and put in a mental asylum) and Mrs Eszter's husband, who is a feeble, isolated foe. The pleasure of the book, and a kind of resistance also, flows from its extraordinary, stretched, self-recoiling sentences, which are marvels of loosely punctuated stream-of-consciousness. These are used with particular brilliance to capture the visionary gropings of Valuska, who wanders through the town thinking cosmic thoughts, and of Mr Eszter: for years, he has been obsessed with tuning his piano to Werckmeister's old harmonic system, and then with choosing one suite of music to play for the rest of his life.

Krasznahorkai can be a comic writer, and comic justice is meted out on Mr Eszter, who finally tunes his piano, sits down to play, and is horrified by the hideous sounds he makes. Eszter thinks of music as a kind of resistance to reality:

> Faith, thought Eszter . . . is not a matter of believing something, but believing that somehow things could be different; in the same way, music was not the articulation of some better part of ourselves, or a reference to some notion of a better world, but a disguising of the fact of our irredeemable selves and the sorry state of the world, but no, not merely a disguising but a complete, twisted denial of such facts: it was a cure that did not work, a barbiturate that functioned as an opiate.

Mental fictions may enrage us, and may lead to madness, but they may also provide the only 'resistance' available. Korin, Valuska and Mr Eszter are, in their different ways, all demented seekers after purity. Alas, though, they are suspended between their 'irredeemable selves and the sorry state of the world', and the 'twisted denial of such facts' that their private paradises constitute. That they cannot exactly describe or enact their private Edens makes those internal worlds not less but more beautiful. Inevitably, as for all of us but perhaps more acutely for them, 'heaven is sad'. And so the rage goes on, can't go on, must go on.

2011

Wounder and Wounded

THE PUBLIC SNOB, the grand bastard, was much in evidence when I interviewed V. S. Naipaul in 1994, and this was exactly as expected. A pale woman, his secretary, showed me in to the sitting room of his London flat. Naipaul looked warily at me, offered a hand, and began an hour of scornful correction. I knew nothing, he said, about his birthplace, Trinidad; I possessed the usual liberal sentimentality. It was a slave society, a plantation. Did I know anything about his writing? He doubted it. The writing life had been desperately hard. But hadn't his great novel, *A House for Mr Biswas*, been acclaimed on its publication, in 1961? 'Look at the lists they made at the end of the 1960s of the best books of the decade. *Biswas* is not there. Not there.' His secretary brought coffee and retired. Naipaul claimed that he had not even been published in America until the 1970s, 'and then the reviews were awful – unlettered, illiterate, ignorant'. The phone rang, and kept ringing. 'I am sorry,' Naipaul said in exasperation, 'one is not well served here.' Only as the pale secretary showed me out, and novelist and servant briefly spoke to each other in the hall, did I realise that she was Naipaul's wife.

A few days later, the phone rang. 'It's Vidia Naipaul. I have just read your . . . *careful* piece in the *Guardian*. Perhaps we can have lunch. Do you know the Bombay Brasserie? What about one o'clock tomorrow?' The Naipaul who took me to lunch that day was different from the horrid interviewee. Stern father had become milder uncle. 'It's a buffet system here. Don't *pile* everything onto one plate. That is vulgar. Put one small thing onto a plate, and when you have finished it they will come and take it away.' I didn't think that he was making amends for his earlier behaviour, nor that he had so admired my piece that he was compelled to meet me off duty. I thought he was merely curious to talk to someone in his late twenties about writing, and that the habits of a lifetime – the brilliant noticer, the committed world-gatherer – were asserting themselves almost automatically: he was working. He was also lecturing, and enjoying it. 'If you want to write serious books,' he said to me, 'you must be ready to break the forms, break the forms. Is it true that Anita Brookner writes exactly the same novel every year?' It is true, I said. 'How awful, how awful.'

The Indian social theorist Ashis Nandy writes of the two voices in Kipling, the saxophone and the oboe. The first is the hard, militaristic, imperialist writer, and the second is Kipling's 'Indianness, and his awe for the culture and the mind of India'. Naipaul has a saxophone and an oboe, too, a hard sound and a softer one. These two sides could be called the Wounder and the Wounded. The Wounder is by now well known – the source of fascinated hatred in the literary world and post-colonial academic studies. He disdains the country he came from – 'I was born there, yes. I thought it was a mistake.' When he won the Nobel Prize in 2001, he said it was 'a great tribute to both England, my home, and India, the home of my ancestors'. Asked why he had omitted Trinidad, he said that he feared it would 'encumber the tribute'. He has written of the 'barbarism' and 'primitivism' of African societies, and has fixated, when writing about India, on public defecation ('they defecate on the hills; they defecate on the riverbanks; they defecate on the streets'). When asked for his favourite writers, he replies, 'My father.' He is socially successful but deliberately friendless, an empire of one: 'At school I had only admirers; I had no friends.'

The Wounder, we learn from Patrick French's superb biography of Naipaul, used and used up his first wife, Patricia Hale, sometimes depending on her, at other times ignoring her, often berating and humiliating her. In 1972, Naipaul began a long, tortured, sadomasochistic affair with an Anglo-Argentinian woman, Margaret Gooding. It was an intensely sexual relationship, which enacted, on Naipaul's side, fantasies of cruelty and domination. On one occasion, jealous because Margaret was with another man, he was 'very violent with her for two days with my hand . . . Her face was bad. She couldn't really appear in public.'

The Wounded Naipaul is the writer who returns obsessively to the struggle, shame and impoverished fragility of his early life in Trinidad; to the unlikely journey he made from the colonial rim of the British Empire to its metropolitan centre; and to the precariousness, as he sees it, of his long life in England – 'a stranger here, with the nerves of a stranger', as he puts it in *The Enigma of Arrival* (1987). This wound is the death that makes possible the great life of the books. Again and again, Naipaul extends a sympathy seemingly reserved only for himself to others, and manages, without condescension or vanity, to blend his woundedness with theirs: the empire of one is colonised by his characters. They range from the major to the minor, from the educated to the almost illiterate, but they are united by their homelessness. They are the men in *Miguel Street* (1959), a book of linked stories rich in comedy and dialect, based on the street in Port of Spain, the capital of Trinidad, where Naipaul spent his formative years. Elias, for instance, dreams of being a doctor. 'And Elias waved his small hands, and we thought we could see the Cadillac and the black bag and the tube-thing that Elias was going to have.' To become a doctor, Elias must escape the island, and to do that he must sit a British scholarship exam. A friend comments excitedly: 'Everything Elias write not remaining here, you know. Every word that boy write going to England.' Elias fails the exam, and sits it again. 'Is the English and litricher that does beat me,' he confesses. He fails it again. He decides to become a sanitary inspector. He fails that exam. He ends up as a cart driver, 'one of the street aristocrats'. And there is Santosh, who narrates one of the stories in *In a Free State* (1971), a servant from Bombay who accompanies his master to Washington, DC, and is quite lost away from his old home. He wanders the American streets, sees some Hare Krishna singers, and for a moment thinks that they are Indians. And his mind yearns for his old life:

> How nice it would be if the people in Hindu costumes in the circle were real. Then I might have joined them. We would have taken to the road; at midday we would have halted in the shade of big trees; in the late afternoon the

sinking sun would have turned the dust clouds to gold; and every evening at some village there would have been welcome, water, food, a fire in the night. But that was the dream of another life.

Instead, as an Indian restaurant owner tells Santosh: 'This isn't Bombay. Nobody looks at you when you walk down the street. Nobody cares what you do.' He means it consolingly – that Santosh is free to do whatever he likes. But Naipaul is alert to Santosh's negative freedom, in which nobody in America cares what he does because nobody cares who he is. Santosh leaves his master, marries an American, becomes a citizen. He is now 'in a free state', but ends his tale like this: 'All that my freedom has brought me is the knowledge that I have a face and have a body, that I must feed this body and clothe this body for a certain number of years. Then it will be over.'

And above all there is Mohun Biswas, the protagonist of Naipaul's greatest novel, *A House for Mr Biswas*, who is born into poverty in Trinidad, begins his professional life as a signwriter ('IDLERS KEEP OUT BY ORDER' is his first commission), miraculously becomes a journalist in Port of Spain, and ends his life at the age of forty-six, lolling on his Slumberking bed and reading Marcus Aurelius – a homeowner but barely housed: 'He had no money . . . On the house in Sikkim Street Mr Biswas owed, and had been owing for four years, three thousand dollars . . . Two children were at school. The two older children, on whom Mr Biswas might have depended, were both abroad on scholarships.' Naipaul ends the short prologue to that novel with a deep autobiographical shudder: imagine if Mr Biswas had not owned this poor house, he suggests to his comfortable readers. 'How terrible it would have been, at this time, to be without it . . . to have lived without even attempting to lay claim to one's portion of the earth; to have lived and died as one had been born, unnecessary and unaccommodated.' How much land does a man need? asks Tolstoy in a fierce late tale. Six feet, just enough to be buried in, is that story's reply. Mr Biswas had a little more than that; but he had so narrowly avoided being the 'unaccommodated man', the naked savage found on the heath in *King Lear*.

Unnecessary, unaccommodated – and unnoticed, until Naipaul made him the hero of his book. The shudder is auto-biographical, because Mr Biswas is essentially Vidia Naipaul's father, Seepersad Naipaul, and the fictional house on Sikkim Street is the real house on Nepaul Street from which Vidia was launched, at nearly eighteen, on his enormous journey to England – 'a box,' writes Patrick French, 'a hot, rickety, par-titioned building near the end of the street, around 7 square metres on two floors with an external wooden staircase and a corrugated iron roof'. Seepersad's father was an indentured labourer, shipped from India to Trinidad in order to fill out the workforce on the sugar-cane plantations. Indentured servitude differed from slavery in that it was theoretically voluntary, and families were allowed to stay together. After five or ten years, the labourer could return to India or stay and take a small plot of land. At the time of Vidia Naipaul's birth, in 1932, the literacy rate among Trinidadian Indians (then about a third of the island's 400,000) was 23 per cent. For the entire island, there were four British government scholarships, which paid for study at a British university, and Vidia felt that this was his only chance to escape. He had won his first scholarship at the age of ten; he won his last in 1949, and left for Oxford the next year.

From this world, Naipaul's father, Seepersad, made a career as a reporter and columnist for the *Trinidad Guardian*, and published a book of fictional stories about his community, written with a simplicity and comedy and attention to detail that his son would admire and emulate. It was an extraordinary achievement, but judged by wider standards it was also a relative failure, because Seepersad never left the island, and had to live vicariously through his clever children, who did. (He died in 1953, aged forty-seven, while Vidia was still at Oxford.) That double assessment – pride and shame, compassion and alienation – is the stereoscopic vision of *A House for Mr Biswas* and, in a sense, of all Naipaul's fiction, and it is why he is a writer who has a conservative vision but radical eyesight. The Wounded, radical Naipaul burns with rage at the cramped colonial horizon of his father's life, and seeks to defend his accomplishments against the colonist's metropolitan sneers; but the conservative Wounder has got beyond the little prison of Trinidad, and now sees, with the colonist's eye and no longer the colonial's, the littleness of that imprisonment. Naipaul is enraging and puzzling, especially to those who themselves come from post-colonial societies, because his radicalism and conservatism are so close to each other – each response is descended from the same productive shame. Naipaul plays the oboe and the saxophone with the same reed.

In his writing, Naipaul is simultaneously the colonised and the colonist, in part because he never seriously imagines that the former would ever want to be anything but the latter, even as he uses each category to judge the other. Thus a pompous English Oxford student of the early 1950s might have seen Seepersad's achievement as absurdly minor, and Vidia Naipaul would certainly have agreed with him; but the bitterness of Seepersad's struggle would also have qualified that Oxonian complacency. How could Vidia not have wanted to defend his father as soon as the Oxonian looked down his nose at him? This dialectic seems familiar because it may have less to do with race and empire than with class; it is the classic movement from province to metropolis, whereby the provincial, who has never wanted to be anywhere but the metropolis, nevertheless judges it with a provincial scepticism, while judging the provinces with a metropolitan superiority. In *A House for Mr Biswas*, the Wounded and the Wounder are hard to disentangle, and Naipaul often adopts a kind of cool summary omniscience that he uses to provoke our rebellious compassion. There is an extraordinary moment early in the book when he offers a flash-forward, and tells us that Mr Biswas's fate would probably be that of a labourer, working on the estates like his brother, Pratap, 'illiterate all his days'. Pratap, he writes, would become 'richer than Mr Biswas; he was to have a house of his own, a large, strong, well-built house, years before Mr Biswas'. And then he changes course:

> But Mr Biswas never went to work on the estates. Events which were to occur presently led him away from that. They did not lead him to riches, but made it possible for him to console himself in later life with the *Meditations* of

Marcus Aurelius, while he rested on the Slumberking bed
in the one room which contained most of his possessions.

Naipaul is here communicating, almost esoterically, with
his presumed non-Trinidadian audience: you are the sort of
people, he seems to say, who might disdain Mr Biswas, but you
are also the kind of people who know that Pratap's 'riches' are
not as important as Biswas's 'riches'; that Marcus Aurelius on
a Slumberking bed, small as it is, is better than a Slumberking
bed without Marcus Aurelius.

V. S. Naipaul spent so much time being disagreeable and
superior, was so masked and armoured, that it can be hard to
remember the young writer's woundedness. The letters he sent
from Oxford to Trinidad, preternaturally confident, occasionally show a chink, as when he writes: 'I want to come top of
my group. I have got to show these people that I can beat
them at their own language.' Patrick French shrewdly dips into
the Oxford student magazine *Isis* to give us an idea of 'these
people', and thus of the world Naipaul had to join and beat.
For instance, the magazine offered a portrait in its 'Americans-
and-Colonials' series, of an Indian undergraduate, Ramesh
Divecha: 'This fine specimen of Hindu manhood is equally at
home theorising on the secrets of his success in Vincent's or
fingering his native chapattis in the Taj . . . He returns to the
jungle in August to study for his Bar Finals.'

To the jungle. Thus joked Pox Britannica.

Naipaul had a breakdown at Oxford, and the years immediately after his graduation as he looked for work in London
were intensely difficult. The hardship was softened by his relationship with Patricia Hale, whom he had met at Oxford in

1952. They were in some ways well matched. Like him, she was from modest circumstances – her father was a clerk in a lawyer's office, and the family lived in a small two-bedroom flat in a suburb of Birmingham. She was the only girl at her school to win a state scholarship to Oxford. They were both twenty-two when they married, and neither family was notified. But whereas Naipaul careered from confidence to anxiety (a year after meeting Pat, he told her that 'from a purely selfish point of view you are the ideal wife for a future G.O.M.' – Grand Old Man – 'of letters'), Pat was stable, supportive, a willing helpmeet. Years later, Naipaul reread his early correspondence with Pat, and made notes. Characteristically, he did not spare himself. He had got too quickly involved with Pat, he wrote; he had been in too deep and could not get out. It would have been better if he had married someone else. Pat 'did not attract me sexually at all'. He decided that the relationship, on his side, 'was more than half a lie. Based really on need. The letters are shallow & disingenuous.'

Pat sometimes seems to have aspired to the condition of the Athenian women adjured by Pericles, in his funeral oration, to 'think it your greatest commendation not to be talked of one way or other'. Her presence in his life was a hush around Vidia's noise; her job was merely to hold the big drum of his ego in the right position, the better for him to strike the vital life-rhythm. 'I am not much good to anyone and Vidia is probably, almost certainly right when he says I have nothing to offer him,' she would write in her diary, many years on in their marriage. Unassertive, Englishly reticent, a little milky and bland, she became steadily obsessed with his writing – even as she would half mockingly call him 'The Genius' in private – and enjoyed being his spur and amanuensis. There are six thrilling pages, in a biography full of intimate and moving revelations, in which Patrick French, with the help of Pat's diaries, shows us the genesis and progress of Naipaul's novel *A Bend in the River* (1979), probably the only rival to *Biswas*. One evening, in the autumn of 1977, after watching television, he informed his wife that he wanted 'to be alone with my thoughts'. Half an hour later she entered his room, and he told her that the novel would begin with these lines: 'My family came from the east coast. Africa was at our backs. We are Indian ocean people.' Then he outlined for her the story and the main characters. Over the next months, he said pleadingly that he could not write the book without her presence, and her diary documents its swift, difficult passage. Sometimes he read to her and sometimes he dictated to her, calling her into his bedroom, like Churchill with his secretaries, at one o'clock in the morning. The novel moved fast, and in May 1978 he asked her to come into his room at twelve thirty at night and 'spoke the end of the book. It took an hour to an hour and a half.'

A Bend in the River is narrated by Salim, a Muslim Indian merchant who has moved to a trading town on the bend of a great river in a newly independent African country. In 1966, Naipaul had spent time in Uganda, Kenya and Tanzania, and in 1975 he travelled to Mobutu's Zaire. In Kisangani, Tanzania, he happened to meet a young Indian businessman whose deracination was striking. The essence of his novel, he said, is: 'What is this man doing here?' Like so many of Naipaul's characters, Salim feels his status to be precarious. 'I was worried for us. Because, so far as power went, there was no difference between the Arabs and ourselves. We were both small groups living under a European flag at the end of the world.' An old friend of Salim's named Indar, who has been educated at a British university, arrives to do research at the town's polytechnic. Indar tells Salim about his journey to England, and once again Naipaul returns to the two beguilingly traumatic stories he has never escaped – the abbreviated short story of his father's journey, and the arpeggiated long story of his own journey. (Indar 'will be me', he told Pat.)

Indar tells Salim that 'when we land at a place like London Airport we are concerned only not to appear foolish'. After university, he tries to get a job with the Indian diplomatic service, but is humiliated at the Indian High Commission in London. The officials there seem to him cringing minor pomposities, yet one of them is bold enough to ask Indar how he can possibly represent India when he comes from Africa: 'How can we have a man of divided loyalties?' Indar tells Salim that 'for the first time in my life in London I was filled with a colonial rage. And this wasn't only a rage with London or England; it was also a rage with the people who had allowed themselves to be corralled into a foreign fantasy.' He decides, in London, that he will be a Naipauline empire of one. He realises that he is homeless, that he cannot go home, that he must stay in a place like London, that 'I belonged to myself alone'. He consoles himself, however:

'I'm a lucky man. I carry the world within me. You see, Salim, in this world beggars are the only people who can be choosers. Everyone else has his side chosen for him. I can choose . . . But now I want to win and win and win.'

Yet near the end of the book, Salim hears that Indar has not exactly won and won and won. His academic gig has folded because the Americans pulled the funding. Now 'he does the lowest kind of job. He knows he is equipped for better things, but he doesn't want to do them . . . He doesn't want to risk anything again.'

The Naipaul who wrote Indar's incandescent monologue is the Naipaul who, many years earlier, had written this fierce letter to Pat:

> I want you to put yourself in my place for a minute . . . If my father had 1/20 of the opportunity laid before the good people of British stock, he would not have died a broken, frustrated man without any achievement. But, like me, he had the opportunity – to starve. He was ghettoed – in a sense more cruel than that in which Hitler ghettoed the Jews. But there was an element of rude honesty in the Nazi approach; and they at any rate killed swiftly. The approach of the Free World is infinitely subtler and more refined. You cannot say to a foreign country: I suffer from political persecution. That wouldn't be true . . . But I suffer from something worse, an insidious spiritual persecution. These people want to break my spirit. They want me to forget my dignity as human being. They want me to know my place.

Naipaul in this letter resembles no writer so much as Frantz Fanon, the radical analyst of the 'insidious spiritual persecution' wrought by colonialism on the colonised. 'The colonized subject', writes Fanon in *The Wretched of the Earth* (1961), is constantly on his guard: Confused by the myriad signs of the colonial world he never knows whether he is out of line. Confronted with a world configured by the colonizer, the colonized subject is always presumed guilty. The colonized does not accept his guilt, but rather considers it a kind of curse, a sword of Damocles.

Fanon is a very different political animal from the conservative Naipaul. Fanon believed in violent revolution, but Naipaul's radical pessimism meets Fanon's radical optimism at that point where the cut of colonial guilt, angrily resisted by both men, is converted into the wound of colonial shame – 'a kind of curse'. And Naipaul's long novella *In a Free State* is practically a working demonstration of Fanon's argument that 'the colonist is an exhibitionist. His safety concerns lead him to remind the colonized out loud: "Here I am master." The colonist keeps the colonized in a state of rage, which he prevents from boiling over.' In that spare, bleak, burning novella, a white Englishman and Englishwoman drive through an African country resembling Uganda. The man is an administrative officer in a government department. In the course of their journey they perpetrate, and also witness, flamboyant acts of colonial rage on black Africans, acts whose *raison d'être* seems to be white self-reassurance. Impotent exhibitionists in Fanon's sense, these white intruders are at once predatory and fearful, constantly supplicating an assumed black 'rage' that they themselves actually feel, and constantly provoke. At a decrepit hotel, an old English colonel humiliates Peter, a black assistant, while his white visitors look on. One day, he warns Peter, you will come to my room to kill me, but you won't get past my door, because I'll be waiting for you: 'I'll kill you, I'll shoot you dead.'

Naipaul's sympathy for the political and emotional fragility of his characters did not extend, alas, to his wife. His brutally fulfilling affair with Margaret Gooding – 'I wished to possess her as soon as I saw her,' he tells his biographer – gradually voided a marriage that had never been sexually fulfilling. In the mid-1970s, husband and wife began to spend more and more time apart as Naipaul travelled on ceaseless journalistic assignments. Naipaul's sister, Savi, suggests that once Pat realised she would not have children and that her husband was committedly unfaithful, she lost her confidence as a woman. Patrick French had access both to Pat's diaries and to searching interviews with V. S. Naipaul, whose candour is formidable: as always, one feels that while Naipaul may often be wrong, he is rarely untruthful, and indeed that he is likely to uncover twenty truths on the path to error. Pat's diaries make for painful reading: 'I felt assaulted but I could not defend myself.' 'He has been increasingly frenzied and sadly, from my point of view, hating and abusing me.' Pat died of breast cancer in 1996. 'It could be said that I had killed her,' Naipaul tells French. 'It could be said. I feel a little bit that way.'

The day after Pat's cremation, Nadira Alvi, the well-heeled daughter of a Pakistani banker, soon to be the novelist's second wife, arrived in Wiltshire, at the house so recently vacated by her predecessor; and Naipaul wrote to his literary agent: 'She is part of my luck, and I would like you to meet her.' This is where French's masterly, mournful book ends, and it seems hideously just, in a story so consumed by social and racial anxieties and so transcendent of them, too, that we should see V. S. Naipaul ending his life with a haughty woman who tells Patrick French that she thinks her husband's relatives are 'jumped-up peasantry' and that her father 'would be shocked that I found happiness with an indentured labourer's grandson'.

In *The Enigma of Arrival*, the long book that Naipaul wrote about the Wiltshire countryside in which he had lived, intermittently, since 1971, there is a searing parenthesis in which he tells us about two derelict cottages he has been converting into a new home. One day, a very old lady is brought by her grandson to look at the cottage where she once spent a summer. Confused by Naipaul's renovations, she thinks she has come to the wrong place. Naipaul is 'ashamed', and so 'I pretended I didn't live there'. But what is the real source of the shame? Is it his building project or his very presence in the English countryside? He lives there but is ashamed to live there; the house for Mr Naipaul in England, as for Mr Biswas in Trinidad, is a homeless house. The man is still unaccommodated.

2008

On Not Going Home

I HAD A PIANO TEACHER who used to talk about the most familiar musical cadence – in which a piece returns, after wandering and variation, to its original key, the tonic – as 'going home'. It seemed so easy when music did it: who wouldn't want to swat away those black accidentals and come back to sunny C major? These satisfying resolutions are sometimes called 'perfect cadences'; there is a lovely subspecies called the 'English cadence', used often by composers like Tallis and Byrd, in which, just before the expected resolution, a dissonance sharpens its blade and seems about to wreck things – and is then persuaded home, as it should be.

I wish I could hear that English cadence again, the way I first properly heard it in Durham Cathedral. I was eleven years old. During the lesson, we choristers had been exchanging notes, probably sniggering at one of the more pompous priests – the one who, as he processed towards his stall, held his clasped hands pointing outwards from his breast, like a pious fish – and then we were up on our feet, and were singing 'O Nata Lux', by Thomas Tallis. I knew the piece but hadn't really listened to it. Now I was struck – assaulted, thrown – by its utter beauty: the soft equanimity of its articulation, like the voice of justice; the sweet dissonance, welcome as pain. That dissonance, with its distinctive Tudor sound, is partly produced by a movement known as 'false relation', in which the note you expect to hear in the harmony of a chord is shadowed by its nearest relation – the same note but a semitone off. As the Tallis was ending, I saw a middle-aged woman with a canvas shoulder-bag enter the shadowy hinterland at the back of the huge building. Standing so far away, a singular figure, she might have been a tentative tourist. But I knew the full bag, that coat I always wanted to be a bit more impressive than it was, the anxious rectitude of my mother's posture. She came every Tuesday afternoon, because the girls' school she taught at got out early then. My parents lived only a mile or so from the cathedral, but I had to board; Tuesday afternoons, before I went back to school, gave me the chance to exchange a few words, and grab whatever she brought in that bag – comics and sweets; and, more reliably, socks.

In my memory this is exactly what happened: the radiance of the music, the revelation of its beauty, the final cadences of the Tallis, and my happy glimpsing of my mother. But it happened thirty-seven years ago, and the scene has a convenient, dreamlike composition. Perhaps I have really dreamed it. As I get older I dream more frequently of that magnificent cathedral – the long grey cool interior hanging somehow like memory itself. These are intense experiences, from which I awake hearing every single note of a piece of remembered music; happy dreams, never troubled. I like returning to that place in my sleep, even look forward to it.

But real life is a different matter. The few occasions I have returned to Durham have been strangely disappointing. My parents no longer live there; I no longer live in the country. The city has become a dream. Herodotus says that the Scythians were hard to defeat because they had no cities or settled forts: 'they carry their houses with them and shoot with bows from horseback . . . their dwellings are on their wagons. How can they fail to be invincible and inaccessible for others?' To have a home is to become vulnerable. Not just to the attacks of others, but to our own massacres of alienation: our campaigns of departure and return threaten to become mere adventures in voiding. I left my home twice – the first time, just after university, when I went to London, in the familiar march of the provincial for the metropolis. I borrowed a thousand pounds from the NatWest bank in Durham (an account I still have), rented a van one-way, put everything I owned into it and drove south; I remember thinking, as I waved at my parents and my sister, that the gesture was both authentic and oddly artificial, the authorised novelistic journey. In this way, many of us are homeless: the exodus of expansion. The second departure occurred in 1995, when at the age of thirty I left Britain for the United States. I was married to an American – to put it more precisely, I was married to an American citizen whose French father and Canadian mother, themselves immigrants, lived in the States. We had no children, and America would surely be new and exciting. We might even stay there for a few years – five at the most?

I have now lived nineteen years in the United States. It's feeble to say I didn't expect to stay as long; and ungrateful, or even meaningless or dishonest, to say I didn't want to. I must have wanted to; there has been plenty of gain. But I had so little concept of what might be lost. 'Losing a country', or 'losing a home', if I gave the matter much thought when I was young, was an acute world-historical event, forcibly meted out on the victim, lamented and canonised in literature and theory as 'exile' or 'displacement', and defined with appropriate terminality by Edward Said in his essay 'Reflections on Exile':

> Exile is strangely compelling to think about but terrible to experience. It is the unhealable rift forced between a human being and a native place, between the self and its true home: its essential sadness can never be surmounted. And while it is true that literature and history contain heroic, romantic, glorious, even triumphant episodes in an exile's life, these are no more than efforts meant to overcome the crippling sorrow of estrangement. The achievements of exile are permanently undermined by the loss of something left behind forever.

Said's emphasis on the self's 'true home' has a slightly theological, or perhaps Platonic, sound. When there is such universal homelessness, of both the forced and the unforced kind, the idea of a 'true home' surely suffers an amount of necessary modification. Perhaps Said's implication is that unwanted homelessness only bears down on those who *have* a true home and thus always reinforces the purity of the origin, while voluntary homelessness – the softer emigration I am trying to define – means that home can't have been very 'true' after all. I doubt he intended that – but nonetheless, in the traditional reading, the desert of exile seems to need the oasis of primal belonging, the two held in a biblical clasp.

In that essay, Said distinguishes between exile, refugee, expatriate and émigré. Exile, as he understands it, is tragic homelessness, connected to the ancient punishment of banishment; he approves of Adorno's subtitle to *Minima Moralia*: *Reflections from a Mutilated Life*. It is hard to see how the milder, unforced journey I am describing could belong to this grander vision of suffering. 'Not going home' is not exactly the same as 'homelessness'. That nice old boarding-school standby, 'homesickness', might fit better, particularly if allowed a certain doubleness. I am sometimes homesick, where homesickness is a kind of longing for Britain and an irritation with Britain: sickness *for* and sickness *of*. I bump into plenty of people in America who tell me that they miss their native countries – Britain, Germany, Russia, Holland, South Africa – and who in the next breath say they cannot imagine returning. It is possible, I suppose, to miss home terribly, not know what home really is any more and refuse to go home, all at once. Such a tangle of feelings might then be a definition of luxurious freedom, as far removed from Said's tragic homelessness as can be imagined.

Logically, a refusal to go home should validate, negatively, the very idea of home, rather in the way that Said's idea of exile validates the idea of an original 'true home'. But perhaps the refusal to go home is consequent upon the loss, or lack, of home: as if those fortunate expatriates were really saying to me, 'I couldn't go back home because I wouldn't know how to any more.' And there is 'Home' and 'a home'. Authors used to be described on book dust-jackets as 'making a home': 'Mr Blackmur makes his home in Princeton, New Jersey.' I have made a home in the United States, but it is not quite Home.

For instance, I have no strong desire to become an American citizen. Recently, when I arrived at Boston airport, the immigration officer commented on the length of time I've held a Green Card. 'A Green Card is usually considered a path to citizenship,' he said, a sentiment both irritatingly reproving and movingly patriotic. I mumbled something about how he was perfectly correct, and left it at that. But consider the fundamental openness and generosity of the gesture (along with the undeniable coercion): it's hard to imagine his British counterpart so freely offering citizenship – as if it were, indeed, uncomplicatedly *on offer*, a service or commodity. He was generously saying, 'Would you like to be an American citizen?' along with the less generous, 'Why don't you want to be an American citizen?' Can we imagine either sentiment being expressed at Heathrow airport? The poet and novelist Patrick McGuinness, in his book *Other People's Countries* (itself a rich analysis of home and homelessness; McGuinness is half Irish and half Belgian) quotes Simenon, who was asked why he didn't change his nationality, 'the way successful Francophone Belgians often did'. Simenon replied: 'There was no reason for me to be born Belgian, so there's no reason for me to stop being Belgian.' I wanted to say something similar, less wittily, to the immigration officer: precisely because I don't need to become an American citizen, to take it would seem flippant; leave its benefits for those who need a new land.

So whatever this state I am talking about is, this 'not going home', it is not tragic; there's probably something a bit ridiculous in these privileged laments – oh, sing 'dem Harvard blues, white boy! But I am trying to describe *some* kind of loss, some kind of falling away. (The gain is obvious enough and thus less interesting to analyse.) I asked Christopher Hitchens, long before he was terminally ill, where he would go if he had only a few weeks to live. Would he stay in America? 'No, I'd go to Dartmoor, without a doubt,' he told me. It was the landscape of his childhood. Dartmoor, not the MD Anderson Cancer Center in Houston. It's not uncommon for expatriates, émigrés, refugees and travellers to want to die 'at home'. The desire to return, after so long away, is gladly irrational, and is perhaps premised on the loss of the original home (as the refusal to go home may also be premised on the loss of home). Home swells as a sentiment because it has disappeared as an achievable reality. Marusya Tatarovich, the heroine of the novel *A Foreign Woman*, by the Russian émigré writer Sergei Dovlatov, comes to the conclusion that she has made a mistake in leaving Russia for New York City, and decides to return. Dovlatov, who left the Soviet Union for America in 1979, and who appears as himself in the novel, tries to talk her out of it. You've just forgotten what life is like there, he says: 'The rudeness, the lies.' She replies: 'If people are rude in Moscow, at least it's in Russian.' But she stays in America. I once saw, in Germany, a small exhibition of Samuel Beckett's correspondence to his German publisher. Many brief note-cards were arranged chronologically, the last written only a few months before his death. Beckett wrote to his publisher not in German but in French, a language in which he had of course made a home; but in the final year of his life, he switched to English. 'Going home,' I thought.

After so many years, life in America, or in my small part of America, has become my life. And life is made up of particulars: friends, conversation, dailiness of all sorts. I love, for instance, that certain New England states alert drivers that they are entering a built-up area with the sign 'Thickly Settled'. I love the Hudson River, its steady brown flow; generally, I like how most American rivers make their European rivals look like wan streams. There is the crimson livery of the Boar's Head trucks. Or the way the mailman, delivering the post in the dark winter afternoon, wears a little miner's lamp on his head, and peers down at his paper bundle. Large American radiators in old apartment buildings, with their hissing and ghostly clanking. A certain general store in New Hampshire that sells winter boots, hand cream, excellent bacon, and firearms. I cherish the phrase 'Take it easy', and the scandalous idea that people would actually say this to each other! I am even fond, now, of things that reliably dumbfound the British – American sports, say; or the fact that the word *fortnight* does not exist; that *fudge* is just chocolate; and that seemingly no one can properly pronounce the words *croissant, milieu* or *bourgeois*.

But there is always the reality of a certain outsider-dom. Take the beautiful American train horn, the crushed klaxon peal you can hear almost anywhere in the States – at the end of my street at night-time, across a New Hampshire valley, in some small Midwestern town: a crumple of notes, blown out on an easy, loitering wail. It sounds less like a horn than a sudden prairie wind or an animal's cry. That big easy loiter is, for me, the sound of America, whatever America is. But it must also be 'the sound of America' for thousands, perhaps millions, of non-Americans. It's a shared possession, not a personal one. I'm outside it; I appreciate it, as something slightly distant. It is unhistorical for me: it doesn't have my past in it, drags no old associations. (We lived about half a mile from the Durham station, and from my bedroom, at night, I could hear the arrhythmic thunder of the big yellow-nosed Deltic diesels, as they pulled their shabby carriages onto the Victorian viaduct that curves out of town, bound for London or Edinburgh, and sometimes blew their parsimonious horns – the British Rail minor third.)

Or suppose I am looking down our Boston street, in dead summer. I see a familiar life: the clapboard houses, the porches, the heat-mirage hanging over the patched road (snakes of asphalt like black chewing-gum), the grey cement pavements (signed in one place, when the cement was new, by three young siblings), the heavy maple trees, the unkempt willow down at the end, an old white Cadillac with the bumper sticker 'Ted Kennedy has killed more people than my gun', and I feel . . . nothing: some recognition, but no comprehension, no real connection, no past, despite all the years I have lived there; just a tugging distance from it all. A panic suddenly overtakes me, and I wonder: how did I get here? And then the moment passes, and ordinary life closes itself around what had seemed, for a moment, a desperate lack.

Edward Said says that it is no surprise that exiles are often novelists, chess players, intellectuals. 'The exile's new world, logically enough, is unnatural, and its unreality resembles fiction.' He reminds us that Georg Lukács considered the novel the great form of what Lukács called 'transcendental homelessness'. I am certainly not an exile, but it is sometimes hard to shake the 'unreality' Said speaks of. I watch my children grow up as Americans in the same way that I might read about, or create, fictional characters. *They* are not fictional, of course, but their Americanism can sometimes seem unreal to me. 'I have an American seventh-grader,' I say to myself with amazement, as I watch my twelve-year-old daughter perform at one of those dastardly school events always held in gymnasiums. Doubtless, amazement attends all the stages of a child's growth – all is unexpected. But there is also that strange distance, the light veil of alienation thrown over everything.

And then there is the same light veil thrown over everything when I go back to Britain, too. When I was first living in the States, I was eager to keep up with life 'back at home' – who was in the Cabinet, the new music, what people were saying in the newspapers, how the schools were doing, the price of petrol, the shape of friends' lives. It became harder to do so, because the meaning of these things grew less and less personal. For me, English reality has disappeared into memory, has 'changed itself to past', as Larkin has it. I know very little about modern daily life in London, or Edinburgh, or Durham. There's a quality of masquerade when I return, as if I were putting on my wedding suit, to see if it still fits.

In America, I crave the English reality that has disappeared; childhood seems breathingly close. But the sense of masquerade persists: I gorge on nostalgia, on fondnesses that might have embarrassed me when I lived in Britain. Geoff Dyer writes funnily, in *Out of Sheer Rage*, about how, when he was living in Italy, he developed an obsession with reading the TV listings in English papers, even though he had never watched telly when he lived in England, and didn't like it.

To hear a Geordie voice on an American news programme leaves me flushed with longing: the dance of that dialect, with its seasick Scandinavian pitch. And all those fabulous words: *segs* (the metal plates you'd bang onto your shoe-heels, to make sparks on the ground and act like a hard-nut); *kets* (sweets); *neb* (nose); *nowt* (nothing); *stotty-cake* (a kind of flat, doughy bread); *claggy* (sticky). The way northerners say *eee*, as an exclamation: 'Eee, it's red-hot today!' (Any temperature over about twenty degrees.) Recently, I heard the old song 'When the Boat Comes In' on National Public Radio, and almost wept.

> Now come here, little Jacky
> Now I've smoked me backy,
> Let's have some cracky
> Till the boat comes in
>
> And you shall have a fishy
> On a little dishy
> You shall have a fishy
> When the boat comes in.

But I really disliked that song when I was a boy. I never had a very northern accent. My father was born in London. It was important to my Scottish petit bourgeois mother that I didn't sound like a Geordie. Friends used to say, with a bit of menace in their voices: 'You don't talk like a Durham lad. Where are you from?' Sometimes it was necessary to mimic the accent, to fit in, or to avoid getting beaten up. I could never say, as the man in the song 'Coming Home Newcastle' foolishly does: 'And I'm proud to be a Geordie / And to live in Geordie-land.'

My town was the university and the cathedral – it seemed that almost everyone who lived on our street was an academic (like my father) or a clergyman; and they didn't sound like Geordies. How vivid all those neighbours are, in my mind! And how strange they were. I think now that in the 1970s I caught the fading comet-end of allowable eccentricity. There was Mrs Jolley, though she was in fact anything but, who walked with three canes, one for the left leg and two (bound together with string) for the right. There was the dry, bony Reader in Classical Epigraphy, Dr Fowler, who was fond of repeating, as a kind of motto, 'Tell it not in Gath!' Next door to us, separated only by a wall, lived a profoundly learned scholar, the university librarian. He knew many languages, and pages of Dickens by heart, and sometimes we would hear him pacing up and down, reciting and laughing. This academic-religious world had obscure prohibitions and rules. There was a historian who for some reason forbade his two slightly green-hued, fearsomely clever daughters from watching *The Forsyte Saga* on television; and a thrifty Professor of Divinity whose household had no television and who, according to my mother, always had sausages, never turkey, on Christmas Day – that family's fantastical drabness sealed in my childish mind by the information that he and his wife and three children exchanged only cotton handkerchiefs as presents. Our headmaster at the Durham Chorister School, also a clergyman, had an elaborate system of mnemonics to help us with difficult Latin words. Whenever the word *unde* appeared in a text, he would suck on his pipe and intone, in Oxonian basso, 'Marks and Spencer, Marks and Spencer!' This was supposed to trigger, 'Where do you get your undies?' 'From Marks and Spencer.' And then lead us to the meaning of the word, which is: 'from where'. As you can see, I haven't forgotten it.

II

A recent editorial in the Brooklyn-based literary journal *n+1* inveighed against so-called 'World Literature'. In their opinion, post-colonial writing has lost its political bite and now fills its toothless face at the trough of global capitalism. *Midnight's Children* gave way, as it were, to the inoffensive Rushdie of *The Ground Beneath Her Feet*. The essay argued that World Literature should really be called Global Literature. It has its royalty, like Coetzee and Ondaatje, Mohsin Hamid and Kiran Desai; its prizes (the Nobel, the Man Booker International), its festivals (Jaipur, Hay) and its intellectual support system (the universities). The success of World Literature, said the editors, is a by-product of successful capitalism, and of a globalised aesthetic that prizes writers who, like Orhan Pamuk, Ma Jian and Haruki Murakami, are thought to have transcended local issues and acquired a 'universal relevance'.

It was hard not to share *n+1*'s derision, once its victim had been so tendentiously trussed. Who could possibly approve of this complacent, festival-haunting, unit-shifting, prize-winning monster? Who wouldn't choose instead, as the editors did, a 'thorny internationalism' over the 'smoothly global', untranslatable felicities over windy width – and Elena Ferrante over Kamila Shamsie? In the end, the journal was really making a wise case for well-written, vital, challenging literature, full of sharp local particularities, wherever it turns up in the world; and so there was inevitably something a bit random about the writers it chose for its preferred canon of Thorny Internationalists: Elena Ferrante, Kirill Medvedev, Samanth Subramanian, Juan Villoro.

Perhaps, though, post-colonial literature hasn't only morphed into a bloated World Lit. One of its new branches may be a significant contemporary literature that moves between, and powerfully treats, questions of homelessness, displacement, emigration, voluntary or economic migration and even flâneurial tourism; a literature that blurs the demarcations offered in 'Reflections on Exile', because emigration itself has become more complex, amorphous and widespread. The editors at *n+1* inaudibly conceded as much in its editorial, when they praised *Open City*, by Teju Cole, a Nigerian-American writer based in New York City, whose first novel is narrated by a young half-Nigerian, half-German psychiatry intern, and which mixes elements of familiar post-coloniality with W. G. Sebald's flâneurial émigré sensibility. Cole, it seems, is approved of, but doesn't quite make the Thorny Internationalist cut.

But to *Open City* could be added W. G. Sebald's work; Patrick McGuinness's *Other People's Countries*; the Nigerian novelist Taiye Selasi; Joseph O'Neill's *Netherland*, which makes acute distinctions between the privileged economic migration of the Dutch banker who narrates the novel and the much less privileged immigration of the Trinidadian trickster who is the book's tragic hero; the work of the Bosnian-American writer Aleksandar Hemon; Marilynne Robinson's *Home*; Mavis Gallant's short stories, written by a Canadian who spent most of her life in Paris; Zia Haider Rahman's formidable first novel, *In the Light of What We Know*; some of the writing of Geoff Dyer; the stories of Nam Le, a Vietnamese-born Australian; the fiction and essays of the Indian novelist Amit Chaudhuri.

The 'great movement of peoples that was to take place in the second half of the twentieth century' that V. S. Naipaul spoke of in *The Enigma of Arrival* was, as Naipaul put it, 'a movement between all the continents'. It could no longer be confined to a single paradigm (post-colonialism, internationalism, globalism, world literature). The jet engine has probably had a greater impact than the Internet. It brings a Nigerian to New York, a Bosnian to Chicago, a Mexican to Berlin, an Australian to London, a German to Manchester. It brought one of *n+1*'s founding editors, Keith Gessen, as a little boy, from Russia to America in 1981, and now takes him back and forth between those countries (a liberty unknown to émigrés like Nabokov or Sergei Dovlatov).

Recall Lukács's phrase 'transcendental homelessness'. What I have been describing, both in my own life and the lives of others, is more like secular homelessness. It cannot claim the theological prestige of the transcendent. Perhaps it is not even homelessness; *homelooseness* (with an admixture of loss) might be the necessary neologism: in which the ties that might bind one to Home have been loosened, perhaps happily, perhaps unhappily, perhaps permanently, perhaps only temporarily. Clearly, this secular homelessness overlaps, at times, with the more established categories of emigration, exile and post-colonial movement. Just as clearly, it diverges from them at times. W. G. Sebald, a German writer who lived most of his adult life in England (and who was thus perhaps an emigrant, certainly an immigrant, but not exactly an émigré, nor an exile), had an exquisite sense of the varieties of not-belonging. He came to Manchester, from Germany, in the mid-1960s, as a graduate student. He returned, briefly, to Switzerland, and then came back to England in 1970, to take a lectureship at the University of East Anglia. The pattern of his own emigration is one of secular homelessness or homelooseness. He had the economic freedom to return to West Germany; and once he was well known, in the mid-1990s, he could have worked almost anywhere he wanted to.

Sebald was interested, however, not in his own wandering, but in an emigration and displacement closer to tragic or transcendental homelessness. In *The Emigrants*, he wrote about four such wanderers: Dr Henry Selwyn, a Lithuanian Jew who arrived in Britain at the beginning of the twentieth century, and who lived a life of stealthy masquerade as an English doctor, before committing suicide late in life; Paul Bereyter, a German who because of his part-Jewish ancestry was prohibited from teaching during the Third Reich, never recovered from this setback and later committed suicide; Sebald's great-uncle, Adelwarth, who arrived in America in the 1920s, worked as a servant for a wealthy family on Long Island, but ended up in a mental asylum in Ithaca, New York; and Max Ferber, a fictional character based on the painter Frank Auerbach, who left his parents behind in Germany in 1939, when he escaped for England.

When *The Emigrants* appeared in Michael Hulse's English translation, in 1996, it was often described as a book about four victims of the Holocaust, which it was not – only two of the emigrants are direct victims. Because the book is deeply invested in questions of fictionality, decipherment and archival witness – and because of the book's teasing photographs – it was also often assumed that these were fictional or fictionalised sketches. Almost the opposite is true. They are more like documentary life-studies; Sebald said in an interview that about 90 per cent of the photographs were 'what you would describe as authentic, i.e. they really did come out of the photo albums of the people described in those texts and are a direct testimony of the fact that these people did exist in that particular shape and form'. Sebald did indeed meet Dr Selwyn in 1970; Paul Bereyter was Sebald's primary-school teacher; his great-uncle Adelwarth emigrated to America in the 1920s; and Max Ferber's life was closely modelled on Frank Auerbach's.

None of this suggests that Sebald doesn't enrich the documentary evidence in all kinds of subtle, slippery, fictive ways. And one of the subtleties involves his relationship, as a kind of emigrant, with his subjects. Henry Selwyn and Max Ferber were, essentially, political refugees, from different waves of twentieth-century Jewish flight; Adelwarth was an economic immigrant; and Paul Bereyter became an inner emigrant, a post-war German survivor who, in the end, did not survive. And Sebald himself? His own emigration would seem to play out in a minor key, by comparison. Officially, he could return to his homeland whenever he wanted. But perhaps he had decided, for political reasons, that he could never go home again, could never return to a country whose unfinished post-war business had so disgusted him in the 1960s.

Sebald is a ghostly presence in *The Emigrants*. We are offered only glimpses of the German academic in England. Yet in another way, the author is strongly present, felt as a steady insistence in regulated hysteria. Who is this apparently well-established professor, so obsessed with the lives of his subjects that he crosses Europe or the Atlantic to interview their relatives, ransack their archives, frown over their photograph albums and follow their journeys? There is a beautiful moment in the first story, about Dr Henry Selwyn, when the text glances at Sebald's own, lesser homelessness, and then glances away, as if politely conceding its smaller claim on tragedy:

> On one of these visits, Clara being away in town, Dr Selwyn and I had a long talk prompted by his asking whether I was ever homesick. I could not think of any adequate reply, but Dr Selwyn, after a pause for thought, confessed (no other word will do) that in recent years he had been beset by homesickness more and more.

Sebald then describes Dr Selwyn's homesickness for the village in Lithuania he had to leave at the age of seven. We hear about the horse-ride to the station, the train journey to Riga, the ship from Riga and the arrival in a broad river estuary:

> All the emigrants had gathered on deck and were waiting for the Statue of Liberty to appear out of the drifting mist, since every one of them had booked a passage to

Americum, as we called it. When we disembarked we were
still in no doubt whatsoever that beneath our feet was the
soil of the New World, of the Promised City of New York.
But in fact, as we learnt some time later to our dismay (the
ship having long since cast off again), we had gone ashore
in London.

I find moving the way in which Sebald's homesickness
becomes Selwyn's, is swallowed by the acuter claims of the
larger narrative. We can only guess at the smothered anguish
in Sebald's primly painful aside, 'I could not think of any
adequate reply.' There is also, perhaps, something touchingly
estranged, unhoused even, about Sebald's language – this
peculiar, reticent, antiquarian prose, in an English created
by Michael Hulse and then strenuously worked over by the
bilingual author.

Sebald seems to know the difference between homesickness and homelessness, between homelooseness and homelessness. If there is anguish, there is also discretion: how
could my loss *adequately* compare with yours? Where exile
is often marked by the absolutism of the separation, homelooseness is marked by a certain provisionality, a structure
of departure and return that may not end. This is a powerful motif in the work of Aleksandar Hemon, who came to
the States from Sarajevo, in 1992, only to discover that the
siege of his home town prohibited his return. Hemon stayed
in America, learned how to write a brilliant, Nabokovian
English (a feat actually greater than Nabokov's because
achieved at a phenomenal pace) and published his first book,
The Question of Bruno, in 2000 (dedicated to his wife, and

to Sarajevo). Once the Bosnian war was over, Hemon could presumably have returned to his native city. What had not been a choice became one; he decided to make himself into an American writer.

Hemon's work stages both his departure and return. In the novella *Blind Jozef Pronek & Dead Souls*, Pronek arrives in America on a student exchange programme. Like Hemon, Pronek is from Sarajevo, is trapped by the war and stays in America. He finds the United States a bewildering, alienating place, full of vulgarity and ignorance. When, near the end of the story, he returns to Sarajevo, the reader expects him to stay. Though the city is terribly damaged, and familiar landmarks have disappeared, he seems to have come back to his 'true home' – where 'every place had a name, and everybody and everything in that place had a name, and you could never be nowhere, because there was something everywhere'. Sarajevo, it seems, is where names and things, words and referents, are primally united. He goes through his parents' apartment, touching everything:

> the clean, striped tablecloth; the radio, with seven ivory-colored buttons and a Donald Duck sticker; the grinning African masks; the carpets with intricate, yet familiar, geo-metric patterns, full of gashes, from under which the par-quet was gone, burnt in the rusty iron stove in the corner; the demitasse, the coffee grinder, the spoons; Father's suits, damp, with shrapnel slashes . . .

But Jozef does not stay, and as the novella closes, we see him in Vienna airport, about to board a flight to America:

He did not want to fly to Chicago. He imagined walking
from Vienna to the Atlantic Ocean, and then hopping
on a slow trans-Atlantic steamer. It would take a month
to get across the ocean, and he would be on the sea, land
and borders nowhere to be found. Then he would see the
Statue of Liberty and walk slowly to Chicago, stopping
wherever he wished, talking to people, telling them stories
about far-off lands, where people ate honey and pickles,
where no one put ice in the water, where pigeons nested
in pantries.

It's as if jet-flight is existentially shallow; a slower journey
would enact the gravity and enormity of the transformation.
Pronek returns to America, but must take his home with him,
and must try to tell incomprehensible stories – pigeons in the
pantries, honey and pickles – of that home to a people who
readily confuse Bosnia with Slovakia, and write off the war
as 'thousands of years of hatred'. And at the same time, he is
making a new home in America. Or not quite: for he will stay
in America, but will, it seems, never rid himself of the idea
that putting ice in the water is a foolish superfluity. And like
Sebald, though in a different register, Hemon writes a prose
that does not sound smoothly native – a fractionally homeless prose. Like his master, Nabokov, he has the immigrant's
love of puns, of finding buried meanings in words that have
become flattened in English, like *vacuous* and *petrified*. One
character has 'a sagely beard', another 'fenestral glasses'. Tea is
described as 'limpid'.

Exile is acute, massive, transformative, but homelooseness,
because it moves along its axis of departure and return, can be

banal, welcome, necessary, continuous. There is the movement of the provincial to the metropolis, or the journey out of one social class into another. This was my mother's journey from Scotland to England, my father's journey from the working classes into the middle classes, my short drive from Durham to London. It is Ursula Brangwen's struggle for departure, in *The Rainbow*, when she quarrels with her parents about leaving her home in the Midlands and becoming a teacher in Kingston-upon-Thames – what her father calls 'dancing off to th'other side of London'.

Most of us have to leave home, at least once; there is the necessity to leave, the difficulty of returning and then, in later life as one's parents begin to falter, the necessity to return again. Secular homelessness, not the singular extremity of the exile or the chosenness of biblical diaspora, might be the inevitable ordinary state. Secular homelessness is not just what will always occur in Eden, but what should occur, again and again. There is a beautiful section at the end of Ismail Kadare's great novel *Chronicle in Stone*, entitled 'Draft of a Memorial Plaque'. Kadare was born, in 1936, in the city of Gjirokastër, in southern Albania, but has spent much of his writing life in Paris. *Chronicle in Stone* is a joyful, comic tribute to the ancient native city he left behind. At the end of the book, Kadare directly addresses his home town: 'Often, striding along wide lighted boulevards in foreign cities, I somehow stumble in places where no one ever trips. Passersby turn in surprise, but I always know it's you. You emerge from the asphalt all of a sudden and then sink back down straight away.' It is Kadare's nicely humdrum version of the moment in Proust when Marcel stumbles on the uneven stones in the courtyard of the Guermantes, and memory opens itself up.

If it didn't trip you up, you wouldn't remember anything. For the émigré writer, returning to live in Gjirokastër is doubtless unimaginable, in rather the way that living in Paris must have seemed unimaginable when Kadare was a young man in Albania. But a life without stumbling is also unimaginable: perhaps to be in between two places, to be at home in neither, is the inevitable fallen state, almost as natural as being at home in one place.

III

Almost. But not quite. When I left England nineteen years ago, I didn't know then how strangely departure would obliterate return: how could I have known? It's one of time's lessons, and can only be learned temporally. What is peculiar, even a little bitter, about living for so many years away from the country of my birth is the slow revelation that I made a large choice many years ago that did not resemble a large choice at the time; that it has taken years for me to see this; and that this process of retrospective comprehension in fact constitutes a life – is indeed how life is lived. Freud has a wonderful word, 'afterwardness', which I need to borrow, even at the cost of kidnapping it from its very different context. To think about home and the departure from home, about not going home and no longer feeling able to go home, is to be filled with a remarkable sense of 'afterwardness': it is too late to do anything about it now, and too late to know what should have been done. And that may be all right.

My Scottish grandmother used to play a game, in which she entered the room with her hands behind her back. You had to guess which hand held a sweet, as she intoned: 'Which hand do you tak', the richt or the wrang?' When we were children, the decision seemed momentous: you *had* at all costs to avoid the disappointment of the empty 'wrang hand'.

Which did I choose?

2014

The Other Side of Silence:
Rereading W. G. Sebald

I MET W. G. SEBALD almost twenty years ago, in New York City. He spoke with me for a public interview at the PEN American Center. Afterwards we had dinner. It was July 1997. He was fifty-three; the brief blaze of his international celebrity had been lit a year before, by the publication in English of his mysterious, wayward book *The Emigrants*. In a laudatory review, Susan Sontag had forcefully anointed the German writer as a contemporary master.

Not that Sebald seemed to care about that. He was gentle, academic, intensely tactful. His hair was grey, his almost-white moustache like frozen water. He resembled the photographs of a pensive Walter Benjamin. There was an atmosphere of drifting melancholy that, as in his prose, he made almost comic by sly self-consciousness. I remember standing with him in the foyer of the restaurant, where there was some kind of ornamental arrangement that involved leaves floating in a tank. Sebald thought they were elm leaves, and was prompted into a characteristic reverie. In England, he said, all the elms had disappeared, ravaged first by Dutch elm disease, the remainder well and truly finished off by the great hurricane of 1987. All gone, all gone, he murmured. Since I had not read *The Rings of Saturn*, I didn't know that he was almost quoting a passage from his own work (where, beautifully, he describes the trees, uprooted after the hurricane, lying on the ground 'as if in a swoon'). Still, I was amused even then by how very Sebaldian he sounded, encouraged by a glitter in his eyes and by a slightly sardonic fatigue in his voice.

During dinner, he returned sometimes to that mode, always with a delicate sense of comic timing. Someone at the table asked him if he might be interested in leaving England for a while and teaching elsewhere. New York, for instance? The great city was at his feet. It was part question, part flattery. Through clear round spectacles he pityingly regarded his interlocutor, and replied with naive sincerity: 'No, I don't think so.' He added that he was too attached to the old Norfolk rectory he had lived in for years. I asked him what else he liked about England. The English sense of humour, he said. Had I ever seen, he asked, any German comedy on television? I had not, and I wondered aloud what it was like. 'It is . . . *unspeakable*,' he said, stretching out the adjective with a heavy Germanic emphasis, and leaving behind an implication, also comic, that his short reply sufficed as a perfectly comprehensive explanation of the relative merits of English and German humour.

Sebald may have been playing with something he had said earlier in the evening, when I had asked him about his relation to his adopted country. He said that although he did not feel at home, he liked 'the almost total absence in that country of any authoritarian structures', and the fierce British respect for privacy. Then he got that glitter in his eyes, and told a funny story:

> A friend of mine once broke an ankle on the beach. There was nobody else there except an elderly English couple sitting in a car, having a cup of tea. He was desperately trying to catch their attention so that they would call an ambulance. In order to do so, he tried to make his way towards them, very much like a soldier in the battlefield. They just looked at him quizzically and didn't say anything. They just thought this is how he goes for his walk and that's fine, it's his business!

Something about the insertion, 'very much like a soldier in the battlefield', is what turns a sweet anecdote into an original piece of English farce.

Comedy is hardly the first thing one associates with the work of W. G. Sebald, but that's partly because his reputation was quickly associated with the literature of the Holocaust, and is still shaped by the two books of his that deal directly with that catastrophe: *The Emigrants*, a collection of four partly fictional, history-haunted biographies, and his last book, *Austerlitz* (2001), a novel about a Jewish Englishman who discovers, fairly late in life, that he was born in Prague but rescued from imminent extermination by being sent at the age of four and a half to England, in the summer of 1939, on the so-called Kindertransport. The typical Sebaldian character is estranged and isolated, visited by depression and menaced by lunacy, wounded into storytelling by historical trauma. But two other works, *Vertigo* and *The Rings of Saturn*, are more various than this, and all of his four major books have an eccentric sense of playfulness.

Rereading him, I'm struck by how much funnier his work is than I first took it to be. Take, for instance, *The Rings of Saturn* (brilliantly translated by Michael Hulse), a kind of comic-mournful travelogue, in which the Sebald-like narrator spends much of the book tramping around Suffolk. He muses on the demise of the old country estates, whose hierarchical grandeur never recovered from the societal shifts brought about by the two world wars. He tells the life-stories of Joseph Conrad, the translator Edward Fitzgerald, and the radical diplomat Roger Casement. He visits a friend, the poet Michael Hamburger, who left Berlin for England in 1933, at the age of nine and a half. The tone is elegiac, muffled, but also curiously intense. The Hamburger visit allows Sebald to take the reader back to the Berlin of the poet's childhood, a scene he meticulously recreates with the help of Hamburger's own memoirs. But he also jokily notes that when they have tea, the teapot emits 'occasional puffs of steam as from a toy engine'.

Elsewhere in the book, Sebald is constantly provoked to humorous indignation by the stubborn intolerability of English service. In Lowestoft, once a prosperous resort but now impoverished and drab, he puts up at the hideous Albion Hotel. He's the only diner in the huge dining room, and is brought a piece of fish 'that had doubtless lain entombed in the deep-freeze for years':

> The breadcrumb armour-plating of the fish had been partly singed by the grill, and the prongs of my fork bent on it. Indeed it was so difficult to penetrate what eventually proved to be nothing but an empty shell that my plate was a hideous mess once the operation was over.

Evelyn Waugh would have been quite content to have written a passage like this, and might have noted that the secret of the comedy lies in the paradox of painstaking exaggeration (as if the diner is trying to crack a safe, or solve a philosophical thesis), enforced by Sebald's calm control of apparently ponderous diction ('operation').

It is the same at the Saracen's Head, in Harleston, where the guest rooms 'were furnished with the most fearful pieces one can imagine', the mirror makes the occupant look 'strangely deformed', and all the furniture seems to be tilting, so that the narrator is pursued even while asleep 'by the feeling that the house was about to fall down.' In *The Emigrants*, Sebald lovingly seizes on eccentric British materials and contraptions. Sebald and his wife dine at the home of Dr Henry Selwyn, the food pushed into the dining room on 'a serving trolley equipped with hotplates, some kind of patented design dating from the Thirties'. (The killer there is 'dating from the Thirties' – this dinner is taking place in the early 1970s.) Later in the same book, Sebald tells the moving story of how he came from Germany in 1966 to England. He was a twenty-two-year-old graduate student, who had studied in Germany and Switzerland, and was now on his way to take up a junior teaching job in the German Department at the University of Manchester. He arrives in the early morning. As his taxi rolls past 'rows of uniform houses, which seemed the more run-down the closer we got to the city centre', Sebald reflects on the fate of this mighty city, one of the engines of the Victorian age, now more like 'a necropolis or mausoleum'. At his small hotel, called the Arosa, he is met at the door by its owner, Mrs Irlam, who is dressed in a pink dressing gown 'that was made of a material found only in the bedrooms of the English lower classes and is unaccountably called candlewick'. (That 'unaccountably called candlewick' being a nice example of how Sebald and his English translators often contrived to make of his prose a strange, homeless melody, neither quite English nor quite German, but some odd mixture of the two.)

Mrs Irlam is a kindly soul, and quickly brings him 'on a silver tray, an electric appliance of a kind I had never seen before', called a 'teas-maid'. This was an ungainly machine, popular at the time, that contained a clock and electric kettle; it could wake you up with morning tea. I remember the one my parents had by the side of their bed, used probably only a handful of times, but reassuring nonetheless. Sebald approaches this cosy English object with mock-solemn gingerliness, as if he were doing anthropology. He places a large photograph of the relic at the centre of his page, and notes that the lime-green phosphorescent glow of the clock face was familiar to him from childhood:

That may be why it has often seemed, when I have thought back to those early days in Manchester, as if the tea maker brought to my room by Mrs Irlam, by Gracie – you must call me Gracie, she said – as if it was that weird and serviceable gadget, with its nocturnal glow, its muted morning bubbling, and its mere presence by day, that kept me holding on to life at a time when I felt a deep isolation in which I might well have become completely submerged. Very useful, these are, said Gracie as she showed me how to operate the teas-maid that November afternoon; and she was right.

How quickly, in this passage, he turns from amusement to something approaching desperation. Sebald's talent for repression – for sounding out the repressions of others and for dramatising his own – is a central element of his writing. When he tells us that the first weeks and months of his time in Manchester were 'a time of remarkable silence and emptiness', his carefully muted adjective simultaneously discloses and hides what must have been an intensely lonely period.

It is hard to imagine how reduced and impoverished life in northern England still was, even in the 1960s; the war dragged a long grey shadow. Sebald knew no one in Manchester, and had applied for the teaching job at the English university largely because he was keen to get out of his native country, and because he had liked the classes given by an Englishman, a former Manchester professor, at his German university, Freiburg. He did not, in fact, stay at the Arosa Hotel, as his lightly fictionalised account has it, but was housed by the university in a single room in a semi-detached 1930s house. After a couple of weeks there, he moved to another single room, this one in a tall, red-brick, turn-of-the-century house about three miles out of the city centre. A black-and-white photograph of this building has a sooty northern grimness that makes it impossible to imagine its version in colour. An academic colleague of Sebald's described the room as 'dark, dingy, and freezing cold'. It contained nothing more than a bed, table and chair. At night, mice ran along the curtain-rail.

The contrast with Sebald's childhood landscape must have been acute. He was born in 1944, in a village in the Bavarian Alps, not far from the Austrian and Swiss borders, and today about two hours by car from Munich – a region of lakes, rivers and mountains that loom over daily life like natural cathedrals. It was an Eden surrounded by flaming swords. Sebald's father was away, fighting in the German army; he didn't return till 1947, having spent two years in a French POW camp. In his study of the Allied bombardment of the German cities, *On the Natural History of Destruction*, Sebald contrasts this remembered paradise with the inferno all around it. 'To this day', when he sees photographs or documentaries dating from the war, he feels 'as if I were its child, so to speak, as if those horrors I did not experience cast a shadow over me, and one from which I shall never entirely emerge':

> I know now that at the time, when I was lying in my bassinet on the balcony of the Seefeld house and looking up at the pale blue sky, there was a pall of smoke in the air all over Europe . . . over the ruins of the German cities, over the camps where untold numbers of people were burnt . . . there was scarcely a place in Europe from which no one had been deported to his death in those years.

Elsewhere in this book, he writes strikingly about how Germany closed civilian ranks after the war, preferring not to examine its crimes but to repress 'the well-kept secret of the corpses built into the foundations of our state, a secret that bound all Germans together in the post-war years, and indeed still binds them'. In interviews, he often said that a large reason for his leaving Germany in 1966 was his awareness that German post-war academic life was as compromised, and as secretive, as life in the home. His work obsessively returns to the horror of foundations that are unfounded; to the idea that, as Walter Benjamin famously put it, every document of civilisation is also a document of barbarism. Sebald expands the definition of 'document' to encompass buildings, states and empires. In *The Rings of Saturn*, he describes at length the murderous machine of Belgian colonialism in the Congo, and pictures modern Brussels, with its 'distinctive ugliness', as 'a sepulchral monument erected over a hecatomb of black bodies'. In *Austerlitz* (translated into English by Anthea Bell), the novel's protagonist, Jacques Austerlitz, realises that the brand-new French national library he is working in, the Bibliothèque Nationale, stands over the old Austerlitz-Tolbiac depot, an enormous clearing house 'to which the Germans brought all the loot they had taken from the homes of the Jews of Paris'. Thus the whole sordid business, he continues, 'is buried in the most literal sense beneath the foundations' of the library.

By most accounts, the young Sebald was an unassuming presence at Manchester (where, when he was not teaching, he worked on an unpublished novel, visited junk shops, and walked a great deal, taking photographs of the city's disused factories and cleared slums). At the University of East Anglia, whose School of European Studies he joined in 1970, and where he spent the rest of his life, he was similarly modest. He taught well-liked classes on Kafka, German cinema, nineteenth-century German fiction and twentieth-century European drama. But many of his colleagues were only faintly aware of the existence of his creative work. The university was well known for its graduate creative writing programme, then one of the few in Britain, but only towards the end of his life, when Sebald's fame was inescapable, was he employed in this area. He had been teaching creative writing for only a term when, on 14 December 2001, near Norwich, he lost control of his car, swerved in front of a truck, and was killed.

He was fifty-seven, and his sudden death came as a desolation. There was to be no more work from a writer who had rapidly established himself as one of the most deeply serious and ambitious contemporary writers, whose fraught intelligence had reckoned, and self-reckoned, with the gravest questions of European history, and who had fearlessly founded a new literary form – combining essay, fiction and photography – in order to probe those questions in new ways.

Like many of his readers, I remember waking up to the blindsiding newspaper report – *W. G. Sebald, Elegiac German Novelist, Is Dead at 57* – and the way the impossible newsprint seemed to cloud before one's eyes. But the loss was acute not only because of his work's undoubted seriousness; the playful side of Sebald's originality made him also a deeply interesting and unpredictable artificer. You wondered what he would do next, what odd precarious success he would come up with; his books were such strange hybrid forms.

Writing and illustration have of course long coexisted, but few writers have ever used photographs in quite the way Sebald does, scattering them, without captions, throughout the text, so that the reader can't be sure exactly how the writing and the photographs relate to each other, or indeed whether the photographs disclose what they purport to. Roland Barthes's great essay on photography, *Camera Lucida* (a book Sebald knew well, and with which his own work is in deep dialogue), is relatively conventional by contrast: the photographs are captioned and clearly reproduced. Sebald's photographs have a fugitive, eccentric atmosphere. They are anti-illustrative, because many of them are low-quality snaps, dingy, hard to decipher, and often atrociously reproduced. He plays with this unreliability in *The Emigrants*, when he includes a photograph of himself standing on a beach in New Jersey, probably taken by his uncle in late 1981 or early 1982. Is it really Sebald? All you can do is stare and stare at it. The photograph is so poor – the author's face little more than a generic blur – that the reader, too, is left standing on loose sand, where all surety is tidally erased and replaced.

And then there is the oddity of Sebald's prose. If you don't care for his writing, you can feel that he's a postmodern antiquarian, a super-literate academic who stitched together a pastiche of his many nineteenth- and twentieth-century influences, and infused the result with doomy melancholy and unease. The English (and half-German) poet Michael Hofmann accused Sebald of 'nailing literature on to a home-made fog – or perhaps a nineteenth-century ready-made fog'. There may be something in that complaint. Probably the most frequent sentence in all of Sebald is some variant of 'Nowhere was there a living soul to be seen'. Wherever the Sebaldian narrator finds himself, the landscape is uncannily unpeopled. He may be walking down an Italian street, or arriving in Lowestoft, or driving through Manchester in the early morning, or meeting Jacques Austerlitz on the promenade at Zeebrugge. Wherever it may be, there is rarely a single 'soul' to be seen, and almost without exception Sebald employs the antique, somewhat 'literary' locution of 'soul' or 'living soul'. (The English translators are loyal here to Sebald's German, where '*lebende Seele*' is the usual term.)

Sebald's work can put you in mind of Diderot selling his library to Catherine the Great: he seems to be downloading everything he has ever read. There is the ghost of the nineteenth-century Austrian writer Adalbert Stifter (the menaced but curious traveller, afoot in a strange, forbidding landscape); of Walter Benjamin (the elaborate analogies and formal diction); of Thomas Bernhard (the tendency to insistent, comic exaggeration); of Peter Handke; and above all of Kafka. As with Kafka's protagonists, the Sebaldian narrator is easily estranged and thrown off balance by what should be customary interactions: booking a hotel room, driving down the New Jersey Turnpike, sitting in a London railway station, taking a train in his native Germany. As in Kafka, there are an unusual number of physically eccentric, deformed or dwarfish figures. In *The Emigrants*, Dr Henry Selwyn is looked after by a housemaid called Elaine, who wears her hair 'shorn high up in the nape, as the inmates of asylums do', and who has the disquieting habit of breaking into 'strange, apparently unmotivated, whinnying laughter'.

At times he overdoes the Gothic pastiche. In *The Rings of Saturn*, the atmosphere at Amsterdam's Schiphol airport strikes the troubled narrator as 'so strangely muted that one might have thought one was already a good way beyond this world'. What the reader might take on faith if encountered in Büchner's *Lenz* (a garish account of a man's fall into madness, written in 1836, which Sebald taught at Norwich), is a little stagey, even portentous, when it concerns merely a modern academic who closely resembles Sebald, a character who happens to be doing a bit of book research and passing through an ordinary European airport.

Yet Sebald also extracts from this self-conscious antiquarianism something unaccountable: a mysterious contemporary stillness, an other-worldliness of the present. His books are celebrated for reproducing old photographs, but his very prose functions *like* an old, unidentified photograph. Consider this troublingly lovely description, from *Austerlitz*, of the German army entering Prague:

> Next morning, at first light, the Germans did indeed march into Prague in the middle of a heavy snowstorm which seemed to make them appear out of nowhere. When they crossed the bridge and their armored cars were rolling up Narodni a profound silence fell over the whole city. People turned away, and from that moment they walked more slowly, like somnambulists, as if they no longer knew where they were going.

Who is speaking? It is characteristic of Sebald's procedures that what we are reading here is not ascribed directly to the author. Jacques Austerlitz, on the hunt for his origins, has travelled to Prague, where he tracks down Vera Rysanova, who was his nursemaid in the 1930s. So in this passage, Jacques Austerlitz is recalling, to the book's narrator (back in contemporary London), what Vera told *him* in Prague about the German occupation of that city: a long chain of at least three story-tellers (Vera–Austerlitz–narrator/Sebald), and more decades. This perhaps accounts for the smothered, recessed diction. The prose has the usual formality of Sebald's work, along with his strain of almost pedantic exaggeration ('and from that moment they walked more slowly'). It is powerful because it is both real and unreal, at once a vivid picture and a frozen allegory. Sebald is here describing a collective death, a falling away; the people in this word-picture, like the felled trees he describes in *The Rings of Saturn*, are as if caught in a kind of swoon. There are people here, but they are in the process of becoming unpeople.

Sebald's petrified or empty landscapes are often places like this, where the living have disappeared into death; or where the living have fallen into the obscurity of death even while still alive. *The Emigrants*, probably Sebald's best book, is a set of four stories about people who have fallen in this way, as if dispossessed by history. They are subject to a kind of inner wasting disease, their lives dwindling like afternoon light. The book is closer to documentary than any of his other creative work. Names and some details have been changed, yet the written lives of these characters follow very closely their actual contours.

The book opens with Dr Henry Selwyn, whom Sebald and his wife encountered in 1970, in the grounds of a country house in Norfolk. A retired physician, Selwyn appears to live like a patrician hermit, having largely abandoned the big house for a stone folly he has built in his garden. Sometime after encountering Sebald and telling the author his life-story, Dr Selwyn committed suicide. There is Paul Bereyter, a character based on one of Sebald's childhood teachers. In 1984, Sebald tells us, he learned of Bereyter's suicide, and set out to discover the reasons. Bereyter was a quarter Jewish, and under Nazi laws was banned from teaching in the mid-1930s, just as he was embarking on his cherished career. A woman he courted, Helen Hollaender, disappeared from his life, and was doubtless deported, 'probably to Theresienstadt in the first instance'. Bereyter never quite recovered from these terrible deprivations. The third story concerns one of Sebald's great-uncles, Adelwarth, a German immigrant who worked as a valet in the United States, and whose life, as an immigrant and closeted homosexual, bore immense strains. Uncle Adelwarth ends up in an Ithaca asylum. The fourth story, 'Max Ferber', probably the most fictive of the four tales, is based on the life of the British painter Frank Auerbach, who at the age of seven was sent from his native Germany to Britain, and whose parents died in the Holocaust.

Sebald's quiet, bashful, mysteriously subaqueous prose brings alive the paradoxical combination of drift and paralysis that has afflicted these lives. These men hid their wounds, but their lives were stained with the effort of that subterfuge. Sebald is generously adept at making these wounds speak. Dr Selwyn, for instance, appears at first to be an eccentric English gentleman, a recognisable Norfolk oddity – at one moment, he fires a rifle from the window of his house, a gun, he explains, that he needed in India when he worked there as a young surgeon. But in the course of little more than twenty pages, a new revelation grows. First, there is the strangeness of the doctor's isolation in the garden folly. Then there is the erotic and emotional deadness of Dr Selwyn's marriage to Elli, a wealthy Swiss heiress. At dinner one evening, Selwyn speaks about the time he spent in the Alps, just after he had graduated from Cambridge in 1913. This was when he developed an intense fondness for his mountaineering guide, a much older man of sixty-five. There is the suggestion, faintly implied but discernible, that Selwyn's admiration was probably love. A year or so later, when Sebald has moved out of Selwyn's house, the two men meet again, and Selwyn tells the author the rest of his story. He was, by birth, a Lithuanian Jew, who left for England in 1899 and changed his name from Hersch Seweryn. For a long time, he concealed his 'true background' from his wife, and now wonders whether the failure of his marriage had to do with 'revealing the secret of my origins, or simply the decline of love'. We realise that Selwyn's life has been structured by repression, beautifully mimicked in this regard by Sebald's writing, which is similarly structured by omission. When Selwyn talks about revealing 'the secret of my origins' (it is the only phrase we are offered), he officially means his Jewishness; but perhaps unconsciously he also means his homosexuality?

Sebald has been an extremely influential writer (in English, Teju Cole, Aleksandar Hemon, Edmund de Waal, Garth Greenwell and Rachel Cusk have all learned from him), and no more so than in the way he writes about whole lives. Released from the formulas of falsity that contaminate much realistic fiction – drama, dialogue, the pretense of 'real time', the cause-and-effect of motive – the writer proceeds like a biographer who sees everything after it has happened; or like the Lord in Psalm 121, who knows 'thy going out and thy coming in'. Sebald understands that a life is an edifice, which we build partly to hide its foundations. And the difference between an edifice and a ruin may be hard to detect. The form of a life is only a frame. Dr Selwyn told the author only what he could bear to tell, a narration honeycombed with elisions: how little we truly know of even a close friend's interiority.

Because we are not God, our narration of another's life is a pretence of knowledge; simultaneously an attempt to know and a confession of how little we know. Most conventional fiction, with its easy inherited confidence, ignores or hides this element of confession, and conceals the epistemological difficulty of the task; that concealment is what we find comfy and consoling about most conventional fiction. Sebald makes the unreliability of this labour a central element of his writing: it is why the stories in his books, like the one Vera tells to Jacques Austerlitz about the Germans entering Prague, tend to be passed along long chains of narration, a narrative traffic that produces, in that novel, the characteristic repetitive formulation 'said Austerlitz', or even 'as Vera had told me, said Austerlitz', or my favourite: 'From time to time, so Vera recollected, said Austerlitz, Maximilian would tell the tale how once . . .' The point of these chains – which resemble those columns of Berliners passing along buckets of rubble just after the war – is that we, the readers, are necessarily at the very end of them. Dr Selwyn tells his repressed tale to the author, who then passes a slightly less repressed version on to us. Likewise with Vera to Austerlitz. Sebald's attempt at decipherment must become, in part, *ours*: we are trying to puzzle this material out, just as he, the fanatical author-researcher, is trying to do.

This effort of retrieval is felt most acutely whenever we stare at one of Sebald's dusky, uncaptioned photographs; and it is not coincidental that photography plays the largest role in the two Sebald books that deal centrally with the Holocaust, *The Emigrants* and *Austerlitz*. In a sense, retrieval is the very theme of *Austerlitz*, whose protagonist grows up thinking of himself as a Welsh boy named Dafydd Elias, only to discover as a teenager that he is a wartime refugee whose true name is Jacques Austerlitz. Even then, it takes many years before Jacques Austerlitz learns exactly how he came to England, and where he came from, and this journey of recovery consumes the entirety of Sebald's dense novel. In the early 1990s, Austerlitz travels to Prague, interviews Vera Rysanova, and learns about his family's fate: that he was put on a train for London in 1939, that his mother was sent to Theresienstadt, and that his father, who escaped to Paris, was last heard of in the French camp of Gurs (from where many Jews were deported to Auschwitz).

Theodor Adorno once suggested that the dead are at our mercy, and memory their only rescuer: 'So the memory is the only help that is left to them. They pass away into it, and if every deceased person is like someone who was murdered by the living, so he is also like someone whose life they must save, without knowing whether the effort will succeed.' This sounds like a confession of survivor's guilt, but Adorno wrote these words before the war, in 1936. From his student days onwards, Sebald was a deep reader of Adorno, though as far as I know he does not quote this sentence anywhere in his work. It might be the epigraph for all his writing. What animates Sebald's project is the apparently paradoxical task of saving the dead; unable to save the dead, we feel judged by them in our failure. That paradox appears at its most acute when we look not at words about people but at photographs of people, since these documents have a presence and palpability that words cannot quite capture. As Roland Barthes suggests, photographs 'attest that what I see has existed'. In photography, he adds, 'the presence of the thing (at a certain past moment) is never metaphoric'. But when we look at old photographs, we are mostly looking at people who are dead: people we failed to rescue. Barthes goes further, and claims that 'whether or not the subject is already dead, every photograph is this catastrophe'.

But if the photograph attests that 'what I see has existed', what happens when a *novelist* inserts into his text uncaptioned photographs of ambiguous veracity? What can 'the presence of the thing' possibly mean in a photograph whose authority we doubt, and which belongs to a text that is itself a hybrid of document and fiction? Isn't a photograph in a novel always 'metaphoric' in some way? Like *The Emigrants*, *Austerlitz* is full of uncaptioned black-and-white photographs – of Wittgenstein's eyes; Breendonk prison, where the Jewish resistance fighter Jean Améry was tortured by the Nazis; Liverpool Street station, where the young children of the Kindertransport first arrived in London; human skeletons; what appears to be an old staircase inside a pre-war apartment building in Prague; the Bibliothèque Nationale, and, notably, a photograph of Jacques Austerlitz as a small boy, a photograph supposedly handed to Jacques by his childhood nursemaid in Prague. This picture, of a fair-haired boy dressed as a page boy, in cape and knickerbockers, adorns the cover of the American edition of Sebald's novel.

Some of these pictures are what they purport to be (Breendonk, Wittgenstein's eyes, the Bibliothèque Nationale); about others, one can't be sure – that staircase, for instance, could be from any number of pre-war apartment buildings, anywhere in Europe. And what does it mean to stare at a photograph of a little boy who is 'supposed' to be Jacques Austerlitz, when 'Jacques Austerlitz' is nothing more than a fictional character invented by W. G. Sebald? Who is the *actual* boy who stares at us from the cover of this novel? We will probably never know. It is an eerie photograph, and Sebald makes Austerlitz say of it (when Vera first hands it to him):

> I have studied the photograph many times since, the bare, level field where I am standing, although I cannot think where it was . . . I examined every detail under a magnifying glass without once finding the slightest clue. And in doing so I always felt the piercing, inquiring gaze of the page boy who had come to demand his dues, who was waiting in the gray light of dawn on the empty field for me to accept the challenge and avert the misfortune lying ahead of him.

The boy does seem to be scrutinising us, demanding something from us, and I imagine that this is why, when Sebald came across it, he chose it. Presumably, he found it in a box of old postcards and snaps, in one of the antique shops he enjoyed rummaging around in. In 2011, I had a chance to examine the Sebald archive – manuscripts, old photographs, letters, and the like – at the Deutsches Literaturarchiv in Marbach am Neckar, and there I found the postcard which bears the boy's image. Eager for 'a clue', I turned it over. On the reverse side, there was nothing more than a price and an English town, written in ink: 'Stockport, 30p.'

Scandalously, in the very area of historical research where documentary fidelity is sacred, Sebald introduces the fraught note of the unreliable. Not of course because he disdained the documentary impulse, but on the contrary, in order to register that he himself, who was not Jewish and had no direct connection to the Shoah, was only a survivor of the survivors – and even then only in a figurative sense. And also perhaps to register that the novelist who writes, of all outrageous things, *fiction* about the Holocaust, cannot, must not, have a comfortable and straightforward relation to the real. For there I was, standing in a German library, searching for clues, peering intently at a photograph of a boy whose name will be forever lost, and replicating the very gesture of decipherment that the fictional character Jacques Austerlitz describes in Sebald's novel.

Sebald has some beautiful words in *Austerlitz* about how, just as we have appointments to keep in the future, it may be that we also have appointments to keep in the past, 'in what has gone before and is for the most part extinguished'. We must go there, he writes, into the past, in search of places and people who have some connection with us, 'on the far side of time, so to speak'. That last phrase puts me in mind of a famous passage from *Middlemarch*, in which George Eliot says that if we were truly open to all the suffering in the world, it would be like hearing the grass grow and the squirrel's heartbeat, and we would die 'of that roar which lies on the other side of silence'. Most of us, she finishes, manage to live by wadding ourselves with stupidity. We survive only by ignoring the faint but terrible roar. In his great work, Sebald visited that far side of time which was also the other side of silence. He could not ignore it.

Becoming Them

NIETZSCHE SAYS SOMEWHERE that the industrious, virtuous English ruined Sundays. I knew this at the age of twelve – that is, the Sunday part, and the ruination part. When I was growing up, Sunday morning was all industry and virtue: the dejected selection of formal clothes (tie, jacket, grey trousers); a quick pre-ecclesiastical breakfast; lace-up shoes handed to my father, master of the polishing arts (that oily Kiwi cake, glistening in its tin like food). Then the eternal boredom of church, with its ponderously enthusiastic adults. And after that, Sunday lunch, as regimented as the Hapsburg Sunday lunches of brisket of beef and cherry dumplings that the Trotta family eats week after week in *The Radetzky March*. A joint of beef, or of lamb, or of pork, with gravy, roast potatoes, and a selection of fatally weakened vegetables (softened cauliflower, tattered Brussels, pale parsnips, all boiled punitively, as if to get the contagion out of them). It was the 1970s, in a small town in the north of England, but it could almost have been the 1870s. The only unusual element in this establishment was that my father cooked lunch. He cooked everything in our family, and always had; my mum was never interested in the kitchen, and gladly conceded that territory.

After lunch, tired and entitled – but sweetly, not triumphantly – my father slumped into the sofa in the sitting room, and fell asleep to classical music on the record player. He fell asleep gradually, not really intending to succumb. He wanted to be awake for one of his favourite composers, a narrow, rich cycle of Beethoven (piano sonatas and string quartets), Haydn (string quartets) and Schubert (lieder, especially *Die Winterreise*). These three masters were as unvarying as the rotation of Sunday beef, lamb and pork. My brother and sister and I were all musical children, so we would be appealed to, as we crept towards the door. 'Don't go yet – you'll miss the next one, "Der Lindenbaum", which Fischer-Dieskau does particularly well. He's got an advantage over Peter Schreier.' My father's musical discussion involved grading performers; though an intelligent auditor, he didn't play a musical instrument. So my memory of those Sunday afternoons is as much a memory of names as of music: 'No one has really approached the young Barenboim, in those late sonatas, except Kempff. But of course Kempff is a completely different pianist. I once heard Solomon play the last two in London. He was very fast and powerful.' Richter, Kempff, Schnabel, Barenboim, Brendel, Ogden, Pollini, Gilels, Arrau, Michelangeli, Fischer-Dieskau, Schreier, Schwartzkopf, Sutherland, Lott, Vickers, Pears – all the precious names of childhood.

I thought of those Sundays when Dietrich Fischer-Dieskau died a few months ago. Some of the obituaries suggested that he became a brand-name for a kind of smooth, dependable quality. That's how he functioned in our household (which isn't to deny his beauty as a singer, or the validity of my father's admiration of him). I grew to be wary of that rich emollience of tone, that tempered, bourgeois liquidity. Just as intolerantly, I got restless with the way my father would look up from the sofa, and calmly utter the double-barrelled guarantee: 'Fischer-Dieskau, of course . . . Marvellous.' The name had the shape and solidity of some dependable manufacturer or department store, a firm that would never go bust. Aston Martin, Rolls-Royce, Harvey Nichols, Austin Reed, Royal Enfield, Fischer-Dieskau. My father had great faith in reliable British companies (often against the evidence, it should be said). It was a joke in our family. Once at dinner, a wall plug exploded, with a mild, odorous flash. Unflappable, imperturbable, my dad went to the wall and examined the plug, like the scientist he was. 'M K and Crabtree, he said, intoning the name of the manufacturer. 'Totally dependable'. We all laughed at this stolid evenness of response, while perhaps gratefully aware that this was the kind of man you would want around in a real crisis. Fischer-Dieskau, like MK and Crabtree, was 'totally dependable', though inconveniently German.

Boredom, Sunday boredom . . . I blamed Christianity. On those English Sundays, the knowledge that all the shops were religiously shut (even the little back-alley record shop, Musicore, where my best friend and I fingered the new LPs) simmered like a sullen summer heat, and made me lethargic. There was nowhere to go, nothing to do. My brother was somehow more adept than I at slipping away; he made it to his bedroom, and I would hear Robert Plant whining up there, the euphoric, demonic, eunuch antidote to

Fischer-Dieskau's settled baritone. (*I should have quit you, long time ago.*) My mother steered clear. So my sister and I would sit with my father, and sometimes when he fell asleep, we would fall asleep too.

For ages, I associated those three composers with that Sunday world. Haydn was killed for me. Even now I can't listen to him, despite the adulatory testimony of musicians and composers I know. For quite a long time, I thought of Schubert only as the composer of snowy, trudging lieder. I refused to hear the limpid beauty of the songs, or the dark anguish; I knew nothing about the exquisite piano sonatas, now among my favourite pieces. Most terribly, I thought of Beethoven as the calm confectioner of the 'Moonlight' Sonata; I heard the beauty, but nothing much more. It was music to go to sleep to, on a Sunday afternoon. A fool's assessment. All the tension and dissonance, the jumpy rhythms, the fantastic experimental fugues and variations, the chromatic storms, the blessed plateaus (the sunlit achievement, once you have got through the storms, as at the end of op. 109 and op. 111) – in short, all the fierce complex modernity of Beethoven was lost to me.

And then Beethoven came back, as probably my father knew he always would, in my early twenties, at a time of solitude and anxiety, came back roaring with the difficult romanticism that my incuriosity had repressed in childhood. I can't now imagine life without Beethoven, can't imagine not listening to and thinking about Beethoven (being spoken to by him, and speaking with him). And like my father, I have quite a few recordings of the piano sonatas, especially the last three, and I listen to the young Barenboim playing, and think to myself, as my father did: '*Not quite as lucid as Kempff, but*

much better than Gould, who's unreliable on Beethoven, and
maybe more interesting than Brendel, and yes, I think I just
heard him make a little mistake, which Pollini certainly never
does . . .'

Sometimes I catch myself and think, self-consciously:
You are now listening to a Beethoven piano sonata, just as your
father did . . . And at that moment, I feel a mixture of satisfaction and rebellion. Rebellion, for all the obvious reasons.
Satisfaction, because it's natural to resemble one's parents, and
there is a resigned pleasure to be had from the realisation. I
like that my voice is exactly the same pitch as my father's,
and can be mistaken for it. But then I hear myself speaking
to my children just as he spoke to me, in exactly the same
tone and with the same fatherly melody, and I am dismayed
by the plagiarism of inheritance. How unoriginal can one be?
I sneeze the way he does, with a slightly theatrical whooshing
sound. I snore like him (identical sinuses). I say 'Yes, yes' just
as he does, calmly. The other day, I saw that I have the same
calves, with the shiny, unlit pallor I found a bit ugly when I
was a boy, and with those oddly hairless patches at the back,
which my father always unscientifically blamed on trouser
cloth rubbing at the skin. Sometimes, when I am sitting
doing nothing, I have the eerie sense that my mouth and eyes
are set just like his. Like him, I am irritatingly phlegmatic at
times of crisis. There must be a few differences: I won't decide
to become a priest in my fifties, as he did. I'm not religious,
don't go to church as he does, so my Sundays are much less
dull than those of my childhood (and the shops are all open
now, a liberty which brings its own universal boredom). I'm
no scientist (he was a zoologist). I am less moral, less ascetic,

far more materialistic ('pagan' would be my self-reassuring euphemism). And I bet he's never googled himself.

This summer I happened to reread a beautiful piece of writing by Lydia Davis, called 'How Shall I Mourn Them?' It is barely two and a half pages long, and is just a list of questions:

> Shall I keep a tidy house, like L.?
> Shall I develop an unsanitary habit, like K.?
> Shall I sway from side to side a little as I walk, like C.?
> Shall I write letters to the editor, like R.?
> Shall I retire to my room often during the day, like R.?
> Shall I live alone in a large house, like B.?
> Shall I treat my husband coldly, like K.?
> Shall I give piano lessons, like M.?
> Shall I leave the butter out all day to soften, like C.?

A few years ago, when I first read this story (or whatever you want to call it), I understood it to be about mourning departed parents, partly because a certain amount of Davis's recent work has appeared to touch obliquely on the death of her parents. I think that the initials could belong to the author's friends – seen, over the years, falling into the habits of grief. It is a gentle comedy of Davis's that those habits of grief are so ordinary (piano lessons, leaving out the butter) that they amount to the habits of life, and that therefore the answer to the title's question must be: 'I can't *choose* how to mourn them, as your verb, "shall", suggests. I can only mourn them haplessly, accidentally, by surviving them. So I shall mourn them just by living.' But I spoke recently to a friend about this story, and she felt I had missed something. 'Isn't it also about *becoming* one's parents, about taking on their very habits and tics after they disappear? So it's also about preserving those habits once they've disappeared, whether you want to or not.' My friend told me that before her mother died, she had had very little interest in gardening (one of her mother's passions); after her mother's death, she began to garden, something that now brings her real happiness.

If you are mourning your parents just by becoming them, then presumably you can mourn them before they are dead: certainly I have spent my thirties and forties journeying through a long realisation that I am decisively my parents' child, that I am destined to share many of their gestures and habits, and that this slow process of becoming them, or becoming more like them, is, like the Roman *ave atque vale*, both an address and a farewell.

My parents are still alive, in their mid-eighties now. But in the last two years my wife has watched her father die, of oesophageal cancer, and seen her mother, only in her late seventies, slip into severe, wordless dementia. She has had one kind of grief for her father; and she has had a different grief for her mother, for an absence that is both a loss and the anticipation of further loss – grief in stages, terraced grief. I say to her: 'I haven't yet had to go through what you've gone through.' And she replies: 'But you will, you know that, and it won't be so long.'

My parents know much better than I do that *it won't be so long*; that their life together is precarious, and balances on the little plinth of their fading health. And there is nothing unique in this prospect: it's just their age, and mine. Twice this year my father has been hospitalised. When he disappears like this, my mother struggles to survive, because she has macular degeneration, and can't see. The second time, I raced over to damp Scotland, to find her almost confined to the dining room, where there is a strong (and pungently ugly) electric fire, and living essentially on cereal; the carpet under the dining table was littered with oats, like the floor of a hamster's cage. When he came out of hospital, my father had a cane, for the first time in his robust life, and seemed much weaker. My brother took him round the supermarket in a wheelchair.

I spent a week at my parents' home, helping out, and it took a couple of days for me to register that something was missing. It nagged at me, faintly, and then more strongly, and finally I realised what it was: there was no music in the house. And I realised that in fact there had been no music for a while; that several previous trips there had been marked by the same lack. I asked my father why he was no longer listening to music, and was shocked to discover that his CD player had been broken for more than a year, and that he had put off replacing it because a new one seemed expensive. He was much less perturbed than I was by this state of affairs. I could hardly imagine my parents' life without thinking of him sitting in an armchair, while Haydn or Beethoven or Schubert played. But of course, this idea of him is itself an old memory of mine, and thus a picture of a younger man's habits – he is frozen as the middle-aged father of my childhood, not the rather different old man whom I now rarely see because I live three thousand miles away, a man who doesn't care too much whether he listens to music or not. So even as I become him, he becomes someone else. Perhaps, I thought, he is simply too busy looking after my mother to have time to relax. And he has a lot to do: he is the cook, the driver, the shopper, the banker, the person who uses the computer, who gets wood or coal for the fire, who mends things when they break, who puts the cat out and who locks up at night. Perhaps he is too busy being anxious about my mother, being slightly afraid for both of them, to sit like he used to do, triumphant and calm and secure.

Or perhaps this is just my fear projected onto him. When I was a teenager, I used to think that Philip Larkin's line, about how *life is first boredom, then fear*, was right about boredom and wrong about fear. What's so fearful about life? Now, at forty-seven, I think it should be the other way round: life is first fear, then boredom (as perhaps the fearful Larkin of 'Aubade' knew). Fear for oneself, fear for those one loves. I sleep very poorly these days; I lie awake, full of apprehensions. All kinds of them, starting with the small stuff and rising. How absurd that I should be paid to write book reviews! How long is *that* likely to last? And what's the point of the bloody things? Why on earth would the money *not* run out? Will I be alive in five years? Isn't some kind of mortal disease likely? How will I cope with death and loss – with the deaths of my parents, or worse, and unimaginably, of my wife, or children? How appalling to lose my mind, as my mother-in-law did! Or to lose all mobility but not one's mind, and become a prisoner, like poor Tony Judt. If I faced such a diagnosis, would I have the courage to kill myself? Does my father have pancreatic cancer? And on and on.

There is nothing very particular about these anxieties. They're banal, even a little comic, as the mother in Per Petterson's novel *I Curse the River of Time* understands when some bad medical news is delivered: 'Good Lord, here I've been lying awake night after night, year after year, especially when the children were small, terrified of dying from lung cancer, and then I get cancer of the stomach. What a waste of time!' It's just the river of time, and a waste of time. But there it is. And sometimes I murmur to myself, repetitively, partly to calm myself down, 'How shall I mourn them?' How indeed? For it sounds like the title of a beautiful song, a German lament, something my father might have listened to on a Sunday afternoon, when he still did.

2013

Don Quixote's Old and
New Testaments

THE WINDMILLS THAT DON QUIXOTE mistakes for giants have something in common with the madeleine that makes Marcel's memory buds salivate: both occur conveniently early in very long books that are, in English at least, more praised than read. And Cervantes may resemble Proust in another way. Both are comic writers, properly snagged in the mundane, whose fiction has too often been etherealised out of existence. Miguel de Unamuno, the relentlessly idealising Spanish philosopher, considered *Don Quixote* a 'profoundly Christian epic' and the true 'Spanish Bible', and correspondingly managed to write about the novel as if not a single comic episode occurred in it. W. H. Auden thought that *Don Quixote* was a portrait of a Christian saint; and Unamuno's unlikely American supporter Harold Bloom reminds us that *Don Quixote*, though it 'may not be a scripture', nonetheless captures all humanity, as Shakespeare does – which sounds more like religious praise than secular caution.

So it is worth reminding ourselves of the gross, the worldly, the violent and, above all, the comic in *Don Quixote* – worth reminding ourselves that we *are* permitted the odd secular guffaw while reading it. If all of modern fiction comes out of the Knight's cape, one reason might be that Cervantes's novel contains most of the major comic tropes, from the farcical to the delicately ironic. First, there is the comedy of egotism – the 'But enough about my work, what do *you* think of my work?' grand manner, brilliantly exploited by Tartuffe, and by Jane Austen's Mr Collins, who proposes to Elizabeth Bennet by listing all the ways in which he will benefit from marriage. Don Quixote is the great chivalric egotist, never more egotistical than when he appears to be most chivalrous. After he and poor Sancho Panza have suffered several adventures, including a beating by some drovers from Yanguas and being tossed in a blanket by a gang of men, Don Quixote has the nerve to tell his servant that these things are evil enchantments and so are not really happening to Sancho: 'Therefore you must not grieve for the misfortunes that befall me, for you have no part in them.' This is the knight who, finding that he can't sleep, wakes up his servant, on the principle that 'it is in the nature of good servants to share the griefs of their masters and to feel what they are feeling, if only for appearance's sake'. No wonder that Sancho elsewhere defines a knight adventurer as 'someone who's beaten and then finds himself emperor'.

The egotist is never very good at laughing at himself, laughable though he often is. Cervantes has a subtle scene in which the Knight and his servant are riding in the hills and are stopped by a loud noise. Sancho Panza weeps with terror, and Don Quixote is moved by his tears. When they finally discover that the noise comes from 'six wooden fulling hammers', pounding away in a cloth mill, Don Quixote looks at Sancho, and sees that 'his cheeks were puffed out and his mouth full of laughter, clear signs that he would soon explode, and Don Quixote's melancholy was not so great that he could resist laughing at the sight of Sancho, and when Sancho saw that his master had begun, the floodgates opened with such force that he had to press his sides with his fists to keep from bursting with laughter'. Don Quixote gets cross with Sancho for laughing at him, and hits him with his lance, complaining, 'In all the books of chivalry I have read, which are infinite in number, I have never found any squire who talks as much with his master as you do with yours.' As so often in Cervantes's novel, the reader travels, in a page or two, through different chambers of laughter: affectionate, ironic, satirical, harmonious.

Don Quixote is the greatest of all fictional enquiries into the relation between fiction and reality, and so a good deal of the novel's comedy is self-conscious, generated when one or more of the characters seems to step out of the book and appeal either to a non-fictional reality or directly to the audience (a staple of pantomime performance and *commedia dell'arte*). The second volume of *Don Quixote*, published in 1615, ten years after the first, throws irony on irony, as the Knight and his sidekick set out once again on their adventures, only to discover that they have become celebrities, because, in the interim, a book about their escapades has appeared – the first volume we have just been reading. Cervantes delights in the epistemological hornet's nest into which Don Quixote and Sancho stumble in this second volume, as they assert their reality by recourse to a prior fiction whose culmination they are now enacting. But in the first volume, long before these complexities arise, Sancho, after being beaten by the drovers from Yanguas, pleads with his master, 'Señor, since these misfortunes are the harvest reaped by chivalry, tell me, your grace, if they happen very often or come only at certain times.' Sancho, as it were, winks at the audience, as if to say, 'I know that I and my master are playing a role.' The awful poignancy of the novel is that the Knight does not.

Sancho's request is perfectly reasonable: if violence is to be cartoonish, the laws of the genre should be observed, and we should be given fair notice – the banana skin seen in advance on the sidewalk. And, certainly, many of the cartoon conventions appear in *Don Quixote*. The two heroes are never, it seems, seriously damaged, despite the thrashings they suffer. They always peel their flattened silhouettes off the ground. There is slapstick, too: at one moment, after Don Quixote has been attacked by the shepherds whose sheep he has attempted to kill, he asks Sancho to peer into his mouth to see how many teeth have been knocked out. As he is doing so, Don Quixote vomits in his face. Sancho promptly vomits back onto Don Quixote. There is plenty of such low comedy, including an inn that, like the cheese shop in the Monty Python sketch, is out of everything that is requested.

Nowadays, it can be tedious to wade through all the needlessly spilled blood: Don Quixote is pounded with a lance by a mule driver who beats him 'as if he were threshing wheat'; another mule driver hits him so hard that his mouth is bathed in blood; 'half an ear' is cut off by a Basque adversary; his ribs are crushed by the drovers from Yanguas; the shepherds knock his teeth out; and he is stoned by the convicts he tries to release. Vladimir Nabokov found it cruel, and never really reconciled himself to the novel. In a Tarantino-tinted age, when 'reality' always seems to get the heavy sideburns of quotation marks, such violence seems less cruel than pointedly unreal, the guarantee of its unreality being the unkillability of its victims. Some of the hysterical realism of modern writers like Pynchon and Rushdie seems to take its cue from Cervantes, the violence having been replaced by perpetual motion.

But Cervantes's violence makes another point, too. It is powerfully anti-idealising. It shows us how the well-intentioned Knight ends up inflicting his good intentions on others. Near the beginning of the book, Don Quixote runs into Andrés, a boy who is being whipped by his master. Certain that his chivalric duty is to free the oppressed, he sends the master packing. Later, Andrés will turn up again, only to explain to Don Quixote and his friends that things turned out 'very different from what your grace imagines'. The boy explains that the master returned and flogged him all the harder, with each blow exulting in how he was making a fool of Don Quixote. As Andrés leaves, he says to Don Quixote that if the Knight ever comes upon him again, even if he's being torn to pieces, 'don't help me and don't come to my aid'. In another incident, Don Quixote attacks a group of priests accompanying a corpse. Convinced that the corpse is that of a knight whose death he must avenge, he charges at the poor priests, breaking the leg of a young man. Quixote introduces himself as a knight whose 'occupation and profession' is to 'wander the world righting wrongs and rectifying injuries'. The young man tartly points out that this can hardly be the case, since he was fine until Don Quixote came along and broke his leg, which will be 'injured for the rest of my life; it was a great misadventure for me to run across a man who is seeking adventures'.

Novel-writing has an entrepreneurial element: to invent a central story that can function at once as a plausible action and as an emblematic or symbolic one is akin to inventing a machine or product, a patent that will run and run. Think of Chichikov travelling around Russia buying up 'dead souls' (Gogol warned a correspondent to garage the novel's subject matter, afraid of giving away his secret invention), or of Bellow's Herzog writing his mental letters to great thinkers and public figures. These are, above all, grand concepts. In *Don Quixote*, a moderately prosperous Spanish gentleman, 'one of those who has a lance and ancient shield on a shelf and keeps a skinny nag and a greyhound for racing', becomes possessed, through reading the stories of chivalric adventures, by the idea that the knights-errant of folklore and fiction were real people; furthermore, it seems 'reasonable and necessary to him, both for the sake of his honour and as a service to the nation, to become a knight-errant and travel the world with his armour and his horse to seek adventures'. When Cervantes invented Don Quixote's madness, and propelled him out onto the Castilian plains to enact it, he set ticking a little hermeneutical clock, by which, miraculously, we are still trying to tell time. Don Quixote's misreadings – his determination to read fiction as reality – license our millions of readings of him, because Cervantes kept the ambition of Don Quixote's journeying as wide and unspecific as possible. We know what Don Quixote thinks he is doing, but what is he really doing? What do his strivings represent? Do his misreadings of the world represent the comic battle of the unsullied Idea doing its best to exist in the brute world of Reality? Or for Idea and Reality should we read Spirit and Flesh? (Poor Sancho, in this scheme, is always seen as Flesh.) Or Literature and Reality? Or is Don Quixote an absolutist artist, striving to shape the recalcitrant world into his vision of it?

That Don Quixote's adventures have been so idealised, not to say Christianised, says more about the idealising tendencies of Christianity than about Cervantes's novel. It is as if those determined to see our foolish Knight as some kind of saint or missionary of the spirit had simply closed their eyes to the mayhem and suffering he causes. Andrés, the flogged boy, is right: Don Quixote's good intentions have perverse consequences. Perhaps Cervantes was interested, then, not only in the pious triumphs of his Knight but also in his pious defeats? And perhaps this interest, despite what may be said about Cervantes's own Catholicism, has a secular, even blasphemous bent? Dostoevsky, who was very interested in Don Quixote, surely saw this when he created the figure of Prince Myshkin, the Idiot, whose Christlike actions have a way of contaminating the world around him. Prince Myshkin is not just too good for the world; he is dangerously too good.

When the young man accompanying the corpse complains to Don Quixote about his broken leg, the two fall into a kind of theological argument, which is really an argument about theodicy – about the ways in which we try to justify God's plan for the world. The young man is a sceptic. He alleges that the dead man was killed by 'God, by means of a pestilential fever'. Don Quixote argues the conventional, orthodox position. 'Not all things . . . happen in precisely the same way,' he says, defending his decision to charge at the priests. For a brief, weird moment, it is as if the young man were likening the Knight to God, to a God whose ways we cannot know, yet whose decisions seem to inflict incomprehensible suffering on us.

Cervantes's novel bristles with little blasphemies like this; it is why the novel is the founder of secular comedy. Don Quixote is often said by his friends and acquaintances to resemble a preacher, a missionary, a holy man. He himself argues that he is doing Christ's work. When he falls into conversation with a priest, the man rebukes the Knight for reading books about chivalry, which are all folly and falsehood. He should instead read the Scriptures. But the great stories of knight-errancy are not fictions, Don Quixote replies. Who could deny, for instance, that Pierres and the fair Magalona really existed? For to this day one can see in the royal armoury 'the peg, slightly larger than a carriage pole, with which the valiant Pierres directed the wooden horse as he rode it through the air'. The priest denies ever having seen this, but the damage is done. Blasphemy hangs like mirage heat. Don Quixote has just defended the reality of ostensible fiction by *arguing from the existence of religious relics*. And the logic is unavoidable: if mere fictions can be taken to be real on the basis of relics, then relics, commonly used to prove the veracity of religion, may be fictions, too. This, in a Catholic country in the midst of Counter-Reformation fervency! Later, Don Quixote will argue that the folkloric 'giant Morgante' must have existed because we all believe – don't we? – that the biblical Goliath existed. Cervantes joins that select company of writers, including Milton, Montaigne and Pierre Bayle, who delight in slipping blasphemy in through the tradesmen's entrance while noisily welcoming divinity at the front gate.

This kind of epistemological teasing continues, as Don Quixote and Sancho find themselves having to prove that they are the legendary figures they claim to be. It is a shame that many readers never get to this second volume, which is both funnier and more affecting than the first. A rough analogy of its action might go like this: Jesus Christ is wandering around first-century Palestine, trying to convince people that he is the true Messiah. It is a difficult task, because John the Baptist, instead of preparing the way for the Messiah, has claimed that *he* is the true Messiah, and has gone and got himself appropriately crucified on Calvary. Since many people have heard of John's death and resurrection, Jesus finds himself being sceptically tested by his audience: can he perform this and that miracle? Moreover, when Jesus hears that John has been crucified on Calvary, he decides to prove his authenticity by changing his plans: he will not now be crucified on Calvary, but will instead travel to Rome to be eaten by lions. Tired, and deeply saddened by the unexpected explosion of his greatest dreams, he sets out for Rome with his dearest disciple and right-hand man, Peter. But Peter, taking pity on him, gets together with some of the disciples and persuades Jesus to give up this Messiah lark, and retire to somewhere nice, like Sorrento. Jesus meekly obeys, arrives in Sorrento, and immediately falls sick and dies, but not before renouncing all claims to divinity and announcing his atheism.

Such a biblical analogy might be the easiest way to decipher the densely subtle games Cervantes plays in the second volume. Don Quixote and his servant are now literary celebrities, because of the publication of Cervantes's first volume, and people want to meet them, put them to the test. Of course, the famous duo have no idea in what light they were depicted by Cervantes, so, in effect, people are laughing behind their backs. Since celebrities prompt mimicry, there is a rival Don Quixote now claiming that he is the real thing, and that our Knight – that is, Cervantes's – is a pretender. But, in addition to all this, Cervantes's novel did, in the real world, inspire an imitation, a book entitled *The Second Volume of the Ingenious Knight Don Quixote de la Mancha*, published in 1614 by one Alonso Fernández de Avellaneda, about whom little is known. Cervantes was already well into the writing of his second volume when he heard about Avellaneda's fraud, and he decided to incorporate it into his own novel. In Chapter 59, Don Quixote hears, through a bedroom wall, two men discussing Avellaneda's book. He is outraged, and quizzes the men about it. When he learns that in Avellaneda's account Don Quixote travels to Saragossa, he decides to travel not to Saragossa (where he had indeed been intending to go) but to Barcelona, 'and in this way I shall proclaim the lies of this modern historian to the world, and then people will see that I am not the Don Quixote he says I am'.

Cervantes's great ironies are false horizons, appearing one after the other. Two fictional characters, in order to prove their 'reality', must appeal to a prior fiction written by the same writer who has now created this second volume of fictional escapades. These fictional characters must then argue with other fictional characters that they are Cervantes's characters and not Avellaneda's. So: there is the novel we are reading (Volume ɪɪ); there is the novel that first created these figures (Volume ɪ); and there is a rival novel about similarly named characters (Avellaneda's actual book). These three books merge to rob 'reality' of its empirical treasure. Reality is simply another broken wall, apparently protecting nobody from scepticism's ravages.

Yet at the moment when Cervantes is at his most playful and self-referential, Don Quixote and Sancho Panza are at their most real. This is the book's great paradox. The second volume belongs to Sancho, who becomes wiser and funnier as the book progresses. His love for Don Quixote is tearfully manifest. And Don Quixote is fighting for his life – which is also to say that he is fighting for his fictionality. It is desperately important for Don Quixote that he be who he says he is, and that everyone believe him. When he gets a traveller, Don Álvaro Tarfe, to agree that he is the *real* Don Quixote and not Avellaneda's, and forces him to sign a certificate to this effect, we laugh but we also shiver at the awfulness of it. Italo Svevo was perhaps thinking of this moment when he had his comic hero Zeno get his doctor to sign a certificate of sanity. Zeno presents it to his father, who, with tears in his eyes, says, 'Ah, then you really are mad!' The reader, with tears in his eyes, says the same as Don Quixote flourishes his certificate. A fantasy that seemed, in the novel's first volume, sometimes a lark, sometimes tedious, often unfathomable becomes, in the second volume, something without which neither Don Quixote nor anyone else can live. All of us want Don Quixote to pursue his madness. We have come to believe in it, partly because, as in Shakespeare, we are made to believe in a character's reality when he himself believes in it so strongly, and partly because we no longer know precisely what 'belief' entails. By the end of the book, we have become little Quixotes, reared on a fictional account of a knight-errant's escapades. We are willing fantasists, unsure of our ground.

It is a tremendous shock when Don Quixote decides to head for home – to retire from his adventuring and become a shepherd. It is an even greater shock when he suddenly dies. He has a fever, is in bed for six days. He sleeps, awakes, and announces himself cured of his madness. He denounces all the 'profane histories of knight errantry'. In one of the greatest comic sentences in the whole book, Cervantes writes that those present, hearing this, 'undoubtedly believed that some new madness had taken hold of him'. Don Quixote calls for Sancho Panza, and asks his forgiveness for 'making you fall into the error into which I fell, thinking that there were and are knights errant in the world'. 'Don't die, Señor' is Sancho's tearful response. Don Quixote makes his will, leaving some money to Sancho, lives on another three days, and then, 'surrounded by the sympathy and tears of those present, gave up the ghost, I mean to say, he died'.

The poverty of the language here, its near-clumsiness and refusal to plume itself up into magnificence, is moving, as if Cervantes himself were overcome with grief at the passing of his creation. Don Quixote has become his own fiction of himself, and cannot live without it. As soon as he renounces it, he must wither away. Yet Sancho Panza remains. And who is Sancho? Earlier in the book, Don Quixote says of Sancho, admiringly, that 'he doubts everything and he believes everything'. Isn't this a fine description of the reader of this novel? Sancho is Don Quixote's reader, who lives on as the book's readers do, all-believing and all-doubting, made both faithful and sceptical by the novel's fidelities and scepticisms, happy inheritors of the Knight's last will and testament.

2003

Dostoevsky's God

I

THE WORLD OF 'THE SLAP' – everyone knows that this is Dostoevsky's world, his 'underground' world of humiliations, affronts, jousts and slights. When, in *The Possessed* (1872), the repulsive revolutionary Peter Verkhovensky visits Kirilov to tell him that he has murdered Shatov, and Kirilov says, 'You've done this to him because he spat in your face in Geneva!', we know we are deep in the underground, profoundly enwebbed, and we know that this spider's psychology is something new in literature.

Consider a few scenes. The narrator of *Notes from Underground* (1864), the underground man, is one day in a tavern when a powerful soldier, an officer, blocked by the narrator, picks him up and moves him out of the way. The narrator is humiliated to have been treated so lightly, and cannot sleep for fantasies about how he will revenge himself. The officer walks every day down the Nevsky Prospect. The narrator follows him, 'admiring' him from a distance. He decides that he will walk in the opposite direction and that when the two men meet, he – the narrator – will not give an inch. But day after day when the moment of physical encounter arrives, he weakens, and moves out of the way just as the officer strides past. At night he wakes up obsessed with the question: 'Why is it invariably I who swerves first? Why precisely me and not him?' Eventually, he does manage to hold his ground, the two men brush shoulders, and the narrator is in ecstasies. He goes home singing Italian arias, feeling properly avenged. The satisfaction, of course, lasts only for a day or two.

In *The Eternal Husband*, a brilliant novella published in 1870, a cuckolded husband, Pavel Pavlovich, whose wife has recently died, travels to Petersburg in order to torment his wife's former lover, Velchaninov. He does indeed torment the lover, not least because the lover does not know for sure if the husband ever discovered the affair. Pavel Pavlovich visits Velchaninov's apartment again and again, teasing and punishing him by withholding the real secret. Does he know of the affair? Yet in typical Dostoevsky fashion, revenge curdles into a sour love. It transpires that the cuckolded husband is really in love with his wife's former lover. He cannot leave him alone, and his 'torture' of him oscillates wildly between expressions of admiration, cringing humility, and savage resentment. The former lover decides that the husband came to Petersburg in order to kill him. He came to Petersburg because he hated him. But, decides the lover, the cuckolded husband loves him too, 'out of spite' – 'the strongest kind of love'. When at the end of the book, the two finally part, the former lover holds his hand out; but the husband cringes away from it. The lover, with derision and insane pride, says, 'If I, if *I* offer you this hand here . . . then you might well take it!'

And finally, a scene from *The Brothers Karamazov*, written in the last years of Dostoevsky's life (1878–81). Fyodor Pavlovich, the old head of the Karamazov family, a clown, buffoon and malefactor, is about to enter a dining room at the local monastery. He has already acted scandalously in the cell of the saintly old monk, Father Zosima. Fyodor decides that he will act scandalously in the dining room too. Why? Because, he thinks to himself, 'it always seems to me, when I go somewhere, that I am lower than everyone else and that they all take me for a buffoon – so let me indeed play the buffoon, because all of you, to a man, are lower than I am'. And as he thinks this, he remembers being asked once why he hated a certain neighbour, to which he had replied: 'He never did anything to me, it's true, but I once played a most shameless, nasty trick on him, and the moment I did it, I immediately hated him for it.'

There is a dark novelty in all this, for sure, but what does it consist of? It is not merely that such characters are, as Dostoevsky believed the Russian soul to be, very 'broad', capable of confusing and unpredictable swervings, full of abysses. Nor is this simply a display of what Stendhal called, in *The Memoirs of a Tourist*, the modern emotions – 'envy, jealousy, and impotent hatred' (Stendhal, after all, is a mere gardener in Dostoevsky's underground, a genial above-grounder by comparison); nor only what is commonly called *ressentiment*. Rousseau may have come closest when he talks of the new inwardness being the replacement of old categories such as virtue and vice with the modern malaise of *amour-soi* and *amour-propre*. For clearly, pride and the deformations of pride are unwashable habits for all but the holiest of Dostoevsky's characters. The underground man, the cuckolded husband and Fyodor Karamazov all seem to act in ways that are against their interests, and what marks their newness, their modernity as fictional characters, is that they do so again and again without cease, and do so, as it were, theoretically: they act like this because their interest is the maintenance of their pride. (By theoretical I mean not that Dostoevsky's interest in psychological oddity is abstract but that it is philosophical; *The Eternal Husband* has indeed a whole chapter of psychological exegesis entitled 'Analysis'.)

When we think of typical Dostoevskian action we surely think of a bewildering mixture of haughtiness and humility, coexistent in the same person, each element oddly menacing. The underground man, that anti-bourgeois banshee, alternately ingratiating and screaming with fury; Peter Verkhovensky, hateful and dominating to his subordinates, but sheepish and adoring with his hero, the child-rapist Stavrogin. And Smerdyakov, the real killer of Fyodor Karamazov, an illegitimate servant who is horrible to his adoptive father but slyly humble before the Karamazov men. And it is not only the menace of pride but the comedy of pride that reverberates throughout Dostoevsky, though comedy is not always associated with Dostoevsky's name. Nothing is funnier in *The Possessed* than the proud, weak governor, Andrei von Lembke, who is being manipulated by Peter Verkhovensky. As the local mayhem mounts, the governor loses his control. He shouts at a group of visitors in his drawing room, 'That's enough!' and marches out, only to trip on the carpet. He stands still for a moment, looks at the carpet, says aloud, 'Have it changed!' and walks out.

Dostoevsky shows us that pride and humility are really one. If you are proud you almost certainly feel humbler than someone in the world, because pride is an anxiety, not a consolation. And if you are humble you almost certainly feel better than someone in the world, because humility is an achievement not a freedom, and the humble have a way of congratulating themselves for being so humble. Pride, one might say, is the sin of humble people and humility is the punishment for proud people, and each reversal represents a kind of self-punishment. Thus Fyodor Karamazov enters the dining room ready to abase himself *because* he disdains everyone else. This sort of logic is hard to find, or hard to find as an explicit psychology, in novelists before Dostoevsky. One has instead to consult the religious weepers and gnashers – Ignatius of Loyola, say, or Kierkegaard – to find anything like it.

But Fyodor enters the dining room, as the underground man walks towards the officer, and as the cuckolded husband comes to Petersburg, for another reason: because he needs other people in order to confirm himself. The underground man admits this; he calls himself 'a retort man', a man who comes 'not from the bosom of nature but from a retort'. This 'dialogism' was most influentially noticed by Mikhail Bakhtin, who posited it as the fundamental principle of Dostoevsky's work. As he writes in *Problems of Dostoevsky's Poetics*:

> What the underground man thinks about most of all is what others think or might think about him; he tries to keep one step ahead of every other consciousness, every other thought about him . . . At all the critical moments of

his confession he tries to anticipate the possible definition or evaluation others might make of him . . . interrupting his own speech with the imagined rejoinders of others.

Thus in Dostoevsky the many pairings, or doublings, in which one character revolves around another, and each is murderously dependent on the other: Peter Verkhovensky and Stavrogin, Raskolnikov and Svidrigailov, Ivan Karamazov and Smerdyakov, Velchaninov and Pavel Pavlovich. In Fyodor's case – and perhaps it is the case with any colossal egotism – other people appear to have become himself. He dislikes his neighbour because of something that he, Fyodor, did to him: 'I once played a most shameless, nasty trick on him, and the moment I did it, I immediately hated him for it.' Clearly, Fyodor longs – however buried the original religious sentiment – to punish himself, because he hates himself. But since other people have merged with himself, he punishes himself by punishing other people, hates himself by hating other people.

And this leads to a Sisyphean repetition of behaviour. Self-punishment means being condemned to re-enact scandal after scandal without cease, because each self-punishment has become indistinguishable from sinning. The sin itself has become the punishment for that sin, and each sin, being another act of outrage, just opens the wound again. Clearly, there is no way that Fyodor Karamazov could ever stop behaving badly to his neighbour, since there is no logic by which he could possibly begin to feel warmly towards him. He would have to like himself, and that is surely not going to happen.

One can go further than the somewhat unreligious Bakhtin, subtle as he always is. The really remarkable aspect of Dostoevsky's celebrated psychology is surely that it is deeply sophisticated and wise in theoretical and human terms, but can only be finally understood in religious terms. His characters, even the very godless ones like Fyodor Karamazov, live under the mottled shadow of religious categories. They are the most complicated modern, secular agglomerations of unconscious motivation and conscious masquerade ever created, and yet there is nothing in Dostoevskian motivation which cannot be also found in the Gospels. They are humbly proud and proudly humble (Mary Magdalene). They sin in order to punish themselves, and know in advance that they will do so (Peter). They doubt in order to be reassured (Thomas). They betray in order to love (Peter, Judas).

Above all, their actions are comprehensible only and finally as efforts to confess, to reveal themselves, to be known. A tiny scene in *The Brothers Karamazov* comes to mind. Katerina Ivanovna, Dimitri Karamazov's fiancée, has taken Grushenka's hand and is kissing it. Grushenka is Dimitri's mistress. Unexpectedly, she extols Grushenka, who appears to bask in the praise. Grushenka takes Katerina's hand as if to reciprocate – and then unexpectedly drops it. 'And you can keep this as a memory – that you kissed my hand and I did not kiss yours.' Katerina calls her a slut, and has her ejected from the house. Once one has gone through all the 'psychological' explanations, once one has burrowed into all the corridors of dialectic, a stubborn inexplicability remains. Why act like this? What is furthered? Grushenka seems to want to annihilate herself. The only explanation is religious.

Grushenka, like so many Dostoevsky characters, wants to be *known*, even if she is not aware of it. She wants to reveal herself in all her dirtiness, her baseness, wants to reveal herself as hateful, proud, bitter, little. She wants to confess, and to be called a slut. The underground man desires, really, not to avenge himself but to *reveal* himself to the officer. Because after all, to let people know what you think of them is also to let them know what you think of yourself. This is the crucial point at which secular psychology meets religious mystery. *The Brothers Karamazov*, which would be the consuming work of Dostoevsky's last years, is precisely concerned with the feebleness of psychological explanation in the face of the oddity and extremism of religious motivation.

II

The final volume of Joseph Frank's magnificent biography opens in 1871, as Dostoevsky returns to Russia after four years abroad. Frank touches quickly upon the earlier years: Dostoevsky's involvement with radicalism and socialist utopianism in the 1840s, which had led to his arrest in 1849 and his mock execution (apparently a little joke of the Tsar's) at the Peter and Paul fortress; his penal servitude in Siberia, from 1850 to 1854; the writing of *Notes from Underground* and *Crime and Punishment* (1866), and the dictation, in one month, of *The Gambler*, to a stenographer, Anna Grigorievna, whom he married in 1867. Frank repeats the emphasis he has made in earlier volumes, on the centrality in Dostoevsky's life of his four years in Siberia. He was doubtless never an atheist – Belinsky had said years before that whenever he mentioned

Christ, the expression on Dostoevsky's face changed, 'just as if he were going to cry' – but he became a devoted reader of the Gospels in Siberia. A copy of the New Testament lay under his pillow for four years. In the prison camp he felt that he discovered the essence of the Russian peasant, and this knowledge funded his later religious nationalism and xenophobia. The Russian sinner, he declared years later, knows that he has committed wrong, while the European is untroubled by his sin, and indeed accepts it as justified. 'I think that the principal and most basic need of the Russian people is the need for suffering, incessant and unslakeable suffering.' Yet the Russian attempt at self-restoration will be 'always more serious than the former urge to deny and destroy the self'. In *The Brothers Karamazov*, he will have Dimitri, charged with murdering his father and facing twenty years of hard labour, exclaim in prison to his brother Alyosha: 'It's impossible for a convict to be without God ... And then from the depths of the earth, we, the men underground, will start singing a tragic hymn to God, in whom there is joy! Hail to God and his joy! I love him.'

But if Dostoevsky had changed, so had Russia when the novelist and his much younger wife returned in 1871. The serfs had been liberated ten years before, and Russian radical thought, which in the 1860s had followed Chernyshevsky's idea of 'rational egotism', and which had exploded into the violent ruthlessness of Bakunin and Nechaev (the model for Peter Verkhovensky), was becoming gentler and broader. Political thought was still divided between the generally conservative Slavophiles and the more radical Westernisers, between those who felt, like Dostoevsky, that Russia needed to offer its own solutions to its own problems, and those who, like Turgenev, saw Europe as the beacon that would illuminate a backward nation.

But in the last decade of his life Dostoevsky discovered that Russian radicalism was not only the secular Westernising kind. There was a new strain, which, while never exactly Christian, seemed sympathetic to certain Christian values. These were people who, without orthodox faith, were yet willing to suspend themselves in the oil of the religious. Some of the Populists, for instance, began to see the rural Russian way of life as treasurable, unique. Dostoevsky, who was conservative but never ideologically fixed in one place, was not automatically anathema to these new, Christianised radicals. Both Dostoevsky and some of the Populists began to envision the transformation of society along the principles of Christian love, charity and selflessness. This was keenly pleasing to Dostoevsky. Once, perhaps, he had believed in the socialist eschatology of a graspable earthly utopia. But his reading of the Gospels had encouraged him to believe that socialism was a kind of blasphemy, an earthbound mimicry of an inimitable divine mission. Socialism 'is also Christianity, but it proposes that it can succeed with reason', he wrote in his notebooks, in the early 1870s. Christianity – and here Dostoevsky and Kierkegaard converge – was not reasonable. It was perhaps a kind of lunacy. It existed not on the bread of reason but on the yeast of faith. The true Christian transformation, Dostoevsky believed, would happen at the end of time, and not by human will. The true Christian, said Dostoevsky, would say to his brother: 'I must share my possessions with my brother and serve him in every way.' But the 'communard' only 'wants to take revenge on society while claiming to appeal to higher goals'.

Those unfamiliar with Frank's earlier volumes may be surprised to find how devoted a husband and father Dostoevsky was. After his death, his wife modestly blacked out the erotic yearnings he expressed in his letters to her. From the status accorded the suffering child in his work, one might well infer that he was a loving father. But Dickens (whom Dostoevsky of course deeply admired) used children in rather similar ways in his novels, and still managed to abandon his wife and children. Frank writes movingly of the pain felt by both parents when their three-year-old son, Aleksey (Alyosha), died from a prolonged epileptic fit in 1878. The couple could not return to the apartment in which he had died. Dostoevsky, wrote Anna in her reminiscences, 'was crushed by this death. He had loved Aleksey somehow in a special way, with an almost morbid love.' In *The Brothers Karamazov*, of course, the avowed hero is the saintly Alyosha (the diminutive of Aleksey), and Ivan's great image of senseless suffering is the child in pain.

Dostoevsky, perhaps, already looked crushed. A few years before, in 1873, when he was made editor of *The Citizen*, a weekly journal, a twenty-three-year-old member of the journalistic staff, Varvara V. Timofeyeva, had described Dostoevsky: 'Very pale – with a sallow, unhealthy paleness – who seemed tired and perhaps ill . . . with a gloomy, exhausted face, covered like a net, with some sort of unusually expressive shadings caused by a tightly restrained movement of the muscles.' He told Varvara that 'the anti-Christ has been born . . . and is *coming*'. And he spoke of the Gospels: 'So much suffering, but then – so much grandeur . . . It's impossible to compare it with any well-being in the world!'

Frank's account of this last decade is really a story of unworldliness, for all that these are the years when Dostoevsky became a social 'prophet'. Until the publication of *The Brothers Karamazov*, whose monthly instalments 'held all of literate Russia spellbound', Dostoevsky was most famous for his *Diary of a Writer*, a monthly publication of sixteen pages, in which he gathered together stories, polemics, replies to his critics, and journalistic commentary on Russian news items such as the latest sensational court case. In the diary, he developed his growing Russian nationalism, in which he saw Russia messianically rescuing the rest of the world by bringing about the union of all Slavs, a mere prelude to a worldwide reconciliation of all humans under Christ, a Christ kept truly alive only by the true Church, the Orthodox Church. There was wild anti-Europeanism, anti-Catholicism and anti-Semitism in this journalism.

Yet for all this, the practical political remedy was becoming more and more ethereal – more religious. Even as Dostoevsky immersed himself in the debates of his country, his politics were thinning into Christological mist. He would tell querulous correspondents, again and again, to turn to Christ, to pray, to love one another, to ask for forgiveness. He pondered more and more deeply the life and teaching of Saint Tikhon Zadonsky, a mid-eighteenth-century Russian monk, who influenced his portrait of Father Zosima in his last novel. Tikhon taught, in Frank's words, 'that humankind should be grateful for the existence of temptation, misfortune and suffering because only through these could humans come to an acknowledgement of all the evil in their souls'. (Frank speculates plausibly enough that Dostoevsky may well have taken these words to be a response to the problem of Job, with whose story Dostoevsky had been obsessed from an early age.) Inwardly, Dostoevsky was preparing himself for the religious transfiguration for which he argues so movingly in his last great novel. For his fifty-eighth birthday, in 1879, Anna gave him a large photographic reproduction of Raphael's *Sistine Madonna*. 'How many times [have] I found him in his study in front of that great picture,' she later wrote, 'in such deep contemplation that he did not hear me come in.'

III

The Brothers Karamazov, for all its 'dialogism', represents a vast Christian exhortation. In *The Possessed*, one of the revolutionary socialists, Shigalev, announces his plan of social transformation. To our ears it is a nightmare out of Orwell. One-tenth of humanity will have unlimited freedom and unrestricted powers over the remaining nine-tenths. These unfortunates must give up their individuality and be turned into a herd of identicals. Peter Verkhovensky, of course, exclaims that Shigalev has 'invented equality', an equality in which 'everyone belongs to all the others, and all belong to everyone. All are slaves and equals in slavery.' To this horrid vision, *The Brothers Karamazov* again and again poses a true Christian equality, in almost identical language (this similarity oddly missed by the omnivorous Joseph Frank): Father Zosima tells his fellow monks that they are 'guilty before all people, on behalf of all and for all, for all human sins'. Later in the novel, when Dimitri Karamazov is falsely accused of killing his father, he offers himself as a scapegoat. He accepts punishment, he says, because he wanted to kill his father and might well have killed him, and is therefore willing to be 'guilty before all'. The forced enslavement and forced equality of Shigalev's proto-communism has been replaced by the willing enslavement and ecstatic equality of Christian penitence.

The Brothers Karamazov tells the story of the unstable and passionate Karamazov family, gentry in a miserable provincial town dominated by a monastery. The hated patriarch, Fyodor, is murdered, and suspicion falls on Dimitri, who had visited the house at the time, and who had emerged covered in blood and apparently three thousand roubles richer. In fact, Fyodor was killed, as we discover late in the book, by his atheistic, skulking servant, Smerdyakov, who is a kind of devil-figure. But each of the three brothers, Dimitri, Ivan and Alyosha, had at one time imagined the murder of his father. Dimitri had attacked Fyodor and had several times threatened to kill him; Ivan, an atheist who believes that in a world without God and immortality, 'everything is permitted', appears to countenance killing Fyodor when he meets the murderous Smerdyakov and informs him that he will be away from the house for a certain period. Certainly Smerdyakov takes Ivan's comment to be an official approval. Even saintly Alyosha, who had been a monk in training at the monastery, admits that he has imagined murder.

The novel, like *Macbeth*, explores the sense that to have imagined a crime is to have already committed it. Macbeth, after all, is changed – his mind is 'full of scorpions', as Shakespeare has it – at the moment he hears the witches' prophecy. Nothing can be the same again. Both works of art live under the shadow of Christ's unfair, even repulsive, admonition that to have looked on a woman with an adulterous heart is to have committed the act. It could be said that all of Dostoevsky's characters, in their febrile determination to turn ideas into action, behave like people who have heard Christ's warning, who deeply believe it, and yet are deeply evading it. The novel seems to come to the conclusion that indeed, as Father Zosima puts it, all are guilty before all. Dimitri, who is fallen, noble, Christ-obsessed, and who has the zeal of the converted sinner, accepts this guilt, and though he professes his actual innocence of the crime, goes willingly to be punished for it.

Yet are not some more guilty than others? Dostoevsky firmly believed that without faith in God and belief in immortality, nothing restrained man's worldly behaviour. Without God, everything is permitted. This is an obviously flawed conclusion, since a glance at world-history shows that *with* God everything already has been permitted. (The Crusades, the Inquisition, burnings at the stake, wars, Christian anti-Semitism, and so on.) Gibbon famously thought that the conclusion might go the other way – that a world without religions might well have been a sweeter place. But Dostoevsky had already written a novel, *Crime and Punishment*, which demonstrated what might go wrong in a man without the Gospel, and here he is at it again in *The Brothers Karamazov*. For although Dimitri and Alyosha have imagined Fyodor's death, and are in some respects 'guilty', it is the atheist Smerdyakov, who borrowed the atheist Ivan's teaching that 'without God everything is permitted', who actually killed the old man. And Smerdyakov is really Ivan's twisted double. Ivan, who has his own nobility, would never have killed his father, but in a sense *his idea did the deed*, via Smerdyakov. An idea is the killer. Atheism did it.

The Brothers Karamazov is a book in love with, and afraid of, ideas. In the end, I think, it proposes the peace of a realm beyond ideas: paradise. This is best seen in the most famous chapter, Ivan's 'Legend of the Grand Inquisitor'. Just before he tells this story to the believer Alyosha, Ivan attacks God for allowing to exist a world in which children suffer. Ivan is one of those atheists who stand on the rung just below faith; he is an almost-believer, and Dostoevsky clearly admires him. In such a man, unbelief is very close to belief, just as in many of Dostoevsky's other characters love is close to hate, punishment to sin, and buffoonery to confession. Religion, Ivan says, tells us that in a future paradise the lamb will lie down with the lion, that we shall live in harmony. But 'if everyone must suffer in order to buy eternal harmony with their suffering, pray tell me what have children to do with it . . . Why do they get thrown on the pile, to manure someone's future harmony with themselves?' He continues: 'I absolutely renounce all higher harmony. It is not worth one little tear of even that one tormented child. They have put too high a price on harmony; we can't afford to pay so much for admission. And therefore I hasten to return my ticket.'

He gets Alyosha, the true Christian, to agree with him. If one could build 'the edifice of human destiny with the object of making people happy in the finale, of giving them peace and rest at last, but for that you must inevitably and unavoid-ably torture just one tiny child . . . and raise your edifice on the foundation of her unrequited tears – would you agree to be the architect of such conditions?' Alyosha says he would not. But, replies Alyosha, there is Christ, who can 'forgive everything, forgive all *and for all*'.

To which Ivan responds with his now famous Legend. It, and the preceding chapter, are deservedly revered. The writing here has the ferocity, the august vitality, the royal perspective, of scriptural writing. It is, truly, a visited prose. In the Legend, Christ is upbraided for allowing humans too much freedom. Humans do not want freedom, says the Inquisitor to Christ, humans are afraid of freedom. They want, really, to bow down to an idol, to subject themselves. They have no desire to live in the freedom to choose between good and evil, between doubt and knowledge.

In these two chapters, Dostoevsky mounts perhaps the most powerful attack ever made on theodicy (the formal term for the effort to justify God's goodness in a world of evil and suffering). In particular, Dostoevsky challenges the two chief elements of theodicy: that we suffer mysteriously on earth but will be rewarded in heaven; and that evil exists because freedom exists – we must be free to do good and evil, to believe in God or not to believe in Him. Any other existence would be robotic, unimaginable. In this scheme, Hitler *must* be 'allowed' to have existed, since we must be free to inhabit every human possibility, good and evil. To the first defence, Ivan says that future harmony is not worth present tears. And to the second – to my mind even more devastating – Ivan says, in effect, 'Why is God so sure that man even wants to be free? What is so good about freedom?' After all – Ivan does not say this, but it is implicit – we will probably not be very free when we get to heaven, and heaven sounds like a nice place. So why are we all so ragingly and horribly free on earth? If there are no Hitlers in heaven, why should it have ever been necessary for there to be Hitlers on earth?

Of course Dostoevsky did not invent these objections. They are as old as rebellion. Furthermore, he knew that theodicy has always been incapable of an adequate response to these hostilities. He merely gave them the most powerful form in the history of anti-religious writing. And this is why many readers think that the novel never manages to escape these pages, that the Christian Dostoevsky, in allowing such power to anti-Christian arguments, really produced not a Christian novel but an unconsciously atheistic one. The philosopher Lev Shestov, for instance, thought that Dostoevsky, for all his orthodoxy, was so corroded by doubt that when he came to imagine the doubter Ivan, he could not help giving him a vitality and appeal far beyond that of the saintly and bland Alyosha. Those of Shestov's mind think that even if the novel demonstrates that atheism is finally a murderous idea because it kills Fyodor, religion is so damaged by Ivan's onslaught that it cannot mount a proper reply.

Dostoevsky, however, very much wanted to reply to Ivan's attack. He worried that Father Zosima and Alyosha would not be what he called, in a letter to an editor, a 'sufficient reply' to 'the negative side' (i.e. the atheistical side) of his book. Well, can there be a reply to Ivan's arguments? Alyosha says what any Christian must, that Christ forgives all of us, that he suffered for us so that we may not suffer, that we do not know why the world has been constructed the way it is. Depending on our beliefs, we will find this adequate or inadequate.

But the novel – and, I think, Dostoevsky intends this – enshrines, in its very form, a further argument. It is that Ivan's ideas cannot be refuted by other ideas. In debate, in 'dialogism', there is no way of defeating or even of matching Ivan, and Alyosha does not really try. At the end of Ivan's Legend, he simply kisses his brother. The only way we can refute Ivan's ideas, the book seems to say, is by maintaining that *Christ is not an idea*. Socialism is an idea, because it is 'reasonable'; atheism, too; but Christianity, so profoundly unreasonable – what Kierkegaard called 'lunacy' – is not an idea. Yet painfully, the only realm in which Christ is not an idea, in which he is pure knowledge, is in heaven. On earth, we are all fallen, and we fall before ideas, we have only ideas, and Christ can always be kicked around the ideational playground.

But Christ is not an idea. This is surely the only way to explain the intellectually nonsensical behaviour of Dimitri, who, though innocent, is willing to be guilty for all and before all; or of Father Zosima's advice that we should ask forgiveness 'even from the birds'; or of Alyosha's final words, which close the book, about how resurrection does indeed exist: 'Certainly we shall rise, certainly we shall see, and gladly, joyfully tell one another all that has been!' Such notions have really fallen off the cliff of ideas and into the realm of illogical, beautiful, desperate exhortation. Belief has smothered knowledge. And this exchange – of the unreason of Christianity for the reason of atheism – means finally that there can be no 'dialogism' in this novel, either of the kind Bakhtin proposed, or of the kind that Dostoevsky so dearly desired. There is neither a circulation of ideas nor an 'answering' of atheism by Christianity. For the answer – the unreason of Christian love – no longer belongs to the realm of worldly ideas, and thus no longer belongs to the novel itself. It exists in Paradise, and in that other, finally un-novelistic book, the New Testament.

2002

Helen Garner's Savage Honesty

IN THE EARLY 1960s, when the Australian writer Helen Garner was a student at the University of Melbourne, she had a brief relationship with a twenty-four-year-old man who was also her tutor. With characteristic briskness, she tells us that she learned two things from him: 'firstly, to start an essay without bullshit preamble, and secondly, that betrayal is part of life'. She continues: 'I value it as part of my store of experience – part of what I am and how I have learnt to understand the world.' A writing lesson and a life lesson: Garner's work as a journalist and novelist constantly insists on the connection between writing about life and comprehending it; to try to do both responsibly and honestly – without bullshit preamble, or bullshit amble, for that matter – is what it means to be alive.

'Honesty' is a word that, when thrown at journalism, unhelpfully describes both a baseline and a vaguer horizon; a legal minimum and an ethical summum. Too often, we precisely monitor the former, and profligately praise the latter. In Helen Garner's case, we should give due thanks for the former, and precisely praise the latter. As a writer of nonfiction, Garner is scrupulous, painstaking and detailed, with sharp eyes and ears. She is everywhere at once, watching and listening, a recording angel at life's secular apocalypses – 'a small grim figure with a notebook and a cold', as she memorably describes herself. She has written with lucid anger about horrifying murder cases, about incidents of sexual harassment, about the experience of caring for a dying friend.

But Garner is, above all, a savage self-scrutineer: her honesty has less to do with what she sees in the world than what she refuses to turn away from in herself. In *The Spare Room* (2008), her exacting autobiographical novel about looking after a friend who is dying from cancer, she describes not only the expected indignities of caring for a patient – the soaked bedsheets, the broken nights – but her own impatience as a host, her own rage: 'I had always thought that sorrow was the most exhausting of the emotions. Now I knew that it was anger.' There seems to be no episode from her own life that she has not analysed. It is characteristic that her reference to her affair with her tutor appears in *The First Stone* (1995), her account of a sexual harassment case in 1991, when two female students at the University of Melbourne accused the master of one of the university colleges of making inappropriate advances: that book is both a report and a deep self-reckoning. Garner's readers are familiar with Mrs Dunkley, who taught her English when she was nine years old; the failure of Garner's three marriages; her two abortions; her dismissal from a teaching job at a Melbourne school (for daring to talk to her thirteen-year-old pupils about sex); her struggles with depression; her feelings about turning fifty, and the complex stitch of fury and liberation at being, now, in her seventies.

The no-bullshit preamble rule is sparklingly employed throughout her work. 'At the turn of the millennium I reached the end of my masochism, and came home from Sydney with my tail between my legs. Single again.' So begins a gentle reflection on learning, once again, how to live alone. 'My First Baby' opens thus: 'This isn't really a story. I'm just telling you what happened one summer when I was young. It was 1961, my first year away from home. I lived at Melbourne University, in a women's college on a beautiful elm-lined boulevard. I was free and happy. Everyone was clever and so was I.' Garner is a natural storyteller: her unillusioned eye makes her clarity compulsive. Take, for example, one of her longer essays, 'Dreams of Her Real Self', in which she recalls her late mother, and illuminates with relentless candour her mother's shadowy presence. Her father, she tells us, is easy to write about; he was vivid, domineering, scornful, and babyishly quick to anger. One of Garner's husbands, having been subjected to a paternal inquisition, described him as a 'peasant'. He was 'an endurance test that united his children in opposition to him'. But she finds it difficult to write about her mother, in part because her father 'blocked my view of her', and in part, we learn, because she was willing to be blocked. So Garner's reminiscence breaks into short, discontinuous sections, as she appraises, from different angles, the unassertive enigma that was her mother. She did not easily show affection, she was patient, timid, unconfident, law-abiding – and, probably, Garner decides, 'she was afraid of me'.

> She did not sense the right moment to speak. She did not know how to gain and hold attention. When she told a story, she felt a need to establish enormous quantities of irrelevant background information. She took so long to

get to the point that her listeners would tune out and start talking about something else. Family shorthand for this, behind her back, was 'and then I breathed'.

What gives the memoir its power, as so often in Garner's writing, is that she is unsparing, in equal measure, of both her subject and herself, and that she so relishes complicated feelings. She chastises herself for not being more responsive to her mother when she was alive; posthumous connection is, after all, too easy. She longs for her to return, but has difficulty regarding her mother's life with anything but horror. She was about twelve, she recalls, when she realised that her mother's existence was divided into compartments. 'None of them was longer than the number of hours between one meal and the next. She was on a short leash. I don't recall thinking that this would be my fate, or resolving to avoid it. All I remember is the picture of her life, and the speechless desolation that filled me.' In some ways, it is a familiar portrait: an educated and liberated intellectual, the beneficiary of higher education and modern feminism, measures, with gratitude and shame, the distance between her mother's opportunities and her own. But it is made singular by Garner's almost reckless honesty, and brought alive by her mortal details: 'She used to wear hats that pained me. Shy little round beige felt hats with narrow brims. Perhaps one was green. And she stood with her feet close together, in sensible shoes.'

'Dreams of Her Real Self' is ultimately an essay about gender and class, categories that have absorbed Garner for much of her work – precisely, it would seem, because gender and class are not categories so much as structures of feeling, variously argued over, enjoyed, endured, and escaped. Her first book,

Monkey Grip (1977), is an intelligent, tautly written novel that chronicles some of Garner's own experiences from the 1970s, in particular her life in what she has called 'the big hippie house-holds' of that era, 'when group dynamics were shaky and we were always having to split and start anew'. But she established her reputation as a non-fiction writer, and established the char-acteristic Garner tone, with *The First Stone*, which tells the story of an incident of sexual harassment in 1991, at Ormond College, the largest and most prestigious residential college of the University of Melbourne. A twenty-one-year-old law student, whom Garner renames Elizabeth Rosen, accused the college's middle-aged Master ('Dr Colin Shepherd', in Garner's telling) of sexual assault. She alleged that during a private meet-ing in his office, Dr Shepherd told her he fantasised about her, and that he put his hand on her breasts. Rosen and another student testified that, later in the evening, at a college dance, Dr Shepherd groped them while dancing with them. Shepherd forcefully denied all the allegations. He was convicted of a single charge of sexual assault, which was overturned on appeal; he resigned anyway, in May 1993.

Garner first encountered the case one morning in August 1992, when she read about it in the Melbourne *Age*. Her early reactions were instinctive. She was puzzled by the young women's recourse to the law. Why didn't the students just sort it out locally, immediately, pragmatically; or get their moth-ers, or friends, to mediate? Garner's own friends, she tells us, 'feminists pushing fifty', were in agreement. Seasoned victims of such fumbled advances (or of far worse), they didn't doubt the veracity of the allegations; but 'if every bastard who's ever laid a hand on *us* were dragged into court, the judicial system of the state would be clogged for years'. Garner wrote to Dr Shepherd, sympathising with his treatment at the hands of 'this ghastly punitiveness'.

The First Stone is subtitled 'Some Questions About Sex and Power', and, in ways both conscious and unconscious, it obsessively pursues the questions raised by Garner's own reflexive response to the case. She defends that initial reaction, but spends the entire book worrying away at it. *The First Stone* attacks and retreats like a bated animal. Garner persists in faulting the students for not acting pragmatically; these were not 'earth-shattering' offences, so why not deal with them swiftly, then and there? A repeated line of attack is that the students and their defenders use the word 'violence' where, in this case, 'it simply does not belong'. To insist on abuses of institutional power, says Garner, nullifies the fact that all relationships contain asymmetries of power, and that there are 'gradations of offence'. And power is always complex, anyway. She seems irritated by Rosen's testimony that Dr Shepherd's advances left her feeling 'humiliated and powerless to control what was happening to her'. Why so powerless? When Dr Shepherd got down on his knees in homage and grasped Elizabeth Rosen's hand, as she alleged, 'Which of them does the word *humiliated* apply to, here?'

But at other moments, as if in retreat, she worries that she has herself changed. An ageing but committed feminist, a child of the 1960s and '70s, she's perturbed that she finds it so easy to side with the man and so hard to sympathise with the women. Perhaps she's punishing the students 'for not having *taken it like a woman* – for being wimps who ran to the law to whinge about a minor unpleasantness, instead of standing up and fighting back with their own weapons of youth and quick wits'. She enriches this rhetorical back-and-forth in other ways. She tells us about her short affair with her tutor; and about an incident in the early 1980s when a masseur, in the middle of a private session, bent down and kissed her on the mouth. Looking back, Garner is clearly astounded that she said nothing to the man. Above all, she was merely embarrassed. And when the massage was over, she said goodbye, went to the reception desk – '*and I paid*'. She usefully explains that Ormond College was for decades a bulwark of male institutional power: women, admitted as full students in 1973, were not always made to feel welcome. She conducts revealing interviews with some of Ormond's most entitled male graduates, who talk casually about their bad behaviour – food fights, public drunkenness, running around naked. After a particularly squalid battle in the dining hall, the Master upbraided the young diners with these telling words: 'The Hall's been raped – you promised me this wouldn't happen.' Without comment, Garner lets that verb hang, or hang itself.

The First Stone quickly became 'controversial', controversial enough that the author felt compelled to write a formal reply to her critics. Alerted to the existence of Garner's letter to Shepherd, the two victims refused to speak to her. It is a refusal Garner returns to, in mounting frustration; her book takes on a curiously blocked, repetitive, almost *victimised* quality, as if she were herself responding to a violation. She attacks modern feminism ('priggish, disingenuous, unforgiving') as if it had put her on trial. Which, in a sense, it had: the victims' allies and defenders soon made their minds up.

Garner was on the wrong side; it was understood that she was writing 'the pro-Shepherd version'. Some feminists boycotted the book when it came out. University professors told their constituencies to avoid it.

The First Stone is, certainly, a very *parental* book: a woman old enough to be the mother of the two students looks on bemusedly, with the advantages of experience and hardened wisdom, and finds herself disappointed that the youngsters just aren't a bit tougher. And even as she writes about the complexities and hidden potencies of gender, Garner comes to the scene – again, like a certain kind of parent – with rather stubborn ideas about male and female roles. She upbraids the victims for avoiding conciliation, a 'feminine – almost a motherly – way of settling a dispute', and, instead, accuses them of charging past conciliation into 'the traditionally masculine style of problem-solving: call in the cops . . . hire a cowboy to slug it out for you in the main street at noon, with all the citizenry watching'. But of course, the gunsmoke of essentialism just reactivates the very warfare Garner seeks to heal. When she rhetorically asks that question about who is *truly* humiliated, the man on his knees in supplication or the woman somewhat distressed in the chair, couldn't the reply be – well, *both*?

Yet more than twenty years after its publication, *The First Stone* also seems a brilliantly prescient book – in its complexity, in the tense torque of its self-argument; and in its very vulnerability and stunned intolerance. Feminism had indeed changed between the 1970s and the 1990s, and Garner's narrative registers, with often uncomfortable honesty, a generational shift. Sexual harassment was coming to be seen as, invariably, a matter of institutional power; there was, as it were, no space left over, no *narrative room*, for Garner's blithe admission of her youthful affair with an older tutor, and certainly not for her appreciation of its educative richness.

In similar ways, Garner's most recent full-length work of non-fiction, *This House of Grief* (2014), makes its complexity out of an honest vulnerability. It recounts the two murder trials of Robert Farquharson, who was charged with murdering his three small children, in 2005. Returning the kids to his ex-wife, after a Father's Day visit, he swerved off the road into a deep dam. The children drowned but Farquharson escaped, abandoning the car in the icy water, and hitching a ride back to his ex-wife's house. Farquharson was convicted of murder in 2007, won a retrial in 2009, and was convicted again in 2010. He was given three life sentences.

Garner's book is superbly alive to the narrative dynamics of the case; she tells a grim story of unhappy marriage, limited social opportunity, bitter divorce and spousal grievance. What consumes the writer are the difficult questions that seem to lie beyond the reach of formal narration: the deepest assumptions of class and gender and power; the problem of how well we ever understand someone else's motives. In her reply to the critics of *The First Stone*, she describes *eros* as 'the quick spirit that moves between people – *quick* as in the distinction between "the quick and the dead". It's the moving force that won't be subdued by habit or law.' That quick spirit is the free devil, the human surplus that she tries to capture in all her best work. The law interests her because its fine calibrations are coarsely developed for this kind of narrative work: the evidence that helps us make sense of a catastrophic and complicated incident is often not the same evidence that helps the law make *its* sense. Paradoxically, the legal process tempts writers (notably Janet Malcolm, Garner's admired model), precisely because trial machinery *appears* to operate like the machinery of narrative, pumping out its near-simulacra for the benefit of reporters, TV journalists, voyeurs and jurors. Garner quotes Malcolm: 'Jurors sit there presumably weighing evidence but in actuality they are studying character.'

At the heart of the Robert Farquharson case is a large narrative question that frequently abuts, but finally diverges from, the smaller legal question before the jury: why? Attracted and repelled, Garner circles around the unspeakable, abysmal horror. Can any story 'explain' why a man might murder his children? She doesn't pretend to possess the explosive answer, and frequently confesses appalled stupefaction; but her book walks us along an engrossing and plausible narrative fuse. Robert Farquharson emerges from Garner's account as limited in intelligence, expression and will. He lived in the small, modest town of Winchelsea (not far from Geelong, where Garner was born). He worked as a cleaner, and had three children with the much more forceful Cindy Gambino, who told the court that Farquharson was 'pretty much of a softie. He always gave in to what I wanted.' Though he was a 'good provider', she found it hard to stay in love with her husband. Cindy eventually left him for a contractor, Stephen Moules, a man more vigorous and successful than Farquharson. She kept the children, and Farquharson had to move out. He was jealous of Stephen's access to the children, fearful of being displaced, and angry that the new lover got the better of the Farquharsons' two cars. An old friend testified that he threatened to kill his children and rob Cindy of her dearest gifts; Garner wonders if Farquharson was really trying to commit suicide.

Her narrative is lit by lightning. Hideous, jagged details leap out at us: the old, child-filled car, swerving off the road and plunging into dark water; the trapped children (the youngest was strapped into a car seat); Farquharson's casual – or shocked – impotence at the crime scene (his first words to Moules, when he arrived, were 'Where's your smokes?'); the slack, defeated, anguished defendant, weeping throughout the trial; the wedding video of the happy couple, Gambino gliding 'like a princess in full fig, head high', and Farquharson, mullet-haired, 'round-shouldered, unsmiling, a little tame bear'; the first guilty verdict, Farquharson's vanquished defence lawyer standing 'like a beaten warrior . . . hands clasped in front of his genitals'.

Garner is a powerful and vivid presence in her non-fiction narratives: she intervenes; she weeps and laughs with the evidence; is scornful, funny, impassioned, gives honest expression to biases and prejudices. (She also avails herself of the full, meaty buffet of Anglo-Australian demotic: 'bloke', 'sook', 'sent to Coventry', 'dobbing in', 'spat the dummy', 'bolshie'.) She powerfully sympathises with Farquharson's thwarted opportunities and flattened will, but she cannot hide her distaste for his weakness, which she expresses in tellingly gendered jabs. In court, she compares Stephen Moules physically to Farquharson ('I was not the only woman' to do so), and admits that Moules 'gave off that little buzz of glamour peculiar to the Australian tradie'. She wonders if there was something in Farquharson, by contrast, that brought out the maternal in women, our tendency to cosset, to infantilize'. In a striking picture near the end of the book, she sees the accused as a big baby, 'with his low brow and puffy eyes, his slumped spine and man-boobs, his silent-movie grimaces and spasms of tears, his big cleaned handkerchief'. It is hard to resist the conclusion that Garner, in full maternal mode, is arraigning him for not being *more of a man*. Is it unfair to wonder if this tough-minded writer was not also unconsciously demanding of the two University of Melbourne women that they, too, act *more like men*?

Some of Garner's prejudices are more unconscious than others, but I suspect she understands perfectly well that narrative truth – what Elena Ferrante calls 'authenticity' (as distinct from mere verisimilitude) – proceeds from a kind of dangerous honesty that is not always conscious but unadmitted, half-disclosed, imperfectly controlled. The author's gradual awakening to her unadmitted anger is what gives Garner's best book, her novel *The Spare Room*, much of its shattering power. Nicola, an old friend who has been diagnosed with stage-four cancer, comes from Sydney to Melbourne, to stay for three weeks with the narrator, who is named Helen. (The novel is closely based on Garner's experience in caring for a terminally ill friend; typically, she said that she kept her first name in the text so that she would be forced to admit to all the shameful, 'ugly emotion' she had actually felt.)

Nicola is charming, elegant and maddening. She pretends to be much healthier than she really is – she gives 'a tremendous performance of being alive', in Garner's savage phrase – and is committed to a kind of social fraudulence that saddens and then gradually enrages her host. Helen longs for Nicola to abandon her bright laugh and fixed social smile, a smile that seems to say, *Do not ask me any questions*. Worse, she has come to Melbourne to seek alternative therapies – vitamin C injections, ozone saunas, coffee enemas – that seem nonsensical to Helen and which only make her friend sicker.

The novel tenderly catalogues that labour of caring which is also the labour of mourning. Helen spends her days and nights washing bedsheets that Helen has sweated through, bringing morphine pills and hot-water bottles, listening outside the bedroom door to Nicola's snoring, which sounds 'like someone choking', driving her friend to the bogus 'Institute' where she undergoes her hopeless remedies. The simple beauty of the novel's form has to do with its internal symmetry: the two women are locked into a relationship which they can escape only if each admits what each finds most difficult to say. Helen must confess to her exhaustion, her despair at not being a better friend and nurse, her anger at Nicola's terrible, terminal time-wasting; and Nicola must admit that time is fading, that she is going to die, that her alternative therapies are an awful distraction, and that she needs proper help, a kind of assistance that Helen is not equipped to give. All my life, says Nicola, 'I've never wanted to bore people with the way I feel.' As in *The Death of Ivan Ilyich* (Garner's book is a contemporary version of Tolstoy's novella), the mortal victim must be brought to comprehend her mortality: Helen tells Nicola that 'You've got to get ready.' There is a deeply moving scene towards the end of the book, when the two friends tearfully embrace in Helen's yard. 'I thought I was on the mountaintop,' says Nicola. 'But I'm only in the foothills':

All day long she kept dissolving into quiet weeping. Sometimes I would put my arms around her; sometimes we would just go on with what we were doing. The hard, impervious brightness was gone. Everything was fluid and melting. There was no need for me to speak. She looked up at me and said it herself, as I put a cup into her hand. 'Death's at the end of this, isn't it.'

After the anger and the tears, the book ends peacefully. Helen flies with Nicola to Sydney, and transfers her to Nicola's very competent niece. The novel closes: 'It was the end of my watch, and I handed her over.' Helen has done as much as she can do. It is a typical Garner sentence – a writing lesson (all novels should end as completely), and a life lesson: spare, deserved, and complexly truthful, both a confession of failure and a small song of success.

2016

The All and the If:
God and Metaphor in Melville

I

WHEN IT COMES TO LANGUAGE, all writers want to be billionaires. All long to possess so many words that using them is a fat charity. To be utterly free in language, to be absolute commander of what you do not own – this is the greatest desire of any writer. Even the deliberate paupers of style – Hemingway, Pavese, late Beckett – have their smothered longings for riches, and make their reductions seem like bankruptcy after wealth rather than fraud before it: Pavese translated *Moby-Dick* into Italian. Realists may protest that it is life, not words, that draws them as writers: yet language at rush hour is like a busy city. Language is infinite, but it is also a system, and so it tempts us with the fantasy that it is closed, like a currency or an orchestra. What writer does not dream of touching every word in the lexicon once?

In *Moby-Dick*, Herman Melville nearly touched every word once, or so it seems. Language is pressed and stroked

in that book with Shakespearean agility. No other nineteenth-
century novelist writing in English lived in the city of words
that Melville lived in; they were suburbanites by comparison. No other novelist of that age could swim in the poetry
of 'the warmly cool, clear, ringing, perfumed, overflowing,
redundant days . . .' And so, despite the usual biographical
lamentations, despite our knowledge that *Moby-Dick* went
largely unappreciated, that in 1876 only two copies of the
novel were bought in the United States; that in 1887 it went
out of print with a total sale of 3,180 copies; that these and
other neglects narrowed Melville into bitterness and blank
daily obedience as a New York customs inspector – despite
this, one says lucky Melville, not poor Melville. For in writing *Moby-Dick*, Melville wrote the novel that is every writer's
dream of freedom. It is as if he painted a patch of sky for the
imprisoned.

Families wallow in detail – in letters, homes, arrange-
ments, travel. For the Melvill family (as they spelt their
name at the time of Herman's birth, in 1819), money was the
bulking detail. Herman's parents, of Scots and Dutch origin,
were the children of wealth, privilege, and Revolutionary
courage. But Alan Melvill, Herman's father, was a deluxe
Mr Micawber, apparently importing French dry goods but
actually threshing his way through the family inheritance. It
is reckoned that, in all, he borrowed $20,000 from his father
and from his parents-in-law. In June 1830 he borrowed $2,500
from his father; a month later, another $1,000; in November
$500 'to discharge some urgent debts'. Nobody knows what
this money satisfied. But when he died, abruptly, in 1832 (he
seems to have suffered some kind of mental collapse), he left

the family deep in debt. Melville was twelve. He was removed from school and sent to work in a bank at $150 a year.

This was a bleak apprenticeship-to-nothing. Melville was a year and a half at the bank, and after the bank came work in his brother's store as a clerk, schoolteaching, and his decision, at the age of twenty, to join a whaling ship. In Polynesia, Melville jumped ship and spent time with a tribe of cannibals. His first novel, *Typee* (1846), is an autobiographical account of his adventures, and was taken as such by contemporary readers. Melville's unsympathetic view of the activity of Christian missionaries in Polynesia guaranteed hostile reviews from certain papers and journals associated with the churches. He was, said one review, 'one of Christianity's most ungrateful sons'. A fuse had been lit: such critics would flash at all future examples of religious scepticism in Melville's writing.

Melville was born into the Calvinism of the Dutch Reformed Church. At his baptism, his parents were asked if they understood that all children are 'conceived and born in sin, and therefore are subject to all miseries, yea to condemnation itself, yet that they are sanctified in Christ, and therefore as members of his Church ought to be baptised'. It was a theology that stressed a quality of helplessness: we are predestined by God's free grace to be chosen, or not chosen, into the elect, but nothing we can do in the way of 'good works' on earth will make any difference. We can be hired or sacked, but it is no good scheming for promotion. In a typically glittering metaphor, Melville writes in *Pierre* (1852), the disastrous novel that followed *Moby-Dick*, that if our actions are 'foreordained . . . we are Russian serfs to Fate'. Pierre is described as someone who is captured by 'that most true Christian doctrine of the utter nothingness of good works', and is therefore inconsolable when tragedy overwhelms him. For he can do nothing to alter his fate. Melville's writing is entirely shadowed by Calvinism, in the way that Nabokov's ape, when given a sheet of paper, drew the bars of his cage. 'But we that write & print', he joked to Evert Duyckinck in 1850, 'have all our books predestinated – & for me, I shall write such things as the Great Publisher of Mankind ordained ages before he published "The World" – this planet, I mean.' Hawthorne best described Melville's struggle with belief. In 1856, Melville was briefly in England, to visit Hawthorne in Liverpool. The two sat on the beach at Southport, and continued the unequal marriage of the last six years – Hawthorne silent and tidy, Melville messy with metaphysics. At this time, wrote Hawthorne, Melville said that he had 'pretty much made up his mind to be annihilated'. He added: 'It is strange how he persists . . . in wandering to and fro over these deserts, as dismal and monotonous as the sandhills amid which we were sitting. He can neither believe, nor be comfortable in his unbelief; and he is too honest and courageous not to try to do one or the other.'

II

Melville, in his relation to belief, was like the last guest who cannot leave the party; he was always returning to see if he had left his hat and gloves. And yet he did not want to be at the party, either. It is just that he had nowhere else to be, and would rather be with people than be alone. He was tormented by God's inscrutable silence. Moby-Dick himself, who is both God and Devil, flaunts his unhelpful silence as God does to Job: 'Canst thou draw out leviathan with a hook?' In the chapter 'The Tail', Ishmael admits that if he cannot really comprehend the whale's rear, then he can hardly see his face: 'Thou shalt see my back parts, my tail, he seems to say, but my face shall not be seen', an appropriation of the verse in Exodus in which God tells Moses that 'thou shalt see my back parts: but my face shall not be seen.' Likewise, Melville was gripped by the torment of the Pyramids and their emptiness. In 1857, while travelling through Egypt, he visited the Pyramids. In his journal, he writes again and again as if, by repetition, to rid himself of the memory of it: 'It was in these pyramids that was conceived the idea of Jehovah.' In *Moby-Dick*, we are reminded by Melville of the 'pyramidical silence' of the whale. In *Pierre*, he will not leave alone this torment and fingers it like a wounded rosary, which is partly why the book is so impacted. It is in *Pierre* that he writes: 'Silence is the only Voice of our God . . . how can a man get a Voice out of Silence?' He jibes at God: 'doth not Scripture intimate, that He holdeth all of us in the hollow of His hand? – a Hollow, truly!' Perhaps, he proposes, all our searches are like this:

> By vast pains we mine into the pyramids; by horrible gropings we come to the central room; with joy we espy the sarcophagus; but we lift the lid – and no body is there! – appallingly vacant as vast is the soul of a man!

More than this, Melville saw that the world did not look like God's world, and that we fail as God's children, because

His standards are cruelly impossible. He has Plotinus Plinlimmon say this in the sermon called 'Chronometricals and Horologicals' in *Pierre*. God keeps one kind of time, says Plinlimmon, and man keeps another, though man is always conscious that he ought to be living his life according to God's time. The difficulty is that, if we really did live in the world according to God's time, we would be thought mad: for this is just what Jesus did. Jesus carried 'Heaven's time in Jerusalem', but the Jews 'carried Jerusalem time', and killed him for his strangeness. Therefore, concludes Plinlimmon, though 'the earthly wisdom of man be heavenly folly to God; so also, conversely, is the heavenly wisdom of God an earthly folly'. And who has not been struck, continues the sermon, by 'a sort of infidel idea, that whatever other world God may be Lord of, he is not the Lord of this; for else the world would seem to give the lie to Him; so utterly repugnant seem its ways to the instinctively known ways of Heaven'.

We can get a sense of the violent bevel on which Melville's faith quivered – half on and half off – if we compare him to two Christians who were writing thoughts exactly like Melville's character Plotinus Plinlimmon at this moment in the middle of the nineteenth century. In Denmark, Kierkegaard strengthened Christianity (as he saw it) by reminding us, like Plinlimmon, that Christianity is a 'folly' for humans, that, as he put it in his *Journals*, 'one must be quite literally a lunatic to become a Christian'. And in England, at almost exactly the same time, Cardinal Newman looked at the world, and, in his *Apologia Pro Vita Sua*, almost agreed with Melville:

I look out of myself into the world of men, and there I
see a sight which fills me with unspeakable distress. The
world seems simply to give the lie to that great truth, of
which my whole being is so full . . . I look into this living
busy world, and see no reflexion of its Creator. This is, to
me, one of those great difficulties of this absolute primary
truth, to which I referred just now. Were it not for this
voice, speaking so clearly in my conscience and my heart,
I should be an atheist, or a pantheist, or a polytheist when
I looked into the world.

Both Kierkegaard and Newman suffered like Melville, and
suffered eloquently, feeling the lack of what Newman beautifully calls 'the tokens so faint and broken of a superintending
design'. But both could hear the voice of God, however thick
its accent. They were full of it. For Melville, however, it was
'Silence'. In his trip to Egypt and to Jerusalem in 1857, God is
an 'idea', a malign 'conception' that cannot be unconceived.
But God is never a voice.

So Melville slapped at God. He could not help playing the
infidel: he is one of the most delvingly sacrilegious writers
who has ever existed. For him, metaphysics could not stop
like a day-trip at some calm watering-place. Dialectic was
always an elastic solitude stretching into the desert. In his
letters to Hawthorne – a writer he self-describingly praised
as one who 'says No! in thunder', for 'all men who say *yes*
lie' – he churns himself into atheistical taunting, using
Hawthorne's reticence as a stand-in for God's. Nobody can
bear truth, he says again and again. He whirls around, magnificently, in 'atmospheric skepticisms'. Why is it, he asks in

a letter written in April 1851, while he was in the middle of writing *Moby-Dick*, that 'in the last stages of metaphysics a fellow always falls to *swearing* so? I could rip for an hour.' Most people, he tells Hawthorne, 'fear God, and *at bottom dislike* Him . . . because they rather distrust His heart, and fancy Him all brain like a watch'. Then he adds an elevated sneer: 'You perceive I employ a capital initial in the pronoun referring to the Deity; don't you think there is a slight dash of flunkeyism in that usage?' He slapped at God; but in some way, he could not do without the idea of being slapped by God in return.

III

Between 1847 and 1850, Melville ecstatically discovered three things: metaphor, metaphysics, and Shakespeare. These were the years in which he grew into the labour of writing *Moby-Dick* (which was written between February 1850 and the summer of 1851). *Mardi* (1849), his third novel but the first in which he indulged in philosophical 'ripping', had been poorly received. Quickly, disdainfully, he turned out two hotcakes for money, *Redburn* (1849) and *White-Jacket* (1850). Intellectually, his mind was abroad. His reading, which had been eager but arbitrary, now took on a systematic wildness. In 1847 and 1848, he bought or borrowed an edition of Shakespeare, a volume of Montaigne, and a volume of Rabelais. In February 1848 he acquired Coleridge's *Biographia Literaria*. In March, he read Sir Thomas Browne (clearly, after Shakespeare, his chief influence) and Seneca; in June, Dante. In 1849 he bought Pierre Bayle's heretical *Historical and Critical Dictionary*. In the same year, he noted in his new edition of Milton that Milton had wandered in his religious belief: 'I doubt not that darker doubts crossed Milton's soul, than ever disturbed Voltair [*sic*]. And he was more of what is called an Infidel.' But it was Shakespeare who troubled him. He could not believe, he wrote to Evert Duyckinck in February 1849, that he had lived so long without properly reading Shakespeare, who now seemed to him like Jesus: 'Ah, he's full of sermons-on-the-mount, and gentle, aye, almost as Jesus. I take such men to be inspired. I fancy that this moment Shakspeare [*sic*] in heaven ranks with Gabriel Raphael and Michael. And if another Messiah ever comes twill be in Shakespere's [*sic*] person.' He found himself drawn to the dark characters in Shakespeare, to Lear, Iago, Timon, the Fools. Through them Shakespeare 'craftily says, or sometimes insinuates the things which we feel to be so ter-rifically true, that it were all but madness for any good man, in his own proper character, to utter or even hint of them!' In his copy, he marks moments of madness.

In the summer of 1850, he met Hawthorne for the first time. His letters begin to sway somewhat maniacally. He assures Hawthorne that 'I am not mad, most noble Festus!' In another: 'This is rather a crazy letter in some respects, I apprehend.' It is simply that he is growing: 'Lord, when shall we be done growing?' he asks. Between 1849 and 1852, he is in a creative temper, flinging around words and ideas. In these letters he turns over, obsessively, the silence of God, and the sense that to speak truthfully in America demands a fit of secrecy. 'Truth is ridiculous to men.' Above all, while he is busy seeing a world stripped of God's presence, he is busy theologising literature. God has disappeared and returns as literature. If the Messiah comes again, it will be as Shakespeare. But the Messiah has come again, and he is called Melville. It is Melville who, in *Moby-Dick*, will follow 'Shakespeare and other masters of the great Art of Telling the Truth'. Here in America, Shakespeares are being born, Christlike creatures who will be crucified for telling the truth. 'Though I wrote the Gospels in this century, I should die in the gutter,' writes Melville in June 1851. Five months later, in November, he is groaning, fretting, racing: 'Appreciation! Recognition! Is Jove appreciated?' In the same letter, he whistles, Whitman-like: 'I feel that the Godhead is broken up like the bread at the supper, and that we are the pieces.' Literature is the new church, and *Moby-Dick* its bible. He is building what he calls (in that novel) 'Noah Webster's ark', a dictionary-ship, a bible-boat.

We hear, in these letters, the hymning, the fattened hysteria of *Moby-Dick*, its leaping exultations. But we also hear the self-pity and self-absorption, the will-to-punishment and self-destruction that make *Pierre* so intensely unlikeable a book. In that novel, allegory points only to itself, and is thus a continual self-advertisement. The entire book is an allegory supposed to remind us that such a book cannot really exist in America. *Pierre* is a kind of Calvinist self-mutilation at the literary, rather than the theological level. It is as if Melville says, in this book: 'Well, if good works really do get you nowhere theologically, here is a good work – this book – that will get me nowhere, because no one will acknowledge it as a good work.' *Pierre* reads as if Melville, anticipating that no one would appreciate his novel, deliberately ruined it (he writes in it that the best writers can never 'unravel their own

intricacies' but instead can only offer 'imperfect, unantici-
pated, and disappointing sequels'). Here writing becomes an
unthanked charity.

During the time that Melville wrote *Moby-Dick*, he
underwent a kind of hysteria of metaphor, an insanity of
metaphor. It was Melville's love of metaphor that drew him
ever further into 'Infidel-ideas'. Metaphor bred metaphysics
for Melville. His metaphors have a life of their own; it is not
only Melville that is 'growing' but also his language. Melville
is the most naturally metaphorical of writers, and one of the
very greatest. He saw the inside of the whale's mouth covered
with 'a glistening white membrane, glossy as bridal satins'; at
sea, the spouting jet of the whale made him look like 'a portly
burgher smoking his pipe of a warm afternoon'. He drew on
the example of late sixteenth- and early seventeenth-century
poetry and prose as naturally as if he were of that age and
not a nineteenth-century American. He saw how metaphor
domesticates and localises (the whale as a burgher) even as it
enlarges. For once we use metaphor, as Sir Thomas Browne
put it in his *Religio Medici* (1642), 'there is all Africa and her
prodigies in us'.

Soaked in theology, Melville was alert to the Puritan
habit of seeing the world allegorically, that is, metaphorically.
The world was a place of signs and wonders which could
always yield up its meaning, like secret ink. Melville did a
certain amount of this sign-gazing himself. Writing to Evert
Duyckinck in August 1850, he mentioned that he was writing
on an old heirloom, a desk of his uncle's. 'Upon dragging it
out to day light, I found that it was covered with the marks
of fowls . . . eggs had been laid in it – think of that! – Is it not

typical of those other eggs that authors may be said to lay in their desks . . .'

More usually, Melville had a way of following metaphor, and seeing where it led him. He wrote to Duyckinck, offering *Mardi* for his library, in the hope that it 'may possibly – by some miracle, that is – flower like the aloe, a hundred years hence – or not flower at all, which is more likely by far, for some aloes never flower'. A year later, writing to Hawthorne, he used an image which has become celebrated:

> I am like one of those seeds taken out of the Egyptian Pyramids, which, after being three thousand years a seed and nothing but a seed, being planted in English soil, it developed itself, grew to greenness, and then fell to mould. So I. Until I was twenty-five, I had no development at all. From my twenty-fifth year I date my life.

Both similes force Melville into dialectic. For, having embarked on them, he must follow their wandering, reverse logic. Thus he writes that his book is like an aloe, that it may flower in a hundred years; but then he is compelled – *compelled by the metaphor he inhabits* – to add that some aloes never flower, and since he has mentioned the flowering of the aloe, he must also mention the aloe's failure to flower. The second simile is more striking, because Melville made this comparison at the very height of his creative fever, while writing *Moby-Dick*. At this pinnacle, he foresees falling into literary decline (as, of course, he did, in real life). Why? Is it because Melville was eerily self-prescient? No, it is because, having likened himself to one of the seeds from the Pyramids, he must follow his own metaphor, and record that these seeds 'grew to greenness, and then fell to mould'. Melville does not really mean to offer a dark prophecy about his development. But the simile he has chosen is a hand-shake with likeness; and it is a handshake that will not let him go. He *must* mention 'mould' because his metaphor forces him to.

Of course, no one is *actually* forced by metaphor, except a madman. But Melville's writing certainly displays an unusual devotion to the logic of metaphor, which is the logic of paral-lelism. Of all writers (Shakespeare and Keats resemble him in this) he understood the independent, generative life that comes from likening something to something else. His work is deeply aware that as soon as you liken x to y, x has changed, and is now x+y, which has its own, parallel life. This is why Melville's similes sometimes seem to be bizarrely elabo-rated, and to continue over sentences and sentences. Like Gogol, who was quite as God-intoxicated as Melville, quite as unstable, who also employs immensely long and detailed metaphors, and whose fiction is similarly tilted towards the allegorical, Melville reads as if he simply cannot tear himself away from the rival life, the alienated majesty, that metaphor offers. If the whale resembles a portly burgher out for a stroll, then Melville feels himself committed to add that the whale's water-jet is the man's pipe: this is how he thinks. Metaphor, in this sense, becomes the very essence of fiction-making, because when a writer commits himself to the independent life of metaphor, he is acknowledging the fictional reality of an imagined alternative. For this is what metaphor is: a fic-tional alternative, a likeness, an other life. Metaphor is the whole of the imaginative fictional process in one move. Keats spoke of how language 'yeasts and works itself up' – *works itself.* This was everything to Melville. Pondering Goethe's advice that one must 'Live in the all, and then you will be happy', he writes: 'This "all" feeling, though, there is some truth in it. You must often have felt it, lying on the grass on a warm summer's day. Your legs seem to send out shoots into the earth. Your hair feels like leaves upon your head. This is the *all* feeling.' What Melville is crediting here is our power to create new life, a life that exists independently from us. And we do this through metaphor. You live 'in the all', when you feel metaphorical, when you feel that your hair is not your hair but has become leaves, your legs not your legs but growing shoots. And once they are growing, who can stop them?

IV

The theological implications of Melville's ravishment by metaphor are immense. Metaphor carries something over, it changes thought. In his letters and in his fiction, Melville thinks through metaphor, uses it to sway his thought. He ends one letter to Hawthorne by saying that he began his letter in a small way, yet 'here I have landed in Africa'. Recall Sir Thomas Browne's 'there is all Africa and her prodigies in us': metaphor transports him, and is then called upon to give image to that very transportation. In his note on Milton's wanderings in religious belief, Melville wrote that 'he who thinks for himself can never remain of the same mind' – Melville wanders, via metaphor, out of 'the same mind' into a different mind, out of sameness into likeness or difference.

The love of metaphor leads Melville astray theologically. His 'wandering' love of language breaks up his God, and he encourages this; his love of language bribes him, turns him against that rival, the Original Author. This can be seen again and again in the work. In Judaea, in 1857, Melville is put into a cold trance by the rockiness of the landscape. 'Is the desolation of the land the result of the fatal embrace of the Deity?' he asks himself. The land must have produced the religion, he feels: 'As the sight of haunted Haddon Hall suggested to Mrs Radcliffe her curdling romances, so I have little doubt, the diabolical landscapes [*sic*] great part of Judea must have suggested to the Jewish people, their terrific theology.' What is terrific is the vulgar blasphemy of the metaphor. Ann Radcliffe wrote Gothic romances. Yet it is because Melville cannot resist the impulse of likeness that he is drawn into comparing the whole of biblical theology to a mere Gothic romance, and ends up implying, thanks to his simile, that Jewish monotheism was just a creative prompting from the landscape, a creative idea for a book – The Book.

Wandering, and the wandering of metaphor, is the subject of Plotinus Plinlimmon's sermon in *Pierre*. In that sermon, Melville likens God to Greenwich Mean Time. God, says Melville, is the universal meridian. We, His creations, are like the chronometers in ships. These chronometers give the time at Greenwich, even when a ship is in the Azores. That is how we are supposed to be, says Melville, carrying God's time throughout the world, even if it contradicts the mere local time. Yet this is impossible, continues Melville. If a man is in China, he should live by local Chinese time, not by Greenwich time. A man who lived according to Greenwich time in China would be mad. But this is exactly what God impossibly asks us to do. He asks us to live as if we were in heaven, and not on earth. This lovely five-page passage combines all of Melville's characteristic tendencies. It is a complaint against God, of considerable philosophical power. It is a metaphor at once homely and grand, which Melville establishes and then commits himself to, elaborating both its allegorical logic and its independent life over many paragraphs, so that the metaphor becomes the vehicle of blasphemous complaint. Once the metaphor is in place, Melville must follow its violent implications to the end. And it is a metaphor about metaphor, for it is an allegory *about* wandering, about straying. Melville's complaint against God is precisely that, like ships, we tend to stray from God's coordinates, and cannot help doing so. To wander is natural – and here, he says, is a wandering metaphor to prove it.

Moby-Dick represents the triumph of this atheism of metaphor. Or perhaps, this polytheism of metaphor. For it is a book in which allegory explodes into a thousand metaphors; a book in which the Puritan habit of reading signs and seeing stable meanings behind them is mocked by an almost grotesque abundance of metaphor. In this book meaning is mashed up like a pudding. The Godhead is indeed broken into pieces. Truth is kaleidoscopically affronted. The whale is likened to everything under the sun, and everything under the moon, too – a portly burgher, an Ottoman, a book, a language, a script, a nation, the Sphinx, the Pyramids. The whale is also Satan and God. The whale is 'inscrutable'. It is so full of meanings that it threatens to have no meanings at all, which is the fear Ishmael confesses to in the celebrated chapter 'The Whiteness of the Whale'. Critics who persist in seeing in Melville an American Gnostic do so because the whale is a demiurge, a bad god (the Gnostic premise was that we are ruled by a bad god). But what, Melville asks, if the whale means nothing at all? What if, at the very heart of the sarcophagus, there is absolutely nothing?

V

By late summer 1851, it was over. This great novel was done. Melville had asked the question: how does an American writer make tragedy worthy of Shakespeare's without setting the story in the remote past? He answered it by making his novel an historical novel whose epoch is the whale – thousands of years old. As Sir Walter Scott filled his novels with the dust of medieval France or Scotland, with clothes, dates, battles, so Melville filled his book with the clothes, dates and battles of the whale. The whale is a country and an age.

How easily it might not have worked! The power is all verbal. Without the language the metaphysics would just be grain. Although one remembers the rhapsodies of poetry, one forgets how precise, how grounded is the language, with what vernacular swing it moves. (Melville founded American vernacular prose equally with Twain: to know this, compare the rhythms of Bellow's *The Adventures of Augie March* with the rhythms of *Moby-Dick*.) Melville Americanises Shakespeare, gives it tilt. Where Shakespeare has Antony like a dolphin, showing its back above the element it lived in, Melville has a democracy of porpoises, tossing their backs to heaven 'like caps in a Fourth of July crowd'. Queequeg, the cannibal, can go anywhere: 'Transported to the Indies, his live blood would not spoil like bottled ale.' Not for nothing does Ishmael pray to 'the great democratic God'. Again and again one is thrilled by the teeter of metaphor, watching it almost fail, and then take like a skin graft. There is a mad persistence to this metaphorising, a fiery pedantry. There is the noise the whale makes, 'an enormous wallowing sound as of fifty elephants stirring in their litter'; the harpooners turning their harpoons in the very quick of the beast, and yet delicately, 'as if cautiously seeking to feel after some gold watch that the whale might have swallowed'. There is Pip, the 'little Negro boy', who falls into the water 'like a traveler's trunk . . . Bobbing up and down in the sea, Pip's ebon head showed like a head of cloves.' There is Ahab's soul, 'a centipede, that moves upon a hundred legs'. And at last, the final chase, the whale sliding like metaphor itself through its fluid of meanings: 'on each bright side, the whale shed off enticings'.

This carnival comes to a chill rest in the chapter called 'The Whiteness of the Whale'. Here Ishmael asks if it is the whiteness of the whale that torments. For whiteness may signify many things (sacredness, purity, superiority) or it may signify nothing. Whiteness 'stabs us from behind with the thought of annihilation . . . whiteness is not so much a colour as the visible absence of colour, and at the same time the concrete of all colors . . . a colorless, all-colour of atheism from which we shrink . . .' Here, in whiteness, is the end of allegory, and therefore the end of metaphor, and therefore the end of language. It is silence, God's Silence, and it sits in the book like some unnamed sea, ready to suck down all who come upon it.

Moby-Dick is the great dream of mastery over language. But it also represents a terrible struggle with language. For if the terror of the whale, the terror of God, is His inscrutability, then it is language that has made Him so. It is Melville's abundance of language that is constantly filling everything with meaning, and emptying it out too. Language breaks up God, releases us from the one meaning of the predestinating God, but merely makes that God differently inscrutable by flooding Him with thousands of different meanings. I think that language and metaphor were a great torture as well as a great joy to Melville. Melville saw – and *Moby-Dick* is the enactment of this vision – that language helps to explain God and to conceal God in equal measure, and that these two functions annul each other. Thus language does not help us explain or describe God. Quite the contrary, it registers simply our inability to describe God; it holds our torment. Yet language is all there is, and thus Melville follows it as Ahab follows the whale, to the very end.

Theologically, metaphor acts like language. It insists on relationship, but to compare one thing with another is also to suggest non-relationship, for nothing *is* ever like anything else. Metaphor always carries the danger of being a wandering away *from* relationship. Thus metaphor, which so promises to illuminate and enlarge, also registers our ultimate inability to compare things. Metaphor, like language, holds our torment, and this explains the peculiar doggedness, almost madness, of Melville's obsession with metaphor. Melville is always using metaphor to solve a problem which metaphor itself only complicates. Melville's metaphors resemble the medieval preference for describing God by His attributes, for describing Him indirectly. But when you have done this, you have not really known Him, and perhaps you have only aggravated the difficulty by bombarding Him with approximations. The very project is futile, and also heretical, because as soon as you liken God to something else, you bring God into the sea of metaphor, on equal status with everything else. You dare the infidel idea that *God is only a metaphor*. No, language is a voice that does not help us get any nearer to the silence of God; it is its own voice.

Melville may have become another messiah in writing *Moby-Dick*; master of meaning, Melville is the real 'great democratic God' to which Ishmael is pledged and by whom he is predestined. But to be a literary god is not to get closer to an actual god, and Melville, who could not entirely release the monitor of God from his life, surely, bitterly knew this. He certainly knew that language is one of the veils of theology, not one of the clarities: 'As soon as you say *Me*, a *God*, a *Nature*, so soon you jump off from your stool and hang from the beam,' he wrote to Hawthorne. 'Yes, that word is the hangman. Take God out of the dictionary, & you would have Him in the street.'

No more than anyone else did Melville manage to get God into the street. He went tidally, between belief and unbelief. Melville has Ishmael argue that life is always a ceaseless tide:

> There is no steady unretracing progress in this life: we do not advance through fixed gradations, and at the last one pause: – through infancy's unconscious spell, boyhood's thoughtless faith, adolescence, doubt . . . then scepticism,

then disbelief, resting at last in manhood's pondering repose of If. But once gone through, we trace the round again: and are infants, boys, and men, and Ifs eternally. Where lies the final harbor, whence we unmoor no more?

Theologically, Melville lived his life in an eternal If, which his love of metaphor only encouraged. Linguistically, in the gorgeous play of metaphor, he lived his life in an eternal All – which was at the same time an eternal If, because it could not console, could not banish the If, and in fact only deepened it. The entity Melville most loved, language, separated him from the entity he most desired, God. A god of a thousand meanings may be as absent as the God of one meaning. Ahab's monomaniacal hunt of the whale is not so far from Ishmael's multiple tolerance of it. Any true life is a blasphemously exhaustive hunt, and Melville lived a true life. Poor Melville, lucky Melville!

1997

Elena Ferrante

ELENA FERRANTE, OR 'ELENA FERRANTE,' is one of Italy's best-known least-known contemporary writers. She is the author of several remarkable, lucid, austerely honest novels, the most celebrated of which is *The Days of Abandonment*, published in Italy in 2002. Compared with Ferrante, Thomas Pynchon is a publicity profligate. It's assumed that Elena Ferrante is not the author's real name. In the past twenty years or so, though, she has provided written answers to journalists' questions, and a number of her letters have been collected and published. From them, we learn that she grew up in Naples, and has lived for periods outside Italy. She has a classics degree; she has referred to being a mother. One might also infer from her fiction and from her interviews that she is not now married. ('Over the years, I've moved often, in general unwillingly, out of necessity . . . I'm no longer dependent on the movements of others, only on my own' is her encryption.) In addition to writing, 'I study, I translate, I teach.'

And that is it. What she looks like, what her real name is, when she was born, how she currently lives – these things are all unknown. In 1991, when her first novel, *Troubling Love*, was about to be published in Italy (*L'Amore Molesto*, its original title, hints at something more troubling than mere trouble), Ferrante sent her publisher a letter that, like her fiction, is pleasingly rigorous and sharply forthright. It lays out principles she has not deviated from since. She will do nothing for *Troubling Love*, she tells her publisher, because she has already done enough: she wrote it. She won't take part in conferences or discussions, and won't go to accept prizes, if any are awarded. 'I will be interviewed only in writing, but I would prefer to limit even that to the indispensable minimum':

> I believe that books, once they are written, have no need of their authors. If they have something to say, they will sooner or later find readers; if not, they won't . . . I very much love those mysterious volumes, both ancient and modern, that have no definite author but have had and continue to have an intense life of their own. They seem to me a sort of night-time miracle, like the gifts of the Befana, which I waited for as a child . . . True miracles are the ones whose makers will never be known . . . Besides, isn't it true that promotion is expensive? I will be the least expensive author of the publishing house. I'll spare you even my presence.

It is hard to argue with the logic of this withdrawal, and the effortful prying of the Italian press – why have you chosen this privacy? Are you hiding the autobiographical nature of your work? Is there any truth to the rumour that your work is really by Domenico Starnone? – has about it the kind of repressed anger that attends a suicide. Ferrante is probably right when she claims that an author who does publicity has accepted, 'at least in theory, that the entire person, with all his experiences and his affections, is placed for sale along with the book'. Our language betrays us: nowadays, you triumphantly *sell* a novel to a publisher; thirty years ago, a publisher simply *accepted* that novel.

As soon as you read her fiction, Ferrante's restraint seems wisely self-protective. Her novels are intensely, violently personal, and because of this they seem – *seem* – to dangle bristling key chains of confession before the unsuspecting reader. There are four novels available in English, each translated by Ann Goldstein: *Troubling Love, The Days of Abandonment, The Lost Daughter* and now *My Brilliant Friend*. Each book is narrated by a woman: an academic in *The Lost Daughter*, and a writer in *The Days of Abandonment*. The woman who tells the story of her Neapolitan youth in *My Brilliant Friend* is named Elena, and seems to cherish the possibilities of writing and being a writer. More than these occasional and fairly trivial overlappings with life, the material that the early novels visit and revisit is intimate and often shockingly candid: child abuse, divorce, motherhood, wanting and not wanting children, the tedium of sex, the repulsions of the body, the narrator's desperate struggle to retain a cohesive identity within a traditional marriage and amid the burdens of child-rearing. The novels present themselves (with the exception of the latest) like case histories, full of flaming rage, lapse, failure, and tenuous psychic success. But these are fictional case histories. One can understand that Ferrante has no interest in adding her privacy to the novelistic pyre.

The Days of Abandonment is Ferrante's most widely read novel in English, with good reason. It assails bourgeois niceties and domestic proprieties; it rips the skin off the habitual. Olga is thirty-eight, is married to Mario, lives in Turin, and has two young children, Ilaria and Gianni. 'One April afternoon, right after lunch, my husband announced that he wanted to leave me.' The calm opening sentence belies the fury and turmoil to come. Olga is blindsided by Mario's announcement. First, there are the obvious responses: loathing, jealousy, despair. She yells without control at Mario: 'I don't give a shit about prissiness. You wounded me, you are destroying me, and I'm supposed to speak like a good, well-brought-up wife? Fuck you! What words am I supposed to use for what you've done to me, for what you're doing to me? What words should I use for what you're doing with that woman! Let's talk about it! Do you lick her cunt? Do you stick it in her ass? Do you do all the things you never did with me? Tell me! Because I see you! With these eyes I see everything you do together, I see it a hundred thousand times, I see it night and day, eyes open and eyes closed!'

What menaces Olga more deeply is the threatened dissolution of her self. What does her life amount to, without the intact family unit? 'What a mistake it had been to close off the meaning of my existence in the rites that Mario offered with cautious conjugal rapture,' she reflects. 'What a mistake it had been to entrust the sense of myself to his gratifications, his enthusiasms, to the ever more productive course of his life.' She is haunted by the memory of a dark figure from her Neapolitan childhood, a woman who lived in her apartment building, whose husband left her, and who, in her abandonment, lost all identity: 'Every night, from that moment on, our neighbour wept . . . The woman lost everything, even her name (perhaps it was Emilia), for everyone she became the "*poverella*", that poor woman, when we spoke of her that was what we called her.' Young Olga was repelled by 'a grief so gaudy', and is desperate, in her own abandonment, not to act like the *poverella*, not to be 'consumed by tears'.

Over the next few weeks, Olga struggles to hold on to reality. The children must be looked after, the dog walked, the bills paid. One day, she sees Mario with his new lover, and realises that it is Carla, a twenty-year-old who is the daughter of an old friend; Mario had tutored her. Olga violently assaults her husband, knocks him down in the street, tears his shirt. Meanwhile, at home, everything is disintegrating. Ants have invaded the apartment; Gianni has a fever; the phone stops working because the bill hasn't been paid; the front-door lock won't work; the dog gets sick. Ferrante turns ordinary domestic misery into an expressionistic hell; she can pull a scream out of thin air. These small trials become a huge symbolic judgement. When Olga sprays insecticide to kill the ants, she does so uneasily, 'feeling that the spray can might well be a living extension of my organism, a nebulizer of the gall I felt in my body'. Her inability to open the front door strikes her as the overwrought emblem of a sexual failure; the workmen who had installed the new lock had seemed to insinuate that locks 'recognize the hand of their master'. 'I remembered the sneer with which the older one had given me his card, in case I should need help,' Olga tells us. 'I knew perfectly well what lock he wished to intervene in, certainly not that of the reinforced door.'

The literary excitement of *The Days of Abandonment* lies in the picture it gives of a mind in emergency, at the very limits of coherence and decency, a mind that has become a battlefield between reason and insanity, survival and explosion. Here

Olga watches Carrano, her downstairs neighbour, a single man, a mild, shy, greying professional cellist:

> So I stood silently watching him from the fifth floor, thin but broad in the shoulders, his hair gray and thick. I felt an increasing hostility toward him that became more tenacious the more unreasonable I felt it to be. What were his secrets of a man alone, a male obsession with sex, perhaps, the late-life cult of the cock. Certainly he, too, saw no farther than his ever-weaker squirt of sperm, was content only when he could verify that he could still get it up, like the dying leaves of a dried-up plant that's given water. Rough with the women's bodies he happened to encounter, hurried, dirty, certainly his only objective was to score points, as in a rifle range, to sink into a red pussy as into a fixed thought surrounded by concentric circles. Better if the patch of hair is young and shiny, ah the virtue of a firm ass. So he thought, such were the thoughts I attributed to him, I was shaken by vivid electric shocks of rage.

In a spasm of self-hatred and need, Olga throws herself at poor Carrano: the scene in which she sadistically seduces him, at once requiring and repulsing his desire, is a tour de force of squalor. Yet Carrano surprises Olga, later in the book, with his gentleness and generosity, and becomes one of the unexpected agents of Olga's eventual survival, her successful race against dissolution.

Ferrante has said that she likes to write narratives 'where the writing is clear, honest, and where the facts – the facts of ordinary life – are extraordinarily gripping when read'. Her prose has indeed a bare lucidity, and is often aphoristic and continent, in Ann Goldstein's elegant, burnished English. But what is thrilling about her earlier novels is that, in sympathetically following her characters' extremities, Ferrante's own writing has no limits, is willing to take every thought forward to its most radical conclusion and backward to its most radical birthing. This is most obvious in the fearless way in which her female narrators think about children and motherhood.

Ferrante's novels could be seen as marked, somewhat belatedly, by the second-wave feminism that produced, among other writing, Margaret Drabble's fiction of female domestic entrapment and Hélène Cixous's theory of *l'écriture féminine*, in the 1970s. (*L'écriture féminine*, or feminine writing, is the project of inscribing 'the feminine' into the language of a text.) Yet there is something almost post-ideological about the savagery with which Ferrante attacks the themes of motherhood and womanhood. She seems to enjoy the psychic surplus, the outrageousness, the terrible, singular complexity of her protagonists' familial dramas. Olga's plight might seem familiar enough, in particular her apprehension that, in throwing her all into being a mother, she has become dangerously null, while her 'ever more productive' husband has only blossomed in the outside world. But the rhetoric with which she expresses her despair and revulsion around motherhood is perhaps less familiar. There is little room for ideological back-and-forth when children are seen as hideous enemies from a horror film: 'I was like a lump of food that my children chewed without stopping; a cud made of a living material that continually amalgamated and softened its living substance to allow two greedy bloodsuckers to nourish themselves, leaving on me the odor and taste of their gastric juices. Nursing, how repulsive, an animal function.' As Olga follows her train of thought, she becomes convinced that the 'stink of motherhood' clung to her and was partly responsible for her husband's defection. 'Sometimes Mario pasted himself against me, took me, holding me as I nearly slept, tired himself after work, without emotions. He did it persisting on my almost absent flesh that tasted of milk, cookies, cereal, with a desperation of his own that overlapped mine without his realizing it. I was the body of incest . . . I was the mother to be violated, not a lover. Already he was searching for figures more suitable for love.' There is a foul brilliance in how Ferrante sticks with the logic of Olga's illogic, so that an ordinary enough complaint about the difficulty of raising children becomes an outsized revulsion, and the stink of motherhood leads inexorably to the incestuous end of all marital eros. But this wayward rigor, engrossing in its own right, also makes absolute sense within the context of Olga's raging jealousy.

Leda, the narrator of *The Lost Daughter* (published in Italian in 2006, and in English in 2008), is a forty-seven-year-old academic who, like Olga, has had to manage both motherhood and professional advancement. She is no longer married to her scientist husband, who lives in Toronto, where her two grown daughters, Marta and Bianca, have also gone to live. About her daughters Leda has ambivalent and often sharply hostile thoughts. Did she, she wonders, really want her children, or was her body simply expressing itself, as a reproducing animal?

I had wanted Bianca, one wants a child with an animal opacity reinforced by popular beliefs. She had arrived immediately,

I was twenty-three, her father and I were right in the midst of a difficult struggle to keep jobs at the university. He made it, I didn't. A woman's body does a thousand different things, toils, runs, studies, fantasizes, invents, wearies, and meanwhile the breasts enlarge, the lips of the sex swell, the flesh throbs with a round life that is yours, your life, and yet pushes elsewhere, draws away from you although it inhabits your belly, joyful and weighty, felt as a greedy impulse and yet repellent, like an insect's poison injected into a vein.

For the narrators of Ferrante's earlier novels, life appears to be a painful conundrum of attachment and detachment. What seems appalling to Leda is that her daughters are so umbilically connected to her own flesh and at the same time are always pushing 'elsewhere', are so alien and other. When her daughters were six and four, Leda abandoned them for three years. 'All the hopes of youth seemed to have been destroyed, I seemed to be falling backward toward my mother, my grandmother, the chain of mute or angry women I came from.' Suspended on a chain of maternity – grandmothers, mothers, daughters, all flesh of one's own flesh – the only thing is to sever the links and get out. Leda feels it is the way to survive: 'I loved them too much and it seemed to me that love for them would keep me from becoming myself.' She remembers standing in the kitchen, her daughters watching her, pulled by them but more strongly pulled by the world outside the home:

I felt their gazes longing to tame me, but more brilliant was the brightness of the life outside them, new colors, new bodies, new intelligence, a language to possess finally as if it were my true language, and nothing, nothing that seemed to me reconcilable with that domestic space from which they stared at me in expectation. Ah, to make them invisible, to no longer hear the demands of their flesh as commands more pressing, more powerful than those which came from mine.

Ferrante may never mention Hélène Cixous or French feminist literary theory, but her fiction is a kind of practical *écriture féminine*: these novels, which reflect on work and motherhood, on the struggle for a space in which to work outside the work of motherhood, necessarily reflect on the achievement of their own writing. To get these difficult words onto the page is to have subdued the demands of the domestic space, quietened for precious intervals the commands of children, and found 'a language to possess finally as if it were my true language.'

Before the writer is an adult, she is a child. Before she makes a family, she inherits one; and in order to find her true language she may need to escape the demands and prohibitions of this first, given community. That is one of the themes that connect Ferrante's latest novel, *My Brilliant Friend*, with her earlier work. At first sight, her new book, published in Italy in 2011, seems very different from its anguished, slender predecessors. It's a large, captivating, amiably crowded *Bildungsroman*, apparently the first of a trilogy. Its narrator, Elena Greco, recalls her Neapolitan childhood and adolescence, in the late 1950s. There is a kind of joy in the book not easily found in the earlier work. The city of Elena's childhood is a poor, violent place (the same city is found in Ferrante's first novel, *Troubling Love*). But deprivation gives details a snatched richness. A trip to the sea, a new friend, a whole day spent with your father ('We spent the entire day together, the only one in our lives, I don't remember any others,' Elena says at one point), a brief holiday, the chance to take some books out of a library, the encouragement of a respected teacher, a sketched design for a beautiful pair of shoes, a wedding, the promise of getting your article published in a local journal, a conversation with a boy whose intellect is deeper and more liberal than your own – these ordinary-seeming occurrences take on an unexpected luminosity against a background of poverty, ignorance, violence and parental threat, a world in which a character can be casually described as 'struggling to speak in Italian' (because mostly people in this book are using Neapolitan vernacular). If Ferrante's earlier novels have some of the brutal directness and familial torment of Elsa Morante's work, then *My Brilliant Friend* may remind the reader of neo-realist movies by De Sica and Visconti, or perhaps of Giovanni Verga's short stories about Sicilian poverty.

Elena meets her brilliant friend at school, in the first grade. Both children are from relatively impoverished households. Lila Cerullo is the daughter of Fernando Cerullo, a shoemaker; Elena's father works as a porter at city hall. Lila first impresses Elena because she is 'very bad'. She is feral, quick, unafraid, vicious in word and deed. For every act of violence meted out to her, Lila has a swift response. When Elena throws stones back at gangs of boys, she does so without much conviction; Lila does everything with 'absolute determination'. No one can really keep pace with that 'terrible, dazzling girl', and everyone is afraid of her. Boys steer clear of her, because she is 'skinny, dirty, and always had a cut or bruise of some sort, but also because she had a sharp tongue . . . spoke a scathing dialect, full of swear words, which cut off at its origin any feeling of love'. Lila's reputation grows when it is discovered that she taught herself to read at the age of three: there is a wonderful scene, indeed the equal of something by Verga, when Lila's schoolteacher excitedly calls in her mother, Nunzia Cerullo, and asks Lila to read a word she has written on the blackboard. Lila correctly reads the word, but her mother looks hesitantly, almost fearfully, at the teacher: 'The teacher at first seemed not to understand why her own enthusiasm was not reflected in the mother's eyes. But then she must have guessed that Nunzia didn't know how to read.'

Elena, who had enjoyed her status as the cleverest girl in the class, has to fall in behind the brilliant Lila, who is as smart at school as she is on the street: she comes first on all the tests, and can do complicated calculations in her head. The two girls seem destined, through education, to escape their origins. In the last year of elementary school, they become obsessed with money, and talk about it 'the way characters in novels talk about searching for treasure'. But *My Brilliant Friend* is a *Bildungsroman* in mono, not stereo; we sense early on that Lila will stay trapped in her world, and that Elena, the writer, will get out – like the academic who, in *The Lost Daughter*, describes her need to leave violent and limited Naples thus: 'I had run away like a burn victim who, screaming, tears off the burned skin, believing that she is tearing off the burning itself.'

In this beautiful and delicate tale of confluence and reversal, it is hard to identify the moments when a current changes course. Perhaps one occurs when Elena's schoolteacher, Maestra Oliviero, tells her that she must take the test for admission to middle school, and that her parents will have to pay for extra lessons to prepare her. Elena's parents, after some resistance, say yes; Lila's say no. Lila tells Elena she is going to take the test anyway, and no one doubts her: 'Although she was fragile in appearance, every prohibition lost substance in her presence.' But Lila eventually loses heart, and does not go to middle school. When Elena later mentions the brilliant Lila to Maestra Oliviero, the teacher asks her if she knows what the plebs are. Yes, Elena says, the people. 'And if one wishes to remain a plebeian,' Maestra Oliviero continues, 'he, his children, the children of his children deserve nothing. Forget Cerullo and think of yourself.'

This warning casts its shadow over the rest of the novel like a prophecy in classical tragedy. In a powerful scene near the end of the book, Lila Cerullo, now sixteen and on the verge of marrying a grocer's son, decides that she wants to take the wedding invitation in person to Maestra Oliviero. Elena accompanies her. The old teacher affects not to recognise the brilliant girl who never made it to middle school, and turns to Elena: 'I know Cerullo, I don't know who this girl is.' With that, she shuts the door in their faces. At Lila's wedding – where, in a characteristically vivid detail, the guests become restive when they realise that the 'wine wasn't the same quality for all the tables' – Elena looks at the modest company and recalls the schoolteacher's question:

At that moment I knew what the plebs were, much more clearly than when, years earlier, she had asked me. The plebs were us. The plebs were that fight for food and wine, that quarrel over who should be served first and better, that dirty floor on which the waiters clattered back and forth, those increasingly vulgar toasts. The plebs were my mother, who had drunk wine and now was leaning against my father's shoulder, while he, serious, laughed, his mouth gaping, at the sexual allusions of the metal dealer. They were all laughing, even Lila, with the expression of one who has a role and will play it to the utmost.

This is where *My Brilliant Friend* ends, with Elena watching the horizon, and Lila being watched by Elena. One girl is facing beyond the book; the other is caught within its pages. Elena Greco, like the women who narrate Ferrante's earlier novels, is a survivor; like them, she has had to wrench her survival out of the drama of attachment and detachment. She feels a kind of survivor's guilt, as if she had robbed the promise of her riches from Lila's treasury. A final irony is coiled in the novel's title, the biggest reversal, a shift in perspective that has taken a whole novel to effect. Before the wedding, when Elena is helping Lila with her wedding dress, the two girls briefly discuss Elena's continued schooling. Lila urges Elena to keep on studying; if necessary she – soon to be a comfortably married woman – will pay for it. 'Thanks, but at a certain point school is over,' Elena says with a nervous, doubtless self-deprecating laugh. 'Not for you,' Lila replies ardently, 'you're my brilliant friend, you have to be the best of all, boys and girls.'

2013

Virginia Woolf's Mysticism

I

THERE IS A STORY that the young Virginia Woolf and others visited Rodin's studio in 1904. The sculptor told the party that they could touch anything except the figures still under sheets. When Woolf began to unwrap one of the sculptures, Rodin slapped her. The story is probably apocryphal; but like the grave of an unknown soldier, we can have it as the emblem of an invisible struggle. Woolf's literary struggle was to uncover figures, in a way that they had never before been denuded. She unwrapped consciousness. To do this, she would have to disobey the generation that stood behind her, its slapping hand outstretched like Rodin's. Woolf's best biographer, Hermione Lee, tells the anecdote in a chapter titled 'Madness': Woolf was on the edge of an attack of mental instability. But there is also what Henry James called the madness of art.

Much about Woolf's childhood can be learned from a ninety-page memoir called 'A Sketch of the Past'. Woolf wrote it in 1939 and 1940, just before she took her life. In it, she looked again at the origins of her literary rebellion, which she found in the impress of her parents, and in the thick air of the family home, at Hyde Park Gate in west London. Virginia Stephen was born in 1882, into the very riot of Victorianism. She wrote that she and her sister, Vanessa, represented 1910 and her parents 1860. All her writing would offer an insubordination to the sure captaincy of the Victorians. They were represented by her mother, Julia Stephen, whom Virginia complicatedly loved, and her father, Leslie Stephen, whom she complicatedly hated. Julia Stephen, a Victorian idealisation of the wife and mother, was unselfish, an emotional wet nurse to her husband, devoted to good works outside the home. When Virginia started writing book reviews in 1905, she felt the ghost of her mother (who had died in 1895) warning her to be femininely decorous, and to soothe male reputations. Woolf, characteristically, wrote at this time that 'My real delight in reviewing is to say nasty things.' Leslie Stephen became Mr Ramsay in *To the Lighthouse*, the needy monolith surrounded by the poor pebbles of his battered family. He was one of the most important agnostics of his generation, a literary critic, a Cambridge rationalist, the author of *The History of English Thought in the Eighteenth Century*. Stephen had a grinding, puritanical mind. 'He would ask what was the cube root of such and such a number; for he always worked out mathematical problems on railway tickets,' wrote Woolf in 'A Sketch of the Past'. Woolf selects one sharp memory which gives us a picture of difficult pleasure. She remembers him stooping from his intellectual labours to mend his little daughter's sailboat, and snorting in embarrassment: 'Absurd! – what fun it is doing this.'

In *To the Lighthouse*, Mr Ramsay is seen struggling to get beyond letter Q in the intellectual alphabet. It is one of Woolf's most beautiful similes: 'It was a splendid mind. For if thought is like the keyboard of a piano, divided into so many notes, or like the alphabet . . . then his splendid mind had no sort of difficulty in running over those letters one by one, firmly and accurately, until it had reached, say, the letter Q. He reached Q. Very few people in the whole of England ever reach Q . . . But after Q? What comes next?' Leslie Stephen acted like a genius but he thought like a merely gifted man. His tantrums, his loud groaning about the difficulty of mental activity, his domestic helplessness, his virile activity (a twenty-mile walk was nothing), the intellectual fez he wore on his head – does it not look, to us, a little like the self-conscious opposite of a dunce's cap? – the foaming beard; all this was sanctioned by the age. It is how 'great men' acted. But Stephen once confessed to his daughter, with his admirable honesty, that he had only 'a good second-class mind', and Woolf wrote: 'He had I think no feeling for pictures; no ear for music; no sense of the sound of words.' Unwittingly, her father trained her in hostility, taught her how to float away from him in his own shallow waters. The way she summed up his limitations would be the way she pounced on the limitations of a whole class of people. Repeatedly, one comes across these portraits in her diaries. Her father was the model 'insider'. He was an institution, which could be abbreviated to 'Eton-Cambridge', places from which she was excluded. Such people were what she called 'Romans' (whereas she was Greek). They kept the Empire spinning, politically and intellectually. They were necessary, she wrote, 'like Roman roads'. But in her father, she found 'not a subtle mind; not an imaginative mind; not a suggestive mind. But a strong mind; a healthy out of door, moor striding mind; an impatient, limited mind; a conventional mind entirely accepting his own standard of what is honest.'

Leslie Stephen can be caricatured, though Woolf never did this. Yet the education he gave his daughter was deep. Virginia Stephen did not go out of the house to school. Her childhood was isolated, and spent in the shadow of her father, who expected that Virginia would 'become an author in time'. Virginia ran through the battery of his books. He read, of course, to the collected family – the thirty-two Waverley novels of Scott, Carlyle's *The French Revolution*, Jane Austen, and the English poets. But Woolf's own reading, under her father's tutelage, constituted her real education. It was like a less heated version of John Stuart Mill's upbringing. She read Greek – Plato, of course – with Walter Pater's sister. Leslie Stephen gave her history and biography. During 1897, when she was fifteen, he chose for her Pepys's *Diary*, Arnold's *History of Rome*, Campbell's *Life of Coleridge*, Macaulay's *History*, Carlyle's *Reminiscences*, and *Essays in Ecclesiastical Biography* by James Stephen, her grandfather. We see Woolf developing that deep, secretive relationship with language that often characterises the solitary child. 'I have spotted the best lines in the play,' she wrote to her brother, Thoby, who was at Cambridge. 'Now if that doesn't send a shiver down your spine . . . you are no true Shakespearean!' And more plaintively, again to Thoby: 'I dont get anyone to argue with me now, and feel the want. I have to delve from books, painfully and alone, what you get every evening sitting over your fire and smoking your pipe with Strachey etc.'

Woolf's background, like a patronymic, was something that marked her publicly. She lived for twenty-two years in her father's house, and escaped only when he died in 1904. This was her first escape – out of Hyde Park Gate, and into Bloomsbury, where she lived with her brothers and sister, in Gordon Square. Her second escape was into literary journalism. The *Collected Essays*, which are still being edited, is the most substantial body of criticism in English this century. They belong in the tradition of Johnson, Coleridge, Arnold and Henry James. This is the tradition of poet-critics, until the modern era, when novelists like Woolf and James join it. That is, her essays and reviews are a writer's criticism, written in the language of art, which is the language of metaphor. The writer-critic, or poet-critic, has a competitive proximity to the writers she discusses. That competition is registered verbally. The writer-critic is always showing a little plumage to the writer under discussion. If the writer-critic appears to generalise about literature, that is because literature is what she does, and one is always generalising about oneself.

In her criticism, the language of metaphor becomes a way of speaking to fiction in its own accent, the only way of respecting fiction's ultimate indescribability. Metaphor is how the critic avoids bullying fiction with adult simplicities. For it is a language of forceful hesitation. Its force lies in the vigour and originality of Woolf's metaphors; its hesitation lies in its admission that, in criticism, the language of pure summation does not exist. One is always thinking through books, not about them. Woolf's father had written 'successfully' *about* books, with a vigorous alienation from his subjects. Leslie Stephen's essays chew through books to the cardboard, grimly intent on the same universal mastication, whether the subject is Pope or the history of the Popes. Therein lay his limitations, and Woolf could surely see this, even if, as a young woman, she could only articulate this limitation as the apprehension that her father's essays were not 'literary' enough. Woolf, by contrast, is 'literary', which is to say metaphorical. She approaches fiction gently, seemingly anxious not to overwhelm it with strong comprehension.

All criticism is itself metaphorical in movement, because it deals in likeness. It asks: what is art *like*? What does it resemble? How can it best be described, or re-described? If the artwork describes itself, then criticism's purpose is to re-describe the artwork in its own, different language. But literature and literary criticism share the same language. In this, literary criticism is completely different from art and music and their criticisms. To describe literature critically is to describe it again, but as it were for the first time. It is to describe it as if literature were music or art, and as if one could sing or paint criticism.

The language of metaphor is the language of this secret sharing, of approximation, of likeness, and of competition. For, as a critic, Woolf was always in competition with what she was reviewing, and her language's proximity constitutes a luxurious squabble. Again and again, her metaphors are used to deliver a judgement which marks both her nearness to her subjects – her ability to use an artistic language –

and her separateness. Forster, she writes, is too fidgety as a novelist, always stepping in to talk about his characters: 'he is like a light sleeper who is always being woken by something in the room'. Dickens, she felt, rather vulgarly made excitement by inventing new, disposable characters: 'Dickens makes his books blaze up not by tightening the plot or sharpening the wit, but by throwing another handful of people upon the fire.' George Moore, she felt, was too literary a novelist: 'Literature has wound itself about him like a veil, forbidding the free use of his limbs.' Many of her essays were written for the *Times Literary Supplement*, whose contributions were, until recently, unsigned. But this anonymity was ideal: surely Woolf knew that her prose had to sign itself. So her essays, both in texture and in content, were self-advertisements. Between 1917 and 1925, she produced her delicate manifestos, which insisted on the break that her generation, the Georgians, must make with the Edwardians. Her generation, as she defined it, meant Lawrence, Joyce, Forster, Eliot, Mansfield. The Edwardians meant Shaw, Galsworthy, Wells, Arnold Bennett. In 'Modem Novels' (1919), 'On Re-Reading Novels', 'Mr Bennett and Mrs Brown' (1923) and 'Character in Fiction' (1924), she argued that character was at the centre of great fiction, and that character had changed 'on or about December 1910'. This was a literary change. Character, to the Edwardians, was everything that could be described; to her generation it was everything that could not be described. The Edwardians blunted character, she felt, by stubbing it into things – clothes, politics, income, houses, relatives. She wanted to sharpen character into the invisible.

First of all, said Woolf, what was 'reality'? To the Edwardians, reality was a furniture sale, everything that could be seen, tagged and marked. But Woolf wanted to break from what she called this materialism, and to look for darker corridors. Reality is 'a luminous halo, a semi-transparent envelope surrounding us from the beginning of consciousness to the end'. It was 'consciousness', and its relation to the 'luminous halo', that was the exquisite distress of Woolf's literary generation. But this new awareness was not a mere evaporation into the aesthetic. Again and again, Woolf insists on her word, 'life'. It was because she felt that life had escaped from Arnold Bennett's novels that she punished them so: 'perhaps without life nothing else is worth while'. She chafed at the vagueness of the word, yet its vagueness was its spur. It was the fate of modernist writing to be merely an advance in failure, because 'life' is so resistant to being broken into words. 'Tolerate the spasmodic, the obscure, the fragmentary, the failure,' she implored her sceptical readers. 'We are trembling on the verge of one of the great ages of English literature.' 'I think', she wrote in her *Diary*, of *The Waves*, 'this is the greatest opportunity I have yet been able to give myself: therefore the most complete failure.'

And certainly, Woolf failed from time to time. *Mrs Dalloway* is not, in the end, as suggestive as it wants to be (Woolf seemed herself to sense this); *The Waves*, though a great book whose last twenty pages are a pure example of secular mystical writing, is too often tediously involved in its own procedures (almost every character has something to say about the difficulty of language); *Between the Acts* seems unfinished. But when Woolf fails it is generally when she is being Victorian, not when she is being Georgian, or modernist. In *Mrs Dalloway*, for instance, she compares twilight in London to a woman changing her clothes for the evening, 'but London would have none of it, and rushed her bayonets into the sky, pinioned her, constrained her to partnership in her revelry'. In *To the Lighthouse* she compares spring to 'a virgin fierce in her chastity, scornful in her purity'. In *The Waves*, she likens the sea to 'a girl couched on her green-sea mattress . . . with water-globed jewels that sent lances of opal-tinted light falling and flashing in the uncertain air like the flanks of a dolphin leaping, or the flash of a falling blade'. Rebecca West thought that *The Waves* was 'pre-Raphaelite kitsch', which is not true. But certainly, in all these cases a cliché of Victorian poetry – twilight, spring and the sea all compared to woman – seeps from Woolf's childhood into her prose and luridly stains its qualities.

When Woolf's prose succeeds, there is no other twentieth-century English novelist who seems so native, so germinally alive, in her language. She wrote of 'words with roots'. She, who loved first and most dearly the Elizabethans and Carolinians – like Melville, she revered Sir Thomas Browne – historicises language. Her rarity is that she has one ear open to metaphor, and the other ear open to adjectives and adverbs. (Melville, again, has this Shakespearean doubleness.) She sees that words, when chosen with an overpowering concentration, begin to turn into abstractions, in the way anything does if it is stared at for long enough: she embarrasses words into confessing their abstract pigments: words begin to seem like colours in her hands. We see this in the fiction and in the superb one-line brushstrokes in the *Diary*. Especially, perhaps, in the *Diary*, where she runs adjectives after each other without the cushion of commas. She looks at the Sussex landscape: 'A heavy flagging windy cloudy day with breadths of sun . . . Lovely are the curves of the grey clouds sweeping; and the long barns lying.' Or this, in *The Waves*: 'Colour returns. The day waves yellow with all its crops.' (This is a great sentence, and simply needs to be repeated again and again.) From *To the Lighthouse*: 'The arrow-like stillness of fine weather . . . Tortoise-shell butterflies burst from the chrysalis and pattered their life out on the window-pane.' And in her *Diary*, she watches people, and throws adjectives at them: 'steamy grubby inarticulate Rex Whistler'. Or Mrs Keppel, a great society hostess: 'a swarthy thick set raddled direct . . . old grasper'. She combines words so paradoxically: 'a nimble secondrate man' (this of a professor of English literature). Of Stephen Spender: 'a loose jointed mind – misty, clouded, suffusive. Nothing has outline. Very sensitive, tremulous, receptive & striding.' Of Edith Sitwell: 'All is very tapering & pointed, the nose running on like a mole.' Of Bunny Garnett: 'that rusty surly slow old dog with his amorous ways and primitive mind'. And then, amidst so much uncertainty and fragility, one finds this little ecstasy, which lights up everything else: 'Dear me, how lovely some parts of The Lighthouse are! Soft & pliable, & I think deep, & never a word wrong for a page at a time.'

II

But Woolf disliked being complimented for her sentences, and wrote that we must go to novelists 'for chapters, not for sentences'. And in truth her achievement is not measured in sentences; and not just measured in chapters. Her break with the Edwardians lies in the way she writes about consciousness. It is here, especially in the flowing form of *To the Lighthouse*, that she did something astonishing. Most readers know Woolf, in the caricature, as a writer who allows her characters to ramble internally, moving randomly, it seems, from thinking about death or memory at one moment to a bowl of fruit at the next. Well, the caricature goes, this was the Bloomsbury way, the soft metaphysics of the upper classes. The caricature has a name for it: stream-of-consciousness. But Woolf's development of stream-of-consciousness is more interesting than that. It allows absent-mindedness into fiction. A character is allowed to drift out of relevance, to wander into a randomness which may be at odds with the structure of the novel as a whole. What does it mean for a character to become irrelevant to a novel? It frees characters from the fiction which grips them; it lets characters forget, as it were, that they are thicketed in a novel. Undoubtedly, Woolf learned some of this from Sterne, and perhaps from Austen. More immediately, she learned it from Chekhov, about whom she wrote in 1917, in 1918, and in 1919. She admired the way, in that writer, 'the emphasis is laid upon such unexpected places that at first it seems as if there were no emphasis at all'.

There is an obvious difference between the fiction she wrote before and after reading Chekhov. But she found her way slowly. In her first novel, *The Voyage Out* (1915), there is a moment which hangs on the verge of stream-of-consciousness. Clarissa Dalloway (who reappears ten years later in *Mrs Dalloway*) is going to sleep. She is reading Pascal, and thinking drowsily about her husband. What would become a current of thought in Woolf's later books, is here stopped, and converted into a dream. She falls asleep, and her dream, which is a fantastic vision of huge Greek letters, wakes her up. At which point she reminds herself that she has been dreaming. The chapter ends, and everything is closed off neatly. In what it allows, this passage is hardly different from the beginning of Chapter 16 (vol. 1) of *Mansfield Park*, in which Fanny Price, highly agitated, also goes to sleep while thinking to herself. Austen writes: 'She fell asleep before she could answer the question, and found it as puzzling when she awoke the next morning.' In both passages, sleep ends internal thought. Random thought, at this stage in Woolf's career, can only exist as drowsiness or as dream. It is not yet daydreaming. In this first novel, if you forget yourself, you must fall asleep. In her best novels, you stay awake and forget yourself.

Everything gathers in *To the Lighthouse*, Woolf's greatest novel, which she wrote between 1925 and 1927. Mr Ramsay, the philosopher, and Mrs Ramsay are on holiday, with their children. James, the youngest, wants to take a boat to the lighthouse. There are houseguests: Charles Tansley, an atheist philosopher and former pupil of Ramsay's; Augustus Carmichael, a lazy old poet who sits all day in a deckchair, purring lovely phrases; and Lily Briscoe, who sits on the lawn painting, painting her 'attempt at something'. Woolf dances between these consciousnesses, so that it seems to be a novel in which everything happens at the same time. Clearly, all these people *are* thinking at the same time, as people do in real life, and the writer's struggle is to outwit narrative-sequence, whereby one is forced to follow the thread of one mind and then the next. Narrative sequence, at bottom, is nothing other than the materiality of words, which forces us to order phrases in sequence, rather than on top of each other. A painter, like Lily Briscoe, can actually mix paints, but a writer cannot do this. The closest a writer can come to this is in the yoking of metaphor, whereby one thing is pushed against another, and a flashing simultaneity is achieved.

But even with metaphor, a novelist cannot literally combine five consciousnesses. Yet if you allow your characters to forget that they *are* consciousnesses, you allow the reader to forget this too. And when you do this, you allow the reader to forget that fictional consciousness, with its severe descriptive limitations, exists at all. Something else comes into being: the unconscious. This is what Woolf does with Mrs Ramsay, three times in the book. The first moment of forgetting is the quietest and the most magnificent, and occurs twenty pages into the novel. For twenty pages, more or less, we see things through Mrs Ramsay's drifting thoughts. She thinks about how much her son wants to go to the lighthouse; she is cross with Tansley for saying that the weather will not be good enough for the boat-trip; she thinks a little about Tansley, and about all her husband's camp-followers – earnest frigid young men who like to discuss university prizes and who has 'a first-rate mind'.

And then a gigantic new climate begins in English fiction. Mrs Ramsay looks out of the window at the lawn, and sees Augustus Carmichael; and then sees Lily Briscoe painting, and decides that Lily is not really a serious artist. And then

Mrs Ramsay remembers that she 'was supposed to be keeping her head as much in the same position as possible for Lily's picture'. In other words, Mrs Ramsay has forgotten, and has only just remembered, that she is at the centre of Lily's painting. So she has forgotten that she is at the centre of the twenty pages we have just read. Yet Mrs Ramsay's forgetting that she is at the centre of the painting, and at the centre of the first twenty pages, has itself taken twenty pages to read! Her forgetting that she is at the centre has been at *our* centre, has been at the centre of what we have just read. We have experienced this forgetfulness with her. We have travelled with her, and in this way out of her. She has been at the centre of the novel all along and we have hardly noticed it, because we have inhabited her own invisibility. Our realisation of this gives a strange new meaning to Mrs Ramsay's keeping her head still, or 'in the same position'. For, although her head might, externally, have been quite still, or in the same position, *inside her head* nothing has been still, nothing has been 'in the same position', indeed, Mrs Ramsay is incapable of keeping her thought in the same position. She has been, in the deepest sense, absent-minded.

When, in real life, we are asked by a friend what we are thinking about, we often say 'Nothing'. Mrs Ramsay would say the same; Woolf informs us later on that Mrs Ramsay hated to be reminded that she had been seen by anyone 'sitting thinking'. Yet Woolf's method shows us that we are never thinking about nothing, that we are always thinking about something, that it is impossible for us not to think, even if the thought is merely the process of forgetting something. She lets her readers not only read this but almost enact it for themselves. It is a perilous process, and some readers decide that it is just a maze of pretty trivia. But it is real; undoubtedly, it brings us closer to what Woolf called 'life'. In her novels, thought radiates outward, as a medieval town radiates outward – from a beautifully neglected centre.

III

But Woolf, who did not properly read Freud until the last few years of her life, was more than a historian of the mind's creases or a novelist of the unconscious; and more than the bold native of English prose. What so moves us in her great novels, and moves us when we picture her at work in her garden hut in Sussex – Bernard in *The Waves* refers to the 'incessant unmethodical pacing' of artistic work – is the constant effort to find a meaning behind 'life'. Was this hidden meaning only aesthetic? Famously, she once wrote that 'behind the cotton wool is hidden a pattern; that we – I mean all human beings – are connected with this . . . that the whole world is a work of art'. This is the formally agnostic side of Woolf that trusted in art, as Pater did, to do somewhat hazily the work of religion. The modernist hope was that such art would best explain the mysteries of things by, precisely, failing to explain them. In place of confident Victorian preaching was the proper stutter of art; in place of system was tangle; in place of solution was compound. Art's failure was its success. The more obscure the 'pattern' behind reality, the more real its obscurity. Woolf's celebrated 'moments of being', in this view, were indescribable clouds which only art could attempt to describe, because art was the true moment of being. Art and reality became one in their mystery. Art, in this sense, acts like ritual rather than doctrine: it cannot define truth, but it nicely ornaments what cannot be known. 'I'm certain that the only meanings that are worth anything in a work of art are those that the artist himself knows nothing about,' Woolf wrote. She disliked the 'mysticism' in *A Passage to India*, because she felt that Forster was an artist who did not trust enough in art alone, who 'despises his art and thinks he must be something more'. Forster was too much of a mystic, or Cambridge Platonist. Thus Woolf the aesthete.

But what of Woolf the religionist? Woolf the Forsterian or Platonist? For there is some evidence that Woolf, without of course despising her art, looked for 'something more', and that she felt that this 'something more' lay beyond or outside art. She felt herself to be 'mystical'. At times she seems to have been looking not so much for the aesthetic pattern behind reality, as for a further metaphysical pattern behind the aesthetic pattern. What this further pattern, so amply recessed, looked like, she could not say. Whether it was also aesthetic, she did not know. She could never describe it. But she suspected that she did not make it herself: it was real, it was revealed, it was given to her. We know this, because she tells us that she sensed this deeper reality in her moments of mental instability. Woolf broke down, mentally, in 1897, in 1904, and most severely in 1913, when she nearly killed herself. In 1926, while finishing *To the Lighthouse*, she again became ill. She would have periods of feverish intensity and insight, followed by weeks of clogged depression. These bouts were terrible. Hermione Lee quotes this self-record: 'Oh its beginning its coming – the horror – physically like a painful wave about the heart – tossing me up.

I'm unhappy unhappy! Down – God, I wish I were dead . . . Wave crashes. I wish I were dead! I've only a few years to live I hope. I cant face this horror any more.'

But once this had passed, Woolf felt that her depression had been 'interesting'. She saw through to some kind of 'truth' while ill. 'I believe these illnesses are in my case – how shall I express it? – partly mystical.' Most significantly, she told Forster that her illness had 'done instead of religion'. She wrote that in periods of intensity, she heard a third voice – not hers, not Leonard's, but another's. Scattered in her writings are moments of mystical feeling. Bernard, at the end of *The Waves*, does not give a Paterian account of the primacy of art, or the ultimate aesthetic pattern of all things (the usual reading), but rather, he undergoes a breakdown which is described in spiritual terms. In September 1926, she wrote of 'the mystical side of this solitude; how it is not oneself but something in the universe that one's left with'. She continues: 'One sees a fin passing far out.' Five years later, in February 1931, amid the triumph of having finished *The Waves*, she writes: 'I have netted that fin in the waste of waters which appeared to me over the marshes out of my window at Rodmell when I was coming to an end of To the Lighthouse.' Now it is difficult to know whether this is a report or an approximation. Did she *see* a fin in 1926, a mystical bulk; or was the idea of a fin merely her image of precisely what she *could not see* but only imagine? Was this a mystical sighting of an actuality, or a lunge at the idea of such? (Verbally, perhaps, it is not accidental that 'fin' is 'end', and is the kernel at the heart of 'finitude' and 'infinitude'.) Repeatedly, she complains of the difficulty of describing this reality. But it was a reality: 'If I could catch the feeling, I would: the feeling of the singing of the real world, as one is driven by loneliness and silence from the habitable world.'

This idea, of a real world behind the habitable world, reminds us of the Victorian Platonism in which Woolf was raised. But Woolf's version is both a fruit of, and a pit shied at, this Platonism. Woolf's father was an agnostic and a rationalist. Victorian Platonism put the good in place of God. This good was an invisible order behind the world of appearances. It could be reached, says Plato in *The Republic*, but only by philosophical thought. Inheriting this tradition, Woolf changes the code: like her father, she did not believe in God. Like the Platonist, she intuited a real world behind the apparent world. But it is not the form of the Good. It is intrinsic, indescribable. And most importantly, it cannot be reached through philosophical reasoning, but only lunged at every so often by that faculty that Plato somewhat despised: the imagination.

So Woolf saw beyond art, and not only in moments of mental brokenness, but in the very midst of that art. Her greatest fiction is moved by the faith that to have visions is to see beyond aesthetic vision. At the end of *The Waves*, Bernard casts off 'this veil of being', and asks: 'What does this central shadow hold? Something? Nothing? I do not know.' Importantly, he feels that he has pierced a silent world without need of language or art, 'a new world . . . without shelter of phrases'. At the end of *To the Lighthouse*, Lily Briscoe sits at her easel, painting 'her attempt at something'. Her attempt at something is more than the attempt to paint a picture. The picture is irrelevant. She reflects that her painting will be hung in an attic or even destroyed. Lily wants, writes Woolf, 'the thing itself before it has been made anything'. Lily's attempt is to grasp time, to restore a moment of the present as it ages before her. This is explicitly not just an aesthetic exertion. That would be tautological: it is art which has gathered this moment, so it would be weak to say that the meaning of this moment is only art. No, what is so moving in this novel is the spreading apprehension that the very vagueness of that invisible 'something' that we are all seeking beyond the senses makes it mystical, pushes it beyond the reach of aesthetic form. The indefinability of the 'something' is what goads Woolf's art into art; but the indefinability is also what exhausts that art. It encourages the very quest it cannot satisfy. This contradictory belief, that truth can be looked for but cannot be looked at, and that art is the greatest way of giving form to this contradiction, is what moves us so intensely. Her work is full of the sense that art is an 'incessant unmethodical pacing' around meaning rather than towards it, and that this continuous circling is art's straightest metaphysical path. It is all art can do, and it is everything art can do. And fin-like, the meaning moves on, partially palpable, always hiding its larger invisibilities.

1997

Job Existed: Primo Levi

PRIMO LEVI DID NOT consider it heroic to have survived eleven months in Auschwitz. Like other witnesses of the concentration camps, he lamented that the best had perished and the worst had survived. But we who have survived relatively little find it hard to believe him. How could it be anything but heroic to have entered hellmouth, and not been swallowed up? To have witnessed it with such lucidity, such reserves of irony and even equanimity? Our incomprehension and our admiration combine to create a writer simplified by our needy amalgam: the writer as hero, saint, witness, redeemer, or a combination of these roles. Thus Levi's account of life in Auschwitz, *If This Is a Man* (1947), whose title is deliberately tentative and tremulous, was rewrapped, by his American publisher, in the heartier, how-to-ish banner, *Survival in Auschwitz: The Nazi Assault on Humanity*. That same edition praises the text as 'a lasting testament to the indestructibility of the human spirit', though Levi often emphasised how quickly and efficiently the camps could destroy the human spirit. A fellow survivor, the writer Jean Améry, mistaking comprehension for concession, disapprovingly called Levi 'the forgiver', though Levi repeatedly argued that he was interested

in justice, not in indiscriminate forgiveness. A German correspondent, an official who had encountered Levi in the camp,
applauded *If This Is a Man*, and found in it 'an overcoming
of Judaism, a fulfilment of the Christian precept to love one's
enemies, and a testimony of faith in Man'. And when Levi
committed suicide, on 11 April 1987, many seemed to feel
that the writer had somehow reneged on his own heroism;
at the time, *The New Yorker* averred that the gesture of Levi's
death cancelled the gesture of his work.

Levi *was* heroic; he was also modest, practical, elusive, dry,
experimental and sometimes limited, refined and sometimes
provincial (he married a woman, Lucia Morpurgo, from the
same class and background he was born into, and died in
the same Turin apartment building in which he had been
born). For most of his life, he worked as an industrial chemist; he wrote some of his first book, *If This Is a Man*, while
travelling to work on the train. Though his experiences in
Auschwitz compelled him to write, and became his central
subject, his writing is varied and worldly and often comic in
spirit, even when he is dealing with terrible hardship: in addition to his two wartime memoirs, *If This Is a Man* and *The
Truce*, and a final, searing enquiry into the life and afterlife
of the concentration camp (*The Drowned and the Saved*), he
wrote realist fiction (a novel about a band of Jewish Second
World War partisans, entitled *If Not Now, When?*) and speculative fiction; also, poems, essays, newspaper articles, and a
beautifully unclassifiable book, *The Periodic Table* (1975).

Primo Levi was born in Turin, in 1919, into a liberal family,
and into an assimilated, educated, Jewish-Italian world. He
would write, in *If This Is a Man*, that when he first learned the

name of his fateful destination, 'Auschwitz' meant nothing to him. He only vaguely knew about the existence of Yiddish, 'on the basis of a few quotes or jokes that my father, who worked for a few years in Hungary, had picked up'. There were around 40,000 Italian Jews; some of them were supporters of the Fascist government (at least until the race legislation of 1938, which announced a newly aggressive anti-Semitism); a cousin of Levi's, Eucardio Momigliano, had been one of the founders of the Fascist Party, in 1919. Levi's father was a member, though more out of convenience than commitment. The interruption of the war aside, Levi never left this world.

Levi gives ebullient life to this comfortable, sometimes eccentric world in *The Periodic Table* – a memoir, a history, an essay in elegy, as well as the best example of his different literary talents. One of the qualities that sets his writing apart from much Holocaust testimony is his relish for portraiture, the pleasure he takes in the palpability of other people, the human amplitude of his noticing. There are funny sketches of Levi's relatives, who are celebrated and gently mocked in the chapter named 'Argon', because, like the gas, they were generally inert: lazy, immobile characters given to witty conversation and idle speculation. Inert they may have been, but colourless they are not – there is Uncle Barbabramín, who falls in love with the goyish housemaid, declares that he will marry her, is thwarted by his parents, and, Oblomov-like, takes to his bed for the next twenty-two years. And there is Nona Màlia, Levi's paternal grandmother, a woman of forbidding remoteness in old age, living in estrangement from her family, now married to a Christian doctor. Perhaps 'out of fear of making the wrong choice', Nona Màlia goes, on alternate days, to temple and to the parish church. Levi recalls that when he was a boy, his father would take him every Sunday to visit his grandmother. The two would walk along the Via Po, Levi's father stopping to pet the cats, sniff the mushrooms, and look at the used books:

> My father was *l'ingengé*, the Engineer, his pockets always bursting with books, known to all the salami makers because he checked with a slide rule the multiplication on the bill for the prosciutto. Not that he bought it with a light heart: rather superstitious than religious, he felt uneasy about breaking the rules of *kasherut*, but he liked prosciutto so much that, before the temptation of the shop windows, he yielded every time, sighing, cursing under his breath, and looking at me furtively, as if he feared my judgment or hoped for my complicity.

But even in this first, light-hearted chapter, Levi announces his theme: his memoir will also be an act of witness, the recording of an old Jewish world 'which I want to set down here before it disappears'. And how careful, even here, is Levi's ironic classicism, which allows his tone to deepen and darken within just half a page. For instance, the third paragraph of *The Periodic Table* begins with a recitation of the history of Levi's forebears, Italian Jews who came originally to the Piedmont countryside from Spain in the sixteenth century, and who would eventually move to Turin after the emancipation of 1848: 'Rejected or given a less than warm welcome in Turin, they settled in various agricultural localities in southern Piedmont, introducing there the technology of making silk . . . They were never much loved or hated; stories of unusual persecutions have not been handed down.' The tone is dry, factual, reportorial. Levi goes on to mention that his father was the target of anti-Semitic mockery at school, though the author judges such teasing to have been 'without malice'. The boys would gather their jackets in their fists to resemble a donkey's ear, and chant: 'Pig's ear, donkey's ear, give 'em to the Jew that's here.' Levi says that the taunt makes an obscure reference to prayer shawls, and then notes, 'in passing', that of course the vilification of the prayer shawl is as old as anti-Semitism: 'from these shawls, taken from deportees, the SS would make underwear which then was distributed to the Jews imprisoned in the *Lager*'. So ends the book's third paragraph, whose tone at the end is as cool as it was at its beginning. Musically, as it were, nothing has changed. But what began with Jews being 'given a less than warm welcome in Turin' centuries ago, has ended with the SS and 'Jews imprisoned in the *Lager*'. What began with settlement and suspicion and mild mockery at school has ended in the camps. *This* is why Levi wants to set something down before a world disappears. And how crushing is Levi's great power of understatement: what histories of suffering are contained and repressed by that modest phrase, 'given a less than warm welcome'.

If you had not read anything else by Primo Levi, you would know, on the basis of the first chapter of *The Periodic Table*, that you were in the hands of a true writer, someone equipped with an avaricious and indexical memory, one who knows how to animate his details, stage his scenes, and ration his anecdotes. It is a book one wants to keep quoting from. With verve and vitality, *The Periodic Table* moves through the phases of Levi's life: his excited discovery of chemistry, as a teenager; classes at the University of Turin with the rigorous but not unamusing 'Professor P.', who scornfully defies the Fascist injunction to wear a black shirt, by donning a 'comical black bib, several inches wide', which comes untucked every time the Professor makes one of his brusque movements. Throughout, there are wittily pragmatic, cleverly original descriptions of minerals, gases and metals, as in this description of zinc: 'Zinc, *zinco, Zinck*: laundry tubs are made of it, it's an element that doesn't say much to the imagination, it's gray and its salts are colorless, it's not toxic, it doesn't provide gaudy chromatic reactions – in other words, it's a boring element.' And Levi writes tenderly about friends and colleagues, some of whom we encounter in his other writing – Giulia Veneis, 'full of human warmth, Catholic without rigidity, generous and slapdash'; Alberto Dalla Volta, who became Levi's friend in Auschwitz, and was one of those rare prisoners who seemed uncannily untouched by the poisons of camp life: 'He was a man of strong goodwill, and had miraculously remained free, and his words and actions were free: he had not lowered his head, had not bowed his back. A gesture of his, a word, a laugh, had liberating virtues, were a hole in the stiff fabric of the Lager . . . I believe that no one, in that place, was more loved than he.'

The most moving chapter in *The Periodic Table* may be the one entitled 'Iron'. It recalls a student friend, Sandro, who studied chemistry with the author, and with whom he explored the joys of mountain climbing. Like many of the people Levi admired, Sandro is physically and morally strong; he is painted as a headstrong child of nature out of a Jack London story. Seemingly made out of iron, and bound to it by ancestry (his relatives were tinkers and blacksmiths), Sandro practises chemistry as a trade, without apparent reflection; at weekends, he goes off to the mountains, to ski or climb, sometimes spending the night in a hayloft. Levi tastes 'freedom' with Sandro – a freedom perhaps from thinking, the freedom of the conquering body, of being on top of the mountain, of being 'master of one's destiny'. Sandro is a powerful presence on the page; aware of this, Levi plays his absence against his presence, informing us, in a beautiful lament at the end of the chapter, that Sandro was Sandro Delmastro, that he joined the military wing of the Action Party, and that in 1944 he was captured by the Fascists. He tried to escape, and was shot in the neck by a raw fifteen-year-old recruit. The elegy closes thus:

> Today I know it's hopeless to try to clothe a man in words, make him live again on the written page, especially a man like Sandro. He was not a man to talk about, or build monuments to, he who laughed at monuments: he was in his actions, and when those ended nothing of him remained, nothing except words, precisely.

The word becomes the monument, even as Levi disowns the building of it.

One of the most eloquent of Levi's rhetorical gestures is the way, as here, he moves between volume and silence, appearance and disappearance, life and death. His pages are full of vivid human beings, some of them fleeting visitors, others vital sustainers or wilful endurers. Repeatedly, Levi tolls his bell of departure: they existed, and then they disappeared. But above all, they existed. Sandro, in *The Periodic Table* ('nothing of him remained'); Alberto, most loved among the camp inmates, who died on the midwinter death march from Auschwitz: 'Alberto did not return, and of him no trace remains'; Elias Lindzin, the dwarf: 'Of his life as a free man, no one knows anything'; Mordo Nahum, 'the Greek', who helped Levi survive part of the long journey back to Italy: 'We parted after a friendly conversation: and after that, since the whirlwind that had convulsed that old Europe, dragging it into a wild contra dance of separations and meetings, had come to rest, I never saw my Greek master again, or heard news of him.' And, of course, the 'drowned', those who went under – 'leaving no trace in anyone's memory'. Levi rings the bell even for himself, who in some way disappeared into his tattooed number: 'At a distance of thirty years, I find it difficult to reconstruct what sort of human specimen, in November of 1944, corresponded to my name, or, rather, my number: 174517.' But the chemist who knowingly uses the scientific word 'trace' – '*Alberto non è ritornato, e di lui non resta traccia*' ('Alberto did not return, and of him no trace remains') – is also the writer whose words make the only traces we have of these abolished lives.

In the autumn of 1943, Levi joined a band of Italian anti-Fascist partisans. It was an amateurish group, poorly equipped and ill-trained, and presented no great difficulty for the Italian Fascist Militia, who captured most of his unit in the early hours of 13 December. Levi had an obviously false identity card, which he ate ('the photograph was particularly revolting'). But the action availed him little: the interrogating officer told him that if he was a partisan he would be immediately shot; if he was a Jew he would be sent to a holding camp near Carpi. Levi held out for a while, and then chose to confess his Jewishness, 'partly out of weariness, partly out of pride'. He was sent to the detention camp at Fossoli, near Modena, where conditions were tolerable – there were POWs and political prisoners of different nationalities, there was no forced labour, and mail was delivered. But in the middle of February 1944, the SS took over the running of the camp, and announced that all of the Jews would be leaving: they were told to prepare for two weeks of travel. A train of twelve closed freight cars left on the evening of 22 February, packed with six hundred and fifty people. Of that number, around five hundred and fifty were selected for death upon their arrival at Auschwitz; the others, ninety-five men and twenty-nine women, entered the *Lager* (Levi always preferred the German word for prison). Levi was imprisoned in Auschwitz-Monowitz, a work camp supposed to produce a rubber called Buna (though it never actually manufactured it). He spent almost a year as a prisoner, and then almost nine months returning home. 'Of six hundred and fifty,' he wrote in *The Truce*, 'three of us were returning.'

Those are the facts, the abominable and precious facts.

There is a Talmudic commentary which argues that 'Job never existed and was just a parable'. The Hebrew poet and concentration camp survivor Dan Pagis surely replies to this easy erasure in his poem 'Homily'. Despite the obvious inequality of the theological contest, says Pagis, Job defeated God without even realising it. He defeated Him with his very silence. We might imagine, Pagis continues, that the most terrible thing about the Job story is the fact that Job didn't understand whom he had defeated, or that he had even won the battle. Not true. For then comes an extraordinary final line: 'But in fact, the most terrible thing of all is that Job never existed and is just a parable.'

I think that Pagis's poem defiantly means: 'Job did exist, because Job was in the death camps. The most terrible thing is not suffering; it is to have the reality of one's suffering erased.' In just this way, Levi's writing insists that Job existed and was not a parable. His famous clarity is ontological and moral: these things happened, a victim witnessed them, and they must never be erased or forgotten. There are many such facts in Levi's books of testament. The reader is quickly introduced to the principle of scarcity, in which everything, every detail, object and fact, becomes essential, for everything will be stolen – wire, rags, paper, bowl, a spoon, bread. The prisoners learn to hold their bowls under their chins, so as not to lose the crumbs. They shorten their nails with their teeth. 'Death begins with the shoes' – infection enters through wounds in the feet, swollen by oedema; ill-fitting shoes can be catastrophic. Hunger is perpetual, overwhelming, and fatal for most: 'The Lager *is* hunger.' In their sleep, many of the prisoners lick their lips and move their jaws, dreaming of food. Reveille, the daily irruption into sleep that haunted Levi for years, is brutally early, at dawn. As the prisoners trudge off to work, they are sent on the way with sadistic, infernal music: a band of prisoners is forced to play marches and popular tunes; Levi says that the pounding of the bass drum and the clashing of the cymbals is 'the voice of the Lager', and the last thing of it he will forget. And present everywhere, there is what he called 'the useless violence' of the camp – the screaming and beatings and humiliations, the enforced nakedness, the absurdist regulatory regime, with its sadism of paradox: the fact, say, that every prisoner needed a spoon, but was not issued one, and had to find it himself on the black market; or the fanatically prolonged daily roll call, which took place in all weathers, and which insisted on militaristic precision from men who were wraiths in rags, already half dead.

Yet many of these horrifying facts can be found in testimony by other witnesses of the horror. What is different about Levi's work is bound up with his uncommon ability to tell a story. It is striking how much writing by survivors does not tell a story, quite; it has often been poetic (Paul Celan, Dan Pagis, Yehiel De-Nur); or analytic, reportorial, anthropological, philosophical (Jean Améry, Germaine Tillion, Eugen Kogon, Viktor Frankl). The emphasis falls, for understandable reasons, on lament, on a liturgy of tears; or on immediate precision, on bringing concrete news, and on the attempt at comprehension. When Viktor Frankl, who like Levi survived Auschwitz, introduces, in his book *Man's Search for Meaning*, the subject of food in the camp, he does so thus: 'Because of the high degree of undernourishment which the prisoners suffered, it was natural that the desire for food was the major primitive instinct around which mental life centered.' Along with this scientific mastering of the information comes something like a wariness of narrative naivety: such writers frequently move back and forth in time, plucking and massing details thematically, from different periods in and outside the camps. This command of the before and after is obviously important, because it communicates, as form, its own assertion of survival. Surely Frankl's rhetoric calmly insists: 'this material did not master me; I master it.'

Levi's prose has a tone of similar command (its composure, its reticence, its order), and in his last book, *The Drowned and the Saved*, he became such an analyst, grouping material by theme rather than telling stories about it. But at the simplest level, *If This Is a Man* and *The Truce* are powerful because they do not disdain story. They unfold their material, bolt by bolt. We begin *If This Is a Man* with Levi's capture in 1944, and we end it with his liberation by the Russians, in January 1945. Then we continue the journey in *The Truce*, as Levi finds his long, Odyssean way home. Everything is new, everything is introduction, and so the reader is placed alongside Levi (as far as that is possible), and sees with his disbelieving eyes. Unlike Frankl, for instance, Levi introduces thirst like this: 'Will they give us something to drink? No, they line us up again, lead us to a huge square . . .' He first mentions the now-infamous refrain 'the only way out is through the Chimney' thus: 'What does it mean? We'll soon learn very well what it means.' To register his ghastly novelties, he often breaks from past tense into a diaristic present.

On its own, Levi's talent for narrative might amount to little more than a trivial literary preference. But a charged relation to novelty becomes important, becomes a kind of ethics, when the writer is constantly registering the moral novelty of the details he encounters. That is why every reader who has opened *If This Is a Man* feels impelled to continue reading it, despite the horror of the material. Levi seems to join us in our incomprehension, which is both a narrative astonishment – how is this possible? what horror is next? – and a moral astonishment: not just at the existence of evil, but at the fact that such evil has been made new, introduced into the writer's world. Levi's writing thus has the form of continuous moral introduction. It is why the victims' ignorance of the name 'Auschwitz' is not a small detail. On the contrary, it tells us everything, actually and symbolically. For Levi, 'Auschwitz' had not, until this moment, existed. It had to be invented, and it had to be introduced into his life. Evil is not the absence of the good, as theology and philosophy has sometimes maintained. It is the invention of the bad: Job existed and was not a parable. Levi registers the same astonishment when first hit by a German officer: 'a profound amazement: how can one strike a man without anger?' It had never happened before. This moral astonishment is felt in some of the book's more celebrated moments, too – when, driven by thirst, he breaks off an icicle, only to have it snatched away by a guard, and asks, 'Why?' To which comes the answer, '*Hier ist kein warum*' ('Here there is no why'). Or when Alex the Kapo, a common criminal, but given limited power over other prisoners, thoughtlessly wipes his greasy hand on Levi's shoulder, as if the other man were not a man. Or when Levi, who was fortunate enough to be chosen to work as a chemist, in the Buna laboratory, comes face to face with his German examiner, Dr Pannwitz, a cold official who raises his eyes to glance at his victim. It is just that, a glance, but Levi has not experienced its like before: 'that look did not pass between two men; and if I knew how to explain fully the nature of that look, exchanged as if through the glass wall of an aquarium between two beings who inhabit different worlds, I would also be able to explain the essence of the great insanity of the Third Reich.'

Levi frequently emphasised that his survival in Auschwitz owed much to his youth and strength; to the fact that he understood some German (many of those who didn't, he observed, died in the first weeks); to his training as a chemist, which had refined his habits of curiosity and observation, and which permitted him, in the last months of his incarceration, to work indoors, in a warm laboratory, while the Polish winter did its own fatal selection of the less fortunate; and to other accidents of luck. Among these last were timing (he arrived relatively late in the progress of the war), and what seems to have been a great capacity for friendship. He describes himself, in *The Periodic Table*, as one of those people to whom others tell their stories. In a world of terminal individualism, in which every person had to fight to live, he did not let this scarred opportunism become his only mode of survival. He was wounded like everyone else; but with resources that seem, to most of his readers, unfathomable and mysterious, he did not lose the ability to heal and to be healed. He helped others, and they helped him. Both *If This Is a Man* and *The Truce* contain beautiful portraits of goodness and charity, and it is not the punishers and sadists but the life-givers, the fortifiers, the endurers, the men and women who sustained Levi in his struggle to survive, who burst out of these pages. Alberto, already mentioned; Steinlauf, who is nearly fifty, a former sergeant in the Austro-Hungarian army and veteran of the Great War, who tells Levi, severely, that he must wash regularly and keep his shoes polished and walk upright, because the *Lager* is a vast machine that exists to reduce its victims to beasts, and 'we must not become beasts'.

Above all, there is Lorenzo Perrone, a stonemason from Levi's own Piedmont area, a non-Jew, whom Levi credited with saving his life. The two met in June 1944 (Levi was work-ing on a bricklaying team, one of whose chief masons was Lorenzo). For the next six months, Lorenzo smuggled extra food to his fellow Italian; more dangerous than even this, he helped him send letters to his family in Turin. (As a 'volunteer worker' for the Reich – i.e. a slave labourer – Lorenzo had limited privileges beyond the dream of any Jewish prisoner.) And more crucial even than the material support – though the daily extra ration of soup was probably decisive in Levi's survival – was Lorenzo's presence, which reminded Levi, 'by his natural and plain manner of being good, that a just world still existed outside ours . . . Thanks to Lorenzo, I managed not to forget that I myself was a man.'

You can feel this emphasis on moral resistance in every sentence Levi wrote: his prose is a form of keeping his boots shined and his posture proudly upright. It is a style that seems at first to be as lucid as glass – an Orwellian windowpane – but which is actually full of undulating strategies. He is acclaimed for the purity of his style, and sometimes faulted for his reticence or coldness. But Levi is 'cold' only in the way that the air is suddenly cold when you pull slightly away from a powerful fire. He is really a passionate writer; his composure is pressurised passion – passionate lament, passionate resistance, passionate affirmation. Nor is he so plain. He is not afraid of rhetorical expansion, particularly when writing forms of elegy – *If This Is a Man* is shot through with sentences of tragic grandeur: 'Dawn came upon us like a betrayal, as if the new sun were an ally of the men who had decided to destroy us . . . Now, in the hour of decision, we said to each other things that are not said among the living.' He loves adjectives and adverbs: he admired Joseph Conrad, and sometimes sounds like him, except that while Conrad can throw his around pugilistically (the heavier the words, the better), Levi employs his modifiers with tidy force. The Christian doctor whom Nona Màlia married is described as 'majestic, bearded, and taciturn'; Rita, a fellow student, has 'her shabby clothes, her firm gaze, her concrete sadness'. In Auschwitz, the drowned, those who are slipping away into death, drift in 'an opaque inner solitude'.

This is a classical prose, the possession of a civilised man who never expected that his humane irony would have to do battle with its moral opposite. But once the battle is joined, Levi makes that irony into a formidable weapon. Consider these words: 'fortune'; 'quiet study'; 'charitably'; 'enchantment'; 'discreet and composed'; 'equanimity'; 'adventure'; 'university'. All of them, remarkably, are used by Levi to describe different aspects of his experiences in the camp. 'It was my good fortune to be deported to Auschwitz only in 1944.' This is how, with scandalous coolness, he begins *If This Is a Man*, calmly deploying the twinned resources of '*fortuna*' in Italian, which combines the senses of good fortune and fate. In the same preface to his first book, Levi promises a 'quiet study' of what befell him. The hellish marching music of the camp is described as an 'enchantment' from which one must escape. In *The Drowned and the Saved*, Levi describes a moment of crisis, when he knows he is about to be selected to live or die. He briefly wavers, and almost begs help from a God he does not believe in. 'But equanimity prevailed,' he writes, and he resists the temptation. Equanimity! In the same book, he includes a letter he wrote in 1960 to his German translator, in which he announces that his time in the

Lager, and writing about the *Lager*, 'was an adventure that has profoundly modified me'. The Italian is *'una importante avventura'*, which Raymond Rosenthal's original translation, from 1987, follows; the newer Collected Edition weakens the force of the irony by turning it into merely 'an ordeal that changed me deeply'. For surely the power of these impeccable words is moral. First, they register their contamination by what befell them (the 'adventure', we think, should not be called that, it *should* be described as an 'ordeal'); and then they gloriously repel that contamination (no, we will insist in calling the experience, with full ironic power, 'an adventure').

In the same spirit of calmly rebellious irony, *If This Is a Man* ends almost casually, like a conventional nineteenth-century realist novel, with cheerful news of continuity and welfare beyond its pages. Its last sentences are: 'In April, at Katowice, I met Schenck and Alcalai in good health. Arthur has reached his family happily and Charles has taken up his teacher's profession again. We have exchanged long letters and I hope to see him again one day.' And that emphasis on resistance is what makes its sequel, *The Truce*, not merely funny, but joyous: the camps are no more, the Germans have been vanquished, and gentler life, like a moral sun, is returning. (There may be nothing more moving in all of Levi's work than a moment, early in *The Truce*, when, after the months in Auschwitz, two Russian nurses help the very sick Levi down from a cart. The first Russian words he hears are *'Po malu!'* – 'gently, gently'; or, even better in the Italian, *'adagio, adagio'*. This soft charity falls like balm on the text.)

Saul Bellow once said that all the great nineteenth-century novelists are really attempting a definition of human nature.

This is pre-eminently true of Primo Levi, even if we feel, at times, that it is a project thrust upon him by fortune. In some respects, of course, Levi's vision is pessimistic, because he reminds us 'how vain is the myth of original equality among men'. In Auschwitz, the already strong prospered – because they were physically or morally tougher than others, or because they were less sensitive, and greedier in the will to live. Only in a utopia is everyone equal, says Levi. (The philosopher Jean Améry, who was tortured by the Gestapo in Belgium, thought that even before pain we are not equal.) On the other hand, Levi is no tragic theologian. He did not believe that 'the pitiless natural selection' that ruled in the camps was the confirmation of man's essential brutishness. The philosopher Berel Lang, in one of the best recent enquiries into Levi's work, argues that this moral optimism makes him a singular figure. Levi, says Lang, can be turned into neither a Hobbesian (for whom the camps would represent the ultimate state of nature) nor a modern Darwinian (who must struggle to explain pure altruism, except as camouflaged biological self-interest). For Levi, Auschwitz was exceptional, aberrant, an unnatural laboratory. 'We do not believe', Levi writes forthrightly, 'that man is fundamentally brutal, egoistic, and stupid in his conduct once every civilized institution is taken away . . . We believe, rather, that the only conclusion to be drawn is that in the face of driving necessity and physical disabilities many social habits and instincts are reduced to silence.'

The life in the camps, such as it was, existed precisely because of its difference from life. In normal existence, Levi argues, there is a 'third way' between winning and losing, between altruism and atrocity, between being saved and being drowned, and this third way is in fact the rule. But in the camp there was no third way. It is this apprehension that expands Levi's understanding for those caught in what he famously named the Grey Zone. He places in the Grey Zone all those who were morally compromised by some degree of collaboration with the Germans – from the lowliest (those prisoners who got a little extra food by performing menial jobs like sweeping, or being night watchmen); through the more ambiguous (the Kapos, often thuggish enforcers and guards who were themselves also prisoners); to the utterly tragic (the Sonderkommandos, Jews employed for a few months to run the crematoria, until they themselves were killed). Again, it is important to note that the Grey Zone, which might itself look like the very proposition of a 'third way', and is sometimes mistaken as such (because it sounds like a place where people are both bad and good, a commingling of virtue and vice, neither white nor black), is no such thing. It is a *mutant realm*, an aberration, a state of impossible, desperate limitation produced by precisely the *absence* of a third way. In ordinary life, there are grey people, for sure; but there is no Grey Zone. Unlike Hannah Arendt, who judged Jewish collaboration in the Grey Zone with infamous disdain, Levi makes a notable attempt at comprehension and tempered judgement. He finds such people pitiable as well as culpable, because they were at once grotesquely innocent and guilty. And he does not exempt himself from this moral mottling: on the one hand, he firmly asserts his innocence, but on the other feels guilty to have survived.

Levi sometimes said that he felt a larger guilt – guilt at being a human being, since human beings invented the world of the concentration camp. Every German must answer for the camps, he said, but so must every person, since the defenceless always clear a way for the strong. But if this is a theory of general shame, it is not a theory of original sin. One of the happiest qualities of Levi's writing is its freedom from religious temptation. He did not like Kafka's work, did not like the darkness of Kafka's vision, and in a remarkable sentence of dismissal, gets to the heart of a certain perverted theological malaise in Kafka: 'He fears punishment, and at the same time desires it . . . a sickness within himself.' Goodness, for Levi, was palpable and comprehensible, but evil was palpable and incomprehensible. That was the healthiness within himself.

Yet on the morning of 11 April 1987, this healthily humane man walked out of his third-floor apartment and either fell, or threw himself, over the bannister of the building's staircase. The act, if suicide, appeared to undo the suture of survival. Some were outraged, others refused to see it as suicide. The implication, not quite spoken, was uncomfortably close to dismay that the Nazis had won after all. 'Primo Levi died at Auschwitz forty years later,' said Elie Wiesel. Wiesel must, in one essential way, be right. But to lament that the Nazis have won every time a survivor of the Holocaust commits suicide is truly a concession that the Nazis have won. Levi was a survivor who committed suicide, not a suicide who failed to survive. The sadness was understandable: Levi himself had seemed to argue against such morbidity, in his chapter on Jean Améry in *The Drowned and the Saved*. Améry, who killed himself at the age of sixty-seven, said that in Auschwitz he thought a great deal about suicide; tartly, and with characteristic irony, Levi replied that in the camp he was too busy for such perturbation. 'The aims of life are the best defence against death: and not only in the *Lager*.'

Most of the contemporary commentators knew little or nothing about Levi's depression, which he struggled with for decades, and which had become desperately severe. In his last months, he felt unable to write, was in poor health, was worried about his mother's decline. In February, he told his American translator, Ruth Feldman, that his depression was, in certain respects, 'worse than Auschwitz, because I'm no longer young and I have scant resilience'. His family was in no doubt. 'No! He's done what he'd always said he'd do,' wailed his wife, when she found his body at the bottom of the stairwell. In this regard, one could see Levi as a survivor twice over, first of the camps, and then of depression. He survived for a very long time, and then chose not to survive, the terminal act perhaps not the negation of survival, but continuous with it: a decision to leave the prison on his own terms, in his own time. Most moving is something said by his friend Edith Bruck, herself a survivor of Auschwitz and Dachau: 'There are no howls in Primo's writing – all emotion is controlled – but Primo gave such a howl of freedom at his death.' This is moving, and perhaps true. Thus one consoles oneself, and consolation is necessary: like much suicide, Levi's death is only a silent howl, because it voids its own echo. It is natural to be bewildered, and it is important not to moralise. For above all, Job existed, and was not a parable.

2015

Marilynne Robinson

GROWING UP IN a religious household, I got used to the sight of priests, but always found them fascinating and slightly repellent. The funereal uniform, supposed to obliterate the self in a shroud of colourlessness, also draws enormous attention to the self; humility seems to be made out of the same cloth as pride. Since the ego is irrepressible – since the ego is secular – it tends to bulge in peculiar shapes when religiously depressed. The priests I knew practised self-abnegation but perfected a quiet dance of ego. They were modest but pompous, gentle but tyrannical – one of them got angry if he was disturbed on a Monday – and pious but knowing. Most were good men, certainly less sinful than the average; but the peculiar constrictions of their calling produced peculiar opportunities for unloosing.

This is probably one of the reasons – putting the secular antagonism of novelists aside – that priests are overwhelmingly seen in fiction as comical, hypocritical, improperly worldly or a little dim. Another reason is that fiction needs egotism, vanity, venality, to produce drama and comedy; we want our sepulchres craftily whited. The seventy-six-year-old Reverend John Ames, who narrates Marilynne Robinson's second novel,

Gilead, is gentle, modest, loving and, above all, good. He is also rather boring, and boring in proportion to his curious lack of ego. At home in the Iowa town of Gilead, in the mid-1950s, aware of his imminent demise, he writes a long letter to his seven-year-old son, which is presented as a series of diary entries. (Georges Bernanos's novel *The Diary of a Country Priest* seems to have been one model.) Mellowly resigned, tired but faithful, he is a man who can serenely exclaim 'how I have loved this life', or inform us that he has written two thousand sermons 'in the deepest hope and conviction'. The reader may roll his eyes at this and think: '*All* two thousand? Not one of them written in boredom or out of obligation?' Yorick, the parson in *Tristram Shandy*, who is so impressed with the eloquence of one of his own eulogies that he can't help writing a self-loving 'Bravo!' on his text, seems closer to the human case, and more novelistically vivid.

As if sensitive to the piety of *Gilead*, Robinson subverted this potential traditional objection by making her novel swerve away from the traditionally novelistic. Ames's calm, grave diary entries contain almost no dialogue, shun scenes, seem to smother conflict before it has taken a breath. Very beautifully, *Gilead* becomes less a novel than a species of religious writing, and Reverend Ames's entries a recognisable American form, the Emersonian essay, poised between homily and home, religious exercise and naturalism.

> This morning a splendid dawn passed over our house on its way to Kansas. This morning Kansas rolled out of its sleep into a sunlight grandly announced, proclaimed throughout heaven – one more of the very finite number of days that

this old prairie has been called Kansas, or Iowa. But it has all been one day, that first day. Light is constant, we just turn over in it. So every day is in fact the selfsame evening and morning. My grandfather's grave turned into the light, and the dew on his weedy little mortality patch was glorious.

The result was one of the most unconventional conventionally popular novels of recent times.

Robinson describes herself as a liberal Protestant believer and churchgoer, but her religious sensibility is really far more uncompromising and archaic than this allows. Her essays, selected in *The Death of Adam* (1998), are theologically tense and verbally lush in a manner almost extinct in modern literary discourse, and which often sounds Melvillean or Ruskinian. She is a liberal in the sense that she finds it difficult to write directly about the content of her belief, and shuns the evangelical childishness of gluing human attributes onto God. As a child she 'felt God as a presence before I had a name for him', she writes, and adds that she goes to church to experience 'moments that do not occur in other settings'. In a way that would seem palatable to many Americans, and certainly to her thousands of liberal readers, her Protestantism seems borne out of a love of religious silence – the mystic, quietly at prayer in an unadorned place, indifferent to ecclesiastical mediation.

But she is illiberal and unfashionably fierce in her devotion to this Protestant tradition; she is voluble in defence of silence. She loathes the complacent idleness whereby contemporary Americans dismiss Puritanism and turn John Calvin, the great originator of Puritanism, into an obscure, moralising bigot. 'We are forever drawing up indictments against the past, then refusing to let it testify in its own behalf – it is so very guilty, after all. Such attention as we give to it is usually vindictive and incurious and therefore incompetent.' We flinch from Puritanism because it placed sin at the centre of life, but then, as she tartly reminds us, 'Americans never think of themselves as sharing fully in the human condition, and therefore beset as all humankind is beset.' Calvin believed in our 'total depravity', our utter fallenness, but this was not necessarily a cruel condemnation: 'The belief that we are all sinners gives us excellent grounds for forgiveness and self-forgiveness, and is kindlier than any expectation that we might be saints, even while it affirms the standards all of us fail to attain,' she writes in her essay 'Puritans and Prigs'. Nowadays, she argues, educated Americans are prigs, not Puritans, quick to pour judgement on anyone who fails to toe the right political line. Soft moralising has replaced hard moralising, but at least those old hard moralists admitted to being moralists.

I do not always enjoy Robinson's founded ecstasies, but I admire the obdurateness with which she describes the difficult joys of a faith that will please neither evangelicals nor secularists. Above all, I deeply admire the precision and lyrical power of her language, and the way it embodies a struggle – the fight with words, the contemporary writer's fight with the history of words and the presence of literary tradition, the fight to use the best words to describe both the visible and the invisible world. Here, for instance, is how the narrator of *Housekeeping*, Robinson's first novel, describes her dead grandmother, who lies in the bed with her arms flung up and her head flung back: 'It was as if, drowning in air, she had leaped towards ether.' In the same novel, the narrator imagines her grandmother pinning sheets to a line, on a windy day – 'say that when she had pinned three corners to the lines it began to billow and leap in her hands, to flutter and tremble, and to glare with the light, and that the throes of the thing were as gleeful and strong as if a spirit were dancing in its cerements'. 'Cerements', an old word for burial cloth, is Robinson in her antique, Melvillean mode, and is one of many moments in her earlier work when she sounds like the antiquarian Cormac McCarthy. But stronger than that fancy word is the plain and lovely 'the throes of the thing', with its animism and its home-made alliteration.

Her novel *Home* begins simply, eschewing obvious verbal fineness, and slowly grows in luxury – its last fifty pages are magnificently moving, and richly pondered in the way of *Gilead*. *Home* has been presented as a sequel to that novel, but it is more like that novel's brother, since it takes place at the same narrative moment and dovetails with its happenings. In *Gilead*, John Ames's great friend is the Reverend Robert Boughton, the town's Presbyterian minister (Ames is a Congregationalist). The two men grew up together, confide in each other, and share a wry, undogmatic Protestantism. But whereas John Ames has married late and has only one son, Reverend Boughton has five children, one of whom is a very prodigal son, Jack Boughton. In the earlier novel, Ames frets over Jack Boughton (now in his forties), who has been difficult since he was a schoolboy: there has been petty theft, drifting, unemployment, alcoholism and an illegitimate child, now deceased, with a local woman. One day, Jack walked out of the Boughton home and stayed away for twenty years, not returning even for his mother's funeral. Recently, we learn,

Jack has unexpectedly returned after all that time away. In the last part of *Gilead*, Jack comes to Ames for a blessing – for the blessing he cannot get from his own father – and spills a remarkable secret: he has been living with a black woman from Memphis named Della, and has a son with her.

Home is set in the Boughton household at the time of Jack's sudden return, and is an intense study of three people – Reverend Boughton, the old, dying patriarch, his pious daughter, Glory, and prodigal Jack. Glory has her own sadness: she has come back to Gilead after the collapse of what she took to be an engagement, to a man who turned out to be married. Like Princess Marya in *War and Peace*, who does daily battle with her father, the old Prince Bolkonsky, she is the dutiful child who must submit to the demands of her tyrannical old father. She is fearful of Jack – she hardly knows him – and in some ways jealous of the freedom of his rebelliousness. Both children differently resent the facts of their return, and their biological loyalty to their father. Robinson evokes well the drugged shuffle of life in a home dominated by the routines of an old parent: how the two middle-aged children hear the creak of the bedsprings as their father lies down for his nap, and then, later, 'a stirring of bedsprings, then the lisp lisp of slippered feet and the pock of the cane'. There are the imperious cries from the bedroom – help with bedclothes, a glass of water – and the hours distracted by the radio, card games, Monopoly, meals, pots of coffee. The very furniture is oppressive, immovable. The numerous knick-knacks were displayed only 'as a courtesy to their givers, most of whom by now would have gone to their reward'. For Glory, who is in her late thirties, there is the dread that this will be her final home:

What does it mean to come home? Glory had always thought home would be a house less cluttered and ungainly than this one, in a town larger than Gilead, or a city, where someone would be her intimate friend and the father of her children, of whom she would have no more than three . . . She would not take one stick of furniture from her father's house, since none of it would be comprehensible in those spare, sun-lit rooms. The walnut furbelows and carved draperies and pilasters, the inlaid urns and flowers. Who had thought of putting actual feet on chairs and sideboards, actual paws and talons?

Much of *Home* is devoted to an attempt to puzzle out the mystery of Jack Boughton's rebellion, his spiritual homelessness. From earliest years, he had seemed a stranger to his relatives. The family had been waiting for him to walk out, and he did, and then this story became their defining narrative: 'They were so afraid they would lose him, and then they had lost him, and that was the story of their family, no matter how warm and fruitful and robust it might have appeared to the outside world.' Even now, now that he has returned, reflects Glory, there is 'an incandescence of unease about him whenever he walked out the door, or, for that matter, whenever his father summoned him to one of those harrowing conversations. Or while he waited for the mail or watched the news.' Over the course of the book, we discover a little of what he has been doing in the twenty years away – as in *Gilead*, we learn about the early illegitimate child, and about his eight-year relationship with Della, who is, ironically enough, a preacher's daughter.

Jack is a suggestive figure – a very literate non-believer who knows his Bible backwards, but who finds it hard to do theological battle with his slippery father. Back home, he dresses formally, putting on his threadbare suit and tie, as if to do his reformed best; but he has a perpetually wary expression and a studied politesse that suggest an existential exile. He tries to conform to the habits of the old home – he tends the garden, does the shopping, fixes up the old car in the garage – but almost every encounter with his father produces a tiny abrasion that smarts and festers. The novel finely mobilises, without explicitness, the major biblical stories of father and son – Esau, denied his birthright, begging for a blessing from his father; Joseph, reunited finally with his father, Jacob; the prodigal son, most loved because most errant.

What propels the book, and makes it finally so power-ful, is the Reverend Boughton, precisely because he is not the gentle sage that John Ames is in *Gilead*. He is a fierce, stern, vain old man, who wants to forgive his son and who cannot. He preaches sweetness and light, and is gentle with Jack like a chastened Lear ('Let me look at your face for a minute,' he says), only to turn on him angrily like a Timon or Claudius. There are scenes of the most tender pain. Robinson, so theo-logically obsessed with transfiguration, can transfigure a banal observation. In the attic, for instance, Glory finds a box of her father's shirts, ironed 'as if for some formal event, perhaps their interment'; and then the novelist, or poet, notices that the shirts 'had changed to a color milder than white'. (The cerements, again.) Father and son clash while watching tele-vision news reports of the racial unrest in Montgomery. Old Boughton imperiously swats away his son's anger with his bland, milky prophecy – 'a color milder than white' – 'There's no reason to let that sort of trouble upset you. In six months nobody will remember one thing about it.' If we have read *Gilead*, we know, as Jack's father does not, why Jack has a special interest in matters of race.

As the old man palpably declines, an urgency sets in. The funnel of the narrative of imminent death should insist on forgiveness, but this is precisely what the father cannot allow. Nothing will change, and Jack will leave again, as his father always knew he would: 'He's going to toss the old gent an assurance or two, and then he's out the door,' he complains. Nothing will change because the family situation rests on a series of paradoxes, which interlock to imprison father and son. Jack's soul is homeless, but his soul is his home, for as Jack tells his sister, the soul is 'what you can't get rid of'. He is condemned to leave and return. If the prodigal son is the most loved because most errant, then his errancy and not his conformity is what is secretly loved, even if no one can admit to that heretical possibility: perhaps a family needs to have its designated sinner? Everyone longs for restoration, for the son to come home and become simply good, just as everyone longs for heaven, but such restoration, like heaven itself, is hard to imagine, and in our lack of imagination we somehow prefer what we can touch and feel – the palpability of our lapses. At least they are palpable, and not other-worldly.

Behind all of Robinson's works is an abiding interest in the question of heavenly restoration. As she puts it in *Housekeeping*, there is a law of completion, that everything 'must finally be made comprehensible. What are all these fragments for, if not to be knit up finally?' But will this restoration ever be enough? Can the shape of the healing possibly fit the size of the wound? The mundane version of this in *Home* is the way in which the novel ponders the question of return. The Boughton children come home to this strange, old-fashioned Iowan town, but the return is never the balm it promises to be, for home is too personal, too remembered, too disappointing. Eden is exile, not heaven:

> And then their return to the *pays natal*, where the same old willows swept the same ragged lawns, where the same old prairie arose and bloomed as negligence permitted. Home. What kinder place could there be on earth, and why did it seem to them all like exile? Oh, to be passing anonymously through an impersonal landscape! Oh, not to know every stump and stone, not to remember how the fields of Queen Anne's lace figured in the childish happiness they had offered to their father's hopes, God bless him.

So as old Boughton is dying, nothing changes, and instead, he petulantly chides his son: 'We all loved you – what I'd like to know is why you didn't love us. That is what has always mystified me.' He continues a little later: 'You see something beautiful in a child, and you almost live for it, you feel as though you would die for it, but it isn't yours to keep or protect. And if the child becomes a man who has no respect for himself, it's just destroyed till you can hardly remember what it was.' Early in the novel, the reverend had seemed to want his son to call him something other than his customary, rather estranged 'Sir' – Papa, or even Dad. Late in the novel, when Jack calls him Dad, he bursts out: 'Don't call me that. I don't

like it at all. Dad. It sounds ridiculous. It's not even a word.'
When he is not rebuking his son, he is complaining about old
age: 'Jesus never had to be old.' He is only calm when asleep:
'His hair had been brushed into a soft white cloud, like harmless aspiration, like a mist.'

In a final encounter of devastating power, Jack goes to his
father to tell him he is going away again. Jack puts out his hand.
'The old man drew his own hand into his lap and turned away.
"Tired of it!" he said.' They are the last words the Reverend
Boughton speaks in this book, an obviously angry inversion of
the last, tired words of serene John Ames in *Gilead*: 'I'll pray,
and then I'll sleep.'

So luminous are this book's final scenes, so affecting, that
it is all the critic can do not to catch from it, as in this review,
the contagion of ceaseless quotation, a fond mumbling.

2008

Ismail Kadare

I

LIKE TRIESTE OR LVOV, the ancient city of Gjirokastër, in southern Albania, has passed its history beneath a sign perpetually rewritten, in different hands, but always with the same words: 'Under New Management'. It enters the historical record in 1336, as a Byzantine possession, but in 1418 was incorporated into the Ottoman Empire. The Greeks occupied it in 1912, yet a year later it became part of the newly independent Albania. During the Second World War, it was taken by the Italians, taken back by the Greeks, and then seized by the Germans: 'At dusk the city, which through the centuries had appeared on maps as a possession of the Romans, the Normans, the Byzantines, the Turks, the Greeks and the Italians, now watched darkness fall as a part of the German empire. Utterly exhausted, dazed by the battle, it showed no sign of life.'

The novelist Ismail Kadare was born in Gjirokastër, in 1936, and those words are from *Chronicle in Stone*, the great novel he drew out of his boyhood experiences of the Second World War. It was published in Albanian in 1971, and in English in 1987. Despite the many horrors it describes, *Chronicle in Stone* is a joyful, often comic piece of work, in which that concentrated irony for which Kadare would become famous – most notably in his later political parables and allegories of communism, like *The Concert* and *The Successor* – is already visible. In this early novel the irony has a more generous, truant warmth. A teenage boy narrates the events, at once wide-eyed and sophisticated: he lives in a large, rambling house, surrounded by relatives, in what appears to be the Albanian Muslim section of a city notable for its Ottoman and Christian influences. War arrives, in the form of Italian bombing, British bombing, and finally the dark rondo whereby Greek and Italian occupiers arrive and depart from the stage like vicars in an English farce: 'At ten in the morning on Thursday the Italians came back, marching in under freezing rain. They stayed only thirty hours. Six hours later the Greeks were back. The same thing happened all over again in the second week of November.'

But in some ways Kadare is more interested in the kinds of stories that the town might have thrown up at any time in the last thousand years. Townspeople talk of spells, witches, ghosts and legends. Our young narrator discovers *Macbeth* and reads it obsessively, seeing parallels between medieval Scotland and modern Gjirokastër. A group of old women discuss a neighbour's son, who has started wearing spectacles, an occurrence that is treated superstitiously, as an ominous disaster. One of the women, Aunt Xhexho, says: 'How I kept from bursting into tears, I'm sure I don't know. He walked over to the cabinet, flipped through a few books, then went over to the window, stopped, and took off his glasses . . . I reached out, picked up the glasses, and put them on. What can I tell you, my friends? My head was spinning. These glasses must be cursed. The world whirled like the circles of hell. Everything shook, rolled, and swayed as if possessed by the devil.' Her interlocutors all agree that a terrible fate has befallen the bespectacled boy's family. 'It's the end of the world,' intones one of the women, regularly. Throughout the novel, these and other neighbours and relatives comment on ordinary events, and this commentary forms a stubborn resistance to the novelty of the occupation. As a mark of how beautifully Kadare blends this atmosphere of the city's traditional antiquity with the rapidity of wartime development, consider something this same woman, Xhexho, says when she first hears an air-raid siren: 'Now we have a mourner who will wail for us all.'

In this novel, Kadare does something very interesting with narrative: he alternates between the first-person 'I' of the young boy who tells the story, and a technique that could be called unidentified free indirect style, whereby he regularly hands off third-person narrative to an implied community, or village chorus, who replace both the boy's perspective and the omniscient perspective of the novelist. On the one hand, the boy is constantly seeing things with the strange, and estranging, perspective of a young writer-to-be (and this is very much a writer's *Bildungsroman*, among other genres). The whole town is anthropomorphised by the narrator – the stones seem to speak, the raindrops are alive, the buildings are like people: 'The fortress was indeed very old. It had given birth to the city, and our houses resembled the citadel the way children look like their mothers.' A villager's house is seen thus: 'It was a somewhat unusual-looking house, with many gable-ends and overhanging eaves. It seemed to me to be dripping with sleep.' But the storytelling also switches from the boy to a diffused third person, the voice of the community itself: 'We've never seen anything like this, said old women who knew the ways of the world and had even been to Turkey.' In the little provincial comic flick of that phrase, 'and had even been to Turkey', we can read, if we want to, the limited viewpoint of the boyish narrator. But I think we are meant to hear, instead, the limits of the town, as if, say, a group of mothers were speaking among themselves, and agreeing that the wisest women in Gjirokastër 'know everything – after all, some of them have even been to Turkey!' This is how Kadare can reproduce a good deal of speech in this book without needing to attribute it to any particular source; it is merely interested commentary from the town:

'What about our anti-aircraft gun? Why doesn't it come on?'

'You're right, we do have an anti-aircraft gun. Why don't we ever hear it?'

The gap between the provincialism of 'and had even been to Turkey' and the cosmopolitanism of the author who is able to see the provincialism of the phrase is ironic, and it is the fond, rueful ironic gap that opens up when an author, raised in a small, relatively peripheral place, leaves it and writes from a larger, relatively more central place: we find this gap, and this kind of ironic-comic 'community' narration, in the Sicilian fiction of Giovanni Verga, in Cesare Pavese's *The Moon and the Bonfire* (narrated by a man who has returned to the rural village of his boyhood), in V. S. Naipaul's *A House for Mr Biswas*, and in some of José Saramago's fiction. Like Naipaul's novel, *Chronicle in Stone* recalls a community that can be remembered by the author but that cannot, practically speaking, be returned to by the author.

Kadare, thankfully, lacks the weight of Naipaul's post-colonial baggage, and his novel has none of the savagery of critique that makes *A House for Mr Biswas* sometimes uncomfortable to read. Whereas Naipaul is both proud and ashamed of Trinidad, seeing it from the viewpoint of metropolitan London, Kadare celebrates his old town, and celebrates its resistance to foreign occupation, its wayward, singular longevity. When, for instance, Kadare describes the old women known as the 'old crones', he essentially praises them for making *all* forms of rule or government, *all* forms of historical imposition or occupation, alien and foreign:

> These were aged women who could never be surprised or frightened by anything any more. They had long since stopped going out of their houses, for they found the world boring. To them even major events like epidemics, floods and wars were only repetitions of what they had seen before. They had already been old ladies in the thirties, under the monarchy, and even before, under the republic in the mid-twenties. In fact, they were old during the First World War and even before, at the turn of the century. Granny Hadje had not been out of her house in twenty-two years. One old woman of the Zeka family had been inside for twenty-three years. Granny Neslihan had last gone out thirteen years before, to bury her last grandson. Granny Shano spent thirty-one years inside until one day she went out into the

street a few yards in front of her house to assault an Italian officer who was making eyes at her great-granddaughter. These crones were very robust, all nerve and bone, even though they ate very little and smoked and drank coffee all day long . . . The crones had very little flesh on their bones, and few vulnerable spots. Their bodies were like corpses ready for embalming, from which all innards likely to rot had already been removed. Superfluous emotions like curiosity, fear and lust for gossip or excitement had been shed along with useless flesh and excess fat.

It is this affection, which can only be called love, that animates much of the comedy of the novel. One thinks of this exchange, for instance, about Stalin:

'They say there's a man called Yusuf, a man with a red beard, Yusuf Stalin his name is, who's going to smash them [the Fascists] all to pieces.'

'Is he a Muslim?' Nazo asked.

Xhexho hesitated a moment, then said confidently, 'Yes. A Muslim.'

Or there is the way the townspeople start orientating their lives around the British bombing raids, as if they were in one of Donald Barthelme's surrealist fictions: 'The English planes paid us regular visits every day. They would loom in the sky almost to a schedule, and people seemed to get used to the bombings as a disagreeable part of a daily routine. "See you tomorrow at the coffee house, right after the bombing." "I'll be up at dawn tomorrow; that way I think I'll have the house cleaned before the bombing." "Come on, let's go down to the cellar, it's almost time." '

And yet, if this novel is certainly a loving tribute to a childhood town, that tribute is never uncomplicated. In an emphasis characteristic of Kadare's wit, the memory of the town's past is regularly burlesqued, too:

> I had heard that the First Crusade had passed this way a thousand years before. Old Xixo Gavo, they said, had related this in his chronicle. The crusaders had marched down the road in an endless stream, brandishing their arms and crosses and ceaselessly asking, 'Where is the Holy Sepulchre?' They had pressed on south in search of that tomb without stopping in the city, fading away in the same direction the military convoys were now taking.

There is something Monty Python–ish about the Crusaders, miles off course, demanding to see the Holy Sepulchre, and the link to the hopelessness of the modern soldiers is deftly made. One enjoys the comedy while wondering, as one is surely meant to, about the accuracy of Xixo Gavo's chronicle. The novel's complexity has to do with the fact that its comedy is tinged with ruefulness: the city outlives its occupiers, but it cannot fight back and gets bombed anyway. The community dreams fruitlessly of revenge. Dino works on his home-made plane, the plane that is going to vanquish the British or Italian bombers, but when the narrator sees it, he is sad – it is just a few bits of wood in a man's living room. Likewise, the city's old anti-aircraft gun excites everyone, but never shoots down anything. Kadare seems to suggest that one has pride, even nationalistic pride, about being Albanian, but it is necessarily tempered – not by Naipaulian shame but by practical irony, an ironic awareness of Albania's littleness and dispensability in the world:

'In Smyrna one time,' the old artilleryman said, 'a dervish asked me, "Which do you love more, your family or Albania?" Albania, of course, I told him. A family you can make overnight. You walk out of a coffee house, run into a woman on the corner, take her to a hotel, and boom – wife and children. But you can't make Albania overnight after a quick drink in a coffee house, can you? No, not in one night, and not in a thousand and one nights, either.' . . .

'Yes, sir,' another old man added. 'Albania is a complicated business all right.'

'*Ex-treme-ly* complicated. It sure is.'

That 'extreme complication' is given voice in many of Kadare's later works – as near farce in his wonderful, boisterous Evelyn Waugh-like novel, *The File on H.*, and as fiercely political allegory in works like *The Successor* and *Agamemnon's Daughter*. Nothing is more complicated in *Chronicle of Stone* than the fact that, in Gjirokastër, foreign war is beginning to veer towards civil war. The Greeks and Italians come and go, the British run their bombing raids, and the Germans arrive as occupiers at the end of the book. But there is a way in which all of these conquerors are ephemeral, and seen almost lightly, from a comic distance. Yet when the Communist partisans start rounding up characters we have known for two hundred or so pages, and executing them in the street, the horror is immediate, local, and potentially limitless, and seems to draw a different kind of attention from the author: one is reminded that this book was written in the 1960s and 1970s, when the Communist regime may well have seemed to Kadare to be agonisingly invulnerable. The novel mentions that one day a notice is posted on a ruined house: '*Wanted: the dangerous Communist Enver Hoxha. Aged about 30.*' Enver Hoxha, the Communist leader who kept a ruthless and paranoid grip on Albania for forty years until his death in 1985, was also born in Gjirokastër, in 1908. The novel does not mention Hoxha again, but his shadow, and the shadow of the regime he would build after the war, falls heavily on the last eighty pages of the book. In one scene, some of the townspeople are deported by the Italians. As a crowd watches, a passer-by asks what they have done. Someone else replies: 'They spoke against.' 'What does that mean? Against what?' asks the passer-by. 'I'm telling you, they spoke against.' The absent, suppressed referent – 'against what?' – is garish in its silence, and Kadare would become a master analyst of this sinister logic of lunacy, in its Communist totalitarian form. Later, one of the partisans shoots a girl by mistake, in a scene that illustrates all of Kadare's power. He has come for the girl's father, Mak Karllashi, whom he calls 'an enemy of the people':

> 'I'm no enemy of the people,' Mak Karllashi protested. 'I'm a simple tanner. I make people's shoes, I make *opingas*.'
>
> The partisan looked down at his own tattered moccasins.
>
> 'Get out of the way, girl,' he shouted, aiming his gun at the man. The girl screamed . . . The gun of the one-armed partisan fired. Mak Karllashi went down first. The

partisan tried to miss the girl, but in vain. She writhed tight against her father as if the bullets had stitched her body to his.

There is the humble detail of the partisan looking down at his moccasins, and the way this detail is picked up and repeated by the extraordinary image of the bullet 'stitching' the daughter to her father (the bullets like needles, but also a beautiful image of how much the daughter wanted to attach herself, sew herself, to her father) – though many great books lay ahead of Kadare when he wrote these words, he has never written better than this.

A page or two later, the same partisan is sentenced to death by fellow partisans for killing the girl (he is accused of 'the misuse of revolutionary violence'). With nice political absurdism, he raises his arm and cries: 'Long live Communism!' and is immediately shot dead. Though *Chronicle in Stone* ends with the German occupation of the city, it gapes, forebodingly, at the post-war Albanian world.

II

At the end of the war, though the nine-year-old Ismail Kadare did not know it of course, he and the thirty-seven-year-old Enver Hoxha were approaching each other like two dark dots on a snowy landscape, still miles apart but steadily converging on the same frozen lake. *Chronicle in Stone* represents an act of political resistance, of the cunning, subtle kind that allowed Kadare to survive Hoxha's regime, even as some of his books were banned. *The Palace of Dreams*, published in 1981, and more obviously antagonistic, is one of those censored novels. Like many of Kadare's books, it is set in an imprecise past shaded by myth, but lit by the glare of totalitarian thought control. The Palace of Dreams is the most important government ministry in the Balkan Empire, where bureaucrats sift and decode the dreams of the Empire's citizens, all of them working to find the Master-Dreams that will help the sultan in his rule. The novel's hero, from a prominent political family, rises up the ranks of the ministry; yet he cannot save his own family from – indeed, he unwittingly precipitates – their political persecution. Enver Hoxha must have known at once that this surreal dystopia vividly conjured up, in carefully deflected form, the secret police apparatus of modern Albania.

The censoring of *The Palace of Dreams* seems to have pushed Kadare beyond the boundaries of suggestion, allegory, implication and indirection. Certainly, the novella *Agamemnon's Daughter*, which Kadare wrote in the mid-1980s, around the time of Hoxha's death, is laceratingly direct and bitterly lucid. It is perhaps his greatest book, and, along with its sequel, *The Successor* (2003), surely one of the most devastating accounts ever written of the mental and spiritual contamination wreaked on the individual by the totalitarian state. Kadare's French publisher, Claude Durand, has told of how Kadare smuggled some of his writings out of Albania, in 1986, and handed them to Durand, camouflaging them by changing the Albanian names and places to German and Austrian ones, and attributing the writing to the West German novelist Siegfried Lenz. Durand collected the rest of this work, on two trips to Tirana, and the manuscripts were deposited in a safe at a Paris bank. As unaware as anyone else that Albanian communism had only five years left to run, Kadare envisaged this deposit as an insurance policy, *d'outre-tombe*. In the event of his death, by natural or unnatural causes, the publication of these works would make it 'harder', in Durand's words, 'for the Communist propaganda machine to bend Kadare's work and posthumous image to its own ends'.

That is a considerable understatement. I'm not sure any regime could bend *Agamemnon's Daughter* to its own ends. It is a terrifying work, relentless in its critique. It is set in Tirana in the early 1980s, during the May Day Parade. The narrator is a young man who works in radio broadcasting, and who has been unexpectedly invited to attend the festivities from inside the Party grandstand. The formal invitation is unexpected, because the narrator is a passionate liberal, strongly (though privately) opposed to the regime, and because he has recently survived a purge at his radio station, resulting in the relegation of two colleagues. On the day of the parade, he cannot stop thinking about his lover, Suzana, who has broken off their relationship because her father is about to be chosen as the supreme leader's designated successor. He has asked his daughter not to jeopardise his career by consorting with an unsuitable man. Chillingly, she tells her lover that when her father explained the situation to her, 'I saw his point of view.'

The novella confines itself to the day of the parade, and is essentially a portfolio of sketches of human ruination; a brief *Inferno*, in which victims of the regime are serially encountered by our narrator, as he walks to the stands and takes his seat. There is the neighbour who watches him from his balcony, 'looking as sickly as ever . . . He was reputed to have laughed out loud on the day Stalin died, which brought his career as a brilliant young scientist to a shuddering halt.' There is Leka B., a former journalist who displeased the authorities and got transferred to the provinces, to run amateur theatricals. He tells the narrator that he put on a play that turned out to have 'no less than thirty-two ideological errors!' Kadare's comment is withering: 'It was as if he were delighted with the whole business and held it in secret admiration.' There is G.Z., another former colleague, who has survived a purge, though no one knows quite how: 'his whole personality and history corresponded in sum to what in relatively polite language is called a pile of shit'. Kadare likens him to the Bald Man in the Albanian folk tale, who is rescued from hell by an eagle – 'but on one condition. Throughout the flight, the raptor would need to consume raw meat.' Eventually, since the journey takes several days, the Bald Man has to offer his own flesh to feed the bird, and by the time he makes it to the upper world, he is no more than a bag of bones.

At the centre of *Agamemnon's Daughter* is an icy reinterpretation of the Iphigenia story. The narrator reflects on Euripides' play, and on Iphigenia's apparently willing self-sacrifice, in order to help her father's military ambitions. He turns around the Greek tale in his mind and blends it with the remembered pain of Suzana's departure. Hadn't Stalin, he thinks, sacrificed his son Yakov, so as to be able to claim that he was sharing in the common lot of the Russian soldier? But what if the story of Agamemnon is really the story of Comrade Agamemnon – the first great account of absolute political tyranny? What if Agamemnon, in 'a tyrant's cynical ploy', had merely used his daughter, so as to legitimate warfare? As, surely, Yakov, 'may he rest in peace, had not been sacrificed so as to suffer the same fate as any other Russian soldier, as the dictator had claimed, but to give Stalin the right to demand the life of anyone else'. The narrator realises, as he watches Suzana's father standing next to the Supreme Guide on the grandstand, that the Supreme Guide must have asked his deputy to initiate his daughter's sacrifice. *Agamemnon's Daughter* ends with this dark, spare, aphoristically alert declamation: 'Nothing now stands in the way of the final shrivelling of our lives.'

Kadare is inevitably likened to Orwell and Kundera, but he is a deeper ironist than the first, and a better storyteller than the second. He is a compellingly ironic storyteller because he so brilliantly summons details that are able to explode with symbolic reality. Anyone who has read *The Successor* cannot forget the moment when the Hoxha figure, called simply the Guide, visits the newly renovated home of his designated successor. The Successor's wife offers to show the Guide around, despite the anxiety felt by others that the lavishness of the renovation may have been a huge political blunder. The Guide stops to examine a new living-room light switch, a dimmer that is the first of its kind in the country.

> Silence had fallen all around, but when he managed to turn on the light and make it brighter, he laughed out loud. He turned the switch further, until the light was at maximum strength, then laughed again, ha-ha-ha, as if he'd just found a toy that pleased him. Everyone laughed with him, and the game went on until he began to turn the dimmer down. As the brightness dwindled, little by little everything began to freeze, to go lifeless, until all the many lamps in the room went dark.

In its concentrated ferocity, this seems like something very ancient: we could almost be reading Tacitus on Tiberius.

III

Alas, there is nothing quite of this high order in Kadare's novel *The Accident* (translated from the Albanian by John Hodgson). The new book is spare and often powerful, but it is a bit too spare, so that the ribs of allegory show through, in painful obviousness. Many of Kadare's familiar procedures and themes are in evidence, beginning with the positing of an enigma that needs decoding. One morning in Vienna, sometime not long after the end of the war in Kosovo, a young Albanian couple is killed in a car accident. The taxi that had been taking them from their hotel to the airport suddenly veers off the autobahn and crashes. The taxi driver, who survives, can give no reasonable account of why he left the road, except to say that he had been looking in his rear-view mirror at the couple, who had been 'trying to kiss', when a bright light distracted him. The accident is suspicious enough to attract various investigators, not least the intelligence services of Serbia, Montenegro and Albania. The dead man, known as Besfort Y., appears to have been an Albanian diplomat, working at the Council of Europe, and may have been involved in NATO's decision to bomb Serbia. Perhaps the woman who died in the car, who was Besfort's girlfriend, and is known in the reports as Rovena St., knew too much, and Besfort tried to kill her, in a botched plan? But why did Besfort seem to refer to Rovena as 'a call girl'? A few months before the accident, he had taken her to an Albanian motel and she had been 'frightened for her life'. So a friend of Rovena's tells inves-tigators. Rovena, says the friend, 'knew the most appalling things . . . She knew the precise hour when Yugoslavia would be bombed, days in advance.'

The security services give up, in the face of the usual Balkan incomprehensibility, and a mysterious, nameless 'researcher' takes over. This authorial stand-in, who works 'without funds or resources or powers of constraint', decides to reconstruct the last forty weeks of the couple's lives, using diaries, letters, phone calls and the testimonies of friends.

> Everywhere in the world events flow noisily on the sur-face, while their deep currents pull silently, but nowhere is this contrast so striking as in the Balkans. Gales sweep the mountains, lashing the tall firs and mighty oaks, and the whole peninsula appears demented.

Kadare feeds off Balkan incomprehensibility: he likes to tease it and tease at it, while simultaneously making fun of people who talk about 'Balkan incomprehensibility'. He is deeply interested in misreading, yet his prose has a classical lucidity, so that much of his power as a storyteller has to do with his ability to provide an extraordinarily clear analysis of incomprehensibility. This analysis veers between the comic and the tragic, and never finally settles in one mode. In both *The Accident* and *The Successor*, we begin with an apparent accident – in the earlier novel, the country's designated successor has been found in his bedroom, shot dead – that allows Kadare to work through rival explanations. (*The Successor* is based on the 'mysterious' death, reported as suicide, of the Albanian prime minister, Mehmet Shehu, in 1981. He had been Hoxha's closest political ally for decades, but after his death he was denounced as a traitor and enemy of the people, and his family arrested and imprisoned.) A question that haunts both novels is: when did it begin? When was 'the accident' inevitable? When did the tide first turn against the Successor? Was it when the Guide failed to come to the Successor's birthday party, for instance? The deconstructive, blackly surreal answer, of course, is that it has always begun; the tide was turning against the Successor even as he was rising up the Party ranks.

Likewise, in *The Accident*, one can see that Besfort and Rovena were always doomed, and that the reason, as in *The Successor*, is murkily ideological. The nameless 'researcher' discovers that Besfort and Rovena have been together for twelve years. Rovena was a student when she met Besfort, who was older than her, and had come to the university at Tirana to teach international law. From the start, the relationship appears to have been electrically erotic, with Besfort as the seducer and dominant partner. The novel hints at very rough sex. They agree to part, but soon reunite. The couple meets in various European cities and expensive hotels, exercising a freedom unthinkable before the collapse of communism, their itinerary largely determined by Besfort's diplomatic travel (where 'diplomat' probably also means 'spy'). But in Graz, for the first time, Rovena feels that Besfort is suffocating her, a feeling that will mount as the relationship progresses. 'You're preventing me from living,' she tells him, and elsewhere she complains that 'he has me in chains . . . he is the prince and I am only a slave'. 'He wanted her entirely for himself, like every tyrant.' To these charges, he replies that she 'took this yoke up yourself, and now you blame me?' He had been her liberator, writes Kadare, 'but this is not the first time in history that a liberator had been taken for a tyrant, just as many a tyrant had been taken for a liberator'. Partly as a game, and partly as an admission of the terminality of their relationship, the couple start speaking of themselves as client and call girl. Besfort thinks of killing her.

The Accident is a difficult novel. It has a very interrupted form, continually looping back on itself, so that dates and place names seem almost scrambled and the reader must work a kind of hermeneutic espionage on the text. Unlike in *Agamemnon's Daughter* and *The Successor*, the analysis of incomprehensibility seems not lucid but opaque. Yet at the same time, the symbolic pressure seems a little too transparent, not suggestively or richly related to the human narrative. One gathers that Kadare is presenting a kind of allegory about the lures and imprisonments of that new post-Communist tyranny, liberty, and he has Besfort bang home this decoding: 'Until yesterday,' he tells Rovena, 'you were complaining that it was my fault that you aren't free. And now you say you have too much freedom. But somehow it's always my fault.' Besfort is the new liberty that Rovena cannot do without, and to which she is willing to be enslaved, and this freedom is dangerous and frequently squalid.

The Accident thus offers an interesting reply to the question with which Kadare closes *Agamemnon's Daughter*. At the end of that novella, the young narrator thinks of the Communist slogan 'Let us revolutionise everything' and asks, rhetorically, 'How the hell can you revolutionise a woman's sex? That's where you'd have to start if you were going to tackle the basics – you had to start with the source of life. You would have to correct its appearance, the black triangle above it, and the glistening line of the labia.' He means that totalitarianism will always be thwarted by some non-ideological privacy, or surplus, beyond its reach. Kundera has repeatedly explored the same question, with regard to a libidinous erotics of resistance. Yet *The Accident* grimly suggests that it is indeed possible to 'revolutionise' a woman's sex, and that capitalism can do it perhaps more easily than communism. After all, the point about Besfort and Rovena, if I am reading the novel right, is that their relationship is thoroughly contaminated by ideology and politics; their very postures of submission and domination are overdetermined.

In a long speech that is surely at the emotional and ideological heart of the book, Besfort tells Rovena, who was only thirteen at the end of the dictatorship, about the kind of madness that prevailed under Hoxha. He describes a world of crazy inversion, reminiscent of Dostoevsky's universe, in which citizens willingly pretended to be conspirators, so as to confess their love for the leader while being simultaneously punished for crimes they had not committed. Each plotter, says Besfort, turned out to be more abject than the last:

> The conspirators' letters from prison became more and more ingratiating. Some requested Albanian dictionaries, because they were stuck for words to express their adoration of the leader. Others complained of not being tortured properly. The protocols sent back from firing squads on the barren sandbank by the river told the same story: their victims shouted, 'Long live the leader!', and as they

conveyed their last wishes some felt such a burden of guilt
that they asked to be killed not by the usual weapons but
by anti-tank guns or flamethrowers. Others asked to be
bombarded from the air, so that no trace of them would
remain . . . Nobody could distinguish truth from fiction
in these reports, just as it was impossible to discern what
the purpose of the conspirators, or even the leader himself,
might be. Sometimes the leader's mind was easier to read.
He had enslaved the entire nation, and now the adoration
of the conspirators would crown his triumph. Some people
guessed that he was sated with the love of his loyal follow-
ers, and that he now wanted something new and apparently
impossible – the love of traitors.

We are back in the world of Leka B., who was oddly proud
of his thirty-two ideological errors, and in the world of *A
Chronicle of Stone*, and the partisan who dies shouting 'Long
live Communism!' Kadare also subtly suggests that this dense,
overwrought speech might itself be evidence that Besfort is a
victim of the totalitarianism he so despises – that he cannot
escape its deformations, its legacies, the memory of its hysteria. But a melancholy thought also casts its shadow. Might
this be true of Kadare, too? It seems poignant that easily the
most powerful section in the novel returns to old ground and
old obsessions, and it seems poignant that this allegory of the
tyranny of liberty is less effective, as a novel, than Kadare's
earlier allegories of the tyranny of tyranny. Perhaps it is in
the nature of freedom, still after all a transitional event in the
history of post-war Albania, that a novelist even of Kadare's
great powers will seem, when trying to allegorise it, to grasp

at amorphousness, will seem to stab at clouds; whereas the old Kadare, who worked within and against totalitarianism, was sustained by the great subject of the Hoxha regime, like a man sitting on a huge statue. Kadare would not be the only novelist who has found, with the collapse of communism, that his world has disappeared, however much he also longed for the destruction of that world. These are early days yet.

2010

Jenny Erpenbeck

EARLIER THIS SUMMER, my family spent a week in an Italian village near Menton, just over the border that Italy shares with southern France. Dry hills, azure Mediterranean, scents of rosemary and lavender, a lemon tree in the garden. Well, lucky us. Daily, we crossed the border into France and back again into Italy. We didn't have to stop, and the listless border guards barely glanced at our respectable little hired car, with its four white occupants. They were a good deal more interested in the African migrants who gathered with persistent hopelessness on the Italian side of the border, just a few feet from the immigration post. We saw the young men everywhere in that Italian hinterland – usually in groups of two or three, walking along the road, climbing the hills, sitting on a wall. They were tall, dark-skinned, conspicuous because they were wearing too many clothes for the warm Riviera weather. We learned that they had made their way from various African countries to Italy, and were now desperate to get into France, either to stay there or to push on further, to Britain and Germany. 'You might see them in the hills. Nothing to be alarmed about. There have been no problems – yet,' said the genial woman who gave us the key to our house. Near that house, there was a makeshift sign, in Arabic and English: 'Migrants! Please do not throw your garbage into the nature. Use the plastic bags you see on the private road.'

I had read moving articles and essays about the plight of people like these – I had read several of those pieces out aloud to my children; I had watched terrible reports from the BBC, and the almost unbearable Italian documentary *Fire at Sea*. And so what? What good are the right feelings, if they are only right feelings? I was just a moral flâneur. From inside my speeding car, I regarded those men with compassion, shame, indignation, curiosity, ignorance, all of it united in a conveniently vague conviction, as Edward VIII famously said about mass unemployment in the 1930s, that 'something must be done'. But not so that it would truly disturb my week of vacation. I am like some 'flat' character in a comic novel, who sits every night at the dinner table, and repetitively, despicably intones, without issue or effect, 'This is the central moral question of our time.' And of course, such cleansing self-reproach is merely part of liberalism's survival dance. It's not just that we are morally impotent; the continuation of our comfortable lives rests on the continuation – on the success – of that impotence. We see suffering only intermittently, and our days make safe spaces for these interruptions.

Jenny Erpenbeck's novel *Go, Went, Gone* is about 'the central moral question of our time', and among its many virtues is that it is alive not only to the suffering of people very different from us, but alive to the false consolations of telling 'moving' stories about people very different from us. Erpenbeck writes about Richard, a retired German academic, whose privileged, orderly life is transformed by his growing involvement with the lives of a number of African refugees – utterly power-less men, unaccommodated men, who have ended up, via the most arduous routes, in wealthy Germany. The risks inherent in making fiction out of the encounter between privileged Europeans and powerless dark-skinned non-Europeans are immense: earnestness without rigour, the mere confirmation of the right kind of political 'concern', sentimental didacticism. A journey of transformation, in which the white European is spiritually renewed, almost at the expense of his darkly exotic subjects, is familiar enough from German romanticism; you can imagine a contemporary version, in which the novelist traffics in the most supple kind of self-protective self-criticism. *Go, Went, Gone* is not that kind of book.

Jenny Erpenbeck, who was born in East Berlin in 1967, is an original writer. In a novelistic tradition still largely dedicated to the treatment of domestic interiority, she does nothing less than attempt readings of the domestic interiority of history. Her first full-length novel, *Visitation* (2010), told the history of the German twentieth century through the lives of the succes-sive inhabitants of a Brandenburg property, rather in the way that Virginia Woolf refracts the First World War through a his-tory of the Ramsays' home, in the 'Time Passes' section of *To the Lighthouse*. Erpenbeck's next novel, *The End of Days* (2014), again recounts twentieth-century history, this time through the long life of a woman who could have inhabited most of its tormented decades – from birth in Galicia at the turn of the twentieth century, to a period in Moscow in the 1930s, ending her days as a nonagenarian in a newly unified Berlin. (I say 'could', because Erpenbeck repeatedly kills off and resurrects her heroine, offering each new phase as an historical hypothetical.)

In *Visitation*, the one character who does not leave, because he does not own or inhabit the house but tends it, is the gardener. As people are displaced, races persecuted, empires demolished and walls erected, the gardener goes about his task of orderly renewal – the unfinished business of visiting clarity on unkempt space. The gardener sees everything lucidly, often with powerful emotion, but from a slight distance. It is a fair image of how Jenny Erpenbeck works. The reader learns to approach her fiction, especially in its early pages, with the same patience she herself deploys. Her narratives are rigorous, prefer the present tense, and are untempted by the small change of contemporary realism (abundant and superfluous dialogue in quotation marks, sharply individuated characters, tellingly selected detail). Her task is comprehension rather than replication, and she uses a measured, lyrically austere prose, whose even tread barely betrays the considerable passion that drives it onward. Among contemporary anglophone writers, this classical restraint brings to mind J. M. Coetzee, the V. S. Naipaul of *The Enigma of Arrival*, and Teju Cole's Naipaul-influenced *Open City*.

That restraint works especially well in *Go, Went, Gone*, where overt passion might so easily become preachment. And it is particularly well suited for establishing the sedate rhythms of our protagonist's daily life, before his transformative encounter. The first pages of Erpenbeck's novel are full of blind banality. Richard has just retired as a professor of classical philology. He is a widower, living alone in a pleasant Berlin suburb, where the only recent disturbance appears to have been an accident in the nearby lake: in the early summer, a man drowned there, and months later the body has not been found. One day in late August, Richard happens to walk past a group of protestors in Alexanderplatz. 'Their skin is black. They speak English, French, Italian, as well as other languages that no one here understands. What do these men want?' But Richard, lost in his own thoughts, barely notices them – he is thinking about an archaeologist friend of his, who has told him that the area is riddled with subterranean tunnels, some dating back to the Middle Ages. At home, his routine closes over him, like the calm waters of the town's lake. For dinner, he makes himself open-face sandwiches with cheese and ham, watches TV, reads his favourite passage from *The Odyssey*. 'Later he drives to the garden supply centre to have his lawnmower blade sharpened.' He eats the same thing for his weekday breakfast, allowing himself an egg only on Sundays.

There is something evasive about his placidity. What is he concealing? What is he guilty of? Erpenbeck does not say, but *we* think: it's the kind of existence that might serve a war criminal's quiet rehabilitation. But of course, Richard, who was just a child during the war, is guilty only of the evil of banality, the moral myopia that dims most of our lucky lives in the West. In fact, like many older Germans, Richard was a victim of what his mother used to call 'the mayhem of war'. He was an infant when his family fled from Silesia for Germany. In the confusion, he was almost separated from his mother, and was handed back to her, through a train window, by a Russian soldier. His father fought in the German army, in Norway and Russia. And for most of his life, Richard was not exactly a child of 'the West': he lived in East Berlin. He and his wife were housed in a street that had been turned into a cul-de-sac by the Wall. They were 'a mere two hundred yards as the crow flies from West Berlin', but their lives were materially and politically distant from their wealthier neighbours. Even now, in a united Germany, Richard's academic pension is smaller than that of his old West German colleagues. He gets lost driving around what used to be West Berlin, because he's unfamiliar with the geography. The dishwasher still makes him smile: for him it's a relative novelty, a toy of privilege.

This is the formation of the man who at first ignores, and then does not ignore, the group of African refugees in Alexanderplatz – a fortunate contemporary European who nevertheless has his own history, however far off, of displacement, warfare, borders and relative impoverishment. Erpenbeck doesn't linger on the reasons for Richard's new attentiveness, but we can surmise that it may be partly academic: after a period of indifference, he is suddenly shocked, ashamed, by his own ignorance. Where are these men from? 'Where exactly is Burkina Faso? . . . What is the capital of Ghana? Of Sierra Leone? Or Niger?' He remembers that his mother used to read to him from '*Hatschi Bratschi's Hot-Air Balloon*,' a kids' book about a 'cannibal boy' from . . . somewhere in Africa. Could he really be no better informed as a retired professor than he was as a child? So, in scholarly fashion, he begins 'a new project', and spends the next two weeks reading books, and making a list of questions to ask the refugees. Painstakingly, Erpenbeck itemises these queries, one after another, rubs our faces in their fathomless ignorance, since by and large this is our fathomless ignorance, too:

> Where did you grow up? What's your native language? What's your religious affiliation? How many people are in your family? . . . How did your parents meet? Was there

a TV? Where did you sleep? What did you eat? What was your favorite hiding place when you were a child? Did you go to school? . . . Did you learn a trade? Do you have a family of your own? When did you leave the country of your birth? Why? . . . What did you think Europe would be like? What's different? How do you spend your days? What do you miss most? . . . Can you imagine growing old here? Where do you want to be buried?

Some of the Alexanderplatz refugees are moved to a former nursing home in Kreuzberg. Richard goes there to interview them, and finally his project is no longer scholarly. Over the next months, he gets to know the handful of characters we in turn get to know. He speaks to them in English or Italian. There is a man whom Richard privately names Apollo, since he looks exactly as he thought the god would look. Apollo is from Niger, is a Tuareg (Richard has only the VW Touareg as a coordinate), and never really knew his parents. Perhaps they sold him? He has worked as a 'slave' for as long as he can recall. There is Awad, born in Ghana, whose mother died giving birth to him. (Richard nicknames him Tristan.) When Awad was seven, his father, who was working as a driver for an oil company, brought him to Libya. Awad got work as an auto mechanic. But Gadaffi's regime began to teeter, and in the civil war 'no one was on our side. Even though I grew up in Libya.' Awad was rounded up by soldiers and put on a boat, along with hundreds of others. Where was the boat going? Malta, Italy, Tunisia? No one knew. They were at sea for days; when someone died, they threw the body overboard. Awad spent three-quarters of a year in a Sicilian camp. Eventually, he flew to Germany, choosing Berlin at random. And there is Rashid, who walks with a limp, and has a scar under his eye. Rashid, who is from Nigeria, was the victim of what appears to have been a Boko Haram attack. He came over to Italy on a boat carrying eight hundred people. When the Italian coast guard tried to rescue them, the boat capsized; five hundred and fifty drowned.

Erpenbeck's novel is usefully prosaic, written in a slightly uninviting, almost managerial present tense, which keeps overt emotion at bay. Just as Erpenbeck does not really examine the causes of Richard's change of heart, so she is wary of bestowing anything like easy 'redemption' on her protagonist (and hence on her novel). Richard is not an intimate creature; he remains somewhat distant to us, and somewhat distant to the African refugees he befriends and ultimately aids. So Richard's 'journey' seems functional rather than spiritual. Though he is spurred to practical action (he ends up making space for twelve refugees in his house), it is not clear that he is a better man at the end of the book than at its start. Two elements seem central to his character: his East Germanness, and his curiosity. The former constantly reminds him of his second-class status in a united Germany, and he uses his sensitivity to this relegation when he begins to interact with the men he befriends. The latter becomes the novel's own curiosity, which is why 'Go, Went, Gone' is as much about the lives of the refugees as it is about Richard's life. Jenny Erpenbeck thanks thirteen interlocutors, whom one assumes to be African immigrants in Germany, for 'many good conversations', and her novel has an air of practical humility, since presumably Richard's questions were once hers, too. What can we discover about these men? What, then, can our discoveries possibly mean? And how do we live – what should we do – once we have modified, however feebly, our colossal ignorance?

Erpenbeck does not force her hand. Though we learn more about the lives of the African refugees by the novel's close, we do not gain intimate access to those lives. And while Richard is keen to learn more, he brings his own assumptions and blindness to his project. For Richard is not simply as ignorant as most of us; his is a highly educated ignorance: 'Richard has read Foucault and Baudrillard, and also Hegel and Nietzsche, but he doesn't know what you can eat when you have no money to buy food.' Out of this literate, well-stocked abyss, Erpenbeck constructs an encounter not only between people, but between cultures. Richard must discover everything about his African interlocutors – family, religion, schooling, customs. And in turn, he will use his own German and classical culture, sometimes defensively, sometimes productively, to begin a process of comprehension that culture might, in fact, impede. He must receive things he may not understand, and he must give things that may not be wanted. Richard brings to bear what is at hand (his cultural inheritance) on what is in front of him (the men whose lives he no longer ignores). But mutual comprehension is by no means guaranteed, or even apparent. At first, he uses his blatantly romantic classical nicknames (Apollo, Tristan, Hermes). Then he sits in on the men's German lessons, and eventually starts teaching them himself. (The novel's blunt, ghostly title is taken from one of these language lessons – *Gehen, ging, gegangen.*)

Erpenbeck beautifully orchestrates a counterpoint, a running line that weaves its way between Richard's established European patrimony and its disruption in the face of the Other.

The novel offers a premonition of this disruption in its early pages, deploying a famous example of it from the classical tradition. Archimedes, drawing geometric circles on the ground, is supposed to have told the Roman soldier who killed him, 'Do not disturb my circles.' Richard refers to this, as an example of how 'You can never count on freedom from mayhem'. He is thinking of the Second World War, and his own childhood. But this nice reflection occurs before he himself has been tested; before his own circles are disturbed by the 'mayhem' of the African refugees he struggles to understand, and whom he later champions. Elsewhere, when one of the men, named Yussuf, tells him that he has worked as a dishwasher in Italy, Richard is uncomfortably aware that this fact spells Yussuf's doom, that he won't get asylum in Germany. (European law allows that since Yussuf entered the continent in Italy, he can be deported back there.) He immediately thinks of a fatal line of Brecht's: 'He who laughs has not yet received the terrible news.'

At the heart of the novel is the friendship – wary, limited – between Richard and a young man from Niger, named Osarobo, who has been three years in Europe. Like the others, Osarobo tells Richard that he wants to work. (The refugees are waiting to apply for asylum, and in this state of limbo are permitted only to receive benefits, not work.) Hearing this, Richard thinks of Mozart's Tamino: 'In front of every door he tries to open, a voice makes him stop: *Go back!*' Osarobo surprises him by saying that he would like to learn to play the piano, and Richard obliges by offering the use of his own instrument. In a vivid scene, he tries to teach him how to play a simple five-finger scale, starting on middle C. For smooth playing, Osarobo must make his hand heavy, but he can't let it fall in the right way:

The black man and the white man look at this black arm and this black hand as if at something that is causing problems for both of them. Your hand has weight, Osarobo shakes his head, yes it does, of course it does, just let it fall. Richard holds Osarobo's elbow from below and sees the scars on his arm that the arm's owner is trying to control, the hand is prepared to jerk back at any moment, the hand is afraid, the hand is a stranger here and doesn't know its way around. Let it fall.

Richard shows Osarobo videos of pianists playing Chopin and Schubert, and one of a pianist who goes unnamed, but who must be Glenn Gould.

Yet this kind of exchange cannot only be one-way. In another poignant moment, a musical reference is, as it were, handed back to Richard by one of the Africans – a reference now altered by its political translation. Facing likely deportation from Berlin, the refugees eventually explode with anger. Yussuf becomes violent, punching anyone who tries to speak to him, including Richard. Shouting in French, Italian and some German, Yussuf yells, 'Leave us in peace, damn it!', and 'I've had enough!' Twenty pages later, Richard suddenly recalls the famous Bach cantata, *Ich habe genug*. But why? 'Maybe it was hearing Yussuf, the flipped-out future engineer, shouting *Ich habe genug* – I've had enough! – in front of the Spandau residence.' Erpenbeck proceeds to quote lines from that celestial cantata – devout language that speaks of leave-taking and religious consolation ('Fall in soft and calm repose! / World, I dwell no longer here'), but which Yussuf's anguish has robbed of such antique sureties.

Once Erpenbeck opens this communication, between privileged European citizen and powerless African refugee,

the asymmetrical structure of the encounter begins to generate its own radical inversions – political and ethical reversals of the kind that Montaigne knowingly uses in his great
essay, 'On Cannibals', or which Shakespeare employs in *King
Lear*, when he has the madly rational king cry out, 'Change
places, and, handy-dandy, which is the justice, which is the
thief?' Each side, for instance, can be as ignorant as the other.
Osarobo has never heard of Hitler, knows nothing about a
world war. Another man, Rufu, has never heard about a wall
dividing East and West Berlin. And when Richard tells him
how the wall worked, he naturally turns the concept upside
down: 'Ah, *capisco*, they didn't want them in the West.' No,
says Richard, 'they didn't want to let them leave the East'. In
this way, Erpenbeck's novel is brilliantly alive to its regime of
ironic inversion. The refugees are not allowed to work, Richard
thinks, but their presence has created 'half-time jobs for at
least twelve Germans thus far'. Why should we have so much,
and they so little? thinks Richard elsewhere. German post-war
prosperity is generally attributed to hard work, native ingenu-
ity and fine organisation. East Germans had little to do with
this economic miracle, yet they are also the lucky beneficiaries.
So, Richard reflects, 'who deserves credit for the fact that even
the less affluent among their circle now have dishwashers in
their kitchens, wine bottles on their shelves, and double-glazed
windows?' He goes further: 'But if this prosperity couldn't
be attributed to their own personal merit, then by the same
token the refugees weren't to blame for their reduced circumstances. Things might have turned out the other way around.'
Richard's friend Sylvia adds: 'I keep imagining that someday
it'll be us having to flee again, and no one will help us either.'

Change places, and, handy-dandy, which is the justice, which is the thief? The East German perspective constantly lends its own difference.

Go, Went, Gone does not merely observe such reversals, but enacts them, and in so doing becomes one of those books, like *The Death of Ivan Ilyich*, or indeed *Open City*, which challenge us not to be mere flâneurs of the text, but to change our lives and the lives of those around us. Such works are always on the verge of becoming scripture or parable, because they announce that to read is to comprehend, and to comprehend is to act. Tolstoy announces this loudly and forcefully; Erpenbeck, like Cole, voices it more quietly. Here, the implied chain of transformation offers its own lesson: just as Jenny Erpenbeck must have been profoundly changed by her encounters with the thirteen African refugees she interviewed in order to write this book, so her fictional protagonist is likewise changed, and so her readers must be likewise changed – we are all part of Richard's 'project'.

Richard is transformed enough to turn his life upside down. In the most conclusive of the novel's reversals, he takes in the stranger – and the stranger ends up cooking his own food for Richard, in the host's house. When the refugees seem likely to be moved by force from Berlin, Richard and his friends act. He arranges to have his house officially recognised as a shelter, and finds room there for as many as twelve refugees. His friends Detlef and Sylvia put three men in their garden guest house. Detlef's ex-wife says that someone can sleep in her tea shop in Potsdam. Richard's archaeologist friend, whose place is empty because he is abroad on a visiting professorship, tells him to ask the neighbours for the key. And so on. 'In this way, 147 of the 476 men now have a place to sleep.'

So *Go, Went, Gone* ends in pealing hope, with the kind of unlikely closures that nineteenth-century novels and children's books indulge in. But Erpenbeck's last-minute rescues are surely not supposed to be realistic; they are supposed to be utopian. This is not how it *went*, but how it *should* go. And curiously, they are utopian without being sentimental: the novel's cool tone never wavers. 'In this way, 147 of the 476 men now have a place to sleep' – does that sentence announce a relative triumph, or a relative failure? Erpenbeck remains hard to read. A clue to the novel's political soul is provided by a decent immigration lawyer, who reminds Richard that two thousand years ago, 'no one was more hospitable than the Teutons'. The lawyer reads aloud from Tacitus' *Germania*, the classical historian's report on the German peoples: 'It is accounted a sin to turn any man away from your door,' wrote Tacitus. 'The host welcomes his guest with the best meal that his means allow . . . No distinction is ever made between acquaintance and stranger as far as the right to hospitality is concerned.' And nowadays? asks Richard. Ah, nowadays, says the lawyer drily, 'we're left with Section 23, Paragraph 1 of the Residence Act'. There is something almost beautiful, Richard thinks earlier, in Osarobo's ignorance of Hitler. Perhaps this innocence could erase the awful past, and transport us 'to the Germany of *before*, to the land already lost forever by the time he was born. *Deutschland is beautiful*. How beautiful it would be if it were true.' If Richard here dreams backwards, this novel also dreams forwards, in a similar gesture of yearning erasure. Make Germany, it seems to say to us, not great again, but beautiful again.

2017

Packing My
Father-in-Law's Library

'Yet, he said, it is often our mightiest projects that most
obviously betray the degree of our insecurity.'
W. G. Sebald, *Austerlitz*

ROUTE 12D, NORTH OF UTICA, New York, south of Fort
Drum and Carthage, runs through poor, shabby countryside.
In the unravelled townships, there are trailers and collapsed
farmhouses. Here and there, a new silo, shining like a chrome
torpedo, suggests a fresh start, or maybe just the arrival of
agribusiness. The pall of lost prosperity hangs heavily. Heavily?
No, to the skimming driver aiming elsewhere, it only falls
vaguely, or vaguely guiltily.

In Talcottville, an example of that lost prosperity can be
seen from the road – a grand, fine limestone house with a
white double-storeyed porch. The house is anomalous, both
in its size and in its proximity to the road. But for a long
time it must have been the house's contents that were truly
anomalous: a careful, distinguished library of thousands of
volumes. For this was Edmund Wilson's family home, built

at the end of the eighteenth century by the Talcotts, one of whom married Wilson's great-grandfather. It was the place the literary critic most happily returned to in later life, though never uncomplicatedly. In his journal of life in Talcottville, *Upstate*, Wilson expresses his love for the region while grumbling, in an old man's crooked jabs, about the bad restaurants and intellectually modest company. 'In a sense, it has always been stranded,' he once wrote of the property. It was here that he died, one morning in June 1972.

I used to drive past Edmund Wilson's house on my way to Canada, where my wife's parents lived after my father-in-law's retirement. Though in apparently reasonable shape, the Wilson home always seemed closed up, forgotten, and in some ways it is the condition of such a house, ignored by a newer road, to seem chronically forgotten. In my mind, I could see into the library, see those shelves and shelves of eloquent, mute books, sunk in themselves like a rotting paper harvest, the ancient, classical authors gesturing in puzzlement to the classical, New World place names of New York State: Rome, Troy, Ithaca, Syracuse.

My father-in-law died last year, and my mother-in-law is ailing, so this summer we drove up to my parents-in-law's house, to empty it for sale. Again we passed the Wilson house, and again I thought about the silent longevity of his books, and the strange incommunicability of that defunct library, so uselessly posthumous, sleeping by the side of this provincial road. I knew that what awaited us in Canada was the puzzle of how to dispose of my father-in-law's library, a collection of about four thousand books, similarly asleep in a large Victorian house in the flat, open fields of rural

Ontario. We would take perhaps a hundred back to Boston, but had no room in our house for more. And then what?

François-Michel Messud, my father-in-law, was a complicated, brilliant man. He was born in France but spent his early childhood in Algiers, and then, nomadically, in Beirut, Istanbul and Salonica. In the early 1950s, he came to America, as one of the first Fulbright Scholars, and stayed on to do graduate work in Middle Eastern studies. He started a PhD on Turkish politics, but abandoned it and went into business, a decision probably born of academic anxiety and patriarchal masochism. He was, in fact, not a tremendously engaged businessman, and retained the instincts of a fine scholar and curious traveller. His mind was worldly, with little hospitality towards literature or music or philosophy. What interested him were societies, tribes, roots, exile, journeys, languages. Educated in an austere French environment, a child of the deprivations of the 1930s and 1940s (he remembered that Jacques Derrida was in the same class as him in junior school in Algiers: 'not then a very good pupil'), he could be difficult. After six in the evening, when cocktails made everything hazardous, one learned to tread carefully, for fear of splashing into an error that might be roughly corrected. Not to know precisely who the Phoenicians were (not to know where they came from and when they flourished); not to know the names of the two most famous mosques in Istanbul, or the history of the civil war in Lebanon, or the ethnic composition of the Albanians; not to recall exactly who said 'Beware of Greeks bearing gifts', or to fluff a French phrase; not to recall why the Sephardim are called the Sephardim, was to court swift disdain.

I was grateful not to be his son; his anxious male authority was so different from my reticent father's that I was alternately impressed and alienated by it. Once, early in my marriage, when I had been living in France for a few months and my ability with the language was improving, we were at dinner, and someone at the table praised me for my increased fluency. Everyone else piously agreed. 'I don't see why I should praise you yet,' my father-in-law broke in, 'it's a very small improvement and you have a long way to go.' I knew he would say it, rather disliked him for it, agreed with him. He himself liked to recount the story of arriving from France, at Amherst College in 1954, and being told by his American room-mate that he would never really master English. 'I could speak it fluently by Christmas,' he would say. Whether the story was true or not, he spoke perfect English, without a French accent, except for a tendency to pronounce 'tongue' as 'tong', and 'swan' as if he were saying 'swam'. He had the foreigner's Nabokovian love of exhuming dead puns; was tirelessly amused, for instance, by the fact that the Archbishop of Canterbury is officially known as 'Primate of all England', and therefore 'should be called Chief Chimp'.

Tribes and societies interested him because he grew up in a tribe, left it for a society and belonged to neither. His tribe was French-Algerian: the *pieds noirs*, the European colonists who went to Algeria in the early nineteenth century, and abandoned it en masse at the end of the war for independence in 1962. Like most *pieds noirs*, he never returned, after independence, to the country of his childhood, so that Algeria – and indeed a whole world of francophone North African experience – could only be experienced in the mind, always practically lost. France, the larger home, was an ambiguous pleasure, as for many of the returning colonists; though his sister settled in Toulon, he never showed much interest in the country, and as a result was refreshingly free of the usual maddening French superiority. Instead, he came to America, where he lived most of his adult life. But he was not an especially eager immigrant, nor a willing democrat; once the early excitements of the Fulbright and graduate school waned, he settled into a familiar European alienation. He lived a lifetime in America, worked here (though for a French company), paid his taxes, read the *New York Review of Books*, bought shirts and underwear at Brooks Brothers, went to new shows at the Metropolitan Museum, but was not an American. Increasingly, American society bewildered and irritated him; the vulgarities and democratic banalities that are merely routinely annoying to educated Americans, or are written off gladly as part of the price of dynamic vitality, gnawed at him. He floated on top of American life, fortunate, wounded, unmoored.

I think that the most important book in his study was a huge atlas, wide open on a wooden lectern, the pages turned daily; sometimes we would catch him standing at the lectern, peering down at the dense, abstract grids of some new-found interest. Travel and reading allowed him to collect a frail library of experience. He travelled widely and systematically. Each trip (to Egypt, Greece, Indonesia, Peru, Morocco, Burma, India, Russia) was thoroughly planned out, prepared for with advance reading and orderly itineraries, and then preserved – usually by his wife – in photographs of buildings and cities: pyramids, temples, mosques, streets, columns, ruins. And he read in the same way: he followed interests, like an army moving along a line of supply, and searched out all the available books on a particular subject. John Berryman made fun of Edmund Wilson's relentlessness, because he used to say, when working on an essay, that he was 'working my way through the oeuvre' of a given writer. There was a similar intellectual voracity. The acquisition of a book signalled not just the potential acquisition of knowledge but something like the property rights to a piece of ground: the knowledge became a visitable place. His immediate surroundings – his American or Canadian surroundings – were of no great interest to him; I never heard him speak with any excitement about Manhattan, for instance. But the Alhambra in 1492, or the Salonica he remembered from childhood (the great pre-war centre of Sephardic Jewry, where, he recalled, there were Yiddish newspapers printed in Hebrew characters), or the Constantinople of the late Byzantine Empire, were . . . what? If I say they were 'alive' for him (the usual cliché), then I make him sound more scholarly, and perhaps more imaginative, than he actually was. It would be closer to the truth to say that such places were facts for him, in a way that Manhattan and Toronto (and even Paris) were not.

And yet these facts were largely incommunicable. He spent his time among businessmen, not scholars. He rarely invited people to dinner, and he could become emphatic and monologic. He tended to flourish his facts as querulous challenges rather than as invitations to conversation, though this wasn't perhaps his real intention. So there always seemed to be a quality of self-defence about the greedy rate at which he acquired books, as if he were putting on layers of clothing to protect against the draughts of exile.

Libraries are always paradoxical: they are as personal as the collector, and at the same time represent an ideal statement of knowledge that is impersonal, because it is universal, abstract, and so much larger, in sum, than an individual life. Susan Sontag once said to me that her essays were more intelligent than she was, because she worked so hard at them, and expanded into them over several months of writing. I murmured something banal about how the critic conducts his education in public, and she bristled. Gesturing towards her huge library, she said, with certainty, 'That isn't what I meant. I've read all these books.' I didn't believe her, since no one has read one's entire library; and it seemed strange of her not to comprehend what I intended to say, which was simply that, like her essays, her library was also more intelligent than she was. This was acutely true of my father-in-law's library, which was not, like Sontag's or Wilson's, a working library, but an underemployed collection for a working mind. My father-in-law's will to completion – his need to encompass a subject by buying all the available books and reading them, and then putting them out – represented an ideal, a kind of abstract utopia, a recovered country free of vicissitudes. A long shelf of careful, brilliant books, all devoted to one subject, was the best possible life that subject could enjoy – a golden life for that subject. Here, for instance, is the first foot of a couple of his shelves on Burma: *Kinship and Marriage in Burma*, by Melford E. Spiro; *Political Systems of Highland Burma*, by E. R. Leach; *Forgotten Land: A Rediscovery of Burma*, by Harriet O'Brien; *Burmese Administrative Cycles: Anarchy and Conquest, c. 1580–1760*, by Victor B. Lieberman; *Return to Burma*, by Bernard Fergusson; *Burma and Beyond*, by Sir J. George Scott; *Finding*

George Orwell in Burma, by Emma Larkin; *A History of Modern Burma*, by Michael W. Charney. And here are the first entries of two or three shelves devoted to Judaism and Jewry: *A People Apart: The Jews in Europe, 1789–1939*, by David Vital; *Vilna on the Seine: Jewish Intellectuals in France Since 1968*, by Judith Friedlander; *Moments of Crisis in Jewish–Christian Relations*, by Marc Saperstein; *The Russian Jew Under Tsars and Soviets*, by Salo W. Baron; *Le Salut par les juifs*, by Léon Bloy; *Les Juifs d'Espagne: Histoire d'une diaspora, 1492–1992*, by Henry Méchoulan. He had three or four hundred books on aspects of the Byzantine Empire, and probably twice that number on Islamic and Middle Eastern subjects.

I spent the first few days in Canada cataloguing the Middle Eastern books, in the hope that we might be able to keep the collection on Islam and Muslim societies intact, and perhaps give them to an institution – a college, a school, a local library, even a mosque. The librarian in charge of Islamic books at McGill University had kindly agreed to look at such a catalogue. It was slow, intricate, engrossing work – fifty-eight books on Egypt alone, from Alfred Butler's *The Arab Conquest of Egypt and the Last Thirty Years of the Roman Dominion*, first published in 1902, to Florence Nightingale's letters from her journey on the Nile, to Taha Hussein's memoir, *An Egyptian Childhood*, originally published in Cairo in 1932. But it soon became apparent that no one really wants hundreds or thousands of old books. Emails sent to the librarians at the local university were unanswered. Someone told us about a public library in a town in Alberta that had burned to the ground. They were going to rebuild, and needed donations. I was ready to ship hundreds. But the website requested only books published in the last two years, which excluded almost everything in my father-in-law's library. Kingston, Ontario, the nearest big town, and the home of Queen's University, had a thriving second-hand book business, so I called one of those shops. Would the owner like to come out to a rural house, about forty minutes from the city, and look over a good library of several thousand volumes? The answer was sympathetic and dismaying. There used to be twelve second-hand bookshops in Kingston, the bookseller told me, and now there are four. 'We have the storage space, but no money. The shop along the street has the money to buy books, but no space. This summer at least three big private collections have come onto the market. So I'm afraid it's just not worth it for me to come out to a house and look at four thousand books.' It wasn't clear who was supposed to feel sorrier for whom.

We had a couple of breaks. An online bookseller, who deals in rare books and first editions, came and picked through what interested him, and filled his old station wagon with boxes. A few days later, an English bibliophile, who teaches philosophy at Queen's, did the same. I enjoyed their obvious excitement, my enjoyment tempered by the sensation that the library was suffering death by a thousand cuts. For in any private library, the totality of books is meaningful, while each individual volume is relatively meaningless. Or rather, once separated from its family, each individual book becomes relatively meaningless in relation to the original collector, but suddenly newly meaningful as the totality of the author's mind. The lovely book *Mecca: A Literary History of the Muslim Holy Land*, by the great New York University scholar F. E. Peters, says little about my father-in-law, except that he bought it; but it represents a distillation of Professor Peters's lifework. In this strange way, our libraries are like certain paintings that, as you get closer to the canvas, become separate and unreadable blobs and daubs of paint.

And in this way, I began to think, our libraries perhaps say nothing very particular about us at all. Each brick in the wall of a library is a borrowed brick, not one made by the bricklayer: several thousand people, perhaps several hundred thousand, own books by F. E. Peters. If I were led into Edmund Wilson's library in Talcottville, from which all the books written by Wilson had been removed, would I know that it was Edmund Wilson's library, and not Alfred Kazin's or F. W. Dupee's? We tend to venerate libraries once we know whose they are, like admiring a famous philosopher's eyes or a ballet dancer's foot. Pushkin had about a thousand non-Russian books in his library, and the editor of *Pushkin on Literature* helpfully lists all those foreign books, from Balzac and Stendhal to Shakespeare and Voltaire. She confidently announces, 'Much can be learnt of a man from his choice of books', and then unwittingly contradicts herself by adding that Pushkin, like many Russians of his class, read mostly in French: 'The ancient classics, the Bible, Dante, Machiavelli, Luther, Shakespeare, Leibniz, Byron . . . all are predominantly in French.' This sounds like the library of an extremely well-read Russian gentleman, circa 1830 – the kind of reading that Pushkin gave to his standard-issue Russian romantic, Eugene Onegin. But what is especially Pushkinian about the library? What does it tell us about his mind?

Theodor Adorno, in his essay 'On Popular Music', pours disdain on the way in which, when we hear a popular hit, we think we are making a personal possession of it ('That's *my* song, the song that was playing when I first kissed X', say), while in fact this 'apparently isolated, individual experience of a particular song' is being stupidly shared with millions of other people – so that the listener merely 'feels safety in numbers and follows the crowd of all those who have heard the song before and who are supposed to have made its reputation'. Adorno, the grand snob, considers this a grave deception. But in a digital age, we surely treat serious classical music in just the same way. And how is a library – in one way of thinking about it, at least – anything but the same kind of self-deception? Isn't a private library simply a universal legacy pretending to be an individual one?

Adorno hated that capitalism, and the branch of it he called the Culture Industry, turned impalpabilities like artworks into things. But there is no escaping that books are most definitely things, and I was struck, working through my father-in-law's books, how quickly I became alienated from their rather stupid materiality. I began to resent his avariciousness, which resembled, in death, any other kind of avariciousness for objects. Again and again, his daughters had begged him to 'do something' about his books before he died. Meaning: *we can't take them*. If he knew that, he did nothing about it, and sorting out his library became sadly indistinguishable from sorting out his pictures or his CDs or his shirts. And though my task was very easy compared to my mourning wife's, the experience made me resolve not to leave behind such burdens for my children after my death.

I remember hearing about an accident that befell the scholar and critic Frank Kermode a few years ago. He was moving house and had put all his most precious books (his fiction, his poetry, signed first editions, and the like) in boxes, on the street. The binmen came by and mistakenly took the boxes, leaving Kermode with a great deal of contemporary literary theory. The story once seemed horrifying to me, and now seems almost wonderful. To be abruptly lightened like that, so that one's descendants might not be lingeringly burdened! After all, can I really contend that my own collection of almost unkillable, inert books, ranged on shelves like some bogus declaration of achievement (for surely the philistine is *right* to ask the cultured owner, 'Have you really read all these?'), tells my children anything more about me than my much smaller collection of postcards and photographs?

The more time I spent with my father-in-law's books, the more profoundly they seemed not to be revealing but hiding him, like some word-wreathed, untranslatable mausoleum. His Algerian childhood, his interesting mind, the diversion of that mind into run-of-the-mill business, his isolation and estrangement in America, his confidence and shyness, pugilism and anxiety, the drinking and the anger and the passion and the pressurised responsibility of his daily existence: of course, in some general way, these thousands of volumes – neatly systematic, proudly comprehensive – incarnated the shape of this life, but not the angles of his facets. The books somehow made him smaller, not larger, as if they were whispering: 'What a little thing a single human life is, with all its busy, ephemeral, pointless projects.' All ruins say this, yet we strangely persist in pretending that books are not ruins, not broken columns.

One of my father-in-law's busy, ephemeral projects fell out of a book about Greek history. A single sheet of paper, with notes written in his careful hand. The date was 2/1/95, and the notes were preparation for a trip to Greece: 'History of Ancient Greece. Jean Hatzfeld and Andre Aymard, N.Y., Norton 1966'. Under this heading were lines in English:

– Greeks establish themselves during second millennium BC: Greece, Black Sea, Asia Minor, Islands, S. Italy.

– Common language and tradition but very divided. *Hellas* = culture, civiliz. ('Hellenes' does not come until 800 BC. 'Greek' is Roman.)

– Geographic identity between Greece and Western Asia Minor: the sea inducted [?] a subsidence which broke up a continent of recent formation and whose structure was very complicated – fjords, deep bays, mountains, capes, islands.

And so on, down the page. Overleaf, he had made a rough drawing of ancient Greece and western Asia Minor (present-day Turkey). It was his entire world: on one side the Mediterranean, and on the other the Aegean, west and east. He had marked the most famous places and circled them: on the Asia Minor side, Aeolia, Lycia, Troy, Smyrna; and on the Greek side, the honeyed, haunted, lost names: Illyria, Attica, Argolis, Corinth, Arcadia.

2011

Acknowledgements

The essays selected in this volume first appeared in *The New Republic*, *The New Yorker*, and the *London Review of Books*, over the last twenty years. The date at the end of each essay is the date of first journalistic publication. I am very grateful to the editors and literary editors of these journals for allowing me, over these twenty happy years, to write at length and seriousness, and for shaping my arguments and sentences when they needed the help.

The following essays were subsequently published in book form:

From *The Broken Estate* (1999):
'What Chekhov Meant by Life'; 'Jane Austen's Heroic Consciousness'; 'The All and the If: God and Metaphor in Melville'; 'Virginia Woolf's Mysticism'.

From *The Irresponsible Self* (2004):
'Saul Bellow's Comic Style'; 'Joseph Roth's Empire of Signs'; 'Bohumil Hrabal's Comic World'; 'Hysterical Realism'; '*Anna Karenina* and Characterisation'; '*Don Quixote*'s Old and New Testaments'; 'Dostoevsky's God'.

From *The Fun Stuff* (2012):
'The Fun Stuff: Homage to Keith Moon'; 'Paul Auster's Shallowness'; 'George Orwell's Very English Revolution'; 'Cormac McCarthy's *The Road*'; '"Reality Examined to the Point of Madness": László Krasznahorkai'; 'Wounder and Wounded'; 'Marilynne Robinson'; 'Ismail Kadare'; 'Packing My Father-in-Law's Library'.

From *The Nearest Thing to Life* (2015):
'Serious Noticing'; 'On Not Going Home'.

'What Chekhov Meant by Life,' 'George Orwell's Very English Revolution', and 'Becoming Them' also appeared in *Best American Essays* (1999, 2010, and 2014, respectively). 'The Fun Stuff: Homage to Keith Moon' also appeared in *Best Music Writing 2011*.

Six essays have not previously appeared in book form; all of them were first published in *The New Yorker* between 2013 and 2017:
'The Other Side of Silence: Rereading W. G. Sebald'; 'Becoming Them'; 'Job Existed: Primo Levi'; 'Helen Garner's Savage Honesty'; 'Elena Ferrante'; 'Jenny Erpenbeck'.

A NOTE ABOUT THE AUTHOR

James Wood is a staff writer at *The New Yorker* and the recipient of a National Magazine Award in criticism. He is the author of four previous essay collections, the novels *The Book Against God* and *Upstate*, and the study *How Fiction Works*. He is a professor of the practice of literary criticism at Harvard University.